MIRRORS AND MIRRORING

Also available from Bloomsbury

AESTHETIC THEMES IN PAGAN AND CHRISTIAN NEOPLATONISM:
FROM PLOTINUS TO GREGORY OF NYSSA
by Daniele Iozzia

ANCIENT MAGIC AND THE SUPERNATURAL IN THE MODERN VISUAL
AND PERFORMING ARTS
edited by Filippo Carlà-Uhink and Irene Berti

BODY LANGUAGE IN THE GREEK AND ROMAN WORLDS
by D. L. Cairns

MAGIC IN ANCIENT GREECE AND ROME
by Lindsay C. Watson

THE ART OF THE BODY: ANTIQUITY AND ITS LEGACY
by Michael Squire

MIRRORS AND MIRRORING

FROM ANTIQUITY TO THE EARLY MODERN PERIOD

Edited by
Maria Gerolemou and Lilia Diamantopoulou

BLOOMSBURY ACADEMIC
LONDON • NEW YORK • OXFORD • NEW DELHI • SYDNEY

BLOOMSBURY ACADEMIC
Bloomsbury Publishing Plc
50 Bedford Square, London, WC1B 3DP, UK
1385 Broadway, New York, NY 10018, USA
29 Earlsfort Terrace, Dublin 2, Ireland

BLOOMSBURY, BLOOMSBURY ACADEMIC and the Diana logo
are trademarks of Bloomsbury Publishing Plc

First published in Great Britain 2020
Paperback edition first published 2021

Copyright © Maria Gerolemou, Lilia Diamantopoulou & Contributors, 2020

Maria Gerolemou and Lilia Diamantopoulou have asserted their right under the Copyright,
Designs and Patents Act, 1988, to be identified as Authors of this work.

Cover design: Terry Woodley
Cover image: Compound Eye © Graham Caldwell

All rights reserved. No part of this publication may be reproduced or
transmitted in any form or by any means, electronic or mechanical,
including photocopying, recording, or any information storage or retrieval
system, without prior permission in writing from the publishers.

Bloomsbury Publishing Plc does not have any control over, or responsibility for,
any third-party websites referred to or in this book. All internet addresses given
in this book were correct at the time of going to press. The author and publisher
regret any inconvenience caused if addresses have changed or sites have
ceased to exist, but can accept no responsibility for any such changes.

A catalogue record for this book is available from the British Library.

Library of Congress Cataloging-in-Publication Data
Names: Gerolemou, Maria, editor. | Diamantopoulou, Lilia, editor.
Title: Mirrors and mirroring from antiquity to the early modern period /
edited by Maria Gerolemou, Lilia Diamantopoulou.
Description: London; New York, NY: Bloomsbury Academic, 2020. |
Includes bibliographical references and index. | Summary: "This volume examines mirrors
and mirroring through a series of multidisciplinary essays, especially focusing on the
intersection between technological and cultural dynamics of mirrors. The international scholars
brought together here explore critical questions around the mirror as artefact and the
phenomenon of mirroring. Beside the common visual registration of an action or inaction,
in a two dimensional and reversed form, various types of mirrors often possess special
abilities which can produce a distorted picture of reality, serving in this way illusion and
falsehood. Part I looks at a selection of theory from ancient writers, demonstrating the
concern to explore these same questions in antiquity. Part II considers the role reflections
can play in forming ideas of gender and identity. Beyond the everyday, we see in Part III how
oracular mirrors and magical mirrors reveal the invisible divine - prosthetics that allow us to
look where the eye cannot reach. Finally, Part IV considers mirrors' roles in displaying the
visible and invisible in antiquity and since"– Provided by publisher.
Identifiers: LCCN 2019037781 (print) | LCCN 2019037782 (ebook) |
ISBN 9781350101289 (hardback) | ISBN 9781350101296 (ebook) | ISBN 9781350101302 (epub)
Subjects: LCSH: Mirrors in literature. | Reflection (Philosophy) in literature. | Mirrors–History.
Classification: LCC PN56.M537 M57 2020 (print) | LCC PN56.M537 (ebook) |
DDC 809/.9335–dc23
LC record available at https://lccn.loc.gov/2019037781
LC ebook record available at https://lccn.loc.gov/2019037782

ISBN: HB: 978-1-3501-0128-9
PB: 978-1-3501-9389-5
ePDF: 978-1-3501-0129-6
eBook: 978-1-3501-0130-2

Typeset by RefineCatch Limited, Bungay, Suffolk

To find out more about our authors and books visit
www.bloomsbury.com and sign up for our newsletters.

CONTENTS

List of Figures   vii
List of Contributors   ix

    Introduction   1

Part I   Philosophy, Reflections and Mirrors   7

1. The Liver and the Mirror: Images Beyond the Eye in Plato's *Timaeus*   *Ava Shirazi*   9
2. Alexander of Aphrodisias on the Reality of Mirror Images   *Katerina Ierodiakonou*   19
3. Catoptrology in Lucretius' *DRN* (4.269–323)   *Myrto Garani*   29
4. Tideus' Theory of Reflection in *On the Mirrors*   *Mikhail Silian*   43

Part II   [Wo]men in the Mirror   57

5. Mirrors of Women, Mirrors of Words: The Mirror in the Greek Papyri   *Isabella Bonati and Nicola Reggiani*   59
6. A Flame on Etruscan Mirrors? Meaning and Function in Daily Life and Religion of the Pattern on the Mirrors' Reflecting Side   *Vittorio Mascelli*   73
7. Portable Love: Ivory Mirror Cases Under the Lens of *fin' amor*   *Loreto Casanueva Reyes*   81
8. 'So Skilfully Mirrored in His Art': (Re)Visiting Mirrors in Oscar Wilde's *The Picture of Dorian Gray*   *Nikolas P. Kakkoufa*   93

Part III   Liminal Mirror   105

9. Mirrors and the Manufacture of Religious Aura in the Graeco-Roman World   *Tatiana Bur*   107
10. The Mirror of Nature   *Daniel Marković*   119
11. 'The Unspotted *Dioptra* of Prophecy': A Mirror Metaphor in Byzantine Literature   *Eirini Afentoulidou*   127

Contents

12. Mirrors and Mirroring in Dreams: Self-Reflection and Liminality in the *Roman de la Rose* and in the *Hypnerotomachia Poliphili*   Efthymia Priki   139

Part IV   Mimetic Mirror   155

13. Plane and Curved Mirrors in Classical Antiquity   Maria Gerolemou   157

14. Reflections on Lucian's Lunar Mirror: *speculum lunae* and an Ancient Telescopic Fantasy   Karen ní Mheallaigh   165

15. Mirroring the Face of God: The Challenge of the 'Invisible Face' and the Metropolitan Crucifixion Ivory   Kallirroe Linardou   177

16. Technologies 'Made in Greece': Konstantinos Simonides' Steampunk Inventions through the Looking-Glass   Lilia Diamantopoulou   189

Notes   199
Bibliography   247
Index   277

FIGURES

6.1	Flames on the extension of the *recto* of Etruscan Hellenistic bronze mirrors	73
6.2	Mirror with Dioscuri in a specular pose, from Norchia, Museo Archeologico Nazionale di Viterbo, inv. 112.305 (*CSE*, Italia, 5, n. 38), first half of the third century BC	74
6.3	Flowers goblet of *Ballota pseudodictamnus* or *acetabulosa* used as a floating wick	78
7.1	Mirror case, ivory, Falconing Party, French (Paris), *ca.* 1330–1360. Height: 9.5 cm, width: 9.5 cm. © The Metropolitan Museum of Art, New York	85
7.2	Mirror case, A Lady Crowning Her Love, French (Paris), *ca.* 1300, ivory. Height: 10.6 cm, Width: 10.3 cm. © Victoria & Albert Museum, London	86
9.1	Detail from the fresco in the Villa of the Mysteries, Pompeii	116
12.1	Oiseuse with her attributes and the dreamer. Bibliothèque nationale de France, fr. 12593 (fourteenth century), f. 6r. Source: https://gallica.bnf.fr/ark:/12148/btv1b6000348j (accessed 18 November 2018)	142
12.2	Amant discovers the rose-garden. Bibliothèque nationale de France, fr. 1558 (early fourteenth century), f. 13v. Source: https://gallica.bnf.fr/ark:/12148/btv1b6000316k (accessed 18 November 2018)	147
12.3	Amant is shot in the eye by Amour's arrow. Bibliothèque nationale de France, fr. 1558 (early fourteenth century), f. 14r. Source: https://gallica.bnf.fr/ark:/12148/btv1b6000316k (accessed 18 November 2018)	148
12.4	The dragon attacks Poliphilo. Glasgow University Library, Sp Coll Hunterian Bh.2.14 (Hypnerotomachia Poliphili, 1499), f. d3v	151
12.5	Poliphilo encounters the Five Senses. Glasgow University Library, Sp Coll Hunterian Bh.2.14 (Hypnerotomachia Poliphili, 1499), f. e2v	152
15.1	Crucifixion ivory, mid-tenth century, Constantinople	178
15.2	Drawing of the Crucifixion ivory by the artist Athanasios Yiotakis (pencil on paper, 2017)	179
15.3	Drawing of the Crucifixion ivory by the artist Ioannis Efthimiou (coal on paper, 2018)	180
15.4	The Metropolitan Crucifixion ivory as exhibited in the Museum show-case	183

Figures

16.1 Front page of the Latin edition of Alhazen's *Book of Optics* (ed. Friedrich Risner, 1572) showing the use of burning mirrors, distorted images caused by refraction in water, rainbows and other optical effects   192

16.2 Ink drawing of a camera obscura from an early seventeenth century illustrated *Sketchbook on military art, including geometry, fortifications, artillery, mechanics, and pyrotechnics* (Rosenwald Coll. ms. no. 27, p. 249; Library of Congress, Rare Books and Special Collections Division)   195

CONTRIBUTORS

Eirini Afentoulidou is a Postdoctoral Researcher at the Austrian Academy of Sciences, Institute for Medieval Research, Division of Byzantine Research, ÖAW.

Isabella Bonati is a Postdoctoral Fellow at the North-West University of Potchefstroom, South Africa.

Tatiana Bur is the Moses and Mary Finely Research Fellow at Darwin College at the University of Cambridge.

Lilia Diamantopoulou is a Professor of Modern Greek Studies in the Department of Cultural Studies at the University of Munich.

Myrto Garani is Assistant Professor in Latin Literature at the National and Kapodistrian University of Athens, Greece.

Maria Gerolemou is a Leventis Research Associate in Hellenic Studies in the Department of Classics and Ancient History at the University of Exeter.

Katerina Ierodiakonou is Professor of Ancient Philosophy at the Department of History and Philosophy of Science of the University of Athens, and Associate Professor at the Department of Philosophy of the University of Geneva.

Nikolas P. Kakkoufa is a Lecturer in the Department of Classics, the Director of Undergraduate Studies for the Program in Hellenic Studies, and an Affiliate Faculty member in the Institute for Research on Women, Gender, and Sexuality at Columbia University.

Kallirroe Linardou is an Assistant Professor in Byzantine and Medieval Art in the Department of Theory and History of Art at the Athens School of Fine Arts.

Daniel Marković is an Associate Professor in the Department of Classics at the University of Cincinnati, OH.

Vittorio Mascelli is a Professor of Etruscan Civilization for the Centro di Servizi Culturali per Stranieri, University of Florence.

Karen ní Mheallaigh is a Professor of Classics at Johns Hopkins University, Maryland.

Efthymia Priki was awarded her PhD in Byzantine Studies from the University of Cyprus in 2016 and her research focuses on comparative medieval literature and text/image studies.

Contributors

Nicola Reggiani is a Researcher of Papyrology in the Department of Humanities, Social Sciences and Cultural Industries at the University of Parma.

Loreto Casanueva Reyes is a Assistant Professor at the Universidad Finis Terrae and a Phd candidate of Philosophy, mention in Aesthetics and Art Theory at the University of Chile.

Ava Shirazi is a Perkins-Cotsen Postdoctoral Fellow at the Princeton Society of Fellows, and a lecturer in Classics and Humanistic Studies at Princeton University.

Mikhail Silian is a PhD student at the Institute of Classical Philology at Humboldt University Berlin.

INTRODUCTION

One of the first acts in our daily routine is to look in the mirror. Irrespective of whether we like what we see or not, in this act something happens that always has concerned man(and woman)kind. 'Without the mirror, a man would not know what his own face looks like' states the modernist poet and art historian Nikolas Calas (1907-1988).[1] Besides this common visual registration of form, action or inaction, various types of mirrors, often possessing special features, can deform, delete and produce new images: for instance, some mirrors shrink or enlarge their reflected objects; curved mirrors or combinations of plane mirrors, in particular, distort or sometimes delete the image of the reflected object, replacing it with a new image; that is to say, mirrors both work for and deny naturalism. However, mirrors also function as transmitters of valuable information not otherwise directly obtainable, revealing hidden aspects of ourselves or offering a holistic picture of the world, i.e. of the divine and the natural, thus marking a divide between what appears to the senses and what really exists. In *Mirrors of the Mind*, Nikolas Calas discusses the attractive interweaving of truth and deception that mirrors can offer. As he puts it: 'The mirror adds to our understanding of reality by providing information about ourselves. While it offers an indispensable element in completing the body image, it simultaneously deceives by giving an inverted version of the self and by suggesting the presence of another, a double.'[2]

By and large, the use of mirrors, their outcomes as well their value, changes through the ages on the basis of technological advances, the use of glass mirrors (rather than metal ones),[3] flat mirrors (as opposed to early metal convex mirrors), large mirrors (as opposed to ancient small mirrors),[4] their introduction to civic life (their monumental character as opposed to their private portable character),[5] and advanced optic or catoptric theories which rationalize the mirror's function,[6] e.g. by explaining visual errors on the basis of light, starting with Alhacen's *De aspectibus* (esp. books 4-6, though he preserves the visual cone with sight at its core) and Kepler (*Ad Vitellionem paralipomena, Dioptrice*), continuing with Descartes (e.g. *Dioptrics The World (or Treatise on Light)* and Newton (*Opticks*).

In classical antiquity, various discussions on mirrors, such as the didactic, prognostic, decorative, liminal and mimetic mirror, describe the effects of mirrors by focusing on the medium of the mirror itself and/or the real or metaphysical character of its products. Two main factors seem to have shaped the narrative on ancient mirrors and reflections. The first is the general anthropocentric character of ancient science:[7] catoptrics, dealing with reflections, is developed in relation to human interaction that is in relation to the viewer, how he is situated towards the visual object. Or, to put it otherwise, the phenomenon of reflection is described via the visual cone which schematizes the adventures of the ray as it passes from one medium (e.g. air) into the reflective or refractive interfaces to finally reach the human eye. The second factor has to do with the structure of the medium itself, specifically its curvature: ancient mirrors are divided into two categories, flat mirrors and spherical mirrors (convex spherical and concave spherical). A flat mirror, though different from contemporary flat mirrors, produces virtual images but right-left reversed; a spherical mirror, while projecting real images, deforms them, by enlarging, reducing or distorting their shape. The first case, that of the plane mirror, is an ideal case; in actual fact, ancient mirrors were made mainly out of metal and were slightly spherical and, thus, the images they produced were always blurred and deformed to some extent.[8]

While mirror images in the ancient world could not be treated as an accurate reflection of a physical object, from the Renaissance onwards mirrors as an imaging technology were, in fact, developed further, not independent of perspectivism, and used to produce accurate reflections and thus serve artistic realism (see the Hockney–Falco thesis regarding Renaissance art[9]), or to attain natural and philosophical truth. Moreover, catoptrical illusions and deformed images from around this point onwards were not the inevitable result of metal, spherical mirrors (as in antiquity), but of playful, conscious optical experiments, with a view to producing amusing marvels and so aesthetic pleasure.[10]

On the other hand, in the Middle Ages mirrors played a central role in folklore, superstition and folk tales, given magical or diabolical attributes and used in fortune-telling and other forms of scrying through reflecting or refractive surfaces. This tradition has been passed on in folk rituals that still endure today, such as the custom of the Klidonas in Greece, celebrated on the 24th of June, at the feast of St John the Baptist: with the help of a water-filled jar, future husbands are revealed to village girls.[11] Moreover, in Byzantium, as most Byzantine texts are theological in nature, when mirror images were mentioned they were set up as moral equivalents of the internal *image* of the viewer, while mirror-gazing was seen as a rather negative pastime.[12] Such ideological reflections are probably further related to the iconoclasm of the eighth and ninth centuries, when pictorial representations and images in general were frowned upon. This is also why pictorial representations of mirrors are quite rare in Byzantine times.[13] From the Early Middle Ages to the Renaissance in both East (Byzantium) and West, there is also a wide range of metaphorical uses of mirrors in the form of instructional manuals for new rulers, widely known as *Specula Regis*;[14] this was part of a widespread genre described as mirror literature (see e.g. *Speculum mundi, – feminarum, – astronomiae, – ecclesiae, – humanae salvationis,– judiciale*, etc.);[15] the title *speculum*, inspired by the small, fragmented captures of reality that mirrors could produce, probably served as an analogy of the truthful, though reductive, approaches to a large subject and phenomenon that the *specula* offered their readers.

In early modern, modern and contemporary philosophy, mirrors and mirroring have mainly been understood as metaphors for logic, thinking and (self-)knowledge, with a strong connection to psychosociology, linguistics and semiotics. By describing, for instance, reality as the totality of facts, Wittgenstein, who used the mirror metaphor for the explanation of the logical form, declaring that reflection is essential for the human thinking, stated that perceptual illusions can be isolated from other facts (in *Tractatus* 1921, 1.1). This leads us to Foucault, according to whom reflections were the result of heterotopian mirroring and had the ability to be 'at once absolutely real [...] and absolutely unreal'.[16] Moreover, mirrors and mirror images create the impression of the simultaneous presence of a second, parallel space and time which annuls the real *chronotopos*, in Bakhtin's wording, that is to say, the barrier between time and space.[17]

Pierre Mabille, who discussed Lacan's mirror-stage already in 1938, rejected the widely accepted division between reality and illusion and proposed that the monistic approach of the medieval realists be re-examined, with illusions treated as part of reality.[18] Notably, since Lacan's theory of the 'mirror stage' it has been impossible to distinguish between 'experience with mirrors and semiosis', as Umberto Eco aptly noted in his examination of mirrors, because they 'seem to be the points of a rather inextricable knot'.[19] Following Baudrillard, who defines Marxism as the mirror of bourgeois society (*Le miroir de la production*, 1973), and postmodern societies as caught up in mechanically produced simulacra that prevent them from approaching social and political reality (*Simulacres et Simulation*, 1981), and Richard Rorty, who develops in his *Philosophy and the Mirror of Nature* (1979) the philosophical idea of knowledge as a mental mirroring of a mind-external world, newer approaches deal with the role of mirrors in self-portraits in online social networks since the media revolution of the so-called 'Selfie Generation'.[20]

The volume at a glance

Mirrors and Mirroring offers the first essay collection on the contextualization of the status of reflections from antiquity to the early modern period on an interdisciplinary basis, giving new insights on mirrors as reflecting media and as material objects, on mirroring as the process of the physical object's reproduction, and on mirror reflections and their relationship to gender, the divine, the natural world and self-perception. Notably, while the mirror as a means of reflection of the self (autoscopy), i.e. as a means of perceiving, evaluating and knowing the self, or as a reflection of the other, as well as in regard to its metaphorical use as an agent of transformation, has received some attention.[21] Less emphasis, however, has been placed on the potential of mirrors as artefacts and imaging technology, thus taking into consideration their technical, mechanical properties for conceptualizing and forming various different images and, thus, realities.[22] The study of mirrors as an imaging technology does not necessarily exclude the notion of mirrors and mirror images invoked metaphorically or figuratively in literature; on the contrary, the volume seeks to demonstrate the dependence on or relationship of the latter to the material and technological character of mirrors and consequently mirroring. Moreover, the thematic comparison of mirror-stories within an interdisciplinary framework helps to further our understanding of the medium of the mirror itself. However, though the composition of the contributions is well-considered, as in any volume of this kind, the reader is welcome to read the essays in a different than the suggested order, since the contributions remain intelligible independently of each other.

In the awareness that a single volume cannot cover the huge amount of sources or interpretations related to mirrors and mirroring throughout the ages, and very conscious of our failure to encompass other traditions which have much to teach on the subject, such as ancient Chinese or Mesoamerican, we hope that this volume, focused, as we have said, on the mirror as medium, artefact and device, will best reflect our aim, to offer glimpses of the technological aspect of mirroring from Antiquity and Byzantium to the Middle Ages and the modern period.

The first part of the volume is dedicated to mirrors and mirroring in classical antiquity. Specifically, the 'Philosophy, Reflections and Mirrors', discusses the practice of mirroring, the status of reflections as well as the mirror itself as a heuristic device useful for stressing the salient features of natural phenomena in an explicit way. The first essay, by Ava Shirazi, argues that the mirror-liver analogy in Plato's *Timaeus*, by taking advantage of all the material attributes of the mirror (smoothness, shininess, brightness and also its ability to reflect numinous images), visualizes the hidden realm of the intellect which keeps the appetitive part of the soul under control. Katerina Ierodiakonou's chapter explores the ontological status of mirror images. Alexander of Aphrodisias (second century CE), by comparing mirror images to colours, bestows upon them a certain reality – though in principle, he challenges the accuracy and reliability of mirror images while acknowledging the fact that they are merely the products of relations among the perceiver, the perceived object, the transparent medium and the surface of the mirror. Myrto Garani's essay argues that, similarly to Plato, Lucretius grants mirrors a heuristic value, in order to demonstrate the reality of nature and the unseen atomic world (the ἄδηλα). To this end, he explains catoptrical mechanics with a view to disassociating mirrors from the wonderful and the deceitful, and, also, from religious practices. The last chapter of this section, by Mikhail Silian, deals with a late antique text by Tydeus, the *De Speculis*, which tries to answer the question why some surfaces reflect bodies better than others by comparing the stages of the process of reflection in the mirror with the stages of seeing and, thus, relating mirrors and mirroring with light (originate from the eye or be reflected by the mirror); the chapter provides an introduction, an English translation (the first to date), and an interpretation of the text.

The second part of the volume, '[Wo]men in the Mirror', discusses the relation of mirroring to gender, and especially the closeness of women to mirrors, which results from the perception of women as objects of desire and their connection with vanity; both the positive relationship of women to beauty and the negative allegories of vanity and luxury are among the reasons why, for instance, the mirror in antiquity is an attribute of Aphrodite, while, on the other hand, in the Middle Ages it is incorporated into the cult of the Virgin Mary as a symbol of her purity and virtue.[23] Specifically, this section studies examples of cosmetic mirrors as well as cases where mirrors act as a medium for perceiving and constructing gender identity. The first chapter (Isabella Bonati/Nicola Reggiani) deals with the mirror as a gendered object, mostly as noted in documentary papyri concerned with the female world, such as lists of paraphernalia and lists of women's goods; next to the established forms for mirror κάτοπτρον and ἔσοπτρον, the chapter takes particular notice of the term ὄσυπτρον. Vittorio Mascelli's essay explores a peculiar decorative pattern on a group of Etruscan mirrors; this could represent a flame 'born' from a flower which, in fact, represents a lighting technique using wicks, revealing an everyday scene in a woman's life, trying to catch her reflection in the mirror, probably during the hours of darkness. Loreto Casanueva Reyes explores mirrors as feminine articles, love tokens and narrative devices in medieval times, and discusses real or fictional ivory mirror cases as a desirable commodity or erotic object in the frame of courtly love. The chapter by Nikolas P. Kakkoufa gives a foretaste and an outlook of the reception of the known story of Narcissus and his reflection in Oscar Wilde's *The Picture of Dorian Gray*. In his text he opens the myth to a Lacanian reading where the discovery of the self is dominant, dealing with the emergence of identity and of the (homo)sexual self.

The chapters in the third part of the volume, 'Liminal Mirror', discuss mirrors as thresholds of liminal spaces, where the real blends with the unreal and, often, with the metaphysical divine. Tatiana Bur's essay on religious mirrors in antiquity investigates how the technology of the mirror supports and produces humanly-manufactured religious aura and specifically miracles such as epiphany and divination, thus bridging the gap between believers and the divine presence. Daniel Marcovic's chapter examines the concept of the mirror as it stands for the process of analogical reasoning regarding the secrets of nature, thereby challenging ideas of seeing and visibility. Eirini Afendoulidou explores the metaphoric usage of the term *dioptra* in the context of mirror metaphors in Byzantine literature and focuses on a late-eleventh-century versified treatise (*Dioptra*) on the state of humans in the visible and invisible, present and future worlds. Finally, Efthymia Priki's chapter deals with oneiric experiences and the use and function of mirrors and reflecting surfaces as a liminal space within the dreams narrated in two works: the *Roman de la Rose* (thirteenth century) and *Hypnerotomachia Poliphili* (1499).

The last section is entitled 'Mimetic Mirror'. This section explores the association of mirrors with mimesis, i.e. mirrors as duplicating devices of reality (and beyond) and covers discussions about the relationship among mirrors, originals, and copies; mirrors, unlike pictorial and plastic arts, instead of merely replicating the world, often challenge or exceed the limits of traditional mimesis, due to the fact that they capture movement, that is, transformation; they thus defy direct vision, by precisely subverting the dynamics of power between subject (perceiver) and object (reflected object). Maria Gerolemou's chapter discusses the potentials and products of plane and spherical mirrors in classical antiquity; whereas the former are the products of mimesis and can be considered ideal reproductions of the real world, the outcome of the second type of mirror is associated with creative *phantasia*, a much more forceful representational tool than mimesis. Karen ní Mheallaigh's chapter discusses how the moon is related to the mirror in antiquity and especially in Lucian's *True Histories*, Plutarch's *On the face of the moon* and Demetrius Triclinius' *On the black figure in the moon*. They all seem to use the mirror as an optical medium; specifically, they study the moon through the function of the mirror and the mirror through the behaviour of the moon, and as cartographical instrument to map the earth and, consequently, 'earthly' reality, literally from a different point of view. Kalliroe Linardou inspects the illusory nature of vision and artistic representation exemplified in a tenth-century carved ivory plaque of the so-called Macedonian Renaissance as a kind of reflection, a materialized eidolon on which the catoptrical illusion enforced by shadows reveals a second image. The volume closes with a chapter by Lilia Diamantopoulou, which explores the forging activities of Konstantinos Simonides, who presents great inventions and technological achievements of modern times, in which mirrors, glasses and polished silver plates play an important role, as if they were already anticipated in late Antiquity or in the early Greek Middle Ages. Driven by personal and socio-political intentions, Simonides tried to shape Greece's image abroad with his forgeries, making his own contribution to nation-building.

To give a concluding remark, *Mirrors and Mirroring* aims to take part in the ongoing general discussion on media and materials *hidden* in literary motifs which presupposes the parallel study of technical/scientific and literary texts. In this light, the editors will consider the volume to have fulfilled its role, if the necessity of a theoretical framework based on the technology of the mirror and the materiality of reflections proposes an interpretation of mirrors as medium of mimesis and at the same time *phantasia*, of mirroring as something that it could be placed beyond the human gaze, and of mirror images as something that could be signified beyond perception. Mirrors played an important role in the history of science and technology not only because they changed human's image of himself, of nature and of the universe, but also because as an optical aid they helped change the ways in which natural philosophy and science were practiced. It is for this reason that we considered it appropriate to organize a conference on 'Mirrors and Mirroring' at the Department of Byzantine and Modern Greek Studies, University of Vienna, held on 6 and 7 October 2017.[24]

We wish to close this introduction with an advice to the medium of mirrors itself, expressed by the author's off-voice in Jean Cocteaus film *The Blood of a Poet* who said that: 'mirrors should reflect a little, before throwing back images'.[25]

PART I
PHILOSOPHY, REFLECTIONS AND MIRRORS

CHAPTER 1
THE LIVER AND THE MIRROR: IMAGES BEYOND THE EYE IN PLATO'S *TIMAEUS*
Ava Shirazi

One of the most curious reflective surfaces in Greek thought is Plato's explicit comparison of the human liver to a mirror in the *Timaeus*.[1] The liver-mirror is a crucial mechanism in Timaeus' account of the embodied soul, a discussion which substantiates on the *Republic* by making the body a vehicle for the tripartite psyche. The characteristics and hierarchies within the soul, as outlined in the *Republic* – reason, spirit, and appetite – remain the same.[2] Each part, however, is assigned to a particular section of the body.[3] The rational and immortal part of the soul rules from atop, in the head. The spirited part is situated close by, just below the neck and above the diaphragm. The appetitive part (also the most disruptive) is fittingly placed far from reason, below the diaphragm and around the digestive system. The organs, such as the heart, the lungs, and more importantly, the liver, assist reason in leading and communicating with the inferior mortal parts of the soul.

The spirit is the most cooperative and the second in command. The appetitive part of the soul is the rebel of the group; or rather (in Timaeus' own words) the 'wild beast' (θρέμμα ἄγριον) that causes turmoil and clamour (θόρυβον καὶ βοὴν) in the body (70e).[4] The appetite is especially choleric (in both senses of the word). It neither understands the discourse of reason nor has the instinct to pay heed to it, even if it could. It does however pay attention to visual forms of communication. Images (in the forms of *eidōla* and *phantasmata*) enchant (ψυχαγωγεῖν) the appetite night and day.[5] Therefore, in order to keep the appetite under control, the gods needed a surface on which the rational part of the soul could communicate with (or at least affect) the appetitive part of the soul through images. Thus, they created the liver.

That the liver can function as a visual, let alone reflective, surface is curious enough. What makes this idea even more extraordinary is Timaeus' rich sensory description of how these images are produced and in turn perceived:

> ... as a plot against this,[6] the god contrived the form of the liver and positioned it in the living quarters of that part [of the soul], making it compact, smooth, and bright, possessing both sweetness and bitterness, so that the force of the thoughts coming from the mind upon it [i.e. the liver], as though upon a mirror that accepts visual impressions and produces perceivable reflections, could scare it. And whenever it uses a part akin to the liver's bitterness, it forcefully conveys its threats, and quickly permeating the entire liver, it displays bile-like colors, and contracting the liver, it makes it entirely shriveled and jagged, bending and

contracting the lobe, the receptacle, and the gates from an upright position, and blocking up the other passages and shutting them close, it produces pain and nausea. However, when a certain gentle breath from thoughts paints opposite phantasms, it produces a rest from the bitterness by wishing to neither move nor fasten upon the nature opposite itself, using on it the sweetness innate within it, and restoring all of it straight, smooth, and unencumbered; it makes the part of the soul placed around the liver gentle and happy, amusing itself at night fittingly, consulting the powers of divination in its sleep, since it does not share in reason or judgement.

... τούτῳ δὴ θεὸς ἐπιβουλεύσας αὐτῷ τὴν ἥπατος ἰδέαν συνέστησε καὶ ἔθηκεν εἰς τὴν ἐκείνου κατοίκησιν, πυκνὸν καὶ λεῖον καὶ λαμπρὸν καὶ γλυκὺ καὶ πικρότητα ἔχον μηχανησάμενος, ἵνα ἐν αὐτῷ τῶν διανοημάτων ἡ ἐκ τοῦ νοῦ φερομένη δύναμις, οἷον ἐν κατόπτρῳ δεχομένῳ τύπους καὶ κατιδεῖν εἴδωλα παρέχοντι, φοβοῖ μὲν αὐτό, ὁπότε μέρει τῆς πικρότητος χρωμένη συγγενεῖ, χαλεπὴ προσενεχθεῖσα ἀπειλῇ, κατὰ πᾶν ὑπομειγνῦσα ὀξέως τὸ ἧπαρ, χολώδη χρώματα ἐμφαίνοι, συνάγουσά τε πᾶν ῥυσὸν καὶ τραχὺ ποιοῖ, λοβὸν δὲ καὶ δοχὰς πύλας τε τὸ μὲν ἐξ ὀρθοῦ κατακάμπτουσα καὶ συσπῶσα, τὰ δὲ ἐμφράττουσα συγκλείουσά τε, λύπας καὶ ἄσας παρέχοι, καὶ ὅτ᾽ αὖ τἀναντία φαντάσματα ἀποζωγραφοῖ πραότητός τις ἐκ διανοίας ἐπίπνοια, τῆς μὲν πικρότητος ἡσυχίαν παρέχουσα τῷ μήτε κινεῖν μήτε προσάπτεσθαι τῆς ἐναντίας ἑαυτῇ φύσεως ἐθέλειν, γλυκύτητι δὲ τῇ κατ᾽ ἐκεῖνο συμφύτῳ πρὸς αὐτὸ χρωμένη καὶ πάντα ὀρθὰ καὶ λεῖα αὐτοῦ καὶ ἐλεύθερα ἀπευθύνουσα, ἵλεών τε καὶ εὐήμερον ποιοῖ τὴν περὶ τὸ ἧπαρ ψυχῆς μοῖραν κατῳκισμένην, ἔν τε τῇ νυκτὶ διαγωγὴν ἔχουσαν μετρίαν, μαντείᾳ χρωμένην καθ᾽ ὕπνον, ἐπειδὴ λόγου καὶ φρονήσεως οὐ μετεῖχε.[7]

In this remarkably dense passage (only one sentence in the Greek), the liver-mirror explains the complex relationship between our physical and psychological experiences, such as fear and pain, tranquility, sleep and even divine inspiration. We can make a crucial observation from the start: according to the *Timaeus*, reason communicates with appetite primarily through the senses. Reason creates sensory impressions for the appetite to see and feel. These impressions are visual (εἴδωλα, φαντάσματα), but they are also qualified and experienced through other sensations such as touch, taste, and feelings of pain, nausea, and restfulness. To use Lorenz's (2006) turn of phrase, the communication between reason and appetite is based on '*non-rational cognition*', that is, it is a form of communication based on the senses.[8]

In what follows, I hope to explicate how the *mirror* informs the visual and other sensory experiences presented within this passage. In other words, why did Plato turn to the mirror for a device of sensory communication between reason and appetite? To fully understand Plato's liver-mirror as a sensory mechanism, however, we first need to understand the significance of the *liver* before and during Plato's time. Therefore, I will first turn to an important overlapping, yet distinct, discourse on the liver in the archaic and classical periods: the practice of hepatoscopy.

The *Liver*-Mirror

While the *Timaeus* associates the liver primarily with the inferior appetites of the soul, as well as with symptoms such as pain and fear, it at the same time bestows upon it a divine honour by identifying it as the organ of divinity. Immediately following his description of the liver-mirror quoted above, Timaeus re-orients the source of the images, as if to redeem the role of the liver (and the appetite) in our bodies. He explains that the lesser gods, remembering the order of their father, the original craftsman, rectified the vile part of us – i.e. the appetite – by establishing the organ of divination, the liver, within it so that it too may have some hold on truth. What then follows is a meditation on the practice of divination, which once again concludes with the statement that the liver was situated in this region for the sake of divination (χάριν μαντικῆς).[9] The liver, therefore, becomes a reflective surface for both the images of reason and the images of the divine.

While Timaeus' association of the liver with divination may seem separate from the liver-mirror mechanism, it is in fact the most fitting cultural link between the liver and the mirror. By identifying the liver as an organ of divination, Plato is explicitly referring to the Greek practice of hepatoscopy, while at the same time, rewriting the tradition for his own philosophic purpose.

Hepatoscopy, the interpretation of animal livers for divine signs, was one of the most important practices of divination in Greek culture, though most scholars believe that the practice began in Mesopotamia and then moved westward towards Greece.[10] Some of our key sources for the practice are model livers, made of either clay or bronze – the latter also being the exclusive material out of which Greeks made mirrors. The models are generally inscribed with what seem like instructions as to what regions of the liver represent favourable or unfavourable omens. With the models dating as early as the eighteenth century BCE,[11] we can note that the liver, long before Plato and long before the mirror,[12] was an important visual surface on which images were interpreted. Model livers, moreover, indicate an interest in how images could be studied on man-made material objects. Interestingly no such model livers have been found in the Greek world.[13] And the surviving evidence for how the Greek exactly practiced hepatoscopy is scarce and quite vague. Thus, while we cannot reconstruct the exact details of the practice, the extant evidence reveals the importance of the visual quality of the liver, such as the smoothness and brightness of its surface, as well as how changes in texture, colour, and form could represent divine signs.[14]

Perhaps one of the most important sets of evidence regarding the Greek practice comes from the iconography on Attic vase paintings, where we actually see a depiction of the liver and the way in which its surface was both a visual and tactile focal point in practices of hepatoscopy.[15] Such depictions are rather formulaic in their representation.[16] At the centre of the images, we find the same representational elements: a young boy carrying a mass of entrails, which he then presents to a hoplite to interpret. Sometimes, the entrails are accented with the colour purple,[17] and at other times, the entrails are marked with incisions or black-lines. The presentation of the young boy vis-à-vis the hoplite is a constant in all the extant images, while the figures on either side change, though even then within a set pattern: we see either an older man or a foreigner on the side of the young boy while a woman or other members of the army stand on the side of the hoplite; often, there is a dog accompanying the men.[18]

The sacrificial entrails – the form of which look quite like and are often identified as the liver – are always in the centre of the image and the point to which all eyes and bodies turn. The significance of the liver, moreover, is emphasized by its size, which always exceeds the size and hold of the young boy's hands. While such images do not provide much detail about the Greek system of hepatoscopy, they nonetheless indicate some key aspects of the interpretive practice. For example, the images seem to indicate that interpreting the entrails was both a matter of vision and touch. Often the hoplite has his hands on the entrails and at times he holds a particular piece in front of his eyes, with his helmet raised, for what seems like a closer look. The overall impression one gets from these type-scenes is that the liver was a special object, one which was meant to be seen and felt, in order to be interpreted. But for what are the hoplites in such images or the *manteis* thought to be looking when examining the surface of the liver?

In a few short passages from the literature of the Classical period, we find an emphasis on the physical qualities of the bile (χολή), the lobe (λοβός) – (generally its shape) – and the 'gates' (πύλαι) of the liver as well as the more general visual qualities such as the organ's smoothness (λειότητα) and complexion (χροιά).[19] Already we can note the similarities between the visual qualities of livers in the context of hepatoscopy and those of the liver-mirror of the *Timaeus*, such as its smooth and bright texture (λεῖον καὶ λαμπρὸν), as well as its colour, which the *Timaeus* describes in greater detail as bile-like (χολώδη χρώματα ἐμφαίνοι). The Platonic text also brings our attention to the liver's lobe as well as its 'gates' which reason bends in order to produce pain and nausea. We can imagine that the liver-mirror in the *Timaeus*, in such a condition, would have probably been read as reflecting unfavourable omens by a *mantis*, much as its condition as such is unfavourable for the general well-being of the body. In fact, Timaeus' description of the liver-mirror is often used to reconstruct practices of hepatoscopy, given that it presents the visual qualities of the liver in much greater detail than any of the texts or images above.[20]

The description of hepatoscopy in the *Timaeus*, however, is nonetheless Platonic in its agenda. First the liver at the centre of Timaeus' account is not that of an animal, but of a human, and moreover Plato rejects the validity of the mantis as interpreter and places the liver explicitly and strictly under the guidance of intellect.[21] But the text also presents the liver as part of a much more complex process than that of hepatoscopy by placing it at the centre of a larger discussion on the production and perception of images in the inner body. Nonetheless, Plato's implicit and explicit evocations of hepatoscopy remind us that long before the *Timaeus*, livers were thought to embody the very challenge of making the imperceptible, perceptible – of making the invisible, visible. The liver was a powerful symbol of visualization in its capacity to make the divine visible to the eye.[22] At this point, then, we can refine our initial question: given that the liver was already an important object for visual communication in Plato's times, why does the *Timaeus* think of the liver as a *mirror*? What particular qualities does this hyphenation, the liver-mirror, lend to Plato's account of sensory perception in relation to the tripartite soul?

The Liver-*Mirror*

It's not difficult to conceptualize the liver in the tradition of hepatoscopy as a sort of 'mirror', where the images on its surface were thought to reflect the will and thoughts of the gods. Plato, nonetheless, is the first to make a direct connection between the organ and the bronze object. There is however one other example where the liver and the mirror are more implicitly compared. On the back of an Etruscan hand-held bronze mirror from the fourth century BCE, we see the engraved figure of a winged haruspex, identified by inscription as Calchas, the mythic Argive seer.[23] With one foot on a rock, Calchas leans forward to inspect and interpret the entrails of an animal. Much like the depictions of the hoplites amidst the act of interpretation in Attic vase paintings, Calchas holds and sets his eyes on a part of the entrails that resembles the liver.[24] We cannot know for certain what quality of the liver Calchas is examining, though his free hand seems to point to either a particular section of the liver (such as the structure of its lobe) or to its colour and texture. His hands remind us of the tactility of the liver (that it was an object often held and felt), while the direction of his eyes reminds us that the liver is a visual surface, meant to be seen and interpreted. With his gaze fixed on the liver, it is clear that he can see something we cannot. The figure of Calchas, moreover, reminds us of another image-type commonly depicted in Attic iconography: that of a woman and her mirror.

The similarities between these two types of images (that is the image of Calchas on the back of the bronze mirror and figures of women on Attic pottery[25]) suggest some of the possible cultural associations between the liver and the mirror (especially given the fact that we see Calchas depicted on the back of a mirror). Like the woman and her mirror, Calchas is depicted in a sort of pictorial isolation: he and the liver appear against a bare background, with the framing ivy leaves further containing the image. The simplicity and lack of any other activity in both images (other than the figure looking at the object in hand) suggest a contemplative moment. Like the mirror in the hands of the woman, moreover, the liver becomes an extension of Calchas' body and a point of visual and mental connection.[26]

As the woman could be contemplating her state of being and general circumstance, perhaps Calchas too is contemplating the significance of the liver's image in relation to greater events. Furthermore, if there is an analogical relationship between the image of Calchas on the back of the mirror and the act of looking into the mirror itself, then the image is perhaps suggesting the following: just as a seer studies a liver and sees divine hidden things, so you (the viewer of the mirror) can see divine (and perhaps favourable) signs in your reflection.[27]

Such parallels between the liver and the mirror may seem quite strange to us today: we neither live in a culture that is interested in the organ as a visual surface, nor do we often see an animal's liver in the raw. Our mirrors, moreover, are not made of bronze. Yet for an ancient viewer the similarities between the liver and the bronze mirror would begin with their outward appearances: both have bright, deep-coloured surfaces that seem to gleam and reflect light.[28] Both of their shiny surfaces are generally attributed to the smoothness of their texture: as we saw earlier, Aeschylus' Prometheus emphasizes the smoothness (λειότης) of the organ while Plato emphasizes the importance of the smoothness and brightness (λεῖος καὶ λαμπρός, 71b) of the liver-mirror in the *Timaeus*.

In general, the textural quality of a bronze mirror's surface was a crucial point of interest for the Greeks. For example, in the *de insomniis*, Aristotle describes the ideal mirror as both smooth and spotless (τὸ καθαρὸν εἶναι καὶ λεῖον) – so much so that it should be sensitive to any contact whatsoever.[29] In the *Timaeus*, Plato conflates these very visual qualities of the mirror (smoothness and spotlessness) with his description of the liver. As noted above, both the texture and the brightness of the liver-mirror are emphasized from the beginning of the passage (λεῖος καὶ λαμπρός, 71b). Furthermore, later (at 72c), as a sort of conclusion to this section, Timaeus compares the function of the spleen – the organ adjoining the liver – to a wiper (ἐκμαγεῖον). This wiper-spleen is laid beside the liver-mirror to keep its surface bright and clean (λαμπρὸν ἀεὶ καὶ καθαρόν – the two adjectives Aristotle uses to describe the ideal mirror). Here, we should recall that spotting on the actual liver was a key visual symbol in the tradition of hepatoscopy. Thus, just as a mirror's unpolished and corroded surface is not ideal for self-reflection, any changes in the liver's texture are not ideal for its function as a visual surface. The *Timaeus* then seems to constantly oscillate between, and in fact conflate, the two demarcated visual surfaces, that of the liver and the mirror.

One could note, however, that there is a significant difference between the liver's function as a visual surface, especially in the tradition of hepatoscopy, and the immediate purpose of a bronze mirror. When the *mantis* looked upon the liver, he would see (as we can reconstruct from the extant evidence) a series of visual stimuli that could then be interpreted as divine signs from an otherwise invisible source, the gods. The liver, in short, reflected images whose referents were otherwise unseen. In this aspect, the liver may seem to stand in sharp contrast with the mirror, an object primarily designed to reflect images of one's self. But the ancient mirror was a far more complicated visual surface than that.[30] On the one hand, there is some evidence in the classical period that mirrors could reflect numinous images, whose referents are otherwise unseen. For example, on a Lucanian nestoris from the fourth century BCE, a reflection of Clytemnestra (who is nowhere in the actual scene) appears to Orestes on the surface of a mirror from the world beyond.[31] In the *Timaeus*, the liver-mirror is also a surface upon which reflection without exact referents are produced: while Timaeus tells us that reason reflects images on the liver-mirror, he does not state that reason reflects images of *itself* – a point to which I shall return shortly.

Even with the similarities between the liver and the mirror (the texture and colour of their surfaces, their significance as two demarcated visual surfaces), the central question still remains: given the rich visual history of the liver in Greek culture, why does Plato compare the liver to a mirror in the first place? What does this man-made object contribute to the passage and how does it expand on and inform the existing cultural conceptions of the liver and the inner body? On the one hand, the liver-mirror seems to serve a similar function as that of the knot-like heart or the spongy lungs earlier in the *Timaeus*.[32] In all these instances, by comparing otherwise hidden and invisible organs of the body to everyday material objects, Plato helps the reader visualize what he cannot otherwise see. But the issue of visualization in this passage goes beyond that of a visual aid for the reader: the analogy of the liver-mirror mechanism not only allows us to visualize (i.e. form a mental image) of what we cannot see (i.e. our liver), but it also is the very tool in our body which helps explain how we are equipped with the power to visualize in the first place. The remainder of this chapter, then, will focus on the distinct attributes of the mirror; that is, the ways in which the liver-mirror, versus the liver alone, presents Plato with an original mechanism for theorizing the process of visualization in relation to his conception of the tripartite soul.

Plato's whole theory of the tripartite soul operates within a remarkably rich conception of non-rational cognition (to once again use Lorenz's terminology) centred on the senses.[33] Put differently, the senses (and sensory perception) are the primary means of communication between these two parts of the soul. First, we need to have a clear understanding of how the liver-mirror functions as a source of visual and sensory communication between reason and the appetite. To summarize the claims in section 71b–d (quoted earlier): Timaeus tells us that the appetitive part of the soul does not understand reason. Rather, both day and night, it is 'bewitched' – literally lead in respect to the soul (ψυχαγωγεῖν) – by images, specifically in the form of *eidōla* and *phantasmata* (71a). Therefore, in order to communicate with appetite, reason must lead this particular part of the soul through a visual medium.[34] In anticipation of this problem,[35] the gods created the structure of the liver (τὴν ἥπατος ἰδέαν συνέστησε),[36] which, like a mirror, is smooth, dense, bright, and capable of receiving visual impressions (τύποι) and reflecting them back so that they can be seen (καὶ κατιδεῖν εἴδωλα παρέχοντι). But how exactly does the rational part of the soul create images on the liver?

According to Timaeus' account, reason seems to be using the liver's mirroring qualities, such as its smooth and bright surface, alongside its own qualities of bitterness (μέρει τῆς πικρότητος χρωμένη συγγενεῖ) in order to reflect bilious-coloured images (χολώδη χρώματα ἐμφαίνοι) that then threaten and frighten the appetitive part of the soul. Later, reason then uses the sweetness inherent in the liver (γλυκύτητι δὲ τῇ κατ' ἐκεῖνο συμφύτῳ)[37] to paint images that are of the opposite kind (αὖ τἀναντία φαντάσματα ἀποζωγραφοῖ), i.e. un-bilious in colour and images which in turn produce a calm and pleasing response. Thus, it is clear that the mirror helps Plato to conjure the materiality of this new reflective surface. By drawing on the material qualities of both the liver and the mirror, Plato reminds us that the rational part of the soul is not casting images on a blank wall, so to speak, but is using crucial material aspects inherent in both objects (smoothness, brightness, sweetness, bitterness) in order to create its images.

Normally in a mirroring situation, there are two components: the mirror and the woman who sees her own image on its surface. Here, however, there are three players: the rational part of the soul is creating reflections on the liver for the appetitive part of the soul to see – much as a parent may create shadow puppets on a wall for a child to see. Thus, we should note that the rational part of the soul is *not seeing itself*, though it seems to be creating a sort of image in light of itself for the appetite to see.[38] In fact, Plato's subsequent mention of painting (*apozōgraphein*) is more appropriate to the situation of viewership: with a painting, you have an image that someone else has created (here the painter would be reason) which then another viewer (here the appetite) sees. The mirror analogy, however, is more suitable to the passage than painting for several reasons. First, in this scenario, reason needs to constantly change the reflections that the mirror surface is producing; thus, unlike a painting which remains fixed in the image it portrays, a mirror surface can quickly present different images for different amounts of time. Its visually flexible surface can work with the forces of reason in order to produce the images necessary to create a variety of psychosomatic experiences.[39]

In this sense, the mirror also does something the liver cannot: the liver, in the tradition of hepatoscopy, would have revealed a fixed set of visual cues that could only be interpreted once for a particular instance; but when conceptualized as a mirror, the liver becomes a surface that can constantly produce new and instantaneous reflections. This is especially important given the function of the liver in the passage as a mediator between reason and the appetite: the liver must constantly reflect different kinds of images in order for the rational part of the soul to keep the appetitive part (which only responds to visual stimuli) under control. The liver, moreover, no longer needs to be removed from the body to be seen and interpreted as in the tradition of hepatoscopy: rather, the new and improved liver-mirror is a constantly active visual organ of perception within us. The liver-mirror, moreover, does not only reflect the visual impressions (*tupoi*) of reason, but this new and improved reflective organ reveals prophetic images when we are asleep,[40] distraught by disease or under some kind of divine inspiration.[41] The liver-mirror, then, is somehow seen as mediating images not only from inside body but also from the divine realm.[42]

Here, we arrive at a final and key attribute of the liver-*mirror* in the *Timaeus*. By placing a mirror inside the body as a central mechanism of psychosomatic experience, Plato equips us with a tool for visualization par excellence. As it is well known, the mirror was a central analogy in theories of vision – that is theories on the mechanisms of sight and the nature of the eye – in the fifth and fourth centuries BCE.[43] In fact, earlier in the *Timaeus* (45d–46b) Plato imagines vision as a process of reflection. In the liver-mirror passage, however, the mirror is not an analogy for the actual process of seeing or for what can actually be seen. Rather, it is an analogy for what can be imagined visually – for the formation of *mental* images. The liver-mirror allows reason to show its power within and on the body. And although it is not quite clear how the appetite actually sees these images, the process points us towards a common human visual experience, that of visualization: our ability to conjure images in our minds without seeing them with our physical eye. And the tool central to our ability to visualize is the mirror – an object that can transform the power and breath of reason (i.e. abstract *logos*) into visual images and impressions.

The mirror-liver in short visualizes the realm of the intellect, and although we never find out what exactly the power of reason looks like, we nonetheless see a rather novel contribution on the part of the *Timaeus*. When visualizing the Platonic world, we are often encouraged to imagine immortal and invisible entities (much like what the rational part of the soul would be) as being without colour, without form – in other words as completely imperceptible, and visible to intelligence alone.[44] In the *Timaeus*, however, it is now *intelligence* (*nous*) that must make itself visible to the eye of the body. In order to do so, it must make itself (or the powers that stem from it) visible; it must make itself both beautiful and ugly, using precisely the flesh and colours of mortal human parts that the one would imagine Plato to otherwise reject.[45] Thus in the human body, *logos*, that is reason, must be visualized in order to be perceived and the mirror is the very mechanism with which it achieves this visualization.

The mirror then emerges from the *Timaeus* as an object of visualization *par excellence*. It is the very tool with which we can give abstract ideas (such as reason) a visual form; with which we can see when our eyes are closed; with which we remember, dream, and see divine inspirations while we sleep. Whether in our hands or embedded deep within the body, it is the producer of the most powerful images: those of the self, the intellect, and the divine.

CHAPTER 2
ALEXANDER OF APHRODISIAS ON THE REALITY OF MIRROR IMAGES[1]
Katerina Ierodiakonou

If nobody is in the bathroom, is the red towel reflected in the mirror? Or, is it only when somebody is in front of the mirror that the red towel is reflected in it? And what does somebody see, when looking at the red towel on the surface of the mirror? Is it the red towel itself, or is it some kind of appearance of the red towel? These are questions that contemporary philosophers raise and try to settle; they concern the reality of mirror images or, to use standard philosophical jargon, their ontological status.[2] But were ancient philosophers also puzzled by what we see in mirrors, and did they have something interesting to suggest on this topic? In particular, do we have any evidence that such issues were among the very many philosophical problems dealt with by Aristotle and his followers?

Aristotle says little about mirror reflections, apart from a few remarks in *Meteorology* 1.5–8 and 3.2–6, where he introduces them in order to explain phenomena such as rainbows and haloes. He seems to claim that what we see by reflection is not an image, but the perceived object itself in a faint manner; for instance, he claims that in the case of the rainbow we see the sun dimly, as if in a mirror, and not colour effects produced by the sun.[3] Alexander of Aphrodisias, on the other hand, the late second-century commentator of many Aristotelian treatises, develops a more elaborate theory of mirroring, which does not simply suggest that what we see in mirrors are the objects themselves but dimly. In his commentary on Aristotle's treatise *On Sense Perception* as well as in his own treatise *On the Soul* and in its *Supplement*, the so-called *Mantissa*,[4] Alexander compares mirror images to colours: colours arise from a particular sort of relation between the perceiver, the perceived object and the transparent medium between them; similarly, mirror images arise from a particular sort of relation between the perceiver, the perceived object, the transparent medium and the surface of the mirror. But if mirroring is understood as gaining a relational property, does this imply that images in the mirror are, according to Alexander, nothing but mere appearances? This is the main question I focus on, here, which has so far received rather little scholarly attention.

Mirror images are false

Let me start with two passages from the *Mantissa*, in which Alexander uses the perception of mirror images for a specific purpose; namely, to rebut the theories of vision advocated by the philosophical adversaries of Aristotle's views. The first passage clearly has as its target the Epicureans:

> How, if what is in the mirror is an image, do so many images again stream off from it, and why are the images in mirrors denser, so that so much streaming off comes from them? Why do these remain and not move? Why, since they do remain, do they not also remain even for a short time when the person who sees them has gone away? Why are images not on the surface of mirrors, but in their depth?[5]
>
> Alexander, Mantissa 135.27–32; trans. Sharples

The second passage seems to be against the Stoics:[6]

> Moreover how is it that after bending, either from mirrors or from transparent things, the effect of the pressure is preserved? This is not possible with a stick; for all things that are bent are made ineffective for pressing, as maimed bodies are for their activities.[7]
>
> Alexander, Mantissa 133.4-8; trans. Sharples. See also, 134.18–27

In the first text Alexander tries to show the inadequacy of the Epicurean theory of vision, according to which seeing takes place when images or effluences (*eidôla*), which are emitted with enormous velocity from the surface of external objects, reach and affect our sense organs.[8] If this were the case, Alexander asks among other things, why do these effluences remain on the surface of mirrors, and also why is it that they do not remain after the perceiver (or, for that matter, the perceived object) has moved away from the mirror? The Stoics, on the other hand, put forward the theory that we see when the innate *pneuma*, which stretches from the soul to our eyes, pricks the surrounding air and forms a continuous substance between our eyes and the perceived object, that is, a visual body in the shape of a cone with its base contiguous to the object; in this way, the visual body is in contact with the object, just like the walking-stick of the blind helps them to perceive external objects by touching them.[9] But Alexander asks the Stoics how come it happens that the bending of the visual body on the surface of mirrors does not turn it completely ineffective, just like the bending of the walking-stick makes it utterly useless.

I do not want to comment, here, on whether Alexander gives a fair description of his opponents' theories nor whether his arguments are good arguments.[10] Rather, what interests me is that mirror images are used by Alexander as evidence against previous theories of vision; and this is particularly unexpected, since Alexander, just like most philosophers in antiquity, generally doubts the accuracy and reliability of mirror images. For instance, there is a passage in his treatise *On the Soul* that manifests Alexander's reluctance to regard mirror images as trustworthy:

> The term 'clear' is applied sometimes to an appearance (*phantasia*) that is both true and strong – that is, to a cognitive appearance – but occasionally also to the one that is simply strong, in distinction to a weak appearance. A strong appearance

carries assent with it, unless it should have been discovered to be false through other criteria: we have this experience when we imagine, for instance, that the stars are not moving, or that one figure in a painting is actually taller than another, or see images in mirrors. We put no faith in such appearances not because they lack strength, but because they are discredited by others; and indeed it often happens that we distrust even some true and strong appearances, if we should somehow have come to be suspicious of them in advance.[11]

Alexander, *On the Soul* 71.13–21; trans. Fotinis modified

And in another passage referring to mirror images, this time in his commentary on the fifth book of Aristotle's *Metaphysics*, Alexander gives us the reason why he thinks that mirror images do not provide us with reliable information about external objects:

But it is in another way that things of the following type are false: those that, although they are beings (*onta*), are nevertheless the source of a false appearance because they appear either not to be the *kind* of thing that they are, or to be things that *are not*. These things are false in a way different from the one just described, for things whose appearance is false are not false [in the same way] as were the things discussed above. For these things are in fact *something* (*tina*), not however the kind of thing that they appear to be. Such are the things in pictures and sketches, which are something, but not what they appear to be; for they appear to be animals although they are not animals, nor any of the other things that the painting might portray. Similarly, the images (*phantasmata*) in dreams are also something (for certain movements take place in those who see the dream-images), but these images are not the kind of thing that they appear to be. For something appears to be walking or conversing, but this is not the case. The images (*emphainomena*) that appear in mirrors are things of this sort and are also false in this way, for they too are something, but not what they appear to be.[12]

Alexander, in *Met.* 432.11–22; trans. Dooley

So, Alexander claims that mirror images are false, in the sense that they do not give us accurate knowledge of, for instance, the position and size of perceived objects, but he insists that they are beings, in the sense that they are something, just like paintings and dream images are something but not what they appear to be. The question that needs to be addressed, of course, is what kind of beings, of something, mirror images are exactly, or in other words, what their ontological status is.

Mirror images, colours and light

There is a passage in Alexander's treatise *On the Soul*, in which he compares mirror images to colours and light. Alexander claims, following closely Aristotle's theory of vision, that the transparent medium between the perceiver and the external objects does not retain their colours after they are gone away, and also the air stops being illuminated as soon as the source of light is no longer present; similarly, mirror images disappear as soon as the reflected objects are removed from in front of the mirror:

> For the colour comes to be present in what is illuminated and in light in the same way that light comes to be present in what is transparent, though what is transparent does not receive light or light colour in virtue of an effluence or in the way matter [receives something]. In fact, when the things that produce these [effects] have gone away, the colour immediately leaves the light as well (in the case where the things that tinge it go away) and light leaves the transparent (in the case where what illuminates it is not present). The sort of change that arises from both sources occurs in what receives them in virtue of a presence and a particular sort of relation (*schesin*), much as [the reflections] in mirrors come to be present in them … This light comes to be by the presence of fire or the divine body in the transparent. For light comes about in virtue of the illuminant's relation (*schesin*) to things whose nature it is to be illuminated. For light is not a body and so comes to be instantaneously.[13]
>
> Alexander, *On the Soul* 42.19–43.11; trans. Caston

If it happens sometimes that human beings continue to see the colour of objects, when the objects themselves are not present any longer, it is because we are ensouled creatures and able to form memories, whereas the transparent medium and mirrors do not retain light or the colours of objects, since they are inanimate:

> The fact that, when the things seen have moved away, some of the colours seem to be left behind in the eyes of those who saw is not a sign of an alteration (*alloiôseôs*). For [the eye] is affected in this way not as being transparent, but as ensouled and able to form images. For this is why it can still preserve for a time the movements that were produced in the sense-organs from external objects. And ensouled [creatures] are even at a subsequent time able to place before their eyes images that they had. At any rate mirrors, even though they are smooth and bright, do not preserve in themselves anything of the colours that appeared in them when either the light or the [source] of illumination or the objects of sight have departed, because they are not affected (*paschei*) and are not ensouled.[14]
>
> Alexander, *Mantissa* 145.7–16; trans. Sharples

So, how does Alexander explain the phenomenon that the transparent medium does not retain light and the colours of perceived objects after they have been removed? Does his explanation apply in the case of mirrors, which also fail to retain the reflected images of objects as soon as these are no longer present?

According to the Aristotelian theory of visual perception, we see an object by means of its colour changing the transparent medium between us and the object perceived. The problem is, of course, how exactly Aristotle understands this change or, as he himself often calls it, 'alteration' (*alloiôsis*). Indeed, this is the main issue on which the attention of contemporary scholars has been focused, during the last decades, with regard to Aristotle's doctrine on sense perception; it concerns the question whether there are, in Aristotle's view, material changes in the transparent medium responsible for the fact that we see colours, or whether Aristotle's doctrine does not involve the assumption of any physical process. The first interpretation is known as the literalist interpretation, whereas the second as the spiritualist or intentionalist interpretation.[15] According to the spiritualist interpretation, seeing colours does not necessarily imply that something actually moves from the coloured object and changes the transparent medium, by starting a material process that enables us to see its colours; what happens, instead, is that the object's colours simply appear through the transparent medium, and this has been described as a quasi-alteration initiated by the object and affecting the medium. In other words, when we see a red towel, the transparent medium becomes in some way red without undergoing a real alteration, i.e. without becoming actually red.

On this highly controversial issue it seems that Alexander sides with the spiritualist interpretation. Indeed, it has been argued that his reading of the Aristotelian account of visual perception represents the first stage of a long process in the history of philosophy of de-materializing Aristotle's theory.[16] For Alexander often repeats that no real alteration or affection (*pathos*) is involved when we see colours, when the transparent medium is illuminated, or when reflections appear on the surface of mirrors. This is after all how he explains, for instance, the fact that two perceivers, one white and one black, are able to see each other, since the transparent medium between them does not change by the colour white in such a way that it would become impossible to register the colour black, or the other way round; similarly, when something is reflected in a mirror, the surface of the mirror does not change in such a way that it would be impossible for other things to be reflected in it, too:

> Even if these two viewers are themselves black and white respectively, and are looking at each other, there is nothing to prevent the air between them from serving at the same time as a medium for their two acts of seeing, since it is not a passive recipient (*mê pathêtikôs*) of the motion imparted to it by the two objects, nor is it a material subject on which they act. There is the further fact that colours appear as reflections in a mirror or in water without producing any change of colour in the reflecting surface; this is evidence that the motion emanating from the sensible object and terminating in these surfaces ceases to operate as soon as the sensible object itself has been removed.[17]
>
> <div align="right">Alexander, <i>On the Soul</i> 62.11–16; trans. Fotinis.
See also, Alexander, <i>Mantissa</i> 147.16–25</div>

But whether or not Alexander's spiritualist interpretation faithfully presents Aristotle's theory of visual perception, there should be no doubt that what actually constitutes a considerable deviation from the Aristotelian text is Alexander's insistence that the emergence of colours, light and mirror images are the result of a particular sort of relation (*schesis*).

The relational character of seeing

To understand Alexander's explanation of the formation of mirror images by virtue of a relation, we need to summon help from passages in his writings in which he does not refer to mirrors, but clarifies the relational character of colours and light. For instance, in his commentary on Aristotle's *On Sense Perception*, Alexander agrees with Aristotle that light is not a body, and further adds that it depends upon the relation between the source of light and the transparent medium:

> If they were to say that what is sent out is light, it would need to be demonstrated to them that it is without body and unable to be sent out and poured forth, as they say. For <light> comes about depending upon a relation (*kata schesin*) between that which is naturally illuminated and that which is able to illuminate. For this reason there is not a movement of light. At any rate, so far as concerns things which can be illuminated from the same distance by <that which naturally illuminates>, we see both the things that are illuminated which are close to the natural illuminant and those which are far away from it at the same time. This would be impossible if light were a body. It is clear that light is a relation (*schesis tis*), and is dependent upon a relation (*kata schesin*) between the illuminant and the illuminated, and is not a substance and body, from the fact that <light> does not persist even for a little while when the illuminant has been turned away.[18]
>
> Alexander, *De sens.* 31.10–18; trans. Towey

Furthermore, in order to explain how light comes about by virtue of a particular sort of relation, and not by virtue of an alteration of the transparent medium, Alexander refers, later on in his commentary, to the relation between father and son, as well as between things on the right and things on the left. For something on the right, for instance, is no longer said to be on the right when the thing on the left changes its position, and similarly light is no longer present in the transparent medium when there is no more luminous source:

> That light depends on a relation (*en schesei*) but not on an alteration is clear from the fact that, whereas things which are altered have not ceased from the affection that is generated in them by that which alters <them> immediately upon its departure (for when that which heats departs that which is heated by it does not immediately cease from the heat that is generated in it by <that which heats>), things that are such by virtue of their relation to something (*kata tên pros ti schesin*) cease to be in the relation to that thing in conjunction with its departure. For the father has ceased being a father when the son has died, and when that which is on

the left has departed that which is on the right is on the right no longer. The same is true of light. For it departs all together in conjunction with the departure of that which naturally illuminates.[19]

Alexander, *De sens.* 134.11–19; trans. Towey

Also, in the *Mantissa*, Alexander stresses that light and colours come about in the transparent medium not by an alteration but by virtue of what he calls a 'modification' (*tropê*), or a 'seeming alteration in accordance with a relation' (*dokousês alloiôseôs kata schesin*); and he parallels, again, this relation to that between things on the right and things on the left:

> The modification [brought about] in the air and in the potentially transparent by fire and by colours is not like that which we say comes about in things that are altered. For alteration is a change and comes about in time and with a transition, but the transparent does not receive light and colours in such a way as to be altered in these respects, but the transparent is said to be affected in the same way as if someone were to say that what comes to be on the right of something has been affected without having been moved itself or received any affection into itself. This is what the modification of the transparent in accordance with light and colours is like too; for it is by the presence of what illuminates or is coloured that the transparent comes to be like this, as [it is] by relation to the [person] who stands alongside on the left that the [person] on the right [comes to be situated on the right]. A sign that this is how it is that, as the [person] on the right ceases to be on the right when the one on the left changes his position, so light ceases when the source of illumination changes its position, and similarly when what is of such a nature as to be seen [does so, the transparent] ceases to be like this, not having received any affection by a change in itself, but when the seeming alteration has happened to it in accordance with a relation.[20]

Alexander, *Mantissa* 143.4–18; trans. Sharples

It is not surprising that Alexander treats light and colours as depending upon a relation, since Aristotle in his *Categories* (ch.7, 6a36–b4) includes perception, and therefore seeing, among the examples of the category of relatives, i.e. the category of *pros ti*: seeing is, according to Aristotle, a relative, in the sense that it occurs when we see its objects and its objects are its objects when we see them; hence, the objects of seeing, namely light and colours, can also be said to depend upon a particular sort of relation. What immediately strikes us, though, is Alexander's terminology. For Alexander characterizes light and colours not only by using the Aristotelian term '*pros ti*', but also by using – in fact, by making abundant use of – phrases involving the term '*schesis*', which is here translated as 'relation'. And this observation turns out to be interesting, since the noun '*schesis*' is found in the surviving Aristotelian treatises only once (*History of Animals* 10.7, 638b17), in a context completely unrelated to the subject of relatives. Aristotle has no noun to denote a relation, but only talks of something being a *pros ti*, i.e. something being directed towards, or relative to, or in relation to something else. On the other hand, the term *'schesis'* becomes after Aristotle a much-used term by Alexander as well as by the other Aristotelian commentators.[21]

Most importantly, in all these passages, Alexander does not only state that light and colours depend upon a relation; in addition, he discusses the kind of relation they depend upon. As it has already been pointed out, he claims that light and colours depend upon a relation that can be compared to the relation between father and son, or between things on the right and things on the left. However, there is also a passage in his commentary (*in De sens.* 126.25–128.6), in which Alexander seems to endorse a different position. After presenting Aristotle's view that seeing is not a *pros ti* of the kind to be found in a relation between equal, unequal or similar things because, unlike such cases, in seeing the position of its objects matters, Alexander first suggests that we should think of seeing as depending upon a relation similar to that between things on the right and things on the left, but later on he makes a different suggestion:[22]

> Or better, seeing needs some relation, though seeing does not consist in the relation (whereas that which is on the right consists in the relation); but it also <needs> that there is some power that is able to apprehend the objects seen. For without this the relation is of no use for seeing. For this reason, <that which is seen is seen> both in being transparent and by virtue of a relation, and seeing is no longer by virtue of a relation.[23]
>
> Alexander, *De sens.* 128.2–6; trans. Towey, modified

That is to say, Alexander seems to propose, here, an alternative interpretation of how to understand seeing as a relative. He now puts forward the view that the relation between things on the right and things on the left is not really helpful for determining the kind of relation we have between that which sees and that which is seen. For he clearly says that what is on the right consists in its relation to what is on the left, whereas seeing depends upon the relation to its objects but it does not consist in it. But in order to figure out what Alexander has exactly in mind in this extremely elliptical passage, we obviously need to become clearer about the distinction between something consisting in a relation and something simply requiring a relation but not consisting in it.

Cases of relatives that consist in a relation, like things on the right and things on the left, have been presented in scholarly discussions as ancient examples of relational change or, in contemporary philosophical jargon, as ancient examples of 'mere Cambridge change'; that is to say, as cases of change which involve acquiring or losing a predicate without undergoing internal alteration.[24] It is actually in Plato's *Theaetetus* (154B–155D) that we first come across the idea of a relative changing merely because its correlative has changed, and not because it has changed in itself: Socrates comes to be shorter than the growing Theaetetus, without any intrinsic change taking place in Socrates himself, and thus he undergoes a merely Cambridge change.[25] So, some scholars have indicated that Alexander probably understands seeing as another case of a mere Cambridge change, since the transparent medium is not really altered, according to him, but it is solely by virtue of its relation to the luminous source or the coloured object that it becomes illuminated and transmits colours.[26] However, Alexander seems not to be content with the view that light and colours depend upon a relation similar to that between things on the right and things on the left; as he himself says, seeing simply requires a relation to its objects, whereas something on the right consists in its relation to something on the left.

Mirror images are real

This is not the occasion to discuss in detail what it means for Alexander, and more generally for the Aristotelian tradition, to treat seeing as a relative of a certain kind. Still, it is important to ask, in this context, why Alexander draws the distinction between a relative that requires a relation and a relative that consists in it, since this distinction seems to affect the way he conceives of the nature of light and colours as well as of mirror images.

In the last quoted passage from his commentary on Aristotle's *On Sense Perception*, Alexander (in *De sens.* 128.2-6) argues that the similarity between seeing and, for instance, things on the right does not go further than the fact that they are both relatives. For there is a crucial difference in the kind of relatives they are: in seeing, he claims, more is required than the relation to its objects, namely the transparent medium as well as a power that is able to perceive the external objects. That is to say, in order for us to see what is needed is something that causes the act of seeing, i.e. its object, but also the perceptual capacity to do so and the transparent medium between us and the perceived object. Similarly, in the case of light and colours: light depends upon the relation between the luminous object and the transparent medium, but it does not consist in this relation, since it also depends upon the presence of a luminous source, namely fire or the divine body. Colours, too, depend upon the relation between the coloured objects and the illuminated transparent medium, but they do not consist in this relation, since they also depend upon the transparency which, according to the Aristotelian theory, characterizes both the medium as well as the coloured objects; for colour is defined by Aristotle as the limit of the transparency in a determinately bounded object (*On Sense Perception* 439b11-12), and the transparency is understood as the common nature that resides in all bodies to a greater or lesser degree depending on the proportion of their constitutive elements (*On Sense Perception* 439a21-25).[27]

Therefore, although light and colours are said to depend upon a relation, there is no obstacle to treat them as real and objective, since they do not simply consist in this relation. In this way, Alexander is perfectly in line with Aristotle's realism, according to which colours are regarded as features of the world that cause us to perceive them, rather than subjective properties of our own experiences. And this is how Alexander seems to understand mirror images, too; although they depend upon a relation, they should not be considered as mere appearances but, rather, as some kind of beings, as something. Does Alexander reserve a special place in the ontology he inherits from Aristotle for such beings, a place that is distinct from perceived objects, so that mirror images can be distinguished from them and still count as something? Unfortunately, Alexander says nothing on this.

To conclude: I think it is quite intriguing how often Alexander stresses the fact that mirror images, just like colours and light, should be understood as depending upon a particular sort of relation, and more specifically a relation that preserves their objective character. Would Aristotle have agreed with the way Alexander interprets and develops his few remarks on mirroring? Ancient thinkers and contemporary scholars share the view that Alexander's readings of Aristotle's doctrines are the most philosophically insightful of antiquity. However, before we accept them as truly expressing the Aristotelian dogma we need to examine them carefully, for they can be rather ambitious and thus tricky at times. At least in the particular case of light, colours and mirror images, it seems to me that Alexander tries to flesh out what he thinks is already implicit in Aristotle's treatises, by introducing sophisticated distinctions that bring out and explicate their relational character.

CHAPTER 3
CATOPTROLOGY IN LUCRETIUS' *DRN* (4.269–323)[1]

Myrto Garani

In the last chapter of his *Naturales Quaestiones* 1, Seneca claims that, even if philosophers are ridiculed, because they rant about the nature of mirrors and reflections, there is no way that nature made such a gift of hard work just *for the sake of luxury* (*Nat. Quaest.* 1.17.1–2):

> *Derideantur nunc philosophi quod de speculi natura disserant*, quod inquirant quid ita facies nostra nobis et quidem in nos obversa reddatur, quid sibi rerum natura voluerit quod, cum vera corpora edidisset, etiam simulacra eorum aspici voluit, quorsus pertinuerit hanc comparare materiam excipiendarum imaginum potentem; non in hoc scilicet ut ad speculum barbam velleremus aut ut faciem viri poliremus (*in nulla re illa luxuriae negotium concessit*).

> Now let people mock philosophers because they discuss the nature of mirrors, because they ask why our appearance is sent back to us, why it faces toward us, what nature was thinking of when, after producing real bodies, she also wanted likenesses of them to be seen, what was the point of producing this material capable of receiving images. It was not, surely, so that we could pluck our beards in front of a mirror, or so that we men could make our faces smooth: she has never in any way served the interests of luxury.

In my chapter I intend to focus only upon the Epicurean approach to catoptrics, in the way this can be tracked down within Lucretius' *De rerum natura*. Lucretius' account of mirrors forms part of his general discussion about sensation in his book 4 (*DRN* 4.26–44):

> Atque animi quoniam docui natura quid esset
> et quibus e rebus cum corpore compta vigeret
> quove modo distracta rediret in ordia prima,
> nunc agere incipiam tibi, quod vehementer ad has res
> attinet, esse ea quae **rerum simulacra** vocamus;
> quae, **quasi membranae summo de corpore rerum**
> dereptae, volitant ultroque citroque per auras,
> atque eadem nobis vigilantibus obvia mentes
> terrificant atque in somnis, cum saepe figuras

> contuimur miras **simulacraque** luce carentum,
> quae nos horrifice languentis saepe sopore
> excierunt; ne forte animas Acherunte reamur
> effugere aut umbras inter vivos volitare
> neve aliquid nostri post mortem posse relinqui,
> cum corpus simul atque animi natura perempta
> in sua discessum dederint primordia quaeque.
> dico igitur rerum effigias tenuisque figuras
> mittier ab rebus summo de cortice eorum;
> id licet hinc quamvis hebeti cognoscere corde.

Now, since I have explained what is the nature of the mind, from what elements it takes its strength when combined with the body, and how when torn away from the body, it returns to its first elements, you shall now see me begin to deal with what is of high importance for this subject, and to show that there exist what we call images of things, which, like films drawn from the outermost surface of things, flit about hither and thither through the air; it is these same that, encountering us in wakeful hours, terrify our minds, as also in sleep, when we often behold wonderful shapes and images of the dead, which have often aroused us in horror while we lay languid in sleep; lest by chance we should think that spirits escape from Acheron or ghosts flit about amongst the living, or that anything of us can be left after death, when body and mind both taken off together have dissolved abroad, each into its own first-beginnings. I say, therefore, that semblances and thin shapes of things are thrown off from their outer surface. This can be recognized by the dullest brain from what follows.

According to the Epicurean theory of visual perception, a constant flow of unseen images, the so-called εἴδωλα (i.e. idols) or – in Latin – *simulacra* or *imagines* is thrown off unremittingly from the outermost surface of things at great speed. Lucretius likens this phenomenon to cicadas shedding their jackets in summer, calves throwing off the caul from their outermost surface at birth and slippery serpents casting off their vesture amongst the thorns: since these things happen, a thin image must also be thrown off from things, from the outermost surface of things (*DRN* 4.57–64). These effluences, which are envisioned as three-dimensional molds of the object they originated from, while retaining the shape, size and colour of that initial object, fall upon our eyes and are considered to be responsible for visual perception.

As far as Epicurus' explicit interest in catoptrics is concerned, apart from the occurrence of the term τὰς [ἀν]ἀκλασεις in his fragmentary Περὶ φύσεως book 2, which deals with the formation and the speed of idols (Epic. fr. [23] [12]1 Arr.), there is no extant catoptrical treatise of his; our doxographical sources offer testimony for a possible Epicurean theory about the formation of mirror-images, which roughly agree with what we read in Lucretius' poem (Apuleius *Apologia* 15):[2]

Quid quod nec ob haec debet tantummodo philosophus speculum invisere? nam saepe oportet non modo similitudinem suam, verum etiam ipsius similitudinis rationem considerare: num, ut ait Epicurus, profectae a nobis imagines velut quaedam exuviae iugi fluore a corporibus manantes, cum leve aliquid et solidum offenderunt, illisae reflectantur et retro expressae contraversim respondeant.

What is more, even these are not the only reasons for a philosopher to look in a mirror. For often he should contemplate not only his likeness but the cause of likeness itself. Are images projected from us, as Epicurus says, flying in a continuous stream from our bodies like a kind of skin, so that, on meeting something smooth and solid, they then rebound on impact and bounce back so as to appear reversed?

Further evidence about this theory can also be gathered from the second century AD fragmentary Epicurean inscription which Diogenes of Oinoanda, in Lycia, carved onto a portico wall, in order to show his fellow-citizens the road to happiness (fr. 9.I.5–II.14 Smith):

I 5   πολ[λ]άκις ὅ[τι εἰκόνες]
      καὶ φάσματα [φύσεις ἀλη]-
      θεῖς ὑπάρχουσιν, καὶ τὰ
      κάτοπτρα μαρτυρήσει
      μοι· οὐ δὴ γὰρ ἀπερεῖ τι
10   ἄ φημι τ[ὸ] εἴδωλον ὃ προσ-
      ομεῖται ἐν τοῖς κατό-
      πτροις. <u>v</u> οὐκ ἂν ἐν ἐκεί-
      νοις ἑαυτοὺ[ς ἑ]ω[ρ]ῶμεν
      καὶ οὐδ' ἂν ἐγείνετο.
II   [τι, εἰ μὴ ἦν ῥεῦμα συνε]
      [χὲς ἀφ' ἡμῶν πρὸς ἐκεῖ]
      [να φερόμενον καὶ] ἡμεῖν
      εἴδωλον ἀναφέρον. <u>v</u> ἀπε-
5   λέν[χ]ει γὰρ καὶ τοῦτο τὴν
      ἀπόροιαν διὰ τὸ ἕκασ-
      τον τῶν μορίων εἰς τὴν
      κατ' εὐθὺ χώραν φέρεσ-
      θαι. <u>v</u> τὰ οὖν ἀπὸ τῶν πρα-
      γμάτων ῥέοντα εἴδω-
      λα, ἐνπείπτοντα ἡμῶν
      ταῖς ὄψεσιν, τοῦ τε ὁρᾶν
      ἡμᾶς τὰ ὑποκείμενα
      αἴτια γείνεται καί, εἰς

[And] often mirrors too will be my witnesses [that likenesses] and appearances are real [entities]. For what I say will certainly not be denied at all by the image which will give supporting evidence on oath in mirrors. We should not see ourselves in them, nor indeed would [any reflection] be created, [if there were not a continual flow being borne from us to the mirrors and bringing back an image] to us. For this too is convincing proof of the effluence, seeing that each of the parts is carried to the point straight ahead. Now the images that flow from objects, by impinging on our eyes, cause us both to see external realities.

We should also bear in mind that despite our meager evidence, for Lucretius' contemporaries mirrors were generally associated with superstitions and the common practice of catoptromancy (or enoptromancy), i.e. the performance of divination by gazing at images reflected into a mirror or another shining surface (e.g. Pausanias 7.21.11–12).[3] We should draw our attention to a fresco in Room 5 of the so-called 'Villa of the Mysteries', which is situated just outside Pompeii on the road to Herculaneum; this famous fresco, which was painted towards the middle of the first century BC and uncovered in 1909, depicts scenes from Dionysiac Mysteries; among these scenes stands out the figure of a young satyr looking intensely into a cup which is held by a Silenus: it is significant that this specific scene, which is contemporaneous to Lucretius' philosophical poem, is generally believed to be one of catoptromancy.[4] It is also worth pointing out that in the second century AD Apuleius (*Apologia* 13–16) rebuts the accusation that, since he possessed a mirror, which was anyway a lavish object difficult to get hold of, he was also involved in the performance of catoptromancy.[5]

It seems, therefore, plausible that Lucretius reserves within his natural philosophical project a special place for his account on mirrors, as a pointed reply to such superstitious practices; this catoptrical account forms part of his endeavour to liberate his pupil, Memmius, from the excruciating shackles of religion and lead him into the Epicurean ideal state of ataraxia, i.e. the ultimate peace of mind. By expounding the intricate catoptrical mechanics, Lucretius suggests that by no means should Memmius think that mirrors are somehow associated either with the deceptively dreadful shadows of the dead or the fictitious ghosts. In other words, for the Epicurean philosopher mirrors have nothing to do with those miraculous functions which are commonly assigned to them by the servants of popular religion such as 'soul-catcher', 'portal to the dead' or 'oracular window on the future' – to use Taylor's phrasing.[6]

As I will demonstrate, far from being just vain objects of luxury, mirrors are incorporated within Lucretius' wide-ranging philosophical argumentation and their otherwise obscure mechanics are eventually endowed with an enlightening *cognitive force*. In this way, Lucretius transforms mirrors from magical tools into tools with indispensable probative and demonstrative value. By initiating his pupil into the catoptrical secrets of nature, Lucretius aims at overcoming the astonishment caused by the limitations that our sensory organs pose.[7] In other words, once their mechanics are deciphered, mirrors are used, in literal and metaphorical terms, as *channels into the unseen atomic world*.

Lucretius explicitly introduces mirrors for the first time in the beginning of Book 4.[8] The reader is already familiar with the fact which was repeatedly touched upon throughout the poem, that in accordance with natural laws, there exist in the microcosmic and macrocosmic world things which are ἄδηλα, since they can never be brought literally before our eyes, either because they are located below our senses due to their size (atoms, atomic structure of things) or too far off for us to obtain a near view of them. That is why, as Lucretius suggests, we have to find *analogical devices*, so as to *metaphorically* elicit and mentally perceive the secrets of nature. Paradoxically, despite the fact that due to their extremely subtle substance, idols are in principle classified among the things which are by nature invisible, Lucretius points to the probative function of mirrors, which disclose the actual existence of idols streaming off objects (*DRN* 4.98–109):

Postremo speculis in aqua splendoreque in omni
quaecumque apparent nobis **simulacra**, necessest,
quandoquidem simili specie sunt praedita rerum, 100
ex ea **imaginibus** missis consistere eorum. 101
sunt igitur tenues formae rerum similesque 104
effigiae, singillatim quas cernere nemo 105
cum possit, tamen adsiduo crebroque repulsu
reiectae reddunt speculorum ex aequore visum,
nec ratione alia servari posse videntur,
tanto opere ut similes reddantur cuique figurae.

Lastly, whatever similitudes we see in mirrors, in water in any bright surface, since they are possessed of the same appearance as the things, must consist of images thrown off from those things. There are therefore thin shapes and like semblances of things, which singly no one can perceive, yet being flung back by *incessant and unremitting repulsion* give back a vision from the surface of mirrors. Nor does there seem to be any other way in which they could be preserved so that figures so like each thing should be given back.

Lucretius makes an appeal to common experience and underscores a tangible fact that anyone can easily attest: as soon as an object is placed in front of a mirror, its idol appears on the mirror. From this point of view, mirrors should be considered to be the essential instrument, thanks to which one can intrude into the unseen world of atoms and perceive the fundamental Epicurean notion of *simulacra*. To put it in different words, mirrors are used as a *window* into the unseen world of atoms, a unique case of visualizing the otherwise ἄδηλα idols.[9]

Whereas the Epicureans believe that sensation is the primary source of truth and hence set great value on sensory evidence (cf. *DRN* 1.423–425), still they warn that one should always make a *distinction* between sense-impressions and the mental formation of beliefs about reality. Despite, therefore, the preliminary *cognitive* value of mirrors, Lucretius makes clear the fact that the mechanics of mirrors are particularly thorny:

since mirrors, depending on their plane, curved or concave shape, may often send back inverted or even distorted images, they may lead one to visual illusions, which are partly responsible for the erroneous magical force attributed to them; that is why one should not rely exclusively upon the idols bounced back from mirrors, without mentally assessing them. Whereas Lucretius deals with various catoptrical problems,[10] I will discuss two of them, which I consider most characteristic of his demonstrative method.

In the first place, Lucretius deals with a case of sensory illusion and explains why reflected idols seem to be on the other side of the mirror (*ultra speculum*, 4.269), as if mirrors have depth (*DRN* 4.269-291):

Nunc age, cur *ultra speculum* videatur **imago**
percipe; nam certe ***penitus remmota*** videtur.
quod genus illa foris quae vere *transpiciuntur*,
ianua cum per se *transpectum* praebet apertum,
multa facitque foris ex aedibus ut videantur;
is quoque enim *duplici geminoque* fit *aëre* visus:
primus enim citra postes tum cernitur aër,
inde fores ipsae dextra laevaque sequuntur,
post extraria lux oculos perterget et aër
alter et illa foris quae vere **transpiciuntur**.
sic ubi se primum speculi proiecit imago,
dum venit ad nostras acies, protrudit agitque
aëra qui inter se cumquest oculosque locatus,
et facit ut prius hunc omnem sentire queamus
quam ***speculum***; sed ubi ***speculum*** quoque sensimus ipsum,
continuo a nobis illuc quae fertur imago
pervenit, et nostros oculos reiecta revisit,
atque alium prae se propellens aëra volvit,
et facit ut prius hunc quam se videamus, eoque
distare *ab speculo tantum semota videtur*.
quare etiam atque etiam *minime mirarier* est par,

illis quae reddunt speculorum ex aequore visum,
aëribus binis quoniam res confit utraque.

Now listen while I tell why the image is seen beyond the mirror; for certainly it seems to be far withdrawn. It is the same as with those objects which are seen in their reality through the doors outside, when the doorway provides an open view through it and allows us to see from the house many things outside. For this vision also is brought about by two distinct stretches of air; for first in this case is seen the air on this side of the doors, next follows the door itself right and left leaf, afterwards the external light brushes the eyes, and the other air, and those things which are seen in their reality through the doors outside. So when the image of the mirror has first thrown itself forwards, while it is on the way to our eyes, it pushes and drives all the air that is between itself and our eyes, and makes us able to perceive all this before we perceive the mirror; but when we have perceived the mirror itself also, at once the image which is carried from us to the mirror reaches it, and being flung back, comes back to our eyes, rolling and propelling before it another air, and makes us see this before we see itself; and that is why it seems to be withdrawn so far off from the mirror. Therefore, again and again I say, it is by no means right to wonder [that this happens both to those things which are seen through doors and also] to those things which give back a vision from the surface of a mirror, since the whole is done by two airs in each case.

In order to demonstrate his theory, Lucretius applies his easily recognizable analogical practice: by taking for granted the universal material homogeneity which is conditioned by the same natural laws, he observes the same or similar natural mechanism which takes place on a coordinated level of reality and appeals to what is manifest, in order to make a deduction about the unseen. In the case under investigation, wherein he draws an analogy with the easily perceptible image of things which are seen through an open doorway and visualizes first the surface of the *mirror as three-dimensional,* he eventually demolishes this illusion. In order to rectify this misconception, the pupil should realize the difference between the two parts of Lucretius' comparison: by means of verbal repetition, he draws attention to the fact that what happens *in reality* is juxtaposed with what just *seems* to take place (4.271 *vere*, 4.278 *vere*; 4.270 *videtur*, 4.288 *videtur*). The details of Lucretius' explanation are rather convoluted – and Sharples' corresponding discussion is very helpful in this respect.[11]

Before we proceed into dissecting the 'scientific' argument of the passage, we should first draw our attention to Lucretius' duplicated claim that he is about to elucidate what 'seems to be far withdrawn' (4.270 *penitus remmota videtur*, 4.288 *tantum semota*). Along the same lines, it is also noteworthy the use of the key-word *transpiciuntur*, a rare compound verb, not found elsewhere in our early extant Latin texts and employed in the present context in its literal sense, meaning 'to see through' (4.271 *transpectum*, 4.278 *vere transpiciuntur*). This expression looks back intra-textually to earlier metaphorical language, which is employed in association with Lucretius' *scientific method* of unveiling the unseen. More precisely, the reader conjures up Lucretius' statement in the prologue to Book 1, regarding the process of cognition of universal constitution, thanks to which his pupil will have the privilege to '*see into the heart* of things hidden' (1.145 *res quibus occultas penitus convisere possis*). Lucretius admonishes his pupil, Memmius, to become 'a penetrating reader' of nature – to use Clay's phrase – in order to *see through* the surface of things and perceive their nature – a process which is suggested over and over again in the course of the poem by the use of compound verbs such as *convisere* or *perspicere*, whose prefix intensifies the notion of intellectual penetration.[12] Along the same lines, Lucretius' first explanation of catoptrical illusion should also be considered to be *programmatic*, regarding the instructions given to his pupil, in the latter's attempt to trespass on the hidden mysteries of nature. The Epicurean pupil is encouraged to *look through* the actual doors and then in philosophical terms to 'think out of the box'; in order to do so, Lucretius puts forward an analogy, by means of which the pupil is assisted to make the necessary mental projection to the mirror, so as to 'restore' the idol back to the *surface of the mirror*.

Despite the programmatic connotations of this catoptrical analogy, it should not pass unobserved the fact that in this context Lucretius significantly inverts his standard metaphorical imagery. Whereas the visual projection to the space out of the door is a *literal* one, in the case of mirrors there is no such a thing as literal – even if invisible – depth beyond the surface of the mirrors to be explored; quite the contrary, the intrusion into the catoptrical unseen world can take place only metaphorically and only so as to unveil the *actual non-existence* of such a *space* endowed *with magical force* reserved for the idols.

As far as his analogical method is concerned, the common denominator of the two parts of the simile, on the basis of which Lucretius forms his conclusion, is *the role of air* in the perception of *distance*. As I have argued elsewhere, Lucretius systematically incorporates within his similes Empedocles' technique of 'inferring conclusions about a particular group of invisible physical phenomena, which involve the presence of an Empedoclean root, by observing its behaviour or action within an accessible container or environment under conditions which are similar to the visible ones.'[13]

Lucretius has discussed earlier in Book 4 the mechanism of perceiving *the distance* of the objects seen; as he argues, the idols drive a current of air before them, by the length of which we judge distance (*DRN* 4.244– 255):

> Et quantum quaeque ab nobis res absit, imago
> efficit ut videamus et internoscere curat;
> nam cum mittitur, extemplo protrudit agitque
> aëra qui inter se cumque est oculosque locatus,
> isque ita per nostras acies perlabitur omnis
> et quasi perterget pupillas atque ita transit.
> propterea fit uti videamus quam procul absit
> res quaeque; et quanto plus aëris ante agitatur
> et nostros oculos perterget longior aura,
> tam procul esse magis res quaeque remota videtur.
> scilicet haec summe celeri ratione geruntur,
> quale sit ut videamus, et una quam procul absit.

And the image enables us to see and takes care that we distinguish how far each thing is distant from us; for when it is sent off, at once it pushes and drives all the air that is between itself and our eyes, and thus this air all streams through our eyes and, as it were, brushes the pupils and thus passes through. This is how we come to see how far off each this is; and the more air is driven before it, the longer the breeze that brushes our eyes, the more distant and far removed the thing is seen to be. Assuredly all this passes in a supremely rapid manner, so that we see all at once both what it is and how far away.

Lucretius disregards the objective difficulties that the validity of this so-called 'air-channel' theory involve and which were pointed out already in antiquity, as we gather from Alexander's of Aphrodisias discussion in his *De sensu* (57.21–26 CIAG Wendland) and in *Mantissa* (136.11–24 Bruns).[14] Instead, he takes it for granted and invites his pupil to observe *the parallel role played by air* in both parts of his analogy (open doors: 4.274 *duplici geminoque* [...] *aere*, 4.275 *primus* [...] *aer*, 4.277–278 *aer alter*; mirror: 4.281 *aera qui inter se cumquest oculosque locatus*; in both cases: 4.291 *aeribus binis*). Assuming that this theory holds true, when we see objects through an open door, (1) we first perceive the air between us and the door, (2) then the door itself, (3) then another current of air outside, and (4) finally the object outside. In a similar way, while (1) the image of the mirror is coming to us, it drives on the air between itself and us, which we perceive first – so, let us call this 'first current of air' – (2) then we see the idol emitted from the mirror itself, (3) then a second current of air – which goes from the object to the mirror and then is driven back to us, performing thus a journey in the reverse direction, (4) and finally the idol of the reflected object. While in the vehicle of the simile, i.e. the open-door, the two currents of air reach us successively in a *straight* line, in the case of the mirror the second current of air is reflected – in a way similar to the idol – and also follows a similar itinerary in a *crooked line*. In other words, the cause of the illusory position of the idol within the mirror is shown to be the trajectory of the second current of air, which is longer, compared to that of the first current of air. As Lucretius suggests, in the case of the mirrors, we should not believe what we see, without further elaborating upon the behaviour of the double currents of air, which results in the visual illusion of depth.

As soon as one perceives the role of double-air of the open-door image, which behaves in a similar – but not identical – way with the air that is stirred in the case of mirrors, the reader realizes that there is *no depth in mirrors* and hence there can be nothing miraculously captured and hidden within them; in fact, Lucretius is once again rather explicit in claiming that everything that falls upon the mirrors is reflected back straight away. Given the fact that the processes in both parts of the simile can be explained on a physical basis, i.e. by means of the behaviour of two currents of air, which similarly control our sense of distance, the passage concludes with the denunciation of the rhetoric of wonder (4.289 *minime mirarier*), which is already familiar to the reader from the discussion of other topics expounded earlier in the poem.[15] Just to give another such a striking example of Lucretius' criticism of bewilderment, towards the end of Book 2 (2.1023–1039) he argues, so as to diminish our wonder at the idea that there exist other worlds apart from our own (cf. 2.1028 *mirabile*, 2.1029 *mirarier*, 2.1035 *mirabile*, 2.1037 *miranda*). As he explains, if we were to see the heavens for the first time, we would similarly be amazed (2.1037 *ita haec species miranda fuisset* 'so wondrous this spectacle would have been'); on the contrary now that we can see it whenever we wish so, we are all literally – in Epicurean, i.e. atomic terms – fed up (*DRN* 2.1038 *fessus satiate videndi* 'wearied with satiety of seeing it'), that is why no one thinks it worthy of looking towards it. Along the same lines, while Lucretius' particularly technical discussion about the absence of depth in the mirrors may conceivably have a nauseating effect upon the unsuspicious addressee, who has just swallowed it like a bitter even if therapeutic drug, being allured by its poetic shell, by the concluding lines, Lucretius explicitly makes his first catoptrical explanation part of his broader goal of banishing astonishment and horror from his addressee, whenever the latter is faced with enigmatic and thus frightening natural phenomena.

Whereas this analogy refers to a single plane mirror, a few lines further down Lucretius sets out to explore the workings of a *series of plane mirrors*, which are disposed in such a way in order to bring into view for an outside observer what lies hidden in the innermost recesses and turnings of a building (*DRN* 4.302–310):[16]

> Fit quoque *de speculo in speculum* ut tradatur imago,
> *quinque* etiam aut *sex* ut fieri *simulacra* suërint.
> nam quaecumque retro *parte interiore* **latebunt**,
> inde tamen, quamvis *torte penitusque* remota,
> omnia *per flexos aditus* educta licebit
> *pluribus* haec *speculis* videantur in aedibus esse:
> usque adeo *speculo in speculum* **translucet** **imago,**
> et cum laeva data est, fit **rursum** ut dextera fiat,
> inde **retro rursum** redit et *convertit* eodem.

> An image may also be transmitted from mirror to mirror, so that as many as five or six images have often been produced. For whatever lies hidden behind in the inner parts of a house, however *tortuous* and *secluded* be the ways in between, may yet be all brought out through these involved passages by means of a number of mirrors and seen to be in the house. So truly does the image shine across from mirror to mirror; and when it has been presented left, it becomes right again, then once more it comes back again and returns to the same position.

Lucretius explains that for such a device to work properly and thus furnish a reliable image of whatever lies hidden in the innermost corners of the building, one should pay attention to certain significant parameters.

Lucretius builds his argument upon the preceding catoptrical explanation, which deals with the pivotal idea of the inversion of right and left in the case of *a single reflection* in flat mirrors (*DRN* 4.292–301):

> Nunc ea quae nobis membrorum dextera pars est,
> in speculis fit ut in laeva videatur eo quod,
> planitiem ad speculi veniens cum offendit imago,
> **non convertitur incolumis**, sed recta retrorsum
> sic eliditur, ut siquis, prius arida quam sit
> cretea persona, adlidat pilaeve trabive,

Catoptrology in Lucretius' *DRN* (4.269–323)

> atque ea continuo rectam si fronte figuram
> servet et elisam retro sese exprimat ipsa:
> fiet ut, ante oculus fuerit qui dexter, ut idem
> nunc sit laevus, et e laevo sit mutua dexter.

Next, that which is the right side of our frame appears in a mirror on the left, for this reason, that when the approaching image hits on the flat of the mirror, it is not turned round unaltered, but is thrust out straight backwards, just as if someone should dash upon a pillar or beam some mask of plaster before it were dry, and if it should at once keep its shape undistorted in front and mould a copy of itself dashed backwards: it will happen that what was formerly the right eye now becomes the left, and that the left becomes right in exchange.

In order to demonstrate this phenomenon, he compares the idol which is dashed against the mirror and then gets reversed straight out in the reverse direction, with a wet plaster-mask when this is hurled against a pillar or beam and then bounced straight back; in this case, what was the left side of the face is now the right and vice-versa, while the mask preserves the features imprinted on its front, but displays them now in reverse: what has been the right eye would now be the left and the left now have become the right. In connection with this analogical image of the mask, we should pay attention to Lucretius' statement that the reflected image that comes back to us inverted *is not unharmed* (*DRN* 4.295 *non ... incolumis*). In this statement, Lucretius conjures up the crucial Epicurean principle which he has put forward already in his Book 1, according to which, when something changes and passes out of its own boundaries, it brings about the death of what it was before (*DRN* 1.670–671):

> nam quodcumque suis mutatum finibus exit,
> continuo hoc mors est illius quod fuit ante.

for whatever by being changed passes outside its own boundaries, at once this is the death of that which was before.

Lucretius embraces this principle about the inversion in the case of a single reflection when he comes to discuss what happens in the case of a series of mirrors. Specifically, he argues that, in order to grasp the true image of the initial hidden object, one should take notice of the *number* of mirrors employed. Since one mirror reverses the image, whereas two mirrors restore the 'real' arrangement, any odd number of mirrors – five in this case – will reverse the image, while any even number such as six will restore it. However, Lucretius blurs the fact that due to these consecutive reflections, the idol that will eventually appear before our eyes will potentially be different, when compared to the atomic structure of the first reflected idol – and therefore it is highly unlikely that the final idol to be perceived will be informative as far as the accurate image of the initial hidden object is concerned. In other words, if we were ready to follow Lucretius' train of thoughts, we would end up with the tricky conclusion that in such a process of multiple reflections, the final reflected image *cannot be unconditionally true* and therefore reliable as regards the process of cognition.

Apart from the *practical scientific value* of the device that Lucretius presents us with – if there is any, and this is a question to be answered by modern physicists, depending on the actual *clarity* of ancient mirrors – I would like to claim that in conjunction with the first passage that we discussed in length, the present description of the series of mirrors should also be considered to be *programmatic* of Lucretius' Epicurean method of inquiry; in fact, while – as I will explain – it vividly bears echoes from corresponding passages with similar connotations, it adds new engaging dimensions.

To begin with, the rhetorical device of polyptoton, which is used here twice (4.302 *de speculo in speculum*; 4.308 *speculo in speculum*) vividly echoes Lucretius' earlier discussion in Book 1 about the process of *progressively bringing into light* the unseen atomic reality (*DRN* 1.1114–1117):

> Haec sic **per**nosces parva **per**ductus opella;
> namque alid ex alio *clarescet* nec tibi *caeca*
> *nox* iter eripiet, quin ultima naturai
> **per**videas: ita res accendent *lumina* rebus.
>
> for one thing will become clear by another, and blind night will not steal your path and prevent you from seeing all the uttermost recesses of nature: so clearly will truths kindle light for truths.

In these verses, which form the epilogue to Book 1, Lucretius resorts – there again twice – to the device of polyptoton (1.1115 *alid ex alio*; 1.1117 *res ... rebus*), in order to demonstrate beyond any doubt that for the Epicureans knowledge is a gradual and cumulative process: the more one learns, the more one's receptiveness to new things is increased. What also dominates is the *imagery of light and darkness*, associated with the philosophical notion of ἐνάργεια.[17]

Turning back to the series of mirrors in Book 4, we should also draw our attention to the verb *latebunt* which plausibly looks back to the dogs' *latebras* in *DRN* 1.408 (*DRN* 1.402–409):

> verum animo satis haec vestigia parva sagaci
> sunt, per quae possis cognoscere cetera tute.
> namque canes ut montivagae persaepe ferai
> naribus inveniunt intectas fronde quietes,
> cum semel institerunt vestigia certa viai,
> sic *alid ex alio* per te tute ipse videre
> talibus in rebus poteris *caecasque latebras*
> insinuare omnis et *verum protrahere* inde.
>
> But for a keen-scented mind, these little tracks are enough to enable you to recognize the others for yourself. For as hounds very often find by their scent the

leaf-hidden resting-place of the mountain-ranging quarry, when once they have hit upon certain traces of its path, so will you be able for yourself to see one thing after another in such matters as these, and to penetrate all unseen hiding-places, and draw forth the truth from them.

In that context, while putting forward the Epicurean principle of the existence of void, Lucretius refuses to offer his pupil more proofs and encourages him to work them out for himself. In order to illustrate this step-by-step process – and here the use of yet another polyptoton should not go unobserved (*alid ex alio*, 1.407) – he compares the keen-scented readers' endeavour to perceive unseen reality with that of hunting dogs finding traces of mountain-ranging prey in the undergrowth, traces that will eventually lead them to its unseen hiding places.[18] Despite the fact that this passage shares with the one which deals with the series of mirrors device Lucretius' general programmatic guidelines, as far as his analogical methodology is concerned, still there is a crucial difference: whereas the so-called 'hunting' or 'venatic' paradigm of investigation invites the pupil to *intrude himself* into the unseen world of the atoms, in order to draw forth the truth (*verum protrahere*), the catoptrical imagery inverts this process: by means of the multiple-mirrors device only a *reflected image* of the unseen reality will be brought in front of his eyes. In other words, one should discover cognitive ways, so as to *bring to the surface* its hidden secrets.

What are the possible consequences in terms of methodology that such an inversion may bring about? In order to answer this question, we should now focus upon the meaning of the verb *translucet* (*translucet imago*, *DRN* 4.308), which is commonly translated by Lucretian scholars to mean 'to shine across' (i.e. to be reflected), instead of its more common static sense 'to shine through, to be translucent' (e.g. Ov. *Met.* 4.353). Let us examine for a moment the possibility that the verb is burdened with the second semantic weight; its prefix *trans-* may conceivably look back to the penetrating cognitive action of the verb *transpicere*, just discussed above in connection with the first catoptrical explanation. If we were willing to keep reading Lucretius' passage in metaphorical terms, then Lucretius would plausibly suggest that in cases of extremely convoluted unseen natural phenomena, it is only by means of such an analogical device of consecutive reflections, that the final image becomes translucent, i.e. comprehensible. But is there a literary device endowed with such a function to be detected within the poem? In this connection, one should bring to mind the so-called 'multi-dimensional similes', thanks to which, whenever a single mirror – i.e. an analogical image – does not suffice in order to shed light upon the phenomenon under investigation, Lucretius simultaneously brings into play two or more vehicles and thus sheds light upon the tenor from different angles, whereas these image are illuminated the one from the other, as if in a chain; in doing so, the straightforward comparison between the tenor and the vehicle is contaminated by the intrusion of a supplementary level of comparison.[19] In fact, we may glean various instances of such 'series of mirrors' throughout the poem. Due to the restriction of space, I will not analyse in length such an example of a multi-dimensional simile.[20] But it is important to point out that if read carefully, this particular Lucretius' catoptrical explanation poses an essential constrain to the application of his analogical scientific method: even if the Epicurean will not literally count the number of 'mirrors' employed, i.e. the analogical images, yet he should be at the alert and evaluate the validity of the final reflected idol perceived: in catoptrical terms, the number of mirrors employed determines whether a viewer will see this final reflected idol which originates from the initial object either restored or reversed – but never unharmed; in a similar way, in case that the pupil cannot handle successfully his analogical tools and correctly evaluate his perceptual data, the analogical image may mislead to a visual illusion and thus his philosophical efforts are destined to fail.

Let us revisit Seneca's question, which has been touched upon in the prologue to this chapter: 'what did nature intend in creating real objects and yet wanting reflections of them to be seen?' In other words, are mirrors of any practical use? Even worse is Lucretius' catoptrical account of any value within the framework of his philosophical poem? Lucretius definitely offers a positive reply to Seneca. As my discussion of mirrors in both literal and metaphorical terms has demonstrated, by the end of this account, the reader is well aware of the fact that an Epicurean mirror has nothing in common with the magical one which was interrogated by the Evil Queen in the Snow White fairy tale and could provide automatic answers: regardless of its repulsive obscurity, by no means can an Epicurean mirror, which is explicitly pieced together out of atoms, be endowed with such a miraculous function. Lucretius turns mirrors into an integral mechanism of his demonstrative and analogical method, by means of which he demystifies further the secrets of nature, in his constant and systematic aim at liberating his pupil from the fear of superstitious religious practices and leading him to the absolute Epicurean pleasure.

CHAPTER 4
TIDEUS' THEORY OF REFLECTION IN *ON THE MIRRORS*
Mikhail Silian

Tideus' short treatise *On Mirrors* (*De Speculis*), which survives only in a Latin translation, presents an original answer to the question why some surfaces reflect bodies better than others. The treatise stands out among ancient and medieval Latin texts on optics.[1] Drawing on the Galenic theory of vision, Tideus provides a more general theory of reflection than that which had been hitherto offered by visual theorists. An otherwise unknown author, Tideus must have been active between Galen's *floruit* in late second century and the translation of *On Mirrors* into Latin in twelfth-century Spain. The medieval manuscripts containing his translation describe Tideus as a doctor from 'Regoui', which is possibly a reference to Reggio di Calabria.

The works of the major scientific authorities of antiquity, above all Ptolemy and Euclid, gave their readers the means of predicting accurately how objects will appear in various kinds of mirrors when they are viewed from different perspectives. However, neither of these authors questioned the concept of a mirror's reflectivity in and of itself. It is precisely in attempting to answer this more fundamental question that makes Tideus' *De Speculis* unusual and fascinating. In the central passages of the treatise, Tideus introduces an authentic concept of the 'basis, material, and seat' of light, assigning this phenomenon to both the eye as the organ of sight and the mirror as the object of reflection. According to Tideus, one can describe any bodily surface as being the basis, material, and seat of the light, if it consists of elements that are in some way akin to clarity and whiteness. Such a body can receive the colours of other objects, using the illuminated air that surrounds it as an instrument. This claim allows Tideus to employ Galenic views on direct vision in his theory of reflection.

In terms of composition, Tideus' treatise falls into three parts. After briefly presenting the main topic of the treatise in the first two introductory paragraphs, Tideus moves to the first part of the treatise (pp. 73–76), in which he elaborates a theory of direct vision. To begin with, Tideus argues that the stages of the process of reflection in the mirror resemble the stages of seeing. Accordingly, one must look for an account of direct vision, which one can subsequently employ as a model for the action of reflection itself. Tideus starts by considering previous theories of vision, similar to those that were upheld by Euclid[2] and Claudius Ptolemy.[3] Euclid claims that direct vision proceeds by casting the visual rays from the eye (cf. Euc. *Opt.*, def. 1–3); this theory is commonly referred to as 'the extramission theory'. Ptolemy in turn developed Euclid's approach to optics, taking over its most basic principles, within what is usually called the discipline of 'geometrical optics'.[4] Along with Euclid, Ptolemy maintains that one can represent the visual field as a cone, with its vertex in the eye and its base at the visual object that is being perceived. Consequently, one can regard various interactions of this cone with bodily surfaces as conic sections. This approach allows Ptolemy and Euclid to consider the question of how a body will appear when it is seen from a certain angle as a specifically geometrical problem. In presenting his own view on direct vision, Tideus keeps some distance from both classical theories of extramission and intramission. On the one hand, he seems to generally agree with Democritus[5] and the Epicureans,[6] who maintained that vision proceeds by the reception of an image of the object (εἴδωλον, *simulacrum*), which enters the eye from the outside. On the other hand, Tideus inscribes their theories into his own reading of Galen's account (although he does not refer to Galen as an influence explicitly).

Claudius Galen employs the concept of *pneuma* (πνεῦμα) to describe the process of vision, and in this he takes the earlier Stoic account as a starting point. The Stoics maintained that a special substance, *pneuma*, fills the human body, and that it is responsible for activities such as movement, perception, and thought. Specifically, visual *pneuma* is responsible for visual perception as it transfers the affections from the eye to the central ruling principle of the seeing agent.[7] Similarly to Euclid and Ptolemy, the Stoics argued that, in the process of seeing, visual *pneuma* emanates from the eye, forming a cone with the vertex in the eye and a base that reaches the bodies which are the object of sight (cf. *SVF* 2.867, 863). Insofar as this cone embraces the air, the visual *pneuma* changes the tension (τόνος, συνέντασις) of the intermediary air (*SVF* 2.844, 864).[8] The air, intensified in this way, reaches the visual object. As a result, the qualities of the observed bodies (such as colour) affect the air, inducing in it an alteration or change of state (ἀλλοίωσις, *SVF* 2.63).[9] According to various sources (e.g., Alexander, Galen, Aetius, and Diogenes Laertius), the Stoics also assimilated the act of seeing to a walking stick; for instance, in Alexander's reading (*SVF* 2.864), the image of the object is 'imprinted' in the base of the visual cone. Based on this textual evidence, one could assume that such an imprint affects the whole body of the visual cone, and in this way it produces an effect on the eye. Afterwards, the affection formed in the eye (πάθος) is transmitted to the ruling principle, which is in turn responsible for the perception of the external object (αἰσθήσεις, αἰσθητικὴ φαντασία) (*SVF* 2.68, 75, 858, 863). In addition to this, the Stoics claimed that each sense-organ, including the eyes, must be somehow similar to its object, in order to be affected by it (*SVF* 2.860). In this way, according to the Stoic account, the eyes are primarily affected by the colours, so they must be 'radiant, pure, and glistening'.[10]

Although Galen's theory of vision clearly relies on the Stoic background, he criticizes a number of Stoic arguments. On the one hand, Galen claims in *De Placitis Hippocratis et Platonis* (henceforth *PHP*) that vision proceeds by means of *pneuma*, appropriating both the language and the explanation of the Stoic theory. On the other hand, unlike the Stoics, he argues that the psychic *pneuma* (this being a kind of *pneuma* that he contrasts with the vital one) reaches only the inside of the eye, and that it does not reach the object itself (*PHP* 7.4.23–25, 452.22–28). Instead, this psychic *pneuma* strikes the air and induces in it a change in state. Galen describes the result of this contact as a 'transfer of the power of alteration' (μετάδοσις δυνάμεως ἀλλοιώσεως), which is similar to the effect of the sunlight on the air. Importantly, in presenting his account of seeing, Galen attacks the Stoic simile of the walking stick. According to Galen (cf. *PHP* 7.41), the Stoics understood the air as an instrument of the eyes, which is itself unable to sense; thus, the visual cone can do no more than give reports about the object, but is not able to form any affection. Galen, in turn, suggests that psychic *pneuma* turns the air within the visual field into a kind of sensing instrument, which performs a function analogous to the visual capacity, and which 'form[s] one body with itself'.[11]

Tideus takes Galen's account as a starting point and develops it by replacing the concept of *pneuma* with the concept of light (*lumen*). Indeed, one can hardly apply Galen's views on direct vision to the theory of reflection without alteration, because it would imply a questionable hypothesis about the presence of *pneuma* in mirrors.[12] That is why Tideus stresses that the intermediary air is needed for seeing, and that air changes its properties in order to become an instrument of seeing. Following Galen, Tideus refutes the Stoic account, maintaining that, if air did not undergo the change of state, the perceptive capacity would only perceive the object indirectly, restricting the viewer to derive the data about the visible object from the sensation of the instrument. In turn, this would mean that the perceptive capacity would need to 'reconstruct' the qualities of the object, based on the interaction between the visual cone and itself. However, this would involve some sort of thinking and reasoning, which would go beyond the capacities of the agent's sense perception.

In the same section of the treatise, Tideus discusses the perception of position, distance, shape, and motion in direct vision. He claims that a viewer can apprehend these qualities, because the visual capacity reaches the object. Tideus seems to imply that the visual capacity manages to do this specifically by using air as an instrument, as well as by using the extension of air between the observer and the object. Hence, the spatial aspect of vision is secured by the fact that the visual capacity forms the cone with a vertex in the eye and a base at the object (in this aspect Tideus is following the tradition stemming from Euclid and Ptolemy). In this manner, the spatial extension of the intervening air embraced by the visual cone guarantees that perception by this means should take into account the relative positions of the vertex of the cone to its base. Although Tideus does not speak directly of the visual cone in the passages presented here, there is textual evidence that he adopted this concept. For instance, in the closing line of the treatise (which I omit in the present translation), Tideus mentions 'strictura pinealis oculi'.[13] Moreover, the reading of P indicates a similar understanding of the argument on behalf of the medieval scribe: 'id est piramidis, quae est ut pinea procedens ab oculo' ('[...] that is, of a pyramid, which is like a cone, proceeding from the eye'). The reading shared by K, B, and L also points in this direction: 'pinealis oculi id est piramidis quae est ut pinea procedens ab oculo' ('[...] "the cone of the eye", which is a pyramid, proceeding from the eye like a pine-cone').

In the second section of *De Speculis* (pp. 76–80), Tideus discusses his theory of reflection. He asserts that it is enough for the air to be illuminated, in order for it to gradually transfer the images of bodies towards the eye or the mirror. Whereas Galen claims that psychic *pneuma* transforms air into a sensing instrument, Tideus assigns this role to light. Such illumination, in turn, is said to either originate from the eye or be reflected by the mirror, which has previously received it from an external light source. This argument clarifies why the mirrors of different shapes and sizes distort the image: when the illuminated air is carrying an image, it can contract or dilate it, depending on the dimensions of the conical light field. Furthermore, Tideus says that some bodies can act as the 'base, material, and seat' of the light, and that both the eye and the mirror belong to this class of bodies. Therefore, they can retain the image communicated by the light and communicate it at further distances.

Moreover, the light from the mirror, just like the light from the eyes, communicates the colours and the image to the source of the light. Tideus calls this source 'the basis, the material, and the seat' of the light. The concept of the basis, material, and seat of the light signifies both the eye and the mirror, emphasizing their ability to receive the visual data that concerns objects by literally casting a light on them. The eye *qua* basis, material, and seat of the light might transmit the image further (possibly, to the ruling principle), while the mirror projects the image upon its own body. Thus, on the one hand, the eye generates the light that instantly turns the air between the observer and the object into a sensing instrument. On the other hand, the mirror cannot produce the light by itself, so it uses the light from an external light source. Nonetheless, like the eye, the mirror changes the air into an instrument by casting the light on it. Thus, in both cases, the air between the basis, material, and seat of the light on the one hand, and the object of reflection in the mirror on the other hand, is instantly filled with light, and the illuminated air around the object receives the colours and the image of this object. As Tideus maintains, 'the colour of the air becomes the colour of the object', which is to say that the air is altered, so that the part of it which lies closest to the object takes on the object's colours. Once the air is changed in this way, the light in the air transfers the alteration to its basis, material, and seat, so that the latter all change correspondingly. Tideus explains such a transmission of change with reference to the principle of 'like to like': in the case of the eye, the moistures within it are of the same kind as whiteness, clarity, and light, and so they can undergo an alteration that would represent the difference of colours in the air. In contrast, the case of the mirror is somewhat more perplexing. Tideus seems to imply that some physical objects are somehow more receptive to light than others.

Furthermore, in the same section, Tideus considers the act of reflection in mirrors of different sizes, at the same time as he presents his original views on the transmission of images by this mode. First, Tideus explains why one sees smaller reflections in smaller mirrors. He implies that the transmission of the image to its base, material, and the seat is a gradual one. It is important for Tideus that the light does not move in the air, but rather instantly changes the entirety of the air which is embraced in the cone of light. In this way, the light can gradually transfer the image 'backwards' within the light field, i.e. from the object to the mirror or the eye. In the previous argument, Tideus has already demonstrated that the image which is equal in size to the object itself must first be formed in the illuminated air. At the next stage, the light transmits the image to the light in the air next to it, then further, and so on, until the image reaches the mirror. 'Contraction and dilation' in the passage means that the light field, which is said to possess a shape of a conical frustum, therefore becomes narrower the closer that it is to the source of the light, and the image closer to the top of the conical frustum becomes smaller. One can also interpret this theory as a comparison between two identical images, inscribed into two circles, namely the top and the base surfaces of the conical frustum. In this case, one figure will be smaller than the other in proportion to the ratio between the diameters of the circles at the two extremes of the conical frustum. Remarkably, if Tideus claimed that the light moves in the air from the source to the object of vision (i.e., that it does not activate the entirety of the air embraced by the visual cone, as Tideus actually argues), the theory of movement of the image 'backwards' to the source of the light would not be possible.

Tideus continues by arguing that a simple change of the size of the object's reflection is just one possibility; the image might also be distorted through the unevenness of the mirror. In this way, the image contained in the sections of the light cone which are closer to the mirror will be brightened and prolonged. Tideus' theory seems to be quite problematic, since it does not fully explain why the prolonged mirror should also prolong the reflection. And as a matter of fact, this does not happen in plain mirrors. One possible explanation is that Tideus has in mind mirrors with a curved surface; Vogt has sided with this suggestion. Melchior-Bonnet also reports that 'nearly always rounded, these [antique] mirrors were either concave or convex'.[14] Another – more complex – clarification of the argument would be that the light between the mirror and the reflected object forms a conical frustum. The form of its top surface should correspond to the default circular form of the mirror. Therefore, the argument is based upon the comparison between the two circles, which are the base and the top surfaces of the frustum respectively. In the default situation with the circular mirror, the mirror will preserve the dimensions of the image received from the base. In this case, the mirror will simply decrease the size of the image of the object, because the top and the base surfaces will both be circular. However, if the shape of the mirror deviates from the circular form, and the base surface remains circular, then the image received by the mirror will be distorted according to the difference in measurements between the base and the top surfaces of the conical frustum. In the third and final section of the work, which is omitted in the present publication (pp. 80–82), Tideus discusses more specific issues concerning direct vision and the physiology of seeing.

This chapter presents the first English translation of the part of Tideus' treatise *De Speculis* in which Tideus discusses the phenomenon of reflection. The translation is based on the first critical edition of the Latin text prepared by Axel Anthon Bjørnbo, and it additionally takes into account the German translation and the comments of Sebastian Vogl.[15] The extant Latin text is very likely to be a translation from an Arabic version of the text[16] dated to the twelfth century, possibly in Toledo, by Gerard of Cremona, whose identity as the translator is corroborated by the fact that the treatise appears on a list of Gerard's works from the *Commemoratio Librorum*.[17] Bjørnbo has argued that the Latin text contains expressions that are characteristic of Gerard.[18] On the whole, it seems plausible that the extant text of *De Speculis* was the work of either Gerard or one of his pupils. Unfortunately, much less can be said about the identity of Tideus himself, who is known to us only as the author of this treatise.

At the current stage of research, we know very little about who Tideus was or about when he composed the *De Speculis*. If we accept that Gerard is indeed the translator of the work from Arabic into Latin, the original work must have been finished before his death in 1187 CE at the latest. The names of Tideus and his father, Theodoros, who is mentioned in the title of *De Speculis*, might suggest that at least an editor of the work might have had a Greek background; nonetheless, one should not lay much weight on this hypothesis, because the names might have been corrupted or falsely added by a scribe. This having been said, it would still not be exceptional for Gerard to translate out of Arabic texts which were originally written in Greek (as was the case with Ptolemy's *Almagest*, Euclid's *Elements*, Aristotle's *Physics*, and Galen's *On the Temperaments*). Hence, one cannot completely rule out the possibility that the text is a double translation, i.e. from Greek to Arabic, and then from Arabic to Latin. On balance, it is difficult to hypothesize about the origins of the text due to the lack of evidence. In any case, the fact that Tideus seems to rely on Galen's *PHP*, which was composed in the second half of the second century CE, helps us to fix a rough *terminus post quem* for the treatise's composition.

It is also possible that the treatise was originally composed in Arabic, and that the title of the treatise, together with the name of the father and the mention of Reggio, was added later. In this case, the Galenic ideas could have reached Tideus, for example, through Hunayn Ibn-Ishaq's *The Book of the Ten Treatises on the Eye* (especially, the third treatise),[19] which was written around the middle of the ninth century. However, Tideus' treatise is clearly less technical and elaborate than the optical works written in Arabic, such as Al-Kindi's *De Aspectibus* or Ibn al-Haytham's *Kitab al-Manazir*. Comparison with such works renders less likely the hypothesis that the treatise was originally composed in Arabic. It is also noteworthy in this connection that in the *De Speculis* we do not encounter arguments found in Ibn-Ishaq's *Ten Treatises* but which are absent in Galen's *PHP*;[20] this evidence speaks for the independence of the *De Speculis* from Ibn-Ishaq, and therefore for an earlier date of its composition. Thus, the original Greek text was likely written at some point between the third and eleventh centuries CE, with a preference being earlier rather than later.

As mentioned above, our only knowledge of Tideus' identity comes from the present work. The title of *De Speculis* tells us that Tideus' hometown was Regoui,[21] which may be a reference to Reggio di Calabria in Southern Italy.[22] One might deduce another possible hint concerning Tideus' occupation from the title of the treatise: it calls Tideus a doctor (*medicus*). This hypothesis seems to be corroborated by Tideus' interest in the physiology of the eye in the closing passage of the work,[23] but the authenticity of the title itself is highly questionable; it might have been added by a later editor of the manuscript. There have been several speculative attempts to identify this Tideus more precisely, but what we learn from the present treatise is all we can say with any degree of certainty.[24]

Although the influence of Tideus' work on the subsequent development of optics was not significant, we do encounter occasional references to *De Speculis* in later works. In this context, it is noteworthy that Roger Bacon (*ca.* 1214–1292 CE) refers to Tideus at least two times in his *Perspectiva*.[25] In a passage, Bacon merely mentions Tideus;[26] elsewhere, he picks up Tideus' argument that the visual capacity (*visus*) must 'embrace the extremities of the object', in order to certify the distance, size, location, and orientation of visible things.[27] In any case, the treatise has survived in fifteen manuscripts,[28] which indicates that it was quite widespread. The critical edition of *De Speculis* is based on nine manuscripts,[29] of which *Cod. Paris.* 9335 (P), which dates from the fourteenth century, is the oldest manuscript that contains the full treatise. Besides P, we find excerpts from Tideus' work in *Cod. Digbean.* 168, which must be somewhat older than *Cod. Paris.*[30] It is also peculiar that *De Speculis* was quite frequently included in the same codices as Ptolemy's *Optics*,[31] Pseudo-Euclid's *De Speculis*,[32] and the optical work of Al-Kindi, *De Aspectibus*.[33] The fact that these four works are included together in six manuscripts suggests that *De Speculis* was regarded as one of the principal ancient works on optics available in Latin translation.[34] It seems possible, moreover, that *De Speculis* was read as complementary to other more technical treatises, insofar as it explains the process of reflection from the standpoint of natural philosophy.

Regarding the secondary literature, *De Speculis* is clearly understudied. Leclerc and Steinschneider contributed to the rising interest in the treatise in the late nineteenth century, but they did not present a detailed analysis of Tideus' theory. The most thorough examination of the work that I am acquainted with is to be found in Peter Brown's doctoral dissertation, *Chaucer's Visual World*.[35] Brown compares Tideus' theory with Galen's account of vision, and he points out the similarity between Galen's concept of visual *pneuma* and Tideus' *virtus videntis* or *virtus visus*. Furthermore, Vogl's translation into German remains the most recent attempt to translate *De Speculis* into a modern language, although it resorts to greater paraphrase than is desirable for the purposes of scholarly work on the treatise.[36] In the present chapter, I aim to provide a consistent and more literal translation that can be used for the purposes of further scholarly work on the treatise.

In the current translation, I leave out pages 80–82 from Bjørnbo's edition, because Tideus does not discuss the issue of reflection there. In the body of the translation, I have chosen to put the Latin words in brackets, either if it is a recurring term used for the first time throughout the text, or in the cases where I deviate from my general policy of translating the term in this chapter. In some of the endnotes, I present my reconstruction of Tideus' ideas, where it might seem necessary. I also provide the full citations from Galen's *PHP* and Roger Bacon's *Perspectiva*, in order to highlight parallels; otherwise, I insert in-text references or abbreviations.[37]

Mirrors and Mirroring

The treatise on what a human being sees in the mirror, and in that which is not a mirror, and on what causes it, gathered from the books of the ancients by Tideus, son of Theodorus, a physician from Reggio

(73) You should know that what a human being sees in a polished fine mirror [made of] iron is seen more truly [than in other objects]. For [it applies to] a fine polished iron, since it is more suitable for reflecting (*redditio*) the light that falls upon it in the surrounding air than most things – just as the magnetic stone is suitable to moving metal objects without the presence of another stone. And, again, just as a small stone can move [if dropped] into vinegar,[38] without other small stones, the polished mirror of fine iron returns (*reddit*) the light falling upon it in the surrounding air in the best way. Therefore, wherever the light is present, the mirror returns it very well.

Consequently, whenever something is opposite to the mirror, and is illuminated somehow (either from its own essence and substance, or from something on which the light from another object falls), the mirror receives the light from the light of the thing in front of it; and then [the mirror], at the same time, most quickly returns this light either to the object itself, or to other things directly opposite to the mirror. And that is what anyone, diligent and experienced in these things, knows.[39] Accordingly, everything, upon which the light from the mirror falls, returns the image of itself, and its own colour, to this light. So, one could say that the light, falling upon the object, receives the image of the object and its colour.

(74)

And, indeed, the wise men hold different opinions concerning the matter. That is to say, some of them have said that the disposition (*dispositio*) [of the image] in the mirror, and of the lights in it, was similar to the disposition of the light of vision (*lumen visus*), when it meets the visible object.[40] And some of them have claimed that the visual capacity (*visus*) perceives either by means of the light coming forth from it, or by the light of the surrounding air, which is spatially extended over thousands of stadia, just as our sight (*aspectus*) reaches the stars in an instant.[41] And we do not encounter a speed of such kind in any other [type of] locomotion of the appearances (*aliqua specierum motuum mobilis de loco ad locum*). And no one can say whether something is cast from the visual capacity, so as to reach the object of vision, or [something is issued] from the object, which we observe, to the visual capacity – since we know that in other kinds of movement such speed is not possible. Hence, the only assumption left is that the visual capacity proceeds by means of the surrounding air, [i.e. by being] scattered between the sight and the visual object.[42] Therefore, the air is related to the visual capacity as the instrument, by means of which [the visual capacity] acts. Furthermore, they have argued, it is impossible for the air to play an active role [in the process of vision]; [i.e.,] that it acts, either by being fixed in terms of [its] disposition, or [by being] altered (*alteratus*) regarding its disposition. [And] if the air is in fact altered, then it is only possible that the alteration is either caused by the observer, or by the object of vision, or by both at once.

If someone said that the air acts, [while] remaining unaltered according to its disposition, and that it perceives the object exclusively with something, with which a human being meets the solid bodies (as it were, with a staff or a stick,[43] by means of which one reaches a blocking object (*res prohibens*) [consisting] of solid bodies, in complete darkness, and discerns it, and senses it by touch), then the reply would be that everything that has this kind of disposition necessarily apprehends (*apprehendit*) the object with the help of judgement (*cogitatio*) and reasoning (*ratiocinatio*). And perceiving (*apprehensio*) by the visual capacity scattered in the air does not involve judgement or reasoning.

And if someone says that the illuminated air is altered, and [that it] is converted (*convertitur*) due to the differences among the colours of the sensible objects, and that when [the air] is changed, its alteration reaches the visual capacity most quickly, and the visual capacity senses and perceives it, – then, it will seem to be detected correctly.[44]

Nevertheless, such perception does not indicate the size (*quantitas*) of the visible object, along with the colour, and this perception shows neither the object's position in its place, nor the distance from the object to the sight, nor the shape of the object, nor its motion. [And] inasmuch as it is true that the visual capacity perceives all these [characteristics], it is hard to deny that the surrounding air, altered in accordance with the colours of the visible objects, signifies (*significet*) the colours of these objects, when the colour of the air becomes the colour of the objects (which is accompanied

(75)

by the alteration in the moistures enclosed by the eye). And these moistures, [in turn,] are altered only because they are of the same kind as whiteness, clarity, and light.[45]

And if it were not possible that the visual capacity perceives the size of object, as well as its position, distance [to the observer], shape, and motion, by means of such signification, the air would return to the visual capacity nothing else but only the colours.[46] However, we experience that the visual capacity, when it meets the object of vision, perceives all these [kinds of] appearances (*species*). And it would be impossible for the viewer (*videns*) to perceive the position of the objects in their places, and their extension (*spacia*), if the power of the viewer (*virtus videntis*) did not reach the object of vision. And the visual capacity, in a similar way, would not apprehend the size of the object, if its power did not contain the object with all its parts. Therefore, it is necessary, in order to perceive visual objects, that one be next to them, and that the objects be perceived in their places.[47] And indeed, it is impossible, that the air plays an active role in the perception, either because the power of the visual capacity, through which the air perceives in the same way as the visual capacity perceives, is in the nature of air, or because the air is converted to the nature of the viewer by what it meets (although one does not encounter it in every [kind of] air, but only in the illuminated one).

And again, similarly, the impact of the light on the visual capacity is actualized, only when either [the visual capacity] meets a shining body, [which is] exposed to the eye, or through the mixing of the external light with the light coming forth from the eye.

And anyone who claims that the thing coming from the eye, [when it] reaches the visual object, does so by itself, is wrong, because we do not encounter any [type of] locomotion of the appearances of such high speed.[48]

And it is hard to object to the one who claims that the brilliant light coming forth from the eye, when mixed with the scattered air, most quickly alters this air to its own essence and substance.[49] Hence, it follows from this argument that the air is an illuminated, scattered, continuous (*continens*) instrument of the visual capacity, with the help of which it perceives all objects. And this is [so], because [the visual capacity] is a creation belonging to the genus [of the air], it is similar to the air, it permeates the air, and it is mixed with the air. And in a similar manner, the dark air overcomes the clear, lucid power of visual capacity (*virtus visus*) coming forth from [the eye], and it alters this power, and it converts this power to its own nature. And that is the reason why one cannot see at night.

And just as sunlight instantly alters air into light, in a similar way the light coming from the eye instantly does it. And again, in a similar way, the light coming forth from the eye is altered by the air instantly.[50]

(76)

And here is the sign that the size of an object, its position, and other similar [characteristics], are perceived only in the object's position and place: if the visual capacity perceived the size of the object and its position, then the power of the visual capacity would reach the object. However, [one knows that, in fact,] the visual capacity perceives the size of the object and its position; therefore, the power of the visual capacity doubtlessly reaches the object. And the similar happens in the rest of the appearances. Accordingly, if the power of the visual capacity reaches the sensible object, [then] it will reach the object either by itself, or by means of the instrument that carries it. And [the power of the visual capacity] does not reach the object by itself, because the movement from one place to another at such speed is impossible. And it happens only with the help of air *qua* instrument, and by the conversion of air to the nature of the visual capacity.

And again they say in a similar way: the light reflected in the air from the mirror does not disappear, unless it returns its own image to the air upon which it falls, and the light receives this image from the air. Thus, when the light of the mirror receives the image of the object, upon which it falls, as well as the colour of this object, it simultaneously returns both [the image and the colour] into the mirror (which is its base (*radix*), material (*minera*), and seat (*sedes*)). And, similarly, all lights take on the images of the objects, upon which they shine, and at once they return these images to the seats, materials, and bases, from which they have departed, as quickly as possible.

However, since there exist multiple elements (of which there are fire, air, water, earth, and the combinations of their parts, the amount of which is innumerable),[51] the light of each of them differs from [the light of] its equals, according to the degree (*quantitas*) of difference between it and the thing, on account of which the lights differ [from each other].[52] And in view of the fact that the lights from various objects differ (i.e., [it is] either the light owing to the nature and the origin of the object, or [the light] falling upon this object from other sources), the reception of each part [of this light] ([i.e., adding] to the object's own light, [which was received] from the light source), and the penetration of the external light into the object depends, [on the one hand,] on the size of the bulk of the body, and its [physical] structure (*permixtio*); and, [on the other hand,] on the level of mixture (*commixtio*) of the light conveyed by that which conveys [the light] for the second time. In such a way, if [pieces of] iron and wood are exposed to the intense sunlight, the iron will retain considerably more

(77)

heat than the wood. Similarly, a polished mirror retains the lights (as well as the images, colours, and figures, returned to it by the lights) in the best way, while other objects, lacking the mirroring nature, would not stand comparison with it.

And what if someone asks: what is the nature of the light? Is it a substance, or an accident? And if it is a substance, then is it a body, or not a body? Furthermore, if it is a body, then is it fire, air, earth, or water? One should say [that] there are multiple answers to this question, and the range of answers is wide. For if we gave a detailed reply, it would prolong the present argument, and it would make us digress from our intention; and [our] intention in this book of ours is to explain the quality of the object seen in the mirror, and in what is not a mirror. Nevertheless, we [shall] mention [something on the matter], according to its value, as briefly as we can.

Some philosophers have argued that light is fire, and that it is a body.[53] And they thought fire was a body, for they claimed [that], since we observe the dilation of a pupil of one eye of the two, when another eye is closed, we know that it wouldn't be the case if a corporeal substance did not fill the eyes.[54] And those, thinking that [the light was] fire, argued [that], when the light is focused by a polished mirror, or a polished body, it kindles.

Now, we return to what interested us in the topic of mirrors, and we claim [that], from every shining object, [the light of which is] lit in the air, and is scattered around this object, the illuminated field is wider than the size of the object, just as when the light from a small candle fills the whole house.[55] And it is the case that, in the mirror just as large, or larger than the face of the observer, one sees his face as neither larger nor smaller [than it really is]; and if the one looks in the mirror smaller than his face, he will see the face [appearing as] small [in the reflection]. It happens because the light [field] of a size [which is] larger than [that from] the face of the observer originates from the large mirror. Therefore, when the light falls at the face of the one looking in the mirror, the image of the face will be formed in that light in the same size [as the real face], just as it would be with a small seal, with which wax or clay is imprinted.[56] [In the latter case,] the wax or clay assumes

(78)

[the imprint] of the seal, in the same size [as the seal]; and what remains of the clay is empty of the figure, having 'run over' [the edge of the seal], i.e. it doesn't have the image [of the seal].[57] Thus, the light returns the image [of the face], as if it assumed this image upon its body, i.e. the mirror; and the face is reflected in the mirror, preserving its real size. So, if the mirror were of the same size as the face, it would be filled with the image of the face, – just as the clay [is] filled up with the seal, [if the seal is] of the same size as it. And if the mirror were larger than the face in size, then the mirror would receive the image, preserving the measurements of the image, and the part [of the surface] of the mirror, that 'ran over', would be empty.

This will happen if the mirror is positioned not far from the face of the observer (i.e. not at a distance), but if it is near to the face, so that the distance between the face and the mirror, as it were, does not extend the size of a palm. However, if the mirror is moved further from the observer, then it will show something different. Thus, if a mirror smaller than the face of the observer were small to such an extent that the [diameter of the] light next [to the face] coming forth from the mirror were wider than the face, then [the following would happen]. When the light from the mirror falls upon the face of the observer, the image of the face is formed in the light, next to the face, preserving the real size [of the face]; and then the light, closest to the face, returns the image to the light following it, and then [that light] will return the image to the light following it, – [and this will go on] continually, until the image reaches the mirror. And this happens with the help of contraction and dilation; and the light requires (*indiget*) this.[58] So, it follows that one looking in a narrow-prolonged mirror sees the image of his face being prolonged, because the light next to the surface of the mirror is considerably wider. Therefore, [the light] falls upon the face, and receives the image [of the face], preserving its real size. Thereafter, [the light] returns it to the narrow-prolonged basis by means of contraction, which [the light] causes in this image, – and by the diminution of the width of the image, as well as by the addition to its height, – until [the light] builds up this image in the measurements, received by the narrow-prolonged mirror. And it is required in the same way as when one requires a prolonged seal in order to give a prolonged shape to the clay, and a rounded seal for a round shape.

And it follows that if one looks in a small mirror from a short distance, as if touching it, one will not see the whole of his own face.[59]

(79)

And when one brings the mirror further from his face, one sees the image of his whole face. [This happens] since, when one brings the mirror nearer to the face, that of the light [reflected by the mirror], which falls upon the face, does not cover the whole face, because the light [field] closer [to the mirror] is narrower than the one next to [the face], and is smaller than it. And when one brings one's face further from that of the light, which falls upon this face from the mirror, this light covers the whole of the face thanks to the width of the light [field] next to it. And if the mirror were so small that the light of it, next to the face of the observer, did not cover the whole of the face, then the observer would not see the image of his whole face, either if he brought the face closer [to the mirror], or if he brought it further. And it would be so, because the light next to the face would not cover the whole face. And yet, one does not understand it well without paying attention to one's own sight, whereas one could, as it were, see that, which we say, clearly. And, truly, the one, who is not [doing] so, is lacking in being a witness and adequate time (*testimonio et mora*).

And what if someone asked: 'How does it happen that the light, when it receives the image of an object, contracts this image, and makes it fit the size of its own body, from which it departs, while this body is smaller than the image of that object?' Well then, avert your truthful souls to a small prolonged mirror, in which what is taken from its width is added to its height; in what way could one believe that a face as large as a span (*palmus*) can be diminished to the size of a knot?

Well, let's pick up an example for our argument. Take it that there is a [burning] candle put in a spacious house, and it fills the whole house with its light.[60] Then, [imagine] someone covers the candle with a leather bag;[61] and, the bag receives that [of the light], which the [whole of the] house received [before]; after that, [suppose] someone covers the candle with a small jug, and this jug embraces the whole of the light [of the candle]. Thus, it is evident that the light is contracted and dilated, – [just] what the example was meant to demonstrate. Consequently, what prevents the image carried by the light from being contracted and dilated? And the fact that the light contracts the image, and brings it together, when [this light] fits

(80)

itself into the body which is its basis, is not more extraordinary than [the fact] that a stone sustains the iron, when [the mirror and the magnetic stone] require it, due to some cause.

<...>

PART II
[WO]MEN IN THE MIRROR

CHAPTER 5
MIRRORS OF WOMEN, MIRRORS OF WORDS: THE MIRROR IN THE GREEK PAPYRI
Isabella Bonati and Nicola Reggiani

> quod petis, est nusquam; quod amas, avertere, perdes!
> ista repercussae, quam cernis, imaginis umbra est:
> nil habet ista sui; tecum venitque manetque...
>
> Ovid. *Met.* III 433–5

Introduction

Greek and Latin papyri recovered from the dry sands of Egypt represent an extraordinary source for shedding light on *realia* over the millennium of Greek and Roman control of Egypt, the so-called 'millennium of the papyri', which lasted from the conquest of Egypt by Alexander the Great (332 BC) to the Arab occupation (middle of the VII century AD). Given their close proximity to everyday life, papyri offer concrete records and valuable testimonies about daily technology and material culture. Papyri are a sort of 'textual mirror' of ancient everyday life and enable us to reconstruct the past in an exceptionally vivid way. Thus, the papyrological evidence cannot be disregarded in the theme of mirrors as material objects. Words denoting the 'mirror' occur mostly in documents on papyrus strictly concerned with the female world, such as lists of *paraphernalia* included in marriage contracts and lists of female goods in pawn. Therefore, documentary papyri provide interesting insights into the material aspects of mirrors owned and used by women in the Egyptian χώρα of the Graeco-Roman period and reveal or confirm physical features of these artefacts that can be compared to the archaeological evidence.

The aim of this chapter is fourfold: (1a) after a brief overview of the terms used in ancient Greek to label the 'mirror', (1b) attention will be focused on the documentary papyri, with a survey of the papyrological attestations of the words for 'mirror' and observations on their phonetic variants, with (1c) a discussion about the issues raised by a specific phonetic variant for 'mirror' during the digitization of the papyrus texts; (2) finally, the emphasis will be on mirror as a 'gender object' in the papyri, its connection with the sphere of women, and its material aspects.[1]

Mirrors and Mirroring

1a. The 'mirror' in ancient Greek

In ancient Greek language and literature, several words are used to label the 'mirror'. They are all noun derivatives from the stem ὀπ- of the verb ὁράω, that means 'to see', 'to look', but also – in the perfect form οἶδα, from the stem εἰδ/οἰδ/ἰδ – 'to know', plus the instrumental suffix -τρον.[2] The combining form -οπτρον originates a family of words preceded by various prefixes. These prefixes mark the direction of the gaze and convey a particular shade of meaning – that is hard to translate into modern languages – to any of these compounds defining the 'mirror':

- κάτοπτρον is the most attested one and etymologically designates a reflecting object for looking 'downwards'. The element κατ-, from the preposition κατά, denoting downward motion, recalls the 'visual sinking' of the gaze in a reflecting surface. This sense of visual *descensio* or κατάβασις expresses the potential of mirrors as a means of metaphorical or symbolic reflection. The etymology of this word retains in its components all the evocative power that the catoptric metaphor had and still has in Western culture and literature, from classical antiquity to modern times. It may be conceptually associated with the tragic myth of Narcissus, the most emblematic and best known Greek myth about mirrors and mirroring,[3] even though the term κάτοπτρον is never referred to this myth in the sources: Narcissus became infatuated with his own image (mostly defined as ὄψις and σκιά) reflected in the surface of a clear pool (πηγή, κρήνη), he looked down into the water, the water acted – literally – as a κάτοπτρον, and he drowned in his reflection;
- εἴσοπτρον / ἔσοπτρον: the form ἔσοπτρον is far more attested, whereas εἴσοπτρον has only a few occurrences in late authors. The prefix εἰς or ἐς embeds the concept of 'object for looking into' or, more loosely, 'to';
- and finally ἔνοπτρον and δίοπτρον, meaning reflecting surfaces for looking 'in' and 'through' respectively. δίοπτρον is the most ancient term to define the Greek 'mirror'. Its first attestation, dating back to the seventh–sixth century BC, is a fragment from the lyric poet Alcaeus of Mytilene, where the word acquires a metaphorical sense since it is said that 'wine is the mirror of the man' (fr. 333 V. οἶνος γὰρ ἀνθρώπω δίοπτρον). The choice of δίοπτρον for 'mirror' entails the image of the gaze that 'passes through': wine, being a δίοπτρον, is a means to probe into the soul and reveal its true nature, according to the well-established τόπος – commonly expressed by the Latin phrase *in vino veritas* – that can be traced back to the *incipit* of another poem by Alcaeus, fr. 366 V. quoted by *schol.* Plat. *Symp.* 217e (p. 65 Greene): οἶνος, ὦ φίλε παῖ, καὶ ἀλάθεα ('wine, dear boy, and truth').[4] The same metaphor of wine as a mirror – referred to as κάτοπτρον in this case – is found in a chiastic verse by Aeschylus, fr. 384 N. κάτοπτρον (γὰρ) εἴδους χαλκός ἐστ', οἶνος δὲ νοῦ ('bronze is the mirror of the form, wine of the heart'). It is noteworthy to remember that the neuter δίοπτρον disappears from the Greek written sources until the age of Hesychius, who mentions it as

interpretamentum of a tool called ἀστραβιστήρ (Hesych. α 7886 s.v. ἀστραβιστήρ· ὄργανόν τι, ὡς δίοπτρον), a word unattested elsewhere that seems to denote an 'instrument used in levelling' (LSJ⁹ 262 s.v.). Here the neuter form is likely to have been influenced by the female technical term διόπτρα, which has the primary meaning of 'optical instrument for measuring angles, altitudes, etc.' (LSJ⁹ 434 s.v.). The very technical nature of the word διόπτρα is confirmed by its specialisation in the technical vocabulary of surgery to define a type of gynaecological instrument, also known as *speculum*: a kind of διαστολεύς, 'dilator', for vaginal examination, as it is explained by Gal. *Ling. s. dict. exolet. expl.* κ (XIX 110,10–1 K.) κατοπτῆρι· τῷ καλουμένῳ ἑδροδιαστολεῖ, ὥσπερ γε καὶ διόπτρα, ὁ γυναικῶν διαστολεύς ('the catopter, which is called the anal dilator, in the same way as the diopter is called the female dilator').[5]

All the Greek names for mirror encompass the notion of seeing, and the prefixes detail different modalities of viewing. The Greek language is, in this case, particularly 'realistic' and 'descriptive', since this technical nomenclature is deeply influenced by the material reality of the shapes of the ancient mirrors. The direction of the gaze is, today, mostly horizontal, whereas in antiquity it was horizontal only when the mirror was hung on the wall or held at face height. The other typologies of the mirror (and the liquid surfaces alike) entailed a gaze mainly directed downwards, usually oblique or vertical.

1b. The 'mirror' in the Greek papyri

Papyrological evidence is basically of a linguistic type and, due to its tight connection with daily life, it can be regarded as a treasure of concrete linguistic information. Special or technical words often refer to a wide range of objects, techniques, and so on, and are not rarely transfigured by linguistic variation, producing orthographic or phonetic variants unattested in other written sources. This has both a linguistic and sociocultural implication since it allows us to trace peculiarities of the pronunciation of Greek by Egyptians as a consequence of the linguistic contact, as well as to identify the different social layers and levels of literacy of the writers (this is especially the case with orthographic mistakes).

The following section is aimed at providing a survey of the attestations of the words for 'mirror' in the Greek papyri from Egypt, in the form of a list of *testimonia* followed by linguistic observations. Amongst the aforementioned Greek words for 'mirror', δίοπτρον and ἔνοπτρον have no occurrence in the papyri.[6] In the documentary papyri, as in literature, κάτοπτρον is the most attested form and occurs 11 times in 10 documents on papyrus ranging in date from the first to the fifth–sixth century AD:

1. P.Mich. II 121, 4,i,3 (AD 42, Tebtynis) *marriage document containing a list of dowry goods* included in the register of the record-office (*grapheion*) of Tebtynis: κάτοπτρ(ον) χ(αλκοῦν)

2. P.Mich.V 343,5 (AD 54–55, Arsinoites) *marriage document containing a list of dowry goods*: κά[τ]οπτρον δίπτυκον

3. BGU III 717,12 (AD 149, Arsinoites) *marriage document containing a list of dowry goods*:[7] κάτοπτ[ρ]ον δίπτυχον

4. P.Oxy. XLIX 3491,7 (AD 157–158) *marriage document containing a list of dowry goods*: κάτοπτρον δίπτυχ(ον) κασιω[τικόν][8]

5. SB XVIII 13176,44–5 (AD 168, ?) *marriage document containing a list of dowry goods*: κάτο|π[τρον] <ἓν>

6. P.Dubl. 14,6 (II–III AD, ?) *list of (perhaps stolen) objects*, probably owned by an artist, like a dancer or a mime:[9] κ]άτοπτρον [ἔ]χων (*l*. ἔχον) ἐπιγραφήν[10]

7. SPP XX 46r,16 (II–III AD, ?) *list of goods in pawn, containing several female dowry articles*:[11] κάτοπτρον χαλκοῦν

8. P.Oxy. XII 1449,21 and 56 (AD 213–217) *return of temple properties* with a detailed list of dedicated offerings: l.56 κάτοπ(τρον) νεωτερικ(ὸν) χα(λκοῦν) δίπ(τυχον) α, whereas in l.21 the term κάτοπτρον is a plausible editorial restoration ([κάτοπτρον] | [χ]αλκ(οῦν) νεωτερ[ικ(όν)])

9. PSI VIII 950,12 (III AD, ?) *list of goods that belonged to a temple*: κατοπτ( ) ... ν ἐσμημένα [, where the *editor princeps* suggests to restore κάτοπτ(ρα) νέον ἐσμημένα [, i.e. "mirrors recently wiped" (see *ed.pr.* p. 131 *ad l.*)

10. P.Genova I 28,7 (V–VI AD, ?) *list of goods probably belonging to a woman*:[12] κάτοπτρον ἐλεφάντινον α.[13]

A further mention of κάτοπτρον is not excluded, but it is too uncertain to be accepted with confidence among the *testimonia* of the term. In P.Coll.Youtie I 7, a Ptolemaic private letter (224 BC, Arsinoites), Amadokos informs Kleon about a highway robbery against some women. In the long list of stolen objects, including many female items, such as toilet articles, garments, ointments and perfumes, there is a word beginning with κα in l.9 and ending with πτρον in l.10: κά[το]|πτρον may be an appealing hypothesis, but το is not readable. The *ed.pr.* (see Scherer 1976: 83 *ad l.*) suggests κάμπτρον as an alternative reading, although this word, a neuter form to be connected with the feminine κάμπτρα, 'case', 'chest', does not have other certain attestations in the papyri (nor in literature). The context itself does not help to clarify the situation since both κάτοπτρον and κάμπτρα often occur in papyrus documents concerned with the feminine world.[14] Regardless, the damaged condition of the text in this point would make too hazardous to consider P.Coll.Youtie I 7 as a sure *testimonium* of κάτοπτρον.

The form εἴσοπτρον, which is scantily attested in literature, as already pointed out, never appears in documentary papyri, being εἴσοπ]τρον conventionally supplied in the tetrad 145 of PSI Congr. XXI 4 col. I,8 (LDAB 5014; MP3 2760.32), a tachygraphic commentary on papyrus from Oxyrhynchus (II–III AD). On the contrary, ἔσοπτρον is attested 8 times in 6 papyri, including the most ancient text on papyrus containing a sure mention of a 'mirror':

11. P.Worp 13, col. II,28 (III BC, ?) *list of goods in pawn*: ἔσοπτρον πρὸς (δραχμὰς) η. This mirror belonged to a woman since it is mentioned in a part of the document recording objects expressly owned by a certain Alexandra[15]

12. P.Mert. II 71,4 (AD 163, Arsinoites) *list of mostly women's articles with prices, probably in pawn*:[16] ἔσοπ<τ>ρον τρίπτυχο(ν) χαλκ(οῦν)

13. SPP XX 15,10 (AD 189, Ptolemais Euergetis) *marriage document recording several dowry goods*: [Ἀφρο]δείτην, ἔσοπτρον δίπτυχον

14. P.Hamb. III 220,7 (AD 223–224, Ptolemais Euergetis ?) *marriage document recording several dowry goods*: Ἀφροδίτη, ἔσοπτρον δίπτυχο[ν]

15. SPP XX 31, col. II,20 (AD 230, Ptolemais Euergetis), *marriage document containing a list of dowry goods*: Ἀφρ[οδίτην, ἔσοπτρον] | [δί]πτ[υχ]ον. Here the word ἔσοπτρον is an editorial restoration, but the presence of a term denoting a 'mirror' is made highly probable both by δίπτυχος (though partially integrated), the most recurring adjective defining mirrors in the papyri (see *infra* § 2), and by the mention of an Ἀφροδίτη, a statuette of Aphrodite, that is frequently found in lists of *paraphernalia*, often preceding a mirror or in close proximity with it.[17] Thus, the restoration is modelled upon the sequence of objects Ἀφροδίτην, ἔσοπτρον δίπτυχον, like in **13** and **14**

16. P.Oxy. XXXI 2603,3, as well as ll.14 and 17 (IV AD) *Christian letter of commendation* in which the term ἔσοπτρον appears three times in a figurative and metaphorical context[18]

From a linguistic viewpoint, what is more relevant is that, besides these well-established words for 'mirror', the documentary papyri bear witness also to another form, ὄσυπτρον, that has no occurrence in literature nor in the inscriptions, and is attested 10 times in 9 documents almost exclusively from the second–third century AD:

17. P.Hamb. III 223,11 (AD 113, ?) *list of goods that are probably part of a dowry*:[19] ὄσυπτρον γυνα[ικεῖον]

18. P.Stras. IV 237r,16 (AD 142, Ptolemais Euergetis) *marriage contract containing a dowry list*: χαλκῆν Ἀφρο||[δί]την, ϙσιπτρον (*l.* ὄσυπτρον) δίπτυχον

19. P.Oxy. XXXVI 2787,4 (II AD) *private letter* mentioning the dispatch of some items, among which an ὄσυπτρον maybe belonging to a woman[20]

20. P.FuadUniv. 8,6 (II AD, ?) *private letter* mentioning some goods, among which an ὄσυπτρον maybe to be sold

21. P.Oslo II 46,7 (III AD, Fayum) *inventory of goods belonging to a dowry*: Ἀφροδείτ[η], | ὄσυπτρον

22. P.Oxy. VI 978,4 (second half–late III AD) *list of household items*, among which an ὄσυπτρον;[21] **8.** (see *supra*) P.Oxy. XII 1449,19 (AD 213–217) *return of temple properties*: ὄσυπτρον ἀργ(υροῦν) π[αιδικ(όν)]. The fact that both ὄσυπτρον and κάτοπτρον (l.56) occur in the same document attests to the contemporary use of both of these forms

23. A remarkable testimony is the Latin transcription *osyptrum*, with the Greek root and the ending adapted and integrated to the Latin morphophonological system. It is attested in Ch.L.A. IV 249r (second half of the second century AD, Philadelphia), a *marriage contract* formulated in Latin legal phraseology but containing various originally Greek technical terms Latinized by the scribe,[22] the majority of which is unparalleled in Latin (e.g. *tribacum, cophinum, heratianon, enotion, catoecicas*). The document enumerates the items of the dowry and *paraphernalia* reproducing the model of Greek marriage contracts, and is written twice on the recto of a single papyrus sheet, according to another typically Greek practice, the practice of the so-called 'double documents': the upper copy (*scriptura interior*) was rolled and sealed by the witnesses so that the text could not be falsified, whereas the lower copy (*scriptura exterior*) was left open to be consulted.[23] Therefore, the word *osyptrum* occurs twice: in the *scriptura interior* (l.9) and in the *scriptura exterior* (l.11)

24. It is also worth mentioning a testimony that can be considered "rediscovered",[24] since it was partially hidden by an editorial misinterpretation. It is found in BGU VI 1300 (republished as C.Ptol.Sklav. II 237), a *private letter* from the late III–beginning of the second century BC written by a woman, Tetos, to her own father, containing a shopping list of luxuries. Most of the items that Tetos asks her father to buy are objects of the *mundus muliebris*, such as precious cosmetics and ointments, garments, and containers for unguents and jewellery. At l.17 an ο[ ]υπτρουθήκην χρυ[σῆν] is mentioned. In the sequence ο[ ]υπτρουθήκην as transcribed by the *editores principes*, W. Schubart and E. Kühn, they conjectured the presence of a compound unattested elsewhere: [κατ]οπτροθήκην. In addition, another *hapax* has been read:[25] ὀ[σ]υπτρουθήκην, i.e. ὀ[σ]υπτροθήκην. This reading is confirmed by the digital image of the papyrus.[26] However, it is highly likely that the sequence is not an unattested compound with the wrong insertion of υ, but two distinct words with the same meaning: ὀσύπτρου θήκην, i.e. 'mirror-box',[27] identifying the even elaborate cases with a cover in which the mirrors were kept. Such a *divisio verborum* implies that this private letter on papyrus contains the oldest attestation of ὄσυπτρον[28]

The spelling ὄσυπτρον has been commonly regarded as a plain mistake, but its frequency of attestations in the papyri, in which it is even more recurrent than ἔσοπτρον and not significantly less recurrent than κάτοπτρον,[29] as well as the existence of the Latin transliteration *osyptrum*, allows us to consider ὄσυπτρον as an independent phonetic variant. This variant was probably typical of the language spoken in the Egyptian χώρα in the second and third centuries AD, although its appearance in **24** proves that it was even known much earlier.[30] Yet another aspect seems to strengthen the impression that ὄσυπτρον is an 'informal' variant influenced by the spoken language: the fact that it is the most attested word for 'mirror' in private letters (see **19, 20, 24**). Indeed, it is true that this variant also occurs in documents like some marriage contracts or inventories of goods belonging to a dowry (see **17, 18, 21, 23**), as well as in a list of dedicated offerings (see **6**), but it is likewise true that – according to the extant evidence – the established forms κάτοπτρον and ἔσοπτρον do not seem to be used in private letters (the only exception being ἔσοπτρον in the figurative context of **16**, and maybe the uncertain testimony of P.Coll.Youtie I 7, see *supra*), whereas they are preferred in more 'formal' documents.

On the phonetic side, by comparing ὄσυπτρον and ἔσοπτρον, the following phenomena may be observed: on the one hand, the interchange of o and ε (ε > o), very common in the Egyptian pronunciation of Greek, especially before the sounds /n/ and /s/;[31] on the other hand, the interchange of υ and ο (ο > υ) that produces the closing of the vowel sound.[32] In this regard, some scholars talked about 'metathesis of vowels in successive syllables' and 'phonetic transposition of the vowels', presuming that εἴσοπτρον was pronounced as *isoptron* and ὄσυπτρον as *osiptron*.[33] But the fact that the form εἴσοπτρον never occurs in the papyri might suggest that it was not used in the spoken language. Regardless, an iotacistic pronunciation of ἔσοπτρον cannot be excluded, since the interchange of ε and ι is well documented, especially before σ,[34] even though a form ἴσυπτρον / ἴσοπτρον is never recorded, whereas the form ὄσιπτρον is attested once (see **18** and *infra* § 3).

As to the Latin transliteration *osyptrum* in **23**, this word (as well as the other originally Greek terms latinized in the document) has relevant sociolinguistic implications. With the exception of only three other Latin marriage or dowry contracts on papyrus,[35] Greek was the language of this kind of documents even when the persons involved were Roman citizens, like the Nomissianus family in this case. Latin was not commonly used in the Hellenized speech community of Philadelphia, where the contract was drawn up, but the persons with Roman *nomina* mentioned in the document probably belonged to a social network – presumably with some connection to the Roman army – in which Latin was the prestige code: this seems to be the reason why they chose to write the contract in Latin. Yet, the more freely formulated part, the dowry list, is heavily based on Greek, thus reflecting a linguistic environment where Greek remained the main spoken language. In such a context, the word *osyptrum* is particularly vivid and telling evidence of the effects of Greek–Latin language contact in Roman Egypt.[36]

1c. The word ὄσυπτρον in the digital editions of the Greek papyri

The digital encoding of the Greek papyri – a well-established practice that since several years during the last years has produced a huge textual databank that is proving to be essential in the multifaceted papyrological scholarly research[37] – has allowed for a general reconsideration of the editorial treatment of many textual and linguistic features of the papyri themselves,[38] and has led to a closer look at the ὄσυπτρον instances described above, which indeed proved very interesting as a test case for the digital reconsideration of phonetic fluctuations.

As mentioned earlier, in the 'traditional' papyrus editions, ὄσυπτρον has always been considered as a misspelling, an outright phonetic deviation from the 'standard' spelling of the word.[39] Regardless, the establishment of such a 'standard' spelling (εἴσοπτρον or ἔσοπτρον?) has been all but certain and consistent, as the regularizations collected in the table printed below, as well as the odd creation of two different lemmas in Sergio Daris' lexical list of the Greek papyri, as if εἴσοπτρον and ἔσοπτρον were two different words,[40] easily show.

As noticed above, the frequency of attestation of the spelling ὄσυπτρον may lead us to suspect that we are dealing with a 'substandard' form, in the terms employed by Trevor Evans to describe 'non-standard' trends consistent with chronological, geographical, or individual uses.[41] Under these circumstances, the papyrological edition should more correctly record and describe the linguistic phenomenon, rather than trying to 'regularize' it to an 'original' version that might be, in fact, unattested (as is εἴσοπτρον in the papyri).

A digital edition can offer the best tools to overcome this issue. While the printed medium must answer to restrictive demands (basically, a philological fixation of the text), the hyperspace must comply to much more complex rules: criteria of searchability, standardization, consistency, all of them cross-depending on each other. From this viewpoint, for example, one 'standard' form should be chosen, thus avoiding unnecessary duplications affecting the search functions of the database.[42] The current way of encoding linguistic variation owes much to printed editions: it works through a 'regularization' tag that binds the 'original' spelling (displayed in the main text) to the 'regularized' one (displayed in the apparatus as a *lege* indication).[43] The inconsistencies in the digital apparatuses (easily visible in the following table) are of course a legacy of the printed editions, but let us consider the occurrence ὄσιπτρον in P.Stras. IV 237,16 (see **18**): shall we consider it – following the printed edition – a different spelling variant of ἔ(ι)σοπτρον, or a further spelling variant of the substandard ὄσυπτρον? Moreover, if we assume that ὄσυπτρον does indeed represent a substandard form, shall we regularize it at all?[44]

Nevertheless, even leaving substandard spellings unregularized may lead to the same digital issues as pinpointed above: for example, one should be aware of all substandards to perform effective searches in the database. Also from the linguistic viewpoint it would be important to establish some connection between substandard forms and their original

Papyrus text	Regularization in the printed edition	Regularization in the digital edition
P.Hamb. III 223,11 [**17**]	ἔσοπτρον in apparatus	*l.* ἔσοπτρον
P.Stras. IV 237,16 [**18**]	*l.* εἴσοπτρον	*l.* εἴσοπτρον
P.Oxy. XXXVI 2787,4 [**19**]	εἴσοπτρον in apparatus (after the P.Oslo [21] comment)	*l.* εἴσοπτρον
P.FuadUniv. 8,6 [**20**]	*l.* εἰσόπτρου	*l.* εἰσόπτρου
P.Oslo II 46,7 [**21**]	εἴσοπτρον in apparatus	*l.* εἴσοπτρον
P.Oxy. VI 978,4 [**22**]	*l.* ἔσοπτρον	*l.* ἔσοπτρον
P.Oxy. XII 1449,19 [**8**]	*l.* ἔσοπτρον	*l.* ἔσοπτρον
BGU VI 1300,17 = C.Ptol. Sklav. II 237 + BL II 32 [**24**]	*l.* ἐσόπτρου	*l.* ἐσόπτρου

starting point. This might be reached by means of a multi-layer architecture, that connects all the possible spelling fluctuations in a lemmatized network where the concepts of 'standard', 'misspelling', 'regularization' lose all meaning[45] and the critical edition ceases to be a simple fixation of an editorial reconstruction, becoming a further step in the fluid transmission of the ancient textual evidence.[46]

2. Mirrors and women's world in the papyri: Between words, objects and culture

Documentary papyri emphasize the mirror as essentially a 'gender object' since most of this papyrological evidence has a clear connection with the feminine world or is related to it in one way or another. In everyday life the connection between mirror and woman was so tight that, perhaps for this reason, the mirror appearing in **17** was defined as γυναικεῖος, 'feminine, belonging to a woman' (ὄσυπτρον γυνα[ικεῖον]). On the one hand, this adjective is quite generic and does not refer to a specific feature of the object, but on the other, its presence seems to circumscribe and characterize its sphere of use and its users.[47] The study of the papyri contributes to illuminate and define the role of mirrors as material objects and reflecting media in the daily life of women in Graeco–Roman Egypt.[48]

Amongst the 24 documentary papyri mentioning mirrors, the connection with the feminine world is: certain for at least 13 *testimonia* (see **1, 2, 3, 4, 5, 11, 13, 14, 15, 18, 21, 23, 24**); highly likely for 7 specimens (see **7, 8, 9, 10, 12, 17, 19**); completely absent in just one case (see **16**); uncertain in a very small number of documents (see **6, 20, 22**), due to the lack of enough elements in the context to ascertain a direct and sure relation to a woman.

The vast majority of these documents are marriage contracts recording dowry goods, the so-called παράφερνα or *paraphernalia*,[49] independent dowry lists, or inventories of objects connected with a dowry. In fact, in the Graeco-Roman world mirrors were commonly correlated to marriage and childbirth, and they often served as wedding gifts. The role of mirrors in the dowry of elite Roman women is also confirmed by the archaeological evidence since these artefacts have frequently been found in the graves of girls who died either before marriage or during childbirth.[50] Moreover, the fact that mirrors were objects of elegance and luxury can tell something about the social status of their owners.

In two other significant cases (see **8** and **9**) mirrors are listed amongst votive offerings. This is consistent with the fact that, from the sixth century BC onwards, mirrors became common votive gifts in the Greek world, and were mostly dedicated to deities concerned with marriage, fertility, and childbirth, in particular, Aphrodite, Artemis, Hera, Demeter, and Persephone.[51] Dowry goods like mirrors were indeed often included in temple inventories on papyrus both because they could be votive gifts to fulfil vows and because they could represent actual objects for worship.[52] The identity of the female worshippers is, of course, often unrecoverable, but it may be assumed that they were classy and had a wealthy status since the bronze or silver mirrors that they dedicated in the sanctuaries were generally expensive.

In addition, the presence of a mirror in a list of household items (see **22**) underscores the function of mirrors within the domestic context, which was the women's realm *par excellence*.

The tight connection between mirrors and women that the documents on papyrus reveal demonstrates the role of mirrors in the *mundus muliebris*, the standard belongings of a woman. 'Physical beauty and personal adornment were intricately linked to issues of identity and status'[53] in antiquity, and mirrors were the best artefacts to both exhibit an individual's reflection and help to manipulate the physical appearance. Their main purpose was, of course, practical and utilitarian: women used them as toilet articles to paint their faces, arrange their hair, dress up and adorn themselves with jewellery. Thus, exactly like today, mirrors were technical instruments for cosmetic and personal beauty care, connected with the most private and intimate aspects of the life of a woman. Their presence in a confined space inside the house marked a decidedly feminine space, in which the mirrors 'functioned as icons of ideal femininity',[54] contributing to the construction of the idea of a woman,[55] and encompassing notions of status, gender and sexuality. Hence, by allowing an actual self-referential experience, the mirror was indispensable to construct not only the exterior appearance but also the individual, gendered identity in a deep way.

This process of self-construction passed through the reflected image. However, that image was very different compared to the one – clear and hyper-realistic – we are accustomed to today. The polished disks employed in the daily toilet ritual of the ancient ladies reflected an image that was very imperfect, sometimes grainy, or even distorting. In a world before photography and mirrors manufactured with an excellent degree of flatness and reflectivity, what a woman gazed into the mirror was not exactly the same as perceived by the others. In addition, in the absence of full-length mirrors, the image was limited and partial due to the small dimension of the reflecting surface, and the view was restricted. Ancient artisans circumvented this problem by resorting to an optical trick: the convex shape of ancient mirrors enabled an expanded viewing area and could 'compress a large scene into a small space',[56] including in the field of vision not only the face but also the entire head and upper chest.[57]

Documentary papyri also contribute to shed light on the material side of mirrors widespread in the Egyptian χώρα of the Graeco-Roman time. In this regard, an overview of the adjectives associated with the words for 'mirrors' proves to be particularly fruitful. The most recurring adjective that defines mirrors in the papyri is δίπτυχος, 'double-folded', 'folding' (see **2, 3, 4, 8, 13, 14, 15, 18**).[58] In literature, this adjective is applied to a mirror only once, in Plu. *Mor.* (*De facie*) 930b,3 διαβάλλεται δὲ τοῖς διπτύχοις κατόπτροις. Therefore, its frequent occurrence in the papyrus documents – in which it is mostly, although not exclusively referred to mirrors[59] – seems to imply that the expression κάτοπτρον / ἔσοπτρον / ὄσυπτρον δίπτυκον was a technical expression of the vocabulary of the material culture in the papyri. The adjective δίπτυκος describes a feature that characterizes a specific typology of mirrors.

The aristocratic ladies of ancient Greece viewed themselves in round disks of polished metal: usually of bronze, sometimes of silver. The earliest Greek mirrors were introduced into Greece, probably from Egypt,[60] in the archaic period. The oldest Greek type is the 'hand mirror', a convex polished disk with an attached, often ornate grip handle. The handle could be either embedded in the disk or made of a separate material, such as ivory (see *infra*).[61] A ring at the top allowed the 'hand mirror' to be hung on the wall. Already found in excavations of Mycenaean sites (about 1400 BC), this typology disappears from the archaeological record from about 1000 BC to 700 BC, then reappears again until about 400 BC. It is followed by the complex and costly 'caryatid' or 'stand mirror', which was popular between 550–450 BC, and was supported by a human – mainly female – figure standing on a base; this elaborate handle could stand on a flat surface and could often be enriched by supplementary decorative attachments.[62] By the late fifth century BC, a new type of mirror was introduced, which was really successful and continued to be manufactured throughout the Hellenistic period and in some areas, among which Graeco-Roman Egypt, well into the Roman era: the so-called 'clamshell', 'case mirror' or 'box mirror', comparable to the modern 'compact'. This type – first invented by the Greeks, then adopted by the Etruscans,[63] and passed on to the Romans – was small (from about 10 to 20 cm), handleless, and easily portable: a decorated lid was attached directly to the polished metal disk of the mirror by a hinge, in order to protect its surface when it was not in use. The box mirrors could be very precious since the hinged cover was often richly enhanced with engravings, relief, or repoussé representations, but scenes could also be engraved on its underside.[64]

The adjective δίπτυχος refers exactly to this folding typology of a mirror. The 'box mirror' remained the most popular type of mirror from the Hellenistic period onwards. The papyrological sources not only confirm this aspect but also integrate the archaeological evidence by adding to the artefacts a valuable textual counterpart and allowing us to return to the physical object the name that it had in antiquity.

Completely in line with what we know from the archaeological finds, bronze is the most mentioned material in the papyri (see **1, 7, 8** ll.21 and 56, **12**), silver only once (see **8** l.19), but in **10** a κάτοπτρον ἐλεφάντινον is listed, literally a 'mirror of ivory'. It is likely that this material refers to a particular part or aspect of the mirror, thus specifying the distinguishing feature of the object. It might identify the presence of an ivory handle, as already mentioned, or otherwise of an ivory case or lid. The κάτοπτρον in **10** would be a 'hand mirror' in the first case, a 'box mirror' in the second. However, the discovery of mirrors with ivory handles, or at least of fragments of ivory handles to be attached to the mirror disks, makes the first option more probable.[65]

The bronze mirror in **12** is not δίπτυχος as usual, but τρίπτυχος, literally 'threefold', 'consisting of three layers'.[66] This seems to point to a characteristic that is not mentioned in any other source. Maybe τρίπτυχος does not define a new, different shape of a mirror (with no parallel in the archaeological evidence), but it might simply indicate that the mirror consisted of three parts assembled together, as it was not uncommon for the hand mirror type.[67] If this interpretation is correct, the adjective τρίπτυχος would not refer to a (so far unknown) typology of Greek mirror, as δίπτυχος does, but to a particular feature of this ἔσοπτρον expressed by a term having the same etymological pattern (τρι- + -πτυχός, from πτύσσω, 'to fold') as the adjective most frequently associated with the mirror in the vocabulary of documentary papyri. Hence, 'threefold' not in the sense of 'foldable three times' (as δίπτυχος is, literally, 'foldable twice'), but 'consisting of three parts'.

Document **6** attests to the fact that mirrors could bear an inscription. Several exemplars of ancient mirrors with inscriptions have been excavated. Although they are mostly interpreted as votive offerings, they could also be employed in everyday life,[68] as this papyrus concretely confirms.

In l.19 of **8**, a silver mirror is followed by a word beginning with π that the *editores principes*, B. P. Grenfell and A. S. Hunt, restore as π[αιδικ(όν)]. The restoration is reasonable since the adjective παιδικός, 'of or for a child', accompanies other objects in the same inventory.[69] In the specific case of ὄσυπτρον in l.19, the adjective might underscore the already mentioned correlation between mirrors and childbirth in Graeco-Roman culture. Thus, the fact that the mirror was literally 'for a child' might mean that it was 'destined to a child for his / her birth' rather than 'owned' by a child. In such a case, the expression ὄσυπτρον παιδικόν could have a sociocultural significance as a direct testimony of that correlation.

Another adjective defining mirrors in **8** deserves special attention since it might be interpreted in a fresh way in the light of the context. In l.56 (and probably also in ll.21–2, see *supra* § **1b**) a κάτοπτρον is referred to as νεωτερικόν. The editors translate νεωτερικός as 'in new style' (p. 141) and comment that 'νεώτερα (is) contrasted with ἀρχαῖα in similar lists' (p. 144). However, no element in the text seems to point to a contrast between a 'new' and an 'old-fashioned' style. Moreover, the comparative νεώτερος[70] and νεωτερικός,[71] an adjective suffixed in -ικός, are not semantically equivalent. The editors also suggest the possibility that νεωτερικός is parallel to παιδικός, but this explanation does not seem convincing enough to justify a term, νεωτερικός, that has no other attestation in the vocabulary of Greek documentary papyri, especially taking into account that there is no real need for a potential synonym to express a concept that could be expressed by using the same παιδικός, as in the aforementioned cases.[72]

The word-formation of νεωτερικός and a particular element in the context might rather suggest an alternative hypothesis and a special meaning of the word in this text. The inventory contained in the papyrus, submitted to local government authorities by priests of various temples at Oxyrhynchus and in the Oxyrhynchite and Cynopolite nomes, mentions a number of deities worshipped at those shrines. One of them is Neotera, who had one of her temples 'in the south-east part of the city' (l.4 [ἐν τοῖς ἀπ]ὸ νότου τῆς π[ό]λεως ἐπ' ἀ[πη]λ(ιώτην)). Her name occurs several times in the inventory, which lists numerous votive offerings to her attesting to longstanding worship. It is indeed specified that some of these offerings are 'in the temple from antiquity' (see l.10) and others are 'dedicated in accordance with ancient custom for vows and reverence' (l.12 ἄνωθ(εν) συνηθ(είας) κατ' εὐχ(ὴν) καὶ εὐσέβ(ειαν) ἀνιερωθέντ(ων)). The identity of the goddess is still a subject of debate and the epithet Νεωτέρα seems to have been linked to many female deities. Most of them are associated with marriage, motherhood and fertility, like the syncretic deity Hathor–Aphrodite, as well as Kore, Persephone, Nephtys, and Isis.[73] The presence of mirrors amongst the votive gifts in **8** does not surprise, given that, as already pointed out, mirrors were often dedicated to deities concerned with marriage and fertility. Our hypothesis is that, in the particular context of this document, the adjective νεωτερικός may have an etymological connection with the theonym Νεωτέρα. This interpretation is linguistically supported by the word-formation in -ικός, a suffix, very productive along the entire history of the ancient Greek language, which expresses relationship and pertinence (i.e. 'having to do with', 'related to', 'pertaining to').[74] Therefore, νεωτερικός in **8** might be modelled on and paralleled by the adjectives formed by a theonym plus the suffix -ικός, such as Ἰσιακός from Ἶσις[75] and Ἀσκληπιακός from Ἀσκληπιός.[76] Hence, the expression κάτοπτρον νεωτερικόν would turn out to mean 'mirror for (i.e. dedicated / related / belonging to) Neotera'.

Finally, the study of the words for 'mirror' in the Greek papyri proves the contribution of the papyrological evidence to refine our knowledge and provide a more accurate interpretation of the material (as well as sociocultural) aspects of the ancient world. Despite the objective difficulty of connecting *verba* and *realia*, papyri from Graeco-Roman Egypt play a decisive role towards reconstructing this complex, and often fragmentary picture thanks to their nature of sources in close proximity to everyday life. Especially when combined with the evidence offered by the archaeological artefacts, the papyri allow us to shed new light on the past. An integrated approach to the study of antiquity, bridging the gap between texts and objects, is thus vital to understand the whole – an entire world as it was, made of objects and words. Not apart, but together. Artefacts may answer questions raised by papyri, papyri may provide a clue to interpreting the artefacts. The effort – and sometimes, hopefully, the outcome – is to strengthen the connection between words and material culture: to give back a name to the *res*, and a shape to the *verba*.

CHAPTER 6
A FLAME ON ETRUSCAN MIRRORS? MEANING AND FUNCTION IN DAILY LIFE AND RELIGION OF THE PATTERN ON THE MIRRORS' REFLECTING SIDE[1]

Vittorio Mascelli

Introduction

A peculiar representation appears on the extension of the *recto* of some Etruscan bronze mirrors dating from the Hellenistic Period: at first sight a floral and lozenge-shaped motif (Fig. 6.1).[2] This pattern has been interpreted by modern scholars as a leaf; a flame on a tripod, symbol of the soul that would turn into a great solar disk;[3] a simple flame;[4] a griffin's tongue with its muzzle facing towards the mirror disk; a hypothetical representation of perfume that rises from acanthus leaves below.[5] The floral pattern (on the reflecting side) usually accompanies depictions of the Dioscuri in a specular pose (on the decorated side, Fig. 6.2) on Etruscan mirrors of the so-called 'standardized production';[6] it also appears on specimens decorated with four characters and a crown of thorns or laurel, and on products attributed to the so-called 'Maestro di Cacu',[7] or to the 'Maestro delle Colonne Flessibili'.[8]

The flame, which rises from a flower, a composition apparently unnatural, but possible, as we will see, is decorated by spark-like dots around its external pyriform profile. Many other Etruscan mirrors have flowers in the same position, but this decoration is particular because it's formed by a lozenge-shaped body enriched by a precise drawing of petals

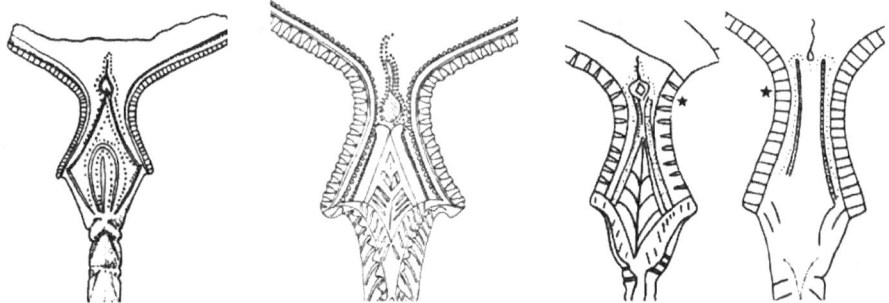

Fig. 6.1 Flames on the extension of the *recto* of Etruscan Hellenistic bronze mirrors.

Fig. 6.2 Mirror with Dioscuri in a specular pose, from Norchia, Museo Archeologico Nazionale di Viterbo, inv. 112.305 (*CSE*, Italia, 5, n. 38), first half of the third century BC.

with a little flame atop that rises upward, surrounded by sparkles. As I argue, though, the connection between the floral pattern and the Dioscuri, carrying religious meaning, cannot be sidestepped. An interpretation that provides a functional reason for its presence on the mirrors could also be considered; as I propose, the flame might represent a light source illuminating the user's reflection in the dark.

Worship of the Dioscuri in Italy and their feminine relevance?

It is possible to identify about one hundred mirrors showing a pattern similar to that of the flame under review.[9] Most of the specimens can be dated between the third and the second centuries BC and show, as mentioned, the presence of the divine twins, a representation that probably had a particular meaning also in religious terms.[10] We know that in antiquity the Dioscuri were worshipped for several reasons, related to their epiphanies on battlefields[11] and to their role as *soteres*, saviours, for sailors during storms (see Alcaeus,[12] Theocritus,[13] and Strabo[14]). But the salvific character of the divine twins on the battlefield cannot explain the presence of the deities as decoration on Etruscan mirrors, which do not appear to be public monuments but rather objects belonging to the private, mostly female, sphere.[15]

The cult of the divine twins had been widely adopted in the Italic and Etruscan territory at least since the Archaic Period, as evidenced by the sinistrorse dedication in archaic Latin from Lavinium with the boustrophedon inscription '*Castorei Podlouqueique qurois*'.¹⁶ However, the element that links the Tyndaridae to the Etruscan religious landscape is undoubtedly the dedication on the bottom of a red-figure cup of Oltos and Euxitheos (510 BC), found in a Tarquinian tomb, that *Venel Atelinas* offered to the sons of Zeus.¹⁷ The dedication is contemporary with other attestations of the Dioscuri in Etruria at the end of the sixth century BC and is considered by G. Colonna as a fulcrum of Etruscan religious history, not only in funerary terms, but also in relation to the cult of the Dioscuri, identified on the inscription in the Etruscan language as *Tinas Cliniiaras*, or sons of *Tinia* (Zeus).¹⁸ The presence of the deities has also been assumed in the decoration of the so-called 'Biga di Castro' and in the paintings of two Tarquinian hypogea: inside the 'Tomba del Barone' and on the *lectisternium* depicted in the 'Tomba del Letto Funebre'.¹⁹ In these contexts the Dioscuri seem to accompany and protect the deceased during the long journey to the afterlife.²⁰ In the fifth century BC, on a stele from Bologna two figures preceding a chariot have superhuman features as psychopompe deities; they are in fact winged, and G. Sassatelli has suggested an identification with the Dioscuri that *'suddenly [. . .] are seen darting through the air on tawny wings'* (*Hymn. Hom.* XXXIII, 13).²¹ Though starting from the middle of the fifth century BC, other deities and eschatological and initiatory religious beliefs seem to be more affirmed in Etruscan religion, including the cult of Dionysus, which offered more satisfactory answers to human needs,²² the widespread presence of the Dioscuri on Etruscan mirrors between the fourth and the second centuries BC is an undoubtable fact, probably in part due to Etruscan contacts with Taranto's sphere.²³

The ancient sources help delineate the complex framework that revolves around the figures of the Dioscuri, for which G. Della Fina has hypothesized an initial cult linked to the Eleusinian Mysteries.²⁴ The aforementioned Homeric hymn to the Dioscuri describes them as winged figures flying, thus overcoming the distance between the human and divine world. Some sources even describe how the twins had the permission from Zeus to come back to life on alternate days in the tomb where they were buried in Therapne,²⁵ or to live every other day in the grave and in the sky.²⁶ These conditions contributed to creating at least in Etruria a liminal association with the Dioscuri, often depicted as intermediate beings between the world of the living and that of the dead, thus obtaining devotion both in the living and funerary spheres.

The role of the Dioscuri as salvific and intermediate divinities between two worlds had already been noted by G. Colonna as an explanation for their cult, in relation to the conception of the sea-journey to the afterlife, witnessed in the pattern of the waves and hippocampi on Tarquinian tombs also of the Archaic Period.²⁷ As is well known, this conception of the journey of the deceased over the sea is also typical of the Hellenistic world, as evidenced on artefacts depicting several marine demons such as Scylla, and various marine patterns, typical of the decorative repertoire of Etruscan Hellenistic art.²⁸ This protective character of the Dioscuri could help us understand the presence of the divine twins on the Etruscan mirrors under examination.

However, the reason for the presence of the Dioscuri on the mirrors seems to require further explanation.²⁹ Etruscan mirrors are generally considered as typically feminine objects and certainly had a place both in a woman's everyday life and in her death.[30] Hence, the decoration on the mirrors is mostly related to the 'feminine imagery' outlined by M. Cristofani,[31] and presents mythological and religious narratives that sometimes highlight women's and brides' virtues.[32] In the past the presence of the Dioscuri on Etruscan mirrors was explained by their role as patrons of athleticism and warfare,[33] or an indication of social status, associating the deceased woman with the equestrian rank,[34] hypotheses rejected by M. Cristofani, who rather than limiting the twins' presence to the census, suggested extending it to the female sphere with deeper meanings.[35]

Regarding the relation of the Dioscuri to women, the sources indicate that the twins were brothers of Helen and that as such they protected her and contributed to her immortality; consider, for instance, the mythical episode of Helen's abduction by Theseus and Pirithous, when the twins intervened to free their sister. This episode had to be well known if, according to Pausanias, it was depicted on the famous ark of Cypselus.[36] Moreover, we know that the Aeginetes sent three golden stars, symbols of Helen and the Dioscuri, on a ship's mast to Delphi, to celebrate the victory of Salamis.[37] On the other hand, the Dioscuri themselves also seem to be involved in women's abductions. Pausanias narrates that one day the Dioscuri introduced themselves in disguise to a man named *Phormion*, who had bought the house where they had once lived. When they asked for his hospitality in a precise room, the man refused, since his maiden daughter slept there, and offered them other rooms. The next day the young woman and all her belongings had vanished, and in their place were images of the Dioscuri and *silphium*, a plant dear to the twins.[38] This is not the only case in which the Dioscuri kidnap a girl. More well-known is the episode of the Leucippids' abduction, told by Pausanias shortly before that of *Phormion*'s daughter, in which the brothers kidnap the daughters of Leucippus, Hilarea and Phoebe.

We should, at this point, also consider the relationship that the Castores had with light: specifically with stars and flames. Such an association could perhaps shed light on the presence of the flame on the Etruscan mirrors under study. The sources tell us that the Dioscuri appeared besides boats or above them as twin stars,[39] in their role of sailors' protectors.[40] Furthermore stars are present both in Greece and in Etruria on artefacts related to the Dioscuri: for instance, on an altar from Thera where stars appear next to two *piloi* (the typical Dioscuri hat) with the dedication by Artemidorus of Perge '*to the Dioscuri who save those who invoke them*' (third century BC),[41] or next to the twins engraved on several Etruscan Hellenistic mirrors. Today it is possible to offer a scientific explanation for the marine epiphanies of these deities. The aforementioned ancient sources describe to us symbolic epiphanies in the form of stars or flames on the tops of ships' masts.[42] These probably described a phenomenon that still occurs today in particular weather conditions, arising from an electroluminescent discharge caused by the ionization of oxygen and nitrogen molecules in the dry air before a thunderstorm, within a strong electric field: the so-called 'St. Elmo's Fire', which often occurs for a few seconds in double or triple jets on ships' mastheads. This was probably interpreted in ancient times as the divine epiphany of the Dioscuri, as in more recent centuries it was interpreted as that of St. Elmo.[43] Stars are also present in the centre of several Etruscan mirrors between the divine twins, and are sometimes symbolized by simple dots; most likely they serve as an allusion to the nature of the Dioscuri as *soteres* that would thus ensure a peaceful journey, also to the underworld.[44] Generally, according to some scholars, it seems plausible to interpret the presence of the Dioscuri in relation to the religious sphere, linked to the moment of transition between the world of the living and that of the dead.[45] This interpretation has intended to lead, however, to the consideration of the mirrors of the so-called 'standardized production', the group to which the mirrors in question belong, as exclusively funerary.[46] If, on the one hand, a funerary nature cannot be excluded for these objects, it seems, however, necessary to underline that a religious symbol accompanies an individual not only in a tomb but also throughout life as an indication of particular beliefs that often involve rituals practiced in life.[47] I believe it more appropriate to consider such objects with mythological-religious motifs as existing within the general sphere of Etruscan religion rather than only within the funerary rituals performed inside the tomb itself.[48]

A flame on Etruscan mirrors: Function and interpretation

Prima facie, it seems plausible to associate the flame on the front of the mirrors under examination with the Dioscuri and their relation to light,[49] also taking into account the importance of their cult in the Etruscan religion and their association with women. However, since the flame is always single (not double as in relation to the twins), set on the apex of a flower, and also appears on some mirrors with Lasas (Etruscan female demons),[50] several doubts may arise about an interpretation exclusively linked to the Dioscuri.[51] I argue that the flame engraved on the mirror's extension, at the base therefore of the polished reflecting side, metaphorically 'helps' the woman to see her own image reflected. Though the presence of the flame, especially through its connection with Dioscuri and Lasas, could carry semantic and religious meanings, we could assume that in absence of daylight, a mirror would need an artificial light behind, below or next to it and in front of the woman's face in order to produce a reflection, and that this light source could be what is here schematically engraved as a flame.[52] This flame, as mentioned above, comes from a funnel-shaped element that clearly evokes a flower. Certainly, the presence of a flame on a flower seems incongruent, which is why other interpretations have been suggested.

However, ancient sources offer a possible explanation for the floral image evoked by the lozenge from which the flame is born: an artificial lighting method that uses a liquid or animal fat as fuel and flowers as wicks. We know from Pliny and Isidore of Seville[53] that wicks could be created with the leaves of particular plants, and this was so common that some of these plants were actually called in ancient times *lychnitis* or *thryallis*, in reference to this use in illumination. A variety of flowers and leaves seems to have been used in antiquity as wicks; one of these is indicated in Pliny's *Naturalis Historia* by the term *phlomos* or *verbascum*,[54] on whose Greek origins (*phlomis*) Dioscorides informs us (III, 100, 101).[55] According to Pliny's account, the plant grows on plains or in the woods and could be white or black; it could be considered wild and has long leaves similar to sage's and woody branches, while two other varieties of *phlomis* have hairy, fat leaves and a third type has thick leaves, which are considered particularly suitable for making wicks (*lumina*) for lamps. This plant bears a 'speaking name' that underlines its intended use, *lychnitis* or *thryallis*. The very name of the wick in Greek, according to Pausanias and others, is in fact θρυαλλίς.[56] Among these plants the *verbascum* or *phlomos* is actually defined as '*herba lucernaris*' (a plant for lamps).[57]

The same concept can be found in Dioscorides about the φλόμος also called *verbascum*.[58] The *verbascum lychnitis* is one of the varieties of this plant, that in Dioscorides' text is cited as φλομίς ή καλουμένη λυχνῖτις.[59]

In the case of our engraved representation, if we accept the identification with a flame, we could relate it to the use of floating wicks described by the ancient sources.[60] Herodotus describes, for example, rites in honour of the goddess Neith in the Egyptian city of Sais, and offers a detailed account of the 'Feast of Lamps', when the inhabitants of Sais light 'oil lamps' formed by simple vases full of oil and salt, with wicks floating on the surface.[61]

The mention of 'λυχνα', lamps, in the account is very interesting in relation to floral wicks: these lamps are described as generic vessels, a general reference which contrasts with the meticulous description of the fuel and wick duration. In other words, Herodotus

Fig. 6.3 Flowers goblet of *Ballota pseudodictamnus* or *acetabulosa* used as a floating wick.

describes λύχνα as generic containers filled with oil and salt.[62] These types of vessels are obviously very widespread in Etruria but have not yet been interpreted as functional to artificial lighting, while the latest lychnological studies are considering the possibility that simple open vessels in the Greek world were functional to artificial lighting.[63]

This particular lighting method that uses natural plant resources for illumination is still used in Italy, with the dried flower goblets of the *Ballota pseudodictamnus* or *acetabulosa* (Fig. 6.3). This use was widespread until the early decades of the twentieth century in Tuscany and in southern regions, so that the plant is better known by the name of 'Luminu' (little lamp) or 'Lumino greco' (Greek little lamp): denomination that speaks of its use outside the peninsula and in particular in Greece where it is also widespread.[64] The funnel-shaped goblet, deprived of seeds, being hollow inside, was collected and dried to be then immersed upside down in open vessels (glass or pottery) in a mixture of oil and water, where, also floating by means of cork supports, it burned and produced light even for a whole day, until the fuel finished and the flame sputtered, leaving no traces of burning on the container (see Fig. 6.3).[65] Since electricity now provides our main sources of light, the little lamp composed of the plant and the mixture of oil and water is mainly used today as a votive candle set next to the images of the beloved deceased and saints, still testifying to a cultural and religious use for this type of artificial light.

Conclusion

Bronze mirrors in Etruscan society had an important function in cosmetic practices, and as prestigious objects they were decorated with mythological or religious themes that had a significant function in a woman's life. Enhancing women's virtues or encouraging pious behaviours or religious beliefs, these representations were not simply decoration, but were bearers of complex messages mainly related to the feminine sphere and to Etruscan religion. At the same time, however, as I argue, mirror-motifs could also be related to real functions. Specifically, the position of this decoration – a flame atop a flower – at the bottom of the polished, reflecting disk, could be related to sources of artificial light, which allowed a woman to see her reflection in the dark. Roman and Greek sources tell us about the possibility to use flowers and plants to produce wicks for lamps, and it seems plausible to see in our representation this particular technique, still used today in the Mediterranean.

Appendix

(Edited mirrors with a flame atop a flower)

The following list obviously does not claim to be complete (many mirrors are still unpublished and stored in museums), but it's an example of some known specimens

Mirrors and Mirroring

published in the *CSE*: about 63 represent the two Dioscuri in specular pose (*CSE* Belgique, n. 2; *CSE* BRD, 1, nn. 8–10, 17, 20–21, 26; *CSE* BRD, 2, n. 33; *CSE* BRD, 3, n. 23; *CSE* DDR, 1, n. 10; *CSE* DDR, 2, nn. 4, 24; *CSE* Denmark, n. 20; *CSE* France, 1.2, nn. 47, 49, 51, 53–54, 56, 58–62; *CSE* GB, 3, nn. 4, 18, 25; *CSE* Hongrie-Tchécoslovaquie, nn. 8, 20; *CSE* Italia, 1.1., nn. 9, 37; *CSE* Italia, 2.1, n. 24; *CSE* Italia, 3.1, nn. 3, 27, 35; *CSE* Italia, 4, nn. 4, 18–19, 25, 31; *CSE* Italia, 5, nn. 15, 17, 21, 38; *CSE* Italia, 6.2, n. 95; *CSE* Italia, 7.1, nn. 10, 79; *CSE* USA, 1, nn. 1, 8, 34; *CSE* USA, 2, n. 39; *CSE* USA, 3, n. 3; *CSE* USA, 4, nn. 9, 10, 12, 24, 32, 40, 42; *CSE* Vaticano, 1, nn. 14, 18, 19); about 11 show four characters, two of which to the side, probably interpretable as the Dioscuri (*CSE* BRD, 1, n. 15; *CSE* Denmark, n. 21; *CSE* France, 1.1, n. 31; *CSE* Italia, 1.1, n. 5; *CSE* Italia, 4, nn. 6, 28; *CSE* USA, 1, n. 28, 36; *CSE* USA, 3, nn. 17–18; *CSE* USA, 4, n. 4); about 24 show the same four-figure scheme (*CSE* Belgique, n. 27; *CSE* BRD, 1, n. 12; *CSE* BRD, 2, nn. 12, 32; *CSE* BRD, 3, n. 22; *CSE* DDR, 1, n. 35; *CSE* France, 1.1, nn. 30, 32, 34, 38–39; *CSE* France, 1.2, nn. 43, 47; *CSE* Italia, 2.1, nn. 18, 21; *CSE* Italia, 3.1, n. 1; *CSE* Italia, 6.1, n. 38; *CSE* USA, 1, nn. 5–6, 24, 27, 33; *CSE* USA, 3, nn. 2, 4); about 6 depict Lasas, female demons (*CSE* BRD, 2, n. 1; *CSE* Italia, 1.1., n. 34; *CSE* Italia, 3.1., n. 26; *CSE* Italia, 5, n. 25; *CSE* USA, 1, n. 10; *CSE* USA, 4, n. 21). There are also some examples of mirrors with a flame, where, unfortunately, the disk is missing (*CSE* France, 1.2, n. 78; *CSE* Italia, 7.1, nn. 9, 91).

CHAPTER 7
PORTABLE LOVE: IVORY MIRROR CASES UNDER THE LENS OF *FIN' AMOR*

Loreto Casanueva Reyes

'Specula sunt, in quibus feminae vultus suos intuantur'.

Medieval German gloss

Opening the mirror

How many functions did a medieval mirror have? In his seminal work *The Medieval Art of Love: Objects and Subjects of Desire* (1998), Michael Camille argued that mirrors, 'like every other object in medieval art, have no single uniform significance but can mean a multitude of things, depending on the context' (1998, 47). For Frelick (2016), for instance, mirrors in the Middle Ages were Janus-like artefacts, that is, they were considered cosmetic or decorative objects as well as textual or pictorial items. This double perception of mirrors also coincides with some medieval mirrors actual two-face features: a glass[1] or polished metal (like copper-alloy) surface and a case made of ivory, which makes them portable. That second feature is the focus of this article.

Beyond its reflecting virtues, portable ivory mirrors were a trendy and desired commodity among women. They were generally acquired as a purchase or given as a gift, but they were also eloquent and meaningful objects in the plot of medieval love treatises and romances. Even though now the looking surface of ivory mirrors is generally missing or broken, cases remain. As a result, they can tell us, on the one hand, about their own curious and luxurious biography in the new 'phantasmagoric' world of objects and, on the other, about the courtly scenes depicted on their front side. Thus, mirrors become both narrative devices and powerful love tokens.

This article has two main purposes: First, the chapter seeks to explain how mirrors and their representations shed light into the Middle Ages' ideals of beauty and love under the lens of *fin' amor*. Second, it aims to show how portable ivory mirror cases are represented in two literary works: *De Amore* (1185) by Andreas Capellanus and *Le Roman de la Rose* (1225–1278) by Guillaume de Lorris and Jean de Meun. To do this, the chapter will begin by providing a brief historical overview of how mirrors were perceived from Antiquity to the Middle Ages; then, it will explore how portable mirrors became a love token; finally, it will provide an analysis of the presence and connotations of mirrors in *De Amore* and *Le Roman de la Rose*.

Mirrors and Mirroring

Mirrors and social reflection

Before exploring its courtly function, I will provide a historical overview of the cosmetic use of mirrors from Antiquity until the Middle Ages by describing antique mirrors. Similar to ivory-case ones, they also carried printed illustrations to model their potential female users.

Since their invention, mirrors were associated with the cosmetic industry because their primary function was to help in the process of styling oneself – what Stephen Greenblatt calls 'self-fashioning'.[2] Although the author coined this concept to refer exclusively to mirrors in the Renaissance, self-fashioning can be traced as far as Antiquity to the present day. Mirrors, especially handheld ones, have always been the main tool for self-fashioning; they are part of the 'system of fashion' from head to toe, but they focus on the user's face. In fact, this self-fashioning function was extremely important after the Crusades, particularly in the first half of the fourteenth century, due to the reintroduction of cosmetics and scented products from Byzantium, where some style customs from the Roman period persisted. For Adlin (2013), 'this renewed enthusiasm for making oneself up and the lack of any specifically designed furniture or interior space for such activity, [made] accessories become the focus of medieval "vanity", from ivory combs and intricately carved mirror cases' (4).[3] Thus, the mirrors' portable size was a virtue considering that women's *toilette* was a modern invention.

Mirrors became essential items, as in the medieval court everyone's skin, hair, and body were on display and under scrutiny when it came to the occurrence of 'courtly love' or *fin' amor*. 'Courtly love' (*amour courtois*),[4] a term coined by Gaston Paris, refers to the kind of love that establishes refined and conscious relationships that are largely channelled by the physical appearance of the lovers and the regulation of their behaviour. This regulation is not only based on gender, but also on the splendour of clothing and cosmetics as well as the lovers' dress and alimentary codes.[5] Courtship was a bridge between lovers, who had to be 'well-dressed for love', assisted by material and aesthetic resources. Framed by the conventions of courtly love, the use of the mirror – compact ones, above all – was essential. By gradually improving its looking surface thanks to technical advances, this miraculous device became a social instrument, especially for medieval women.

As Stewart (2017) points out, make-up, hairstyle, and clothing reflected the wealth and health of their bearers, while hair and skin held a privileged place under the lens of *fin' amor*:

> the nature and condition of the skin and hair went further [than clothing], defining an individual's social position and temperament but also offering important clues to his or her physical wellbeing, something not so easily to interpreted from what someone might be wearing. This makes the skin and hair as well as the make-up used to protect, to embellish and potentially improve these bodily features, particularly significant.[6]

The quote above shows how the portable mirror was a cosmetic device with a social function. Nevertheless, once this function was depicted in literary works, it became more complex. In *Le Roman de la Rose*,[7] for instance, mirrors are an instrument for grooming and a garment, but also a bauble. In *De Amore*, as we will see, they are portable love tokens.

Other authors like Lee (2015) define the medieval mirror as a tool for users to realize about how they were seen by others, 'in a world before photography and webcams, the hand mirror provided a rare glimpse of how the dressed individual was perceived by others' (167). In addition to the aforementioned perceptions of compact mirrors, there are four other features and functions of these mirrors that are shared among the Hellenistic period, the Roman period, and the Middle Ages: portable mirrors were a feminine attribute, they contributed to the performance of female users' sexual identity, some of these mirrors were even self-referential in terms of sight and gaze, and finally, mirrors worked as a *speculum* when they included (mostly female) human figures in their covers – like *boudoir* scenes starred by ideal maidens, which invited comparison and emulation.

What these four similar functions across periods show is that the connections surrounding handheld mirrors, that is, connections to women's dressing, erotic love, and *speculum* were not new in the Middle Ages. However, what is new is the relation between ivory mirrors and a unique kind of portable object, such as a prayer book and a love token; the ivory mirror's medium and size; and its presence in some literary sources, such as romances and treatises, which expands portable mirrors' significance by being framed by the theories and practices of *fin' amor*. The next section explores why and how portable mirrors, particularly ivory ones, became love tokens.

Portable love, readable mirror

There are several reasons why portable mirrors came to be considered portable love tokens: they are portable as love tokens, but more effective due to the power of the gaze; they work as narrative devices as much as books; and many of them are made of ivory, which was an expensive and therefore valued gift to be given by a lover. We will now analyse each of these reasons.

When comparing portable mirrors to love tokens, we can see that a love token also must be handheld, carried discretely, and hidden everywhere and anywhere, like a secret.[8] Although ivory mirrors are also handheld, due to their shape and size they were much more portable than any love token. For this reason, portable ivory mirrors became the perfect, most sensitive, and sophisticated token to be exchanged by lovers. More important than their shape and size, however, is mirrors' reflecting surface. For courtly love, sight was the most important sense involved, as love is born and burns from the gaze of the lover. In fact, love is even described as a dart, or an arrow. The mirror is a medium to both look at oneself – to look beautiful in preparation to meet the lover and to invoke his or her image – and also be reminded of the lover (and giver). As a gift, the giver looked upon its surface, so his or her image still lives in it, as a living portrait,[9] or as a Bologna stone.[10]

Indeed, of all of the gifts that represented the code of courtly love, the mirror was the item that best depicts this allegory;[11] it does so to such an extent that some medieval mirrors have mirrors sculpted in their cases, which show the grooming process and emphasize the mirrors' own condition as visual instruments. For instance, there are some eloquent examples of ivory mirrors cases that represent Narcissus or the Lady and the Unicorn; both are stories about medieval love and gazing in which their characters use a mirror or look deep into its reflective surface.

The second reason that made portable mirrors become love tokens is their function as narrative devices that work as testimonies of medieval courtship rituals just as much as books at the time. Similar to portable mirrors, portable books were new artefacts in the Middle Ages, and in fact, they both underwent a significant transformation in the late medieval period. They came in different formats, sizes and shapes, and some of them became smaller and more suitable for travel or private use. Moreover, books and mirrors have been closely linked in cultural history, particularly miniature books and ivory mirrors because of the literary scenes carved upon them.

In the case of mirrors, ivory artisans (*pigniers*, 'comb-makers' in French) carved this material to make a refined group of objects, such as mirror cases, combs and caskets, reaching its peak between the thirteenth and fourteenth centuries. Given elephant ivory's exotic origin, any object made of this material was expensive; therefore the owners of ivory objects were aristocratic women who received them as courtship, betrothal or wedding tokens. The content sculpted on the front of the mirrors were scenes of courtly love (lovers playing chess, hunting or embracing) as well as chivalric literary motifs (Tristan and Isolde); the 'subject matters reflect[ed] the activities and interests of their owners',[12] as much as modern pocket mirrors contain images of our favourite band or idyllic landscapes. These images testify to the strong relation between courtly narrative and objects, since some artisans created a range of daily life objects (such as tableware, rugs, writing cases, and women's accessories) that included literary scenes and motifs.

Portable mirrors also became love tokens due to their promotion of courtly social codes and the shaping of the lover's behaviour. Mirrors' amorous imagery had a didactic function: they performed as a *speculum*, especially to a feminine audience. Courtly ladies were not just influenced by other women, but by customs depicted in chivalric literature and culture, like the fashion styles of some feminine characters.[13] It could be argued that this influence was greater under the glimpse of ivory carved mirrors. In fact, as Smith (2017) explains in 'The Gothic Mirror and the Female Gaze', 'the female viewer was encouraged to take up a viewing position in which she saw herself not only as a desired object, but also as a desiring subject, able to enact a certain degree of agency'.[14]

Generally, the women depicted in these scenes were looking actively at a male figure, as can be seen in a French ivory mirror case, from The Metropolitan Museum of Art, New York, which shows couples surrounded by some attendants in a typical scene of falconry (Fig. 7.1). Hunting had been a topic in amatory literature since Antiquity, but in the Middle Ages falconry was meaningful because of two reasons. It was not only one of

Fig. 7.1 Mirror case, ivory, Falconing Party, French (Paris), *ca.* 1330–1360. Height: 9.5 cm, width: 9.5 cm. © The Metropolitan Museum of Art, New York.

the traditional and sophisticated customs of courtly society, but also an allegory of *fin' amor*: falcons used to be temporarily blind during the hunt, as were the lovers under the effects of Love. In the two scenes, the couples are looking at each other intensely while holding falcons in their hands. Despite being accompanied, they are enclosed in their amorous gaze, as if they were unable to see anything other than themselves. The character of the mirror as an instrument for vision was reinforced with this kind of motifs. The intensity of the loving gaze acts as if the lady and the gentleman were prey and hunter – or vice versa – and it can also represent the lovers' blindness, embodied by the symbolism of falcons.

Ladies were not just owners and beholders of ivory mirrors, but also readers of literary scenes that they knew perfectly because of their cultural background. Their hands held their mirrors as if they were silent miniature books – like prayer books – that could be opened or closed.[15] This takes us back to the main theme of this chapter: portable love. Because of its versatility, according to Rebold (2009),

> ivory is a dense material that is carved with relative ease. Due to its collagen content, ivory has a smooth texture and a natural sheen, its oiliness permitting it to be highly polished … Ivory is especially suitable for small portable items intended for an individual's private devotions, the diminutive size inviting close scrutiny of the subject depicted, thereby aiding personal contemplation and reflection.
>
> (p. 100)

As we have stated before, ivory mirror cases were small, from two and one-half inches to six inches in diameter. This size allowed keeping them inside caskets or purses when closed, while they offered a private encounter when open. Mirrors were useful to arrange one's image due to its personal intimate use, but they also worked as a love token, as a gate to 'call the lover to the mind' and even as a memorial of a secret love affair that one can hide anywhere, like Victorian reliquaries or lover's eyes.[16]

In addition to the material and size, portable ivory mirrors' as love tokens are determined by their shape, which is just as meaningful as the other features. As Camille puts it (1998), there are affinities between chaplets (a decorative head garland) and mirrors, as they are both courtly objects and feminine garments that symbolize never-ending love thanks to their circular form. For instance, a French ivory mirror case, 'A Lady Crowning her Lover', from Victoria and Albert Museum, London (Fig. 7.2), whose date is circa 1300, depicts a woman investing her suitor with a chaplet while he is kneeling and offering his heart to the lady.

A last revision of ivory as material is needed here to close the circle – or the mirror – which sheds light into the last reason for portable ivory mirrors to become love tokens. As we have seen, the mirror was an aid for grooming; on the other hand, ivory mirrors in particular had a cosmetic function that is further emphasized by the fact that for late medieval women white was the ideal skin colour. Camille notes that ivory is a 'substance suggestive of flesh – creamy, undulating, and soft – and probably, after wax, the most flesh-like of all artistic media' (1998, 57). By looking themselves in their mirrors, courtly ladies touched and gazed a material that embodied a superior beauty goal: Having a white and desirable skin. Indeed, the use of gloves and the practice of painting the skin with wheat flour to whiten it aimed to achieve that goal. Hence, the double didactic purpose of ivory mirrors comes to light, as their backs personify courtly love as well as beauty ideals through the carved scenes and the white, fleshy material that ivory was.

Fig. 7.2 Mirror case, A Lady Crowning Her Love, French (Paris), *ca.* 1300, ivory. Height: 10.6 cm, Width: 10.3 cm. © Victoria & Albert Museum, London.

The next and final section brings together the first and second sections by analysing the presence of portable ivory mirror cases in two literary works: *De Amore* and *Le Roman de la Rose*. The analysis seeks to explain these mirrors' significance in terms of how, through these representations, mirrors provide a glimpse at courtly love in medieval times.

Ars Amandi as *speculum* or the art of love is a mirror

In the courtly context, from the XII to the XIV centuries, the mirror was considered a tool that promoted the convenience of grooming one's appearance as a courtship strategy. Through the allusion to and the representation of mirrors, both *Le Roman de la Rose* and *De Amore* we can perceive the values attributed to these artefacts as well as their multiple uses. As both works are written on the basis of *fin' amor* and thus exalt and/or disapprove the protocols of this sentimental code, these works operate as discourses characteristic of the classical *Ars Amandi* literary tradition and its subsequent cosmetic didactics. The following section will unravel the cosmetic and ethic functions of the mirrors represented in these literary texts. First, I will briefly refer to the works' production contexts and their courtly affiliation; then, I will analyse specific passages that are essential to determine the uses and judgements attributed to mirrors, whether negative (vanity, lust) or positive (beauty, love tokens).

Le Roman de la Rose is a French poem written by two authors: the first part was written by Guillaume de Lorris between 1225 and 1230, and the second part was added by Jean de Meun between 1269 and 1278. If the first part is a compendium of the imagery of courtly love and an allegory of love itself – where a Lover (Amant) learns the amorous code – the second is a refutation and a critique of the *fin' amor*. Even though the poem shows unity through its subject and formal techniques, the same cannot be said of the tone: it is a reflection of the contexts of production and reception of each of the authors. On the one hand, Lorris, a *troubadour*, portrays a romantic vision of love and promotes courtly love as sentimental education; on the other, De Meun creates a satirical voice against pleasure for life's sake. This is because according to him, love should only be made for the purpose of procreation.[17] Similarly, the two parts show handheld mirrors that appear as feminine objects desired by women and designed for them; however, these mirrors have miscellaneous functions. For Lorris, the mirror is a symbol and an instrument of beauty, but for De Meun, it is a useless vanity object. Despite the differences between their notions of mirrors, one operates as a key to the other.

In the first part, Guillaume de Lorris introduces the figure of a tangible mirror after the description of Idleness' (Oiseuse) body and clothing,[18] in the section 'The Garden of Pleasure' (463–713).[19] Idleness, the gatekeeper, represents the perfect courtly lady, but also the goddess of Luxuria. Under the lover's gaze:

> there was no need to search in any land for a more beautiful female form. She had a charming gold-embroidered chaplet; no maiden ever had one more elegant or

unusual. I could not describe it properly if I took all day. On her gold-embroidered chaplet she had a garland of fresh roses, in her hand she held a mirror, and she had arranged her hair very richly with rich braid ... When she had combed her hair carefully and decked herself out in her fine clothes, her day's work was done. She spent her time in a happy and carefree manner, being troubled or anxious over nothing except attiring herself nobly.

(549–574)

Idleness' mirror is not just a mirror, but also a garment: a beautiful tool of beauty that enhances the beautiful body, hair and skin of the bearer.[20] Besides the onomastic explanation – Idleness' life consists in grooming herself, which is an idle but also active life by sculpting her image – and the depiction of the well-dressed lady, framed by the courtly rules of fashion, we may be asking ourselves: What was the mirror – her main beauty tool – like? Was it round, compact and made of ivory? The poet does not tell us, but some of the manuscripts show us how miniaturists imagined that mirror. The two manuscripts from the Bibliothèque Nationale de France (fr. 801 and fr. 24391) present Idleness with a hand mirror. While fr. 801, 8v, shows a mirror with a square shape, fr. 24391, 1r, displays a rounded one. A folio of a manuscript from the Bodleian Library, MS Selden Supra 57, 10r, depicts a rounded mirror as well. The manuscript 1945-65-3 from the Philip S. Collins Collection at the Philadelphia Museum of Art portrays in its folio 11r a more sophisticated mirror that has a stand, so it is not a handheld mirror. Moreover, fr. 801, fr. 24391 and MS Selden Supra 57 also depict the lady combing her hair, while the surface of the mirror of the Selden Supra shows the reflected face. Considering the shape and size of these illustrated mirrors, it is possible to assert that ivory mirrors were in fashion at the time.

In the second part of the poem, another occurrence of mirrors as portable objects shows them under a pessimistic light that reflects upon the idea of courtly love. The section 'The Advice of Friend' (9101–9492) was written by De Meun with the rhetoric aim to explain the author's naturalistic concept of love. The Husband (Mal Marié) states that his wife wears her clothing not to protect her body but to seduce other men. Through a list of highly prized and appealing adornments for women, which are considered baubles by men, the Husband accuses mirrors of inciting indecency:

What use to me are these headbands, these caps striped with gold, these decorated braids and ivory mirrors, these carefully crafted golden circlets with their precious enameling ... These clasps of gold and precious stones at your throat and on your bosom, these fabrics and these girdles whose fittings are worth as much as gold or seed-pearls, what are such baubles worth to me?

(9271–9288)

The list of female items is longer and its length emphasizes the worthlessness and lust for them; the list also displays the tension between necessary and decorative articles. In the Husband's speech, the ivory mirror is only one item in a dozen of accessories. What this shows is that the mirror is not fundamental for the plot, unlike other mirrors along the poem, such as Narcissus' fountain or Idleness' mirror. The attention paid to mirrors in the latter may be because in that context mirrors are related to lust and vanity, and because they always depict a woman with her comb and mirror. The Husband, as a projection of De Meun, condemns the reign of luxury and the abuse of these tools by women.

Mirrors, combs, and the *mundus muliebris* in general, link *Le Roman de la Rose* with the textual tradition of *Ars amandi*. For example, in some Ovidian sources, 'all women are narcissists whose self-appreciation is fully contingent on the use of a mirror'.[21] After all, mirrors were new artifacts in medieval contexts. It should be noted that although looking surfaces and mirrors are as old as humanity, the new techniques promoted a wider circulation of these objects during the Middle Ages, which made it easier for women to purchase and use them, as they became progressively more common and affordable. In fact, late medieval literature depicts this circulation and represents it in its plots. According to Mark Pendergrast, 'gradually . . . mirrors invaded secular literature'.[22]

In this context, mirrors were reported as instruments of *vanitas* as well as appreciated keepsakes. Their uses were codified by treatises like *De Amore*, written circa 1185 by French author Andreas Capellanus, which we will now turn to. In its *liber secundus*, chapter VII, titled 'On various judgments about love', countess Maria de Champagne asks Andreas about proper gifts for ladies to accept from their lovers, and he records the bestowal or exchange of them as a common custom in his time[23] by enumerating all of the appealing presents that ladies may freely accept from their lovers:

> A handkerchief, a fillet for the hair, a wreath of gold or silver, a breastpin, a mirror, a girdle, a purse, a tassel, a comb, sleeves, gloves, a ring, a compact, a picture, a wash basin, little dishes, trays, a flag as souvenir, and, to speak in general terms, a woman may accept from her lover any little gift which may be useful for the care of the person or pleasing to look at or which may call the lover to her mind, if it is clear that in accepting the gift she is free from all avarice.
>
> (paragraph XXI, 49)

All of these objects inhabited the feminine toilet, cupboard or casket: they were garments and cosmetics 'useful for the care of the person,' pleasing *bric-à-bracs* 'to look at', and also small and portable memorials that 'call the lover to her mind', or love tokens, as Capellanus points out in his text. These objects had such emotional power because they came, literally, from the hands of the sender or giver. As Burns (2002) states, gifts operate as a synecdoche of the lover. When Burns discusses the wide range of pieces of clothing and their symbolism in medieval courtly atmosphere as well as their status as love tokens, she states that when a lover accepts any of these as gifts, they are accepting the love of the giver and also welcoming their body, since the object previously touched the lover's skin and will be touched by the owner. It seems as no coincidence that the greater part of the catalogue of gifts consists of artefacts related to the body and its embellishment.[24] When the mirror is given, so too the lover is transferred.[25] Amorous gifts like the ones listed by Andreas Capellanus were bridges between lovers, their bodies, and their feelings. In her article, 'Gazing at Gawain: Reconsidering Tournaments, Courtly Love, and The Lady Who Looks' Elizabeth L'Estrange (2008) notes that 'a woman may have read the scenes they depicted [in ivory mirrors] as an allusion to the real access to the male body . . . as a prelude to the pleasures that would take place outside of the public arena' (86–87). Ultimately, mirrors, pieces of clothing and other artefacts embody the lover and express her or his erotic emotion, a source of affection, memory, and commitment to the beloved.

Closing the mirror

This chapter has given a historical overview of mirrors as artefacts and also their connotations from Antiquity until the Middle Ages. The analysis has gone beyond the mirrors' 'self-fashioning' function to focus on portable ivory mirrors as symbols of the *fin' amor* experience. The amorous code printed in the scenes that decorate the back of those ivory mirrors and the manufacturing material itself make a mirror an object in two senses of the term: the portable ivory mirror is an artefact but also a unique *object of study*. Undoubtedly, these mirrors are different and more complex than their Greek and Latin counterparts. Their elegant and luxurious material evoked the wealth and sophistication of French courts, the cozy size created an intimate atmosphere, the colour and texture expressed both a cosmetic aim and a promise of an erotic encounter, and the motifs carved on their fronts told the amorous stories that ladies and gentlemen read and heard as part of their courtly culture.

We have also explored how portable ivory mirrors became love tokens. In this regard, we have argued that compact mirrors can be observed, and also read. A mirror becomes a device that just as treatises and literary works do, models a certain amorous behaviour; in other words, following the logic of traditional *Ars Amandi*, it becomes a *speculum*. When a woman looks herself in this mirror, she not only sees herself and prepares for the amorous encounter, but also longs for becoming one of the heroines portrayed in the mirror's case and experiencing love as it occurs in courtly literature. She is a mirror user as well as a reader and disciple of Love. This view is further supported by Sand (2011), who declares, the user – the pupil – of an ivory mirror interacts deeply not only with its reflective surface but also with the imagery of its non-reflective parts. The Janus-like metaphor echoes again: ivory mirrors were reflective and non-reflective and both sides were meaningful under the lens of courtly love.

The chapter has shown that compact ivory mirrors are part of a rich range of interconnected meanings, which transcend their cosmetic functions to have other applications and to resemble other objects, such as portable love tokens. Indeed, the literary sources analysed – *Le Roman de la Rose* and *De Amore* – are significant and relevant testimonies of such assertion. On the one hand, for Andreas Capellanus and many other scholars, mirrors had positive associations, as they were feminine garments, love tokens, narrative devices and *specula* of loving behaviour and performance. On the other hand, for Jean de Meun, mirrors were mere baubles.

Therefore, mirrors have not only been subjected to cosmetic practices and judgements, but also ethical ones. On that basis, their literary allusions, descriptions, and representations provide a literary work with an aesthetic sense; this is possible because the mirror becomes an artefact capable of articulating meaningful metaphor, synecdoche, and allegory in relation to love and sight. Ultimately, the virtue that makes it possible for the ivory mirror to multiply its complementary functions is its portable character, as observed both in the material medieval culture and in the literary works analysed.

The portable ivory mirror's ornamental, erotic, narrative, and modelling uses are indeed motivated by ivory's versatility and certainly by the skilfulness of artisans that made them. In the end, it seems as if ivory's noble character itself and its suitability to adapt to a hand's palm, a purse, or a wall had extended even further to adjust to the laws of a courtly love creed disseminated in an iconographic and literary manner.

CHAPTER 8
'SO SKILFULLY MIRRORED IN HIS ART': (RE)VISITING MIRRORS IN OSCAR WILDE'S *THE PICTURE OF DORIAN GRAY*
Nikolas P. Kakkoufa

'I can quite understand your objection to art being treated as a mirror. You think it would reduce genius to the position of a cracked looking glass. But you don't mean to say that you seriously believe that Life imitates Art, that Life in fact is the mirror, and Art the reality?' Cyril asks Vivian in *The Decay of Lying* (1891).[1] Oscar Wilde will give (part of) an answer this question in his 1891 preface to *The Picture of Dorian Gray* by claiming that 'it is the spectator, and not life, that art really mirrors'.[2] This tension between art and life, between mirrors and mirroring, and the text and its reader/spectator is a common *topos* not only in the *fin de siècle* literature, as a way to support the dogma 'art pour l'art', but also in much earlier texts that are trying to understand the connection of art with the real world of objects. It has already been supported that in *The Picture of Dorian Gray*, in particular, these two forms of art – painting and writing – are more closely connected to the *art of mirroring* than in any other literary work of the *fin de siècle*, especially in regards to understanding one's self and his own sexuality at its inception.[3]

This chapter's aim is not to extensively discuss this rich tradition of writing in relation to mirrors and mirroring, but to revisit *The Picture of Dorian Gray* in an effort to enrich existing scholarship on the topic by focusing on the use of the mirror within the text, not only as a signifier of Narcissism or a trope for talking about sexuality, but also as a physical object (including its various transformations), and, most importantly, its use as a learning mechanism.[4] In doing so, it employs the tale of Narcissus and Echo, in the Ovidian narrative, and Lacan's *Mirror Stage*.[5] My emphasis is on the Ovidian version of the myth because, as shown by Louise Vinge, Ovid is not only the first and best known author to give a full account of Narcissus' (homo)sexual chronicle, but he is also the first one to incorporate Echo's (hetero)sexual story in this narrative.[6] I shall argue that Wilde uses both Narcissus (Dorian, Basil) and Echo (Lord Henry, Sibyl Vane), and in effect both types of mirroring – visual and acoustic – in the narrative of his story and in Dorian's quest to know himself.

Narcissus is probably the first and best known example of the consequences of over exaggerated admiration of one's self via its mirror reflection.[7] The myth appears in various ancient Greek and Roman writers: the earlier Greek sources are by Parthenius of Nicaea in Bithynia (a Greek grammarian and poet), and Pausanias (a Greek traveller and geographer of the second century AD),[8] but the interpretation that has haunted our western thought and imagination comes from Ovid's *Metamorphoses*. In brief, the boy ends up falling in love with his own reflection – which, at first, he does not recognize – and at the end he drowns himself in order to connect with his love and in his place instead of a body they find a flower.

Of special interest to this chapter is the Tiresian prophesy to Narcissus' mother that precedes the unfolding of his story and is an Ovidian deviation from the earlier versions of the story (3:339);[9] when Liriope inquires regarding the longevity of her son's life, Tiresias gives her the following answer: 'si se non noverit' (if he shall himself not know). This use of the verb *nosco*, which could be interpreted as a process of knowing one's self, opens the myth to a different interpretation. If we take this as the reason behind the unfolding of the story then Narcissus is not destroyed by his self love but by his recognition of himself. At the same time, vision, and especially the process of mirroring seems to be the way in which the youth not only falls in love with himself but also the way in which he acquires access to knowing himself.

Writers, poets, sculptors, and painters alike have been inspired by Narcissus' myth. But beyond its artistic reappropriations, the figure of Narcissus has also become the emblem of (negatively viewed) self love and specifically of homosexuality and has entered the register of popular culture.[10] At the end of the nineteenth and the first half of the twentieth century Narcissus enters the realm of psychoanalysis and becomes a 'mental state', usually associated with women and 'effeminate' men.[11] Sigmund Freud believed that the narcissistic stage is an unavoidable one in the early stages of someone's life, since it represents the necessary fascination of loving and knowing one's self where later the adult version of the *I* moves away from it and loves (an)other. It is therefore a normal infantile characteristic.[12] In following this thought, and by examining the folklore, supernatural and superstitious charms associated with the mirror, Géza Roheim concludes that 'the mirror is a representative of Narcissism', and identifies the mirror with Narcissus.[13] Those who have followed in Freud's footsteps, take this a step further and connect it with the inability to leave the narcissistic stage. Sadger, in his *Die Lehre von den Geschlechtsverirrungen* (*Psychopathia Sexualis*), observes that 'we can say of homosexuality that it is the Narcissistic perversion *par excellence*'.[14] These early psychoanalytic comments and references use literature as an evaluation of their theories; Otto Rank (1911) refers to Oscar Wilde's *The Picture of Dorian Gray* as displaying various aspects of Narcissism, 'to a greater extent probably than any other imaginative work in English literature' and goes on to quote Schlegel's saying that 'the poet is always a Narcissus' and Freud's view that 'paranoia is a fixation of Narcissism'.[15]

The Picture of Dorian Gray (1890; 1891) exists in a number of versions; readers only gained full access to his initial typescript of the novel in 2011 when Harvard University Press published the typescript under the title: *The Picture of Dorian Gray: An annotated, uncensored edition*. The censored, and in effect amputated, first publication was not only a result of the now infamous strict Victorian censorship, but also of the text's strong homosexual nuances. This era, which was eloquently described by Eve Kosofsky-Sedgewick as 'the era of homosexual panic',[16] permeated not only the openness of the book and its necessity to find 'pronouns that tell and hide', to borrow from C. P. Cavafy's famous line,[17] but also affected the inaugural discourses on modern homo/heterosexuality in medicine, psychiatry, language and law and its dealings in literary texts.[18] The first time that the word 'homosexuality' enters the English language was in 1892, after the novel's publication, via the translation of Richard Krafft-Ebing's book *Psychopathia Sexualis* – and only as an adjective, whereas as a noun it is only being used in 1912.[19] Until then, both writers and critics used coded language to refer to such actions: unhealthiness, sin, insanity, uncleanliness, etc.

Having these in mind one understands the necessity of openly employing the tale of Narcissus and Echo, and a number of other codes, in order to express and apprehend issues of sexuality.[20] The book, from its first pages, and in various instances after that, clearly associates Dorian Gray with Narcissus and this topic has been examined by a number of scholars,[21] who have aptly showed how Oscar Wilde uses Narcissus and how his re-incarnation of the myth is about a closeted affair of homosexual bodies and homosexual desire. The three main characters – Dorian Gray, Basil Hallward and Lord Henry Wotton – create a triangle of homosocial/homosexual behaviour. They supplement each other – the intellectual, the artist and the object of desire and art – and they are linked through mirroring processes. Basil and Dorian are mirrored through the portrait while Lord Henry is linked with Dorian via the small mirror that he gives to him and through Lord Henry's words that Dorian echoes throughout the novel.[22]

The novel early establishes the portrait as a mirror: 'As he [Basil] looked at the gracious and comely form he had so skilfully mirrored in his art, a smile of pleasure passed across his face, and seemed about to linger there.'[23] This skilful mirroring process is then extended between the object of art and the artist. When Basil is told that he should exhibit the portrait, his answer is negative, but his wording is indicative of what is argued here: 'I know you will laugh at me [...] but I really can't exhibit it. I have put too much of myself into it.'[24] How could the portrait have too much of Basil in it, and why would this be a reason not to exhibit it? What is it that the portrait holds that could be used against Basil? The answer comes from Basil himself (my emphasis):

> Harry, every portrait that is painted with feeling **is a portrait of the artist, not of the sitter.** The sitter is merely the accident, the occasion. It is not who is revealed by the painter; **it is rather the painter who**, on the coloured canvas, **reveals himself**. The reason I will not exhibit this picture is that **I am afraid that I have shown with it the secret of my own soul.**[25]

If the painter is also simultaneously reflected in the painting, then can we consider Dorian's painting as a self-portrait of Basil as well? And, if so, what are the identical elements between these two that might allow us to make such a claim other than their underlying homosexuality and, in effect, the relationship between the self that desires and the self that is desired? Basil's confession not only invokes the idea of the writer as a Narcissus but also the idea of the painter as one. This idea of the poet, and the creator in general, as a Narcissus is not a conception of the nineteenth century but of the Renaissance.[26] During the Renaissance, and before acquiring various negative connotations in psychoanalysis and popular culture, Narcissus was also considered the inventor of painting. In particular, Leon Battista Alberti's choice of Narcissus as the inventor of painting in his 1435 book *De Pictura* has stirred a long discussion in the scholarship regarding visual culture in early modernity,[27] but of interest, here, is Alberti's definition of painting: 'the act of embracing by means of art the surface of the pool'.[28] If we equate painting, and in our case the portrait, with the surface of the pool doesn't it make it then a mere reflection? Is the painting a mirror? In the late fourteenth and fifteenth centuries we have a proliferation of texts that discuss the relationship between the mirror and painting. Such discussions included the limitations of perspective, the origins of painting, the analogy between the mirror image and the painted image, and, the concept that the mind of the painter resembles a mirror. Leonardo Da Vinci, in particular, who writes extensively on the difference between mirrors and portraits, argues that the painter not only acts as a mirror but also 'transmutes' himself (if we identify the creator with the mirror) into the material by which the painting is made.[29] Seen as such, the painting is always a self-reflection of the artist; but where Da Vinci believes that the artist is reflected in the choice of colours, Basil and, in effect Oscar Wilde, claims that the artist is reflected though his erotic desire. In both cases, though, the painting also becomes, more or less, a self-portrait.

Lucian Freud's self-portraits have been considered as exemplary in self-revealing a figure's soul, rather than just nudity, mainly because of his method of working from the centre to the edge of a drawing as a way of revealing the 'inside' of his figures. Ernst Van Alphen's analysis of Lucian Freud's self-portraits, is to the point (my emphasis):

> **The mirror is thought to be the site of an absolute but momentary return.** In my view, it is not so much that 'the temporality of simultaneity' is the object of desire but, rather, that its **transience** is the disenchanting reality behind an illusion: **the simultaneity of a mirror reflection can only be temporal, fleeting, because what the mirror holds and returns must be present.**[30]

The emphasis to the fleeting element of the reflection brings to mind the narrator's question in Narcissus story: 'you simple boy, why strive in vain to catch a fleeting image?'[31] If, indeed, the mirror, and any type of mirror from the lake in Narcissus' tale to the modern mirrors, only allows for momentary and temporal returns and the traditional portrait is a mirror reflection without such shortcomings then how are we to understand Dorian's magical portrait? In my view, this portrait is somewhere in between: though atemporal, at times, it still manages to reflect the internal transformations of both characters under discussion. We do not see Basil's physical body in the portrait but his desire for Dorian and in effect the use of the portrait as a learning device for himself. In Dorian's case, the portrait reflects his internal beauty, that of his 'soul'. And, in a similar vein to Narcissus and Echo's story, Dorian's reflection changes according to his relationship to Sibyl Vane.

Echo, in the Ovidian tale, 'was still a body, not a voice, but talkative as now, and with the same power of speaking only to repeat, as best she could, the last of many words'.[32] In her brief (hetero)sexual encounter with Narcissus, she is only wanted by him when she repeats his words; the moment she touches him 'to throw her longing arms around his neck'[33] Narcissus rejects her physical love by yelling 'keep your arms from me',[34] which results into the decline and eventual disappearance of her physical body.[35] The same story occurs with Dorian Gray and Sibyl Vane, as he falls in love with her only when she is on stage – repeating the words of others – and when she tries to have a physical (hetero)sexual relationship with him as herself, she is rejected by Dorian and then takes her own life. Both incidents are instrumental for the unravelling of their individual plots, of the way in which both young men end up knowing themselves, and, finally, of the consequential punishments of both Narcissus and Dorian.

The difference in *The Picture of Dorian Gray*, however, is that both Basil and Dorian are reflected in the portrait and both of them die. Therefore, should we understand Dorian's portrait as a reflection of the painter on the one hand and of the object on the other? Can they both be reflected in the portrait without being present? And could the portrait reflect the painter if, as Lord Henry states, there is no physical resemblance between the two: 'I can't see any resemblance between you [...] and this young Adonis. Why my dear Basil, he is a Narcissus, and you – well, of course you have an intellectual expression, and all that'?[36] And if so, can we then read Basil's – and Dorian's later refusal – to exhibit the portrait as an effect of what Lacan defines as the mirror stage through the identification of 'the transformation that takes place in the subject when he assumes an image'?[37]

The moment, therefore, that Basil becomes knowingly mirrored in the portrait he transforms and acquires a different understanding of himself and of his own sexual id(entity) in particular. The real Dorian, or rather Basil's Dorian, is identified with and reflected through desire and therefore his physical form is not necessary to be present for him to be in the painting. That is why later Basil claims that (my emphasis):

> Dorian Gray is merely to me a motive in art. **He is never more present in my work than when no image of him is there**. He is simply a suggestion, as I have said, **of a new manner**.[38]
>
> Then why won't you exhibit his portrait?
>
> Because I have put into it all the **extraordinary romance** of which, of course, I have never dared to speak to him. He knows nothing about it. But the world might guess it; [...] **There is too much of myself in the thing, Harry, too much of myself!**[39]

According to the above claim, the object becomes a motive: Dorian is the suggestion of a new manner. A motive for what though? For honesty? For accepting one's feelings? And what is this new manner? The answer comes in Basil's confession about the extraordinary romance of himself that is reflected in the painting and must remain a secret. How could the world guess it, if it is not visible? How can one understand someone else's reflection in the 'mirror'? We should remember an important aspect from Ovid's tale: Narcissus, at the beginning, does not fall in love with himself but with 'another image' which he then recognizes to be himself: 'not knowing what he sees, he adores the sight'.[40] As Yves Bonnefoy puts it, 'Narcissus must first believe that he loves another in order to be able to love himself'.[41] But the narrator's intervention, in the Ovidian myth, is of particular salience for what we are discussing here:

> You see a phantom of a mirrored shape;
> Nothing itself; with you it came and stays;
> With you it too will go, if you can go![42]

Could this analogy be applicable to *The Portrait's* story? Basil only understands himself through Dorian and in his effort to create Dorian's portrait he ends up realizing that the portrait of someone else, Dorian's a-temporal reflection at this point, is the reflection of him, and specifically of his desire and sexuality, more than of Dorian's. The Ovidian 'if you can go' signifies the unavoidability of the situation, since the subject cannot get away from his now known self. Is the ever concealed 'symbolic displacement of the erotic onto the aesthetic' as present as Cohen argues?[43] Later in the novel, Basil confesses to Dorian (my emphasis):

> I will sit in the shadow, and you shall sit in the sunlight. Our lives are like that. **Have you noticed in the picture something that you did not like? Something that probably at first did not strike you, but revealed itself to you suddenly?** It is quite true that I have worshipped you with far more romance of feeling **than a man should ever give to his friend**. Somehow, I had never loved a woman. I suppose I never had time. [...] From the moment I met you [...] **I quite admit that I adored you madly, extravagantly, absurdly**. It was to have been my masterpiece. It is my masterpiece. But, as I worked at it, every flake and film of colour **seemed to me to reveal my secret**. There was love in every line, and in every touch, there was passion.[44]

The painting mirrors nothing other than the painter's homosexual identity and desire. In a metaphorical manner, the painter lives in the fear of his homoerotic reflection being noticed by the world (shadow) whereas Dorian lives in the light, because with the advice of Lord Henry he is yielding to his temptations. But is it possible to think of this reflection of erotic desire as one of a 'specular image'? You cannot have a shadow without the light, and at the same time, there's no object without a shadow. According to Lacan 'such jubilant assumption of his specular image [...] would seem to exhibit in an exemplary situation the symbolic matrix in which the *I* is precipitated in a primordial form, before it is objectified in the dialectic of identification with the other, and before language restores to it, in the universal, its function as a subject'.[45] This is why Basil's question is of great importance; because it emphasizes the fact that when one sees his mirroring he unexpectedly understands himself, him and his erotic desires, by eventually escaping the 'primordial from' of his image in a way that when verbalized it asymptomatically (suddenly) becomes self-revealing.

The portrait, then, helps Basil understand the reason behind his desire to paint Dorian in the first place and why he wanted this to be his masterpiece. The abstract element of the mirrored image helped him not only to understand his erotic self – though he does not understand why he never loved a woman – but also forced him to overcome the fear of confessing such a desire. What we would now call a 'coming out' process. This is why the confession is introduced by the phrase 'Let us sit down. I will sit in the shadow, and you will sit in the sunlight. Our lives are like that.' How different is the reference to a phantom in the Ovidian myth and the shadows in *The Portrait*? Both are illusions that play with reality; the game between light and darkness in Wilde's novel is of great importance in unlocking the relationship between the two. An object needs to emit its own light to be visible, and if not, it must reflect light in order to be seen. And, according to catoptrics, reflection involves two rays – an incoming or incident ray and an outgoing or reflected ray. In my view, Basil and Dorian are not only reflected in the same painting, but they also need each other in order to be really seen as (homo)sexual and desiring subjects – and to borrow from Ovid's phrase Dorian is – 'nothing himself; with you it came and stays' and vice versa. Wilde here encapsulates an important reality: whereas Basil emerges from the shadows through his confession (coming out to Dorian) and now understands that 'art conceals the artist far more completely than it reveals him', Dorian starts to hide the reflection of his 'true' self in the portrait and starts using actual mirrors in an effort to create his *Gestalt*.

After Basil comes into being as a homosexual subject, what Lacan would call *le devenir*,[46] Dorian delves further into 'sin' and becomes the talk of the town. People refuse to sit or to be seen with him or even to be with him in the same room. He becomes a byword for indecency, which was a word used for homosexuality. The person that has mirrored his beauty on the famous portrait, and which has set his story in motion, now becomes the medium through which the public's mirroring of Dorian Gray, what Lacan would call his *imago*, is constructed by giving Dorian a complete view of the form of his body. When they meet again, Basil feels the need to dissociate himself from Dorian's image, both because he is (no longer) the one creating it and, because 'he does not believe them when he sees him':[47]

> Yes, it was Dorian himself. But who had done it? He seemed to recognize his own brush work, and the frame was his own design. [. . .] In the left-hand corner was his own name.[48]

This is the point where the mirror becomes a painting, and the painting becomes a mirror as the reflected – now fully aware of his body through this temporal dialectic – is projected into history.[49] Now that their secret is 'out in the open' other people have the power of creating and dominating Dorian's (and in effect Basil's) public image. And that is how the atemporal frame by which the initial painting was protected – paintings usually represent a specific mirroring in time – now becomes Dorian's prison. An inescapable mirroring of himself – of either who he thinks he is or who society thinks he is. Image and soul become one through his reflection on the painting. This mirroring reversal is then transformed into the novel's narrative: Basil becomes the object and Dorian becomes the spectator. As the narrator informs us 'There was simply the passion of the spectator, with perhaps a flicker of triumph in his [Dorian's] eyes. He had taken the flower out of his coat, and was smelling it, or pretending to do so.'[50] Can we read this reference to the flower as a turning point for Dorian's complete transformation into Narcissus? Or even more so, as an indirect reference to him not being Narcissus? A passage from the 1891 edition of the novel, not republished by Frankel as it is not part of the initial typescript, may aid in elucidating this; it is part of Basil's first confession to Dorian, where among envisioning him as a historically beautiful figure by name – Paris and Adonis – he continues:

> You had leant over the still pool of some Greek woodland, and seen in the water's silent silver the marvel of your own face. And it had all been what art should be, unconscious, ideal, and remote. One day, a fatal day I sometimes think, I determined to paint a wonderful portrait of you as you actually are, not in the costume of dead ages, but in your own dress and in your own time.[51]

The description of Narcissus in the extract above is quite obvious; all the basic elements of Ovid's tale are present: the still pool, the idyllic location and the reflection of the boy's beauty in the silver of the lake. Why would Basil name the first two and not Narcissus? Dorian has already been identified with Narcissus by Lord Henry earlier in the novel. Is it because Narcissus has already acquired all the negative connotations that the term now has and Basil, being in total awe of Dorian's beauty, didn't want to attribute these negative elements on Dorian? The last sentence, beyond its presaging element through the reference to the fatality of this choice, also shows Basil's determination to portray Dorian 'as he actually is' and not in the costume of dead ages. This can be read in two ways; on the one hand, we may read this as Basil's effort to protect Dorian as all names mentioned had a tragic death – the same he tries to do with the frame of the painting – but, on the other hand, it could also be a deliberate choice, on Wilde's part, to go against the masks of homosexuality by bringing his erotic desire towards him to the front. The whole context guides us towards this as Basil expresses his adoration towards the young man. The triggering effect that leads to Basil's assassination is located at the beginning of their encounter. In particular, when Basil tries to touch Dorian he reacts by saying 'Don't touch me. Finish what you have to say.'[52] This might also explain the different ending of Dorian's story.

Dorian is not just enjoying the mirroring of his beauty but actively seeking to prolong it through his wish – even prayer – to change places with his portrait as his reflection would grow older and Dorian would remain young and beautiful. Is it possible to read the picture's current monstrous condition in a Lacanian way by tracing the distinction between Dorian and his painting in his own and in the public's perception of himself? And if so, was the damage created in Dorian's image the result of a society that does not accept homosexuality? Was the sin written across his face or was it forced upon it just because homosexuality is considered 'gross indecency'?[53] In the final scene of the novel, they are both locked in Dorian's 'room of shame', where he hides his portrait. The room acts as a *glass closet*, in Eve Kosofsky-Sedwick's terms, as Dorian tries to hide something that people already know (they all talk about him as if he is a monster):

'You told me that you had destroyed it.'
'I was wrong. It has destroyed me.'
'I don't believe it is my picture.'
'Can't you see your romance in it?'
'My romance, as you call it...'
'As you called it.'
'There was nothing evil in it, nothing shameful. This is the face of a satyr.'
'It is the face of my soul.'
'Christ! what a thing I must have worshipped! This has the eyes of a devil.'[54]
[...] 'My God! if this is true [...] and this is what you have done with your life, why, must you be worse than those who talk against you fancy you to be!' [...]
'Good God, Dorian, what a lesson! What an awful lesson!'[55]

Their stichomythic dialogue is based on mirrored reversals of their reality in the same way that objects are reversed when reflected in the mirror. One of the reasons for this, if we accept that Basil and Dorian are mirrored reflections of each other as we have argued here, is that the mirrored image – though it seems identical – is actually reversed in the direction perpendicular to the mirror surface. This is why the destroyed reflection of Dorian in the portrait is destroying him and that is also why Basil's romance is reflected as a one way feeling. The opposites continue with the purity of Basil's emotion – or in fact its initial reflection on Dorian's painting – and his current state in which he is identified with a satyr and even the devil himself. The reason for this, according to Basil is their exaggerated admiration for the young boy: 'I worshipped you too much. I am punished for it. You worshipped yourself too much. We are both punished.'[56] Again – a reflection of the same action. Basil's admiration for Dorian ended up into the latter's imprisonment in that frame of beauty that has forced him to worship himself, and in effect to destroy him as Dorian claims. The portrait kept him hostage, not only to the temporal phenomenology of his beauty, but to the signification of its frame. This is the very image that will cause its creator's destruction: 'Dorian Gray glanced at the picture, and suddenly an uncontrollable feeling of hatred for Basil Hallward came over him. [...] he loathed the man who was seated at the table, more than he had ever loathed anything in his whole life.'[57]

An interesting reformation process then begins as Dorian tries to reverse all the negative that he has done in the past when it comes to treating people, and especially to women. He describes a story in which he met a young girl and decided to break up with her before breaking her heart – 'I won't bring her to shame. And I determined to leave her as flowerlike as I had found her.'[58] A reverse mirror image of the Sibyl Vane story with a perhaps alternative ending. In his discussion with Lord Henry, his intellectual mentor, Dorian tries to say – and even believe – that he will be a new man, a better man and while Lord Henry pushes back on this Dorian remains adamant to his position. Instead of believing this, though, and moving on with his life he believes that his soul's reflection in the picture must have changed – in the same way that he has changed. Earlier in the book we also find that:

> [Dorian] would creep upstairs to the locked room, open the door with the key that never left him, and stand, with a mirror, in front of the portrait that Basil Hallward had painted of him, looking now at the evil and ageing face on the canvas, and now at the fair young face that laughed back at him from the polished glass.[59]

Two mirroring devices (the mirror and the painting), two different reflections (the aged/evil and the fair young face), but one person.[60] This is the paradox of *The Picture of Dorian Gray*, and a deviation from the Ovidian tale; Narcissus' face never turns malign or ugly – the same with Basil's feeling that never had anything evil or shameful. The sharpness of the contrast gives pleasure to Dorian until the moment he hears of Basil's confession that ends up with his killing. That moment is an important rite of passage for Dorian, because the next time that he will revisit his 'magic mirror', after his self-proclaimed life as a good man, he will decide that this decrepit mirroring is no longer representative of who he is but 'an unjust mirror, this mirror of his soul that he was looking at'.[61] It has been giving him nightmares and sadness and no pleasure anymore, because 'it had been like conscience to him. Yes, it had been conscience'.[62] And that is why he decided to use the same knife with which he killed Basil to destroy his painting: 'As it had killed the painter, so it would kill the painter's work, and all that that meant'.[63] When Dorian destroys the painting he also kills himself – the reflection of the painter's work and in his place, instead of a beautiful flower they find an ugly man that they only recognize from his rings.

Let us briefly gloss the 'all that that meant' phrase. What is it that it really meant? To borrow again from Ovid, 'For long his words seemed vain; what they concealed / the lad's strange death and stranger love revealed'.[64] These are the two verses that follow Tiresias' prophecy regarding Narcissus longevity. Can the same be applied to Wilde's strange story? 'It was from within, apparently, that the foulness and horror had come. Through some strange quickening of inner life, the leprosies of sin were slowly eating the thing away' the narrator informs us.[65] Both Basil's and Dorian's deaths then were an effect of knowing themselves; the common denotator in this was the painting and its ability not only to represent beauty and ugliness but also to mirror and reflect the reality of their feelings and their desires. The 'within' can be applied to all three of them; within Basil, within Dorian and within the painting. It can be understood as the reverse to what we now call the toxicity of hiding who you really are. Basil liberates himself through his confession, but that does not save his life. In a similar way, though Dorian tried to reverse his wrongdoings, it was in vein because the answer to his story was given long before that; on the 'fatal day' that Basil decided to paint his portrait. Though the plot of the story is driven by 'invert' desire – Basil's for Dorian, Lord Henry's for Dorian and Dorian's for himself – there is no sex involved. That makes sense, if we accept the argument that Basil and Dorian are mirror reflections of each other; they are two sides of the story. They represent the newly nascent homosexual subject that finds itself torn between the mirror image of who they think they are, the one that they are, and the one that the society thinks they are – just like in Lacan's mirror stage.

The mirror image becomes an affirmation of identity;[66] self-doubling (as in the case of Basil and Dorian) and self-representation are in *The Picture of Dorian Gray* a method by which we can 'multiply our personalities' and experience more fully the 'myriad lives and myriad sensations' that constitute our identity. And Wilde, as himself, comes to confirm this a few years later, in 1894, when he writes to a young admirer: 'Basil Hallward is what I think I am; Lord Henry what the world thinks of me; Dorian what I would like to be – in other ages, perhaps'.[67] What I have hoped to briefly show here is that the tale of Narcissus and Echo is not only used as a way to code 'inversion' or to show the consequences of self-admiration, but also as a necessary rhetorical device and a vehicle in understanding one's self. Instrumental in this has also been the use of mirrors and the process of reflection, self-reflection, and echoing.[68]

PART III
LIMINAL MIRROR

CHAPTER 9
MIRRORS AND THE MANUFACTURE OF RELIGIOUS AURA IN THE GRAECO-ROMAN WORLD[1]

Tatiana Bur

Ναί, ἔφη, φαινόμενα, οὐ μέντοι ὄντα γέ που τῇ ἀληθείᾳ

'Yes', he said, 'things we can perceive, but not, I think, things that are real in the true sense.'

Plato, *Republic* 10.596e[2]

Religion has a problem: how to make the divine present.[3] Different religions respond to this problem in different ways, and even within a single religious system, various solutions – centred around words, performances and objects – often co-exist comfortably.[4] The mirror, as one such object, has proven to be a useful medium to bridge the gap between the sacred and profane realms over a great stretch of time, space and cultures. This chapter asks why mirrors might be suitable for fabricating religious aura at all, and in Greek religion in particular.

I use a comparative ethno-anthropological approach to explain how mirror images can work to assist humans in making contact with the divine. I then turn to the ancient Greek material to suggest that a broader cultural curiosity with the ontology of reflection underscored the use of mirrors in ancient religious contexts. This is put to the test by combining a close reading of an ancient catoptric manual – Pseudo-Hero's *Catoptrica* – with anecdotal evidence which testifies to the deployment of mirrors in ancient religious contexts. Understanding the way that the mirror and reflection work to address the problem of divine presence in ancient Greek religion moves us beyond an antiquarian fascination with the mirror, prompting us to look at the ways in which man-made objects constructed, and were constructed by, broader human understandings of the world.

Mirrors and religious aura

Mirrors can be understood as objects which embody the properties of reflection. Reflection has both physical and metaphysical properties: it can intensify light, create heat and iridescence, but it can also act as the perfect tool for mimesis, and raise questions about the truth value of what one is seeing. While it is easy enough to observe in a number of cultures that reflection has been harnessed as a technique to manufacture divine presence, it is somewhat harder to understand the exact features of the technology that are foregrounded, or the specific way in which the technology evokes a sense of divine enchantment.[5] Two case studies will represent the ends of the spectrum as to the uses of reflection to manifest the supernatural: ancient indigenous Mesoamerican religion, and modern Hinduism. The comparative analysis will serve to put into stronger relief the subsequent exploration of the use of the technology of reflection to manufacture ancient Greek religious aura, and what this could have meant for ancient Greek worshippers and their sense of experiencing and believing in the divine.

For the ancient indigenous societies of Mesoamerica, the religious potential of the mirror lay in its capacity to reflect light, rather than to produce images. From as early as 1500 BC, obsidian – a naturally occurring volcanic rock – was polished to take advantage of its shiny blackness, and then used in the creation of a number of objects including mirrors.[6] Amerindian gods were bright spirits who lived in a light-infused realm, and reflective objects were symbolically precious to their worshippers because they embodied the substance and essence of the divinity.[7] The eyes of deities themselves are often depicted as reflective surfaces in Classic Maya art.[8] The *Florentine Codex*, written by a sixteenth-century Franciscan missionary eight years after Cortés' arrival in Mexico, helps us reconstruct the ways in which obsidian and other materials featured in the physical and religious landscapes of indigenous Amerindian society, and in particular the central place of brilliance, shine and iridescence in Amerindian cosmology.[9] The chapter on precious stones emphasizes their chromatic and luminous effects, and leaves no doubt that these stones were valued precisely on account of the reflective properties of their material.[10] It was thanks to reflection's connection to light that obsidian mirrors could help solve the problem of presence in ancient Mesoamerica.

The use of mirrors in Hindu religion is entirely different. According to Hindu mythology, the well-being of the world is understood to depend on the gaze of the deities, and it is for this reason that the all-seeing gods are said never to close their eyes.[11] Worshippers, in turn, must keep their eyes open to make reciprocal contact with the divine. The mirror thus becomes a medium used in Hindu rituals and incorporated into religious images to help manufacture and propagate *darśan*: the sense of ritual connectedness with the divine through the gaze.[12] Reflection is harnessed as a way to extend the field of vision and create two-directional visual contact between deity and worshipper.

The following Jain mirror ritual (*darpaṇa pūjā*) offers a clear illustration. The worshipper stands in the main pavilion of the temple and holds a mirror so that they can see in it the divine image (*mūrti*). They then dab sandalwood paste onto the forehead of the reflected image. The intention behind this ritual is that by seeing the face of the deity – above all, their innately dispassionate qualities – the worshipper might also become free of passion and hatred.[13] The mirror here is a tool to unite the deity and the worshipper in a single visual frame; to achieve an unparalleled sense of proximity to the deity; and to connect with the virtual image as a mimetic exemplum. This is facilitated by specular reflection and further enhanced by the haptic connection with the deity's virtual image projected in the mirror. Reflection quite literally brings the supernatural to the worshipper's fingertips, something which is possible in a religion which, critically, understands the divine *not* as ontologically separate in realm or substance from mortals.[14]

In both modern-day Hindu religious traditions and ancient indigenous Mesoamerican religion, the technique of reflection was harnessed to make the divine present to the worshipper. Yet to collapse under a single explanatory framework these disparate, culturally specific uses of the mirror would be misleading. Mesoamerican obsidian mirrors were theologically useful for their materiality and shininess. They were able to affect a sense of religious enchantment through their relationship with light and, as a result, with those intangible cosmological powers believed to be diffused abstractly through reflective objects. For modern Hindu pilgrims, reflection allows direct contact with the supernatural through the power of the eyes and of the gaze. Reflection in Hinduism is closely linked to sight, and divinities are drawn both physically and metaphysically closer to the worshipper through the use of mirrors and reflection. When we turn to the Greek counterparts of these examples, we find the technology of reflection is harnessed differently again: in the case of ancient Greek religion, the everyday capturing of the ontologically familiar in an ontologically distinct reflection was used as a way to bridge the gap between man and god.

(The ontology of) reflection in Greek thought

From philosophy to oratory, history to poetry, art to theatre, there is no genre in Classical antiquity that did not ponder the rich potential – both literal and symbolic – of reflective surfaces. One of the themes which unites these otherwise disparate genres is a recurring curiosity about the ontology of the reflected object. The epigraph with which I opened the chapter presents this notion as it is perhaps most famously formulated: in book 10 of Plato's *Republic,* Socrates explains to Glaucon the distinction between forms, artefacts and images as part of a larger argument denouncing 'imitative' arts – visual art and poetry.[15] The mirror in this instance is a tool which allows objects to be easily and quickly 'manufactured' through reflection. However, the philosopher stresses that what appears will only ever be at a remove from the truth. Anxieties about the truth value of the virtual image have a lasting historical imprint extending into Christian and Neoplatonic thought. This is evident in *De Mysteriis,* for example, where despite endorsing the use of light in certain divinatory contexts,[16] Iamblichus firmly denies that apparitions in mirrors could have theological relevance.[17]

Yet this very same distance between the virtual image and its real counterpart is not always envisioned as opening up space for deceit. The earliest literary reference to the mirror comes from the archaic Greek poet Alcaeus, who states that wine is a mirror to man (οἶνος γὰρ ἀνθρώπω δίοπτρον).[18] Alcaeus' metaphor – clearly playing on the duality of wine's potential as a reflective surface alongside its inebriating effect – foregrounds the capacity of the mirror to make apparent something initially hidden to the naked eye, just as wine proverbially does, too. Reflection offers the viewer a deeper understanding of reality than the faculty of vision does unassisted and this relies on the reflected image existing as separate to the 'live' image in question.

Reflection's distinct ontological status allowed it to exude different agency from the object to which it was tied not only in terms of perceived truth value, but also in relative strength. At times, for example, reflections exceeded reality in their persuasiveness. This is true in the case of Narcissus who would not have fallen in love with himself unassisted, but whose reflection is detached enough from his real existence for him to be emotionally, even erotically, overcome by it. On the other hand, the myth of Perseus and Medusa can be read as a foil to the Narcissus tale; where, crucially, the reflected image is a weaker, less effective version which allows Perseus to behead Medusa without her gaze turning him to stone.[19]

Though ontologically distinct, reflections are temporally tied to the original. This is already clear in Plato's discussion (mirrors allow for the *instant* production of images),[20] and other examples abound. Demosthenes, for instance, famously practising declamation in front of a mirror, finds reflection useful as a tool for live-time feedback on visual performance, bringing to the fore this temporal connection between the reflected image and the original object.[21] Since viewers are conscious – then as now – that reflections must be tied to something present in a particular space, they rely on them to make deductions about what is in the space in the moment they see the reflection, all the same remaining instinctively wary of the ontology of the form.

The mirror was useful at least as a literary (and artistic) device for the virtual image it created and the cognitive gymnastics these effects allowed in interpreting reality whether imitating, enhancing, weakening, or misrepresenting it. We could extend this discussion into an enormously rich catalogue of examples demonstrating how the polysemous nature of the mirror was enthusiastically explored in ancient literature. Some sophisticated work has been undertaken on unpacking the significance of the mirror in Graeco-Roman art and text over the last thirty or so years.[22] Although the focus and breadth of the studies differ, taken together they show that the mirror was popular in antiquity above all for the paradoxes inherent in the object and its accompanying metaphors.[23] Yet this takes us only so far since, as we have noted, the cultural value of the effect of reflection cannot be taken for granted. That light is marginalized, colour and iridescence absent, images crucial, and distortions frequent are all distinctive features of the Greek uses of and understandings of reflection. I turn now to an exploration of how this was conceived to work in practice through the examination of a genre which bridges the literary and the material: ancient technical manuals.

Ancient catoptric manuals

Technical texts are particularly useful for our present purposes since, unlike anecdotal evidence, they offer insight into the mentality behind the construction of mirrors, the interest in arrangement and erection of mirrors, and clues as to why and how the effects created through geometrical optics were applied in the specific context of ancient Greek religion. These are texts that have, to date, largely been excluded from the discourse on the cultural value of the mirror and its metaphors in antiquity.[24] Understanding the catoptric 'programme' – the ways in which authors perceived that they could put the effects of geometrical optics to use – is, however, imperative if we are to interpret correctly the agency of these objects. Like their philosophical counterparts, technical texts combine vision (essential physiologies of seeing, at least as it was then understood) and visuality (how vision could be employed socially and culturally), and thus deserve a more nuanced analysis than they have hitherto received.[25] While philosophers often talk about visuality in metaphorical terms, the mathematical authors give practical applications of their theories of vision.[26]

As a genre, catoptric treatises describe various arrangements which combine three types of mirrors: concave, convex and plane. These usually progress from most simple (proving the laws of reflection) to more sophisticated arrangements which problematize the relationship between the virtual image and reality through various visual techniques: magnification, distortion, multiplication, or omission.[27] If we conceive of objects as embodiments of technical systems – as the work of Alfred Gell encourages us to – it is precisely the discrepancy between processes of production and the viewer's understanding of these processes which enables technology to provoke a sense of enchantment.[28] Technical manuals as a genre, therefore, are interested in explaining techniques of catoptric manipulation which might make the viewer question the ontological nature of reflected objects, since there is a discrepancy between what is seen when an object is directly perceived, and what is seen when an object is seen in a mirror. Though the technician's position is one of privileged knowledge, the viewer was not necessarily not aware of the techniques involved, leading to the 'enchantment' of the technology.

In the introduction to his *Catoptrica*, Pseudo-Hero offers a fairly lengthy introduction where he justifies the value of the study of reflection (as opposed to just optics and dioptrics):[29]

> *videntes autem et katoptricum negotium esse dignum studio – habet enim quandam admirabilem speculationem.*
>
> We see too that the topic of catoptrics is also worthy of study – for it possesses a certain wonderful observation.[30]

It is helpful to render *speculatio* here not as a 'theory' (as translated by Jones) but, staying closer to the etymological sense of 'reflection', to think of it as a way that an otherwise intangible sense (sight) can be made observable.[31] In other words, Pseudo-Hero makes the explicit statement that catoptrics deserves attention precisely because the observable product of geometrical optics – the reflection – provokes wonder.[32] Contrary to what we might believe, this is not because of the mirror's mimetic potential, but because it shows things contrary to expectation, exploiting the difference between the real image and its reflection.[33] While in the *Florentine Codex*, for example, the application of light and the effects of luminous properties of reflective surfaces are of most interest because they are consistent with (and in turn help reinforce) indigenous conceptions of the world, for the Greek mathematician the epistemological value of studying reflection lies in understanding the way the projection of image works.[34] Greek catoptric manuals are chiefly concerned with the way that the reflection of rays produce different visual experiences, and how this can be manufactured and manipulated. For Pseudo-Hero, at least, reflection gave humans a way to observe what was not typically observable, whether this was a human body in unexpected form, something happening behind you, or what your neighbour was doing across the street.[35] Hero's 'dextral mirror', for example, makes clear that the same arrangement, depending on how it is erected, can be a tool for proper proportion and realism, or for monstrous distortion, reversal, inversion, and tilting.[36] Catoptric knowledge allowed for the human production of this ontologically slippery thing that was reflection, and this, in turn, provoked wonder.

We have seen, therefore, that mirrors are trans-historically and trans-culturally useful tools to create religious aura and that, specifically in the ancient Greek world, reflections are considered temporally tied to, yet ontologically distinct from, the original. Catoptric manuals offer a unique perspective for understanding how the effects generated by geometrical optics were regarded as technologies of the marvellous applied to negotiate human responses to their surroundings.[37] Due to their prioritizing of the technical, the contexts of use are almost absent in these manuals, but the few clues that are scattered throughout do, perhaps not so coincidentally, hint at religious settings.[38]

Mirrors and ancient Greek religious aura

I now turn to how the concern for the ontology of the reflection, which we have seen to be pervasive in Greek thought and literature, is played out in anecdotal evidence specifically relating to the religious realm. This final section asks: what is the evidence for the construction and deployment of mirrors in ancient religious contexts, and, given the previous discussion, how might we best read these episodes in order to understand how the mirror solved the problem of presence in Greek religion?

Mirrors are attested for use in rituals that actively seek to connect with the divine, as well as in episodes of unsolicited contact with the divine. The former category includes divination with mirrors (known as catoptromancy), and the latter the erection of mirrors as media for divine epiphany. In general, these two categories – epiphany and divination – are closely related since they both rely on redirecting the supernatural from another 'world' to the human world. Catoptromancy and catoptrically induced epiphany work in the same way – by manufacturing religious aura through reflection('s production of ontologically distinct images) – to pull the realms of the mortal and human together in meaningful ways.

An early parody of the ritual of catoptromancy is found in Aristophanes' *Acharnians*:

Λα. κατάχει σύ, παῖ, τοὔλαιον. ἐν τῷ χαλκίῳ
ἐνορῶ γέροντα δειλίας φευξούμενον.
Δι. κατάχει σὺ τὸ μέλι. κἀνθάδ' ἔνδηλος γέρων
κλάειν κελεύων Λάμαχον τὸν Γοργάσου.

Lamachus: *Boy, you pour on the oil. In the bronze, I see an old man who will be prosecuted for cowardice.*

Dicaeopolis: *And you, pour on the honey. On here too an old man is manifest, telling Lamachus, son of Gorgasus, to cry like a baby!*[39]

The focus on sight in the comic scene is marked. Polishing the surface with a viscous substance allows the image to be better reflected (the more substance is poured on, the more can be seen) which links the effectiveness of reflection as a religious medium to sight, not, for example, to light as it was interpreted by Armand Delatte.[40] This is consistent with Pseudo-Hero's statements relating to materiality and reflection. The author explains that mirrors need to be highly polished, and that any gaps in the reflective surface will need to be filled with an adequate material, *to ensure there are no holes in the visual frame*.[41] Polishing, then, is important insofar as it will allow a greater amount of light to reflect on the surface to create a better, more complete image, but not to capitalize on the glary effect. Further, Aristophanes' joke relies on the fact that divination in general was fraught with errors of interpretation and here, despite all the buffing in the world, the bronze still remains an abstruse surface through which to see the divine precisely because of – and thanks to – its ability to display a distorted image. Sight, then, though critical in the process, does not lead to disambiguation.[42] This stands in contrast, for example, to the way that sight in Hinduism is tied to (mimetic) clarity.

The absence of a religious specialist in the Aristophanic parody serves to highlight the role of the interpreter in catoptromancy (and in other gazing rituals) perhaps even more so than in other forms of divination. Indeed, of all techniques of divination available to ancient Greek worshippers, catoptromancy is one far less concerned with answers and far more concerned with enchantment through abstract divine presence which the object engenders.[43] An often cited example of catoptromancy from a sanctuary to Demeter in Patras in Northern Achaea, however, provides a rare case where we do in fact have the sense that the worshipper is coming with some sort of question, or at least a very broad issue on which the god's opinion is solicited – life or death (and, it must be said, only that: οὐ μὲν ἐπὶ παντί γε πράγματι, ἀλλὰ ἐπὶ τῶν καμνόντων).[44] Pausanias describes in detail the oracle consulted by the ill, as well as its surroundings and its construction around a spring.[45] The oracle is arranged so that a mirror attached to a cord is suspended above the spring with the rim just touching the surface of the water. After praying and burning incense, the worshipper looks into the mirror to see the sick person alive or dead. If we think about the arrangement practically, we can imagine how the transparency of the water offered the potential to project something below the water surface onto the mirror floating above as a sort of visual enhancement.[46] Additionally, the undulating water surface continuously distorting the shapes of the reflections would have further enhanced the contraption's enchanting effect. Distortion and visual manipulation are crucial in order to facilitate the separate ontologies of real and reflected which underlie the use of catoptrics as a religious technology. Lucian is surely satirizing this sort of oracle in *A True Story* when he describes a mirror suspended over a well which, he says, shows every city and nation (πάσας μὲν πόλεις, πάντα δὲ ἔθνη).[47] Presumably for the parody to resonate, mirror contraptions in oracular settings must have held some place in the collective experience; and the Lucianic satire works precisely because of the existent anxieties of the truth value of the mirror. When he stares into it himself, Lucian does not just see any nation or people, but sees his own family and his native land. The specificity of the images in Lucian's tale, both in terms of content and form, is to be taken as highly ironic given that catoptric projection in mantic contexts does not, in fact, rely on mimesis or clear projection of specific visions, but works through distortion, ambiguity, and interpretation.

The underlying idea with which the Lucian passage toys – that of the range and specificity of the projection – is an interesting one for pushing further our analysis of reflection, especially when read against the description of Pseudo-Hero's 'multiview' mirror. Pseudo-Hero presents this mirror as the so-called *polytheoron* (probably how it was named in the Greek original), and the thirteenth-century translator presumably then glossed it as the *multividum*.[48] Despite the difficult manuscript, I think there is something to be made of the fact that this mirror – a fairly simple arrangement of two bronze, rectangular, plane mirrors connected along one side with a hinge – was named according to its perceived ability to manufacture *more* in image than in reality. It seems that this is not just more in number, but also in intensity and genre. The text at this point is unfortunately full of lacunas, yet thanks to Schmidt's work on the translator's marginal jottings in Greek, we can make out a connection with a religious setting:[49]

> *speculum construere quod dicitur polytheoron, id est multividum. facit autem dextra dextra apparere, adhuc autem et* (lacuna) *motum facit apparere,* (lacuna) *attestatur quia Pallas genita fuit ex vertice Iovis, multas facies [manifestat], unum digitum facit multos, deinde* (lacuna) *distracta bovum manifestat.*

> To build a mirror which is called a 'polytheoron': it is a 'multiview'. It makes right appear as right, also three-headed Zeus, it makes motion appear, it produces dancing victories, it attests that Pallas was born from the brow of Zeus, it [shows] many faces, it makes one finger many, and lastly it shows distorted bulls' heads.[50]

Of all the possible designs, the author has chosen to harness technical knowledge in practical form to stage Greek myth and animate iconography. Hero says that the multiview can be made with 2:1 height to breadth proportions, but is equally possible with a different ratio. The practical detail does not matter so long as the final montage has 'good proportions', says the author, and that it is made without wobbling at all, and with the images unobstructed.[51] These remarks highlight that it is the effect which matters most to the technician of Greek catoptrics, and that this effect relies on an effective transmission of images. The movement associated with the projection of the virtual images is also striking. As opaque as the description is, there is a clear sense of action: motion appears, Athena is born, the victories dance. This brings us back to the idea that the mirror can act as a 'live feed' of images and that the immediacy of the vision leads the viewer to deduce that the virtual spectacle must actually be present and occurring in the moment they see it, giving cognitive reliability to the presence of the divine which appears in an ontologically distinct form: a reflection.

Pliny – who is likely to have been writing contemporaneously with Hero, or close to it – describes similar mirrors consecrated at a temple at Smyrna that show strange or monstrous (*monstrifica*) forms.[52] One wonders whether such mirrors were placed inside the temple as votive offerings, or whether they formed part of the architecture of the temple. In any case, their place within a sacred space likely marks them as tools to solve the problem of divine presence, and it is worth highlighting once more that in Pliny's narrative it is the distorting effect that reflection engenders which is foregrounded within this. Anthemius, later in the sixth century AD, picked up on the same catoptric potential in his description of mirrors which show right as left, two heads on one body, and four eyes.[53]

Pseudo-Hero's most elaborate description is of how to construct a mirror 'so that everyone who approaches will see neither himself nor someone else, but only whatever picture someone has chosen in advance.'[54] The author specifies that the actual object whose image is to be reflected should be hidden, and that the viewer should be physically unable to move past the optimal viewing point. This indicates a clear concern for the spectacle of the miracle, and an imperative for the viewer to be fully convinced by the effect of the miracle.[55] The author also says that his text gives only the bare bones of the catoptrics involved, but that, as regards things external to the arrangement, everything should be organized as is appropriate for the place and the fabricator's purpose.[56] Whatever these other elements may have been, the comment certainly indicates that we are far from an armchair invention. Rather, the arrangement was part of a more complete experience where technology was used to provoke a psychological reaction in its human 'user'.

The first arrangement of Euclid's *Catoptrica* is based on the same geometric problem, and Anthemius' fourth arrangement also describes a similar piece.[57] The most intriguing case for comparison, however, comes from Pausanias' description of the sanctuary to Despoina at Lykosoura in Arcadia:

> ἐν δεξιᾷ δὲ ἐξιόντι ἐκ τοῦ ναοῦ κάτοπτρον ἡρμοσμένον ἐστὶν ἐν τῷ τοίχῳ· τοῦτο ἤν τις προσβλέπῃ τὸ κάτοπτρον, ἑαυτὸν μὲν ἤτοι παντάπασιν ἀμυδρῶς ἢ οὐδὲ ὄψεται [τὴν] ἀρχήν, τὰ δὲ ἀγάλματα τῶν θεῶν καὶ αὐτὰ καὶ τὸν θρόνον ἔστιν ἐναργῶς θεάσασθαι.

> On the right as you go out of the temple there is a mirror fitted into the wall. If anyone should look into this mirror, he will see himself very dimly indeed or not at all, but the actual images of the gods and the throne can be seen vividly.[58]

The mirror here has been incorporated into the permanent architecture of the temple. The way that Pausanias constructs his narrative makes it sound as if the mirror is positioned strategically near the exit so that it capitalizes on the sense of religiosity the worshipper feels coming out of the sacred space. The catoptric arrangement subverts the worshipper's assumptions of real and reflected when what they expect to see (their own image) becomes either superimposed or entirely replaced by images (*agalmata*) of the gods or the throne. Likely within moments of engaging in a ritual which aimed to make contact with the divine, the worshipper sees the images of the god dominating over or replacing their own physical form and in this very moment, the divine presence – which they experience in a way that makes evident the ontological difference between man and god – is felt more strongly than ever.[59]

Catoptric manipulation seems to have been harnessed in other religious contexts, too, possibly mystery or initiatory which involved intense, ecstatic experiences.[60] Since this is the topic best treated by scholars already, I limit myself to a single concluding example: a compelling piece of evidence which is embedded in the well-known fresco of the Villa of the Mysteries in Pompeii thought to have been painted in the first century BC. The fresco has been variously interpreted, yet by all accounts it depicts a religious rite, possibly related to initiation to the cult of Dionysus. The scene that is of interest to us shows an older satyr seated and holding a bowl out in front of a younger satyr who peers over, wide-eyed and curious, while another young satyr holds up a mask in the background (Fig. 9.1). This scene has been understood in a number of ways. Certain scholars held that the satyr was being offered a drink from the bowl, while others have argued that this was more likely to be a scene of divination by gazing (*lecanomancy*).[61] The most telling element of this scene, and the element most unique to it, is the satyr in the back who is holding up a mask at the exact correct angle for its reflection to be projected into the bowl into which the other satyr is gazing. This is an instance of humanly-manufactured divine epiphany capitalizing on the potential of reflection. The painter of the fresco has captured the exact moment when the human hand participates in creating religious enchantment through technical knowledge. The artist hints at the 'problem of presence'

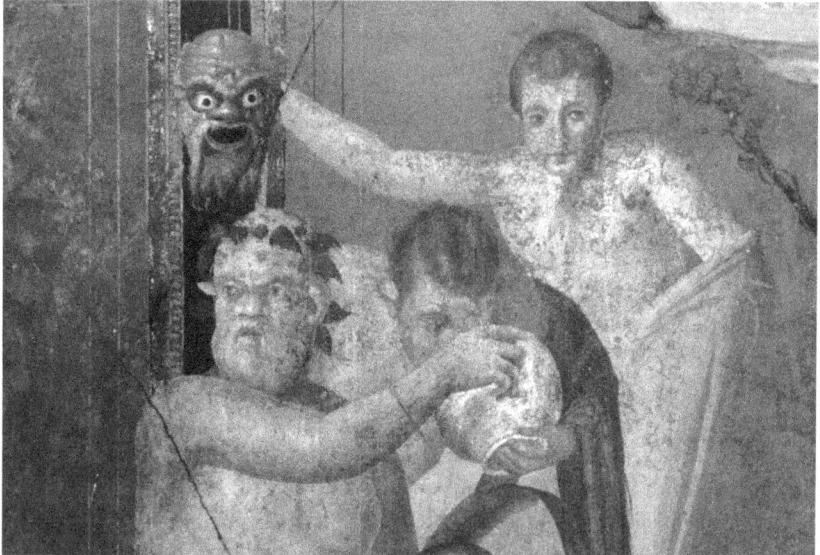

Fig. 9.1 Detail from the fresco in the Villa of the Mysteries, Pompeii.

and has painted for us one of its solutions: reflection as a tool for the creation of a divine epiphany. This is, in its own genre, much the same as the way in which ancient technical manuals are keen to divulge how catoptrics plays with ontology and provides further evidence for the use of mirrors for divine apparition.[62]

Before we turn strictly to conclusions, one issue remains to be addressed and that is chronology. Is it possible to trace diachronic developments in the use of catoptric technologies for the production of religious aura in Graeco-Roman antiquity? Over the course of the chapter, we have seen that our evidence for the use and interpretation of mirrors and reflection extends from the Classical texts of Aristophanes and Plato, through Hellenistic and Roman mathematicians, the literature of the Roman Empire, and beyond into late antiquity. Of course, theological discourse shifts in all sorts of ways over the course of this period and one particularly relevant *longue-durée* change is the gradual – though not complete – move towards de-materializing religion and privileging word and spirit over matter.[63] For the majority of the Patristic authors, the image of god remains a critical theological frame of reference, but it is the *logos* of God that becomes a tool to evaluate the world, and a guide to redress the individual after the fall of man with the aim to reflect the image of God according to which humans were created.[64] Reflection and the divine by no means become divorced in the Christian tradition, but they coalesce in new ways.[65] The mirror not only becomes an object symbolic of vain adornment, but, critically, within the much broader theme of the rejection of Pagan avenues to connect with and embrace the divine, specular reflection is singled out by Clement of Alexandria as an inappropriate medium for direct epiphany, and one which is specifically used to fool initiates in the context of the Mysteries of Dionysus, for example.[66]

Conclusions

The first point that this chapter seeks to make is quite simply that mirrors and reflections were used in ancient Greek religion. Already, this goes some way towards characterizing the ancient religious experience. It shows an inclination towards the creation of religious aura through technical means and should be considered within a larger picture of other applications of techniques and technical knowledge for similar purposes. Such religious technologies – of which catoptrics formed part – did not only allow and organize access to the transcendental, but their use tells intriguing tales about the nature of the gods, and the organization of the cosmos in ancient Greek religion. The second aim of the chapter, and the place of departure for the discussion, was to understand how the same laws of geometrical optics, and same objects through which these laws are materialized, could do different things according to different religious systems within which they existed. Reflective surfaces in Greek antiquity offered a connection with the supernatural not by enabling the worshipper to see and be seen by the divine in an intensely direct manner as in modern Hinduism, not by diffusing a cosmological charge through an emphasis on light as was the case in ancient Mesoamerica, but by creating and manipulating the ontological gap between the real and the virtual image.

CHAPTER 10
THE MIRROR OF NATURE
Daniel Marković

This chapter examines four instances of the idea of 'the mirror of nature' (*speculum naturae*, κάτοπτρον φύσεως) in Latin and Greek literature. Recent discussions of mirrors and their symbolism in antiquity have not discussed this concept systematically,[1] mainly because they have been focused on the general questions of morality (self-reflection, self-knowledge, and introspection)[2] and the problems of reciprocity and double.[3] But even if the concept of 'the mirror of nature' does not shed much light on these particular questions, it is interesting in its own right. The four instances of the phrase that will be discussed here come from Lucretius, Cicero (two), and Plutarch. Two of these are found in explicitly Epicurean context (Lucretius and Cicero) and, since they are chronologically earlier, this might be meaningful. As I hope to show, the concept seems to be associated particularly with Epicurus's views on natural phenomena and could be of Epicurean origin; it also anticipates the use of mirrors in modern optical instruments. As an instrument that produces likenesses of natural phenomena, in these four examples the mirror is imagined as a source of analogies that brings the principles of nature to light. This kind of analogical reasoning, in which inferences about the invisible work of nature are made on the basis of what is evident, is the foundation of Epicurean atomistic physics.

1) Lucretius 3.972–75

Our first instance of the phrase 'the mirror of nature' comes from the end of the third book of Lucretius's *De rerum natura* (*DRN*). The lines in question echo the opening passage of the concluding part of the book, where Lucretius corroborates Epicurus's tenet that death is of no concern to us by arguing to his Roman audience that just as they felt nothing before they were born, for example in the times of the Second Punic War, they will not be able to feel anything after their death.[4] After eliminating every theoretical possibility that the soul can survive death, Lucretius turns to wrong beliefs. He brings to the stage a personified Nature to rebuke humans for the sorrow they feel when they think about death.[5] In a short but passionate harangue, Nature argues that humans should stop mourning and weeping over the prospect of death. Regardless of the kind of life they have had up to that point, Nature claims, their sorrow is entirely irrational. If so far they have been happy in their lives, they should depart from life satisfied, as a guest would depart from a banquet. But if they have not, they should not delay the departure that will bring them relief from pain.

Mirrors and Mirroring

At this moment an elderly man is introduced; he is not persuaded by the logic of Nature's twofold alternative and still mourns the prospect of death. Nature scolds him for living his life in a way that leaves him unprepared for his inevitable exit. Continuing in the voice of narrator, Lucretius adds that the old man should depart from life as soon as possible and make room (and thus also provide the material) for new life. Countless generations have already died, Lucretius points out, and countless generations will die; we all hold life as tenants not owners. Closing the section, the narrator adds:

Respice item quam nil ad nos anteacta vetustas
temporis aeterni fuerit, quam nascimur ante.
hoc igitur speculum nobis natura futuri
temporis exponit post mortem denique nostram.
numquid ibi horribile apparet ? num triste videtur
quicquam? non omni somno securius exstat?

Look back also and see how the ages of everlasting time past before we were born have been nothing to us. This therefore is the mirror which nature puts in front of us, showing the time to come after our eventual death. Is there anything horrible in that? Is there anything gloomy? Is it not more peaceful than any sleep?

(Trans. after Rouse-Smith)

In these lines, 'the mirror of Nature' is conceived as an instrument that makes natural laws and their consequences for us easier to grasp. These natural laws remain the same across the spectrum and operate uniformly at different points in time. Lucretius thus repeats here the argument that opened the concluding part of the book, namely that our experience of emotional detachment from the distant past in the present moment can provide a good analogy for the attitude we should adopt toward our prospects in the future. If we do not worry about what happened before we were born, why should we worry about the events that will take place after our death? From this perspective, the two extremes in the continuum of time are analogous and can be seen as mirroring each other.

The image of mirror stands here for the process of analogic reasoning. It provides a good conceptual metaphor: two things compared in an analogy can be seen as an object and its likeness in a mirror – i.e., two entities facing each other along the same continuum or axis. Analogic reasoning is firmly grounded in Epicurean epistemology and operates in Lucretius's poem both along the axis of magnitude and along the axis of time.[6] On the one hand, it allows the poet to deduce the laws that regulate the microscopic realm of atoms by observing the laws of macroscopic natural phenomena (for example atomic motion through the image of particles of dust in a sunbeam);[7] on the other, it enables him to construct the attitude toward the unknown future on the basis of the present attitude toward the remote past. Ultimately, the point of the reasoning is to liberate the reader from the excessive concerns that traditionally accompany the idea of death as an unknown that lies in the future.

In his commentary on these lines of *DRN* 3, Heinze adduces a similar place in Pliny the Elder.[8] Discussing burial practices, Pliny uses the same Epicurean argument, namely that one's condition after the moment of death is exactly the same as one's condition before the beginning of life. Pliny may have had Lucretius's passage in mind and, although his language does not contain the mirror metaphor, it is helpful in terms of explaining the meaning of Lucretius's image. Rejecting the preservation of dead bodies and the idea that the dead will live again, Pliny concludes his analogy with the following words: *at quanto facilius certiusque sibi quemque credere, specimen securitatis ante genitali sumere experimento!* (How much easier and more certain it is for each man to trust himself and to take a specimen of security from the experience of his condition before birth!).[9] In place of Lucretius's *speculum*, Pliny has *specimen*, a cognate word (derived from the root *spec-*) that indicates a visible sign of something that could be hidden from view.

2) Cicero, *De finibus* 2.32

The preceding example presented an argument based on the analogy between two points that lie outside the trajectory of individual human life. The following two examples will make a similar comparison bringing together two points *within* the continuum of individual human life. The first example directly connects the phrase 'the mirror of nature' with Epicurus.

In the second book of *De finibus*, Cicero criticizes Epicurus's teaching on pleasure. Epicurus's notion of pleasure is ill-defined, Cicero explains, because it confuses pleasure with the absence of pain. In the section that precedes the quotation below, Cicero says that Epicurus explains his concept of the supreme good (*summum bonum*) with reference to young children who are still not corrupted by age. It is precisely in children, according to Epicurus's argument, that one can see how humans naturally seek pleasure as the ultimate good and avoid pain as an evil. This explanation, Cicero points out, neglects Epicurus's own distinction between kinetic and static pleasure. Children simply do not exemplify the pursuit of static pleasure, or the state of being free from pain, the pleasure that Epicurus thinks is the highest pleasure of all. Cicero continues his argument:

> *Nec tamen argumentum hoc Epicurus a parvis petivit aut etiam a bestiis, quae putat esse specula naturae, ut diceret ab iis duce natura hanc voluptatem expeti nihil dolendi. nec enim haec movere potest appetitum animi, nec ullum habet ictum, quo pellat animum, status hic non dolendi, itaque in hoc eodem peccat Hieronymus. at ille pellit, qui permulcet sensum voluptate. itaque Epicurus semper hoc utitur, ut probet voluptatem natura expeti, quod ea voluptas, quae in motu sit, et parvos ad se alliciat et bestias, non illa stabilis, in qua tantum inest nihil dolere. qui igitur convenit ab alia voluptate dicere naturam proficisci, in alia summum bonum ponere?*

Indeed Epicurus could hardly have obtained proof of this equation from looking at young children or even at animals, though he regards them as mirrors of nature. He could hardly have claimed that natural instinct leads children to seek the pleasure of feeling no pain. This is not the sort of thing that can arouse appetitive desire. The static condition of freedom from pain produces no motive force to impel the mind to act (on this point Hieronymus is also mistaken). Only the caress of sensual pleasure has this effect. So, it is the fact that kinetic pleasure is attractive to young children and animals that Epicurus relies on to demonstrate that pleasure is what we naturally seek. He makes no appeal to static pleasure, which consists simply in the absence of pain. Surely, then, it is inconsistent to say that nature proceeds from one kind of pleasure, but supreme good from another.

(Trans. Woolf)

Cicero explicitly attributes to Epicurus the notion that children and animals are 'mirrors of nature'; he does not object to this general idea, but only to the inconsistent way in which Epicurus uses the idea in his argument, claiming that the analogy supports his teaching on pleasure as the *summum bonum*. Epicurus is wrong, Cicero claims, because the behaviour of infants is not consistent with his ultimate conclusions about *static* pleasure as the highest good. Static pleasure is the pleasure that is enjoyed after a desire is satisfied and all pain has been removed. Kinetic pleasure is the pleasure enjoyed in the process of satisfying desire; Epicurus thought that this pleasure was inferior in quality to the static one because it involves a certain amount of pain, namely the pain that is being removed. Since children and animals strive for this kind of pleasure, Cicero objects, they do not provide a good argument for his theory. Despite the objection which turns Epicurus's own teaching against his claims, it appears that Cicero and Epicurus would agree on the general premise that children display behaviour that allows us to draw inferences about human nature. They both believe that a fixed human nature operates uniformly across the spectrum of age, so that the inborn or natural notion of the highest good can already be seen in the behaviour of children.

3) Cicero, *De finibus* 5.61

This example is closely connected with the preceding one, even if it does not come directly from an Epicurean context. In book five of *De finibus*, the Peripatetic Piso also uses the analogy between adult men and children, but this time for the argument that the *summum bonum* is not pleasure but virtue or moral excellence:

> *Hoc autem loco tantum explicemus haec honesta, quae dico, praeterquam quod nosmet ipsos diligamus, praeterea suapte natura per se esse expetenda. indicant pueri, in quibus ut in speculis natura cernitur. quanta studia decertantium sunt! quanta ipsa certamina! ut illi efferuntur laetitia, cum vicerunt! ut pudet victos! ut se accusari nolunt! quam cupiunt laudari! quos illi labores non perferunt, ut aequalium principes sint! quae memoria est in iis bene merentium, quae referendae gratiae cupiditas! atque ea in optima quaque indole maxime apparenti in qua haec honesta, quae intellegimus, a natura tamquam adumbrantur.*

For the present I shall only explain that what I am calling morality is desirable in its own right and not just because we love ourselves. This is shown by the case of children, where we can see nature at work as clearly as in a mirror. Consider how keen their rivalries are, and how fierce the contests where those rivalries are pursued! Consider their elation at winning and their shame in defeat; their aversion to blame and their love of being praised; their willingness to endure anything so long as they come out on top! Consider how well they remember those who have shown them kindness, and their own eagerness to repay it. These traits are most apparent in the best characters, where what we understand as the moral qualities are already being drawn in outline by nature.

(Trans. Woolf)

Although it is meant to support a different conclusion, the argument rests on the same assumption as the argument of Epicurus, namely that children's behaviour reveals human nature. In his account, Piso relies on Antiochus of Ascalon, an eclectic philosopher (and also one of Cicero's teachers). Antiochus's argument apparently began from the notions of self-love and instinct for self-preservation as basic traits of human nature, claiming that these are developed and refined throughout life. In the course of his account of the argument, Piso uses the example of children several times, for example to illustrate the innate human love of learning and the innate desire for constant activity.[10] After he makes the latter point, Piso adds the following justification of his method of reasoning: 'All the ancient theories, especially the one I espouse, visit the cradle, in the belief that the easiest way of understanding nature's intentions is to look at early childhood' (*omnes veteres philosophi, maxime nostri, ad incunabula accedent, quod in pueritia facillime se arbitrantur naturae voluntatem posse cognoscere*).[11] This view could also be described as a version of diachronic analogy, which we have seen in the example from Lucretius. The analogy posits that the laws of nature are uniform and that the principles that can be observed on one side of the continuum of human life also apply to the other.

4) Plutarch, *Moralia* 967d5–e1

In book five of *De finibus*, Cicero's Piso claimed that the desire for constant activity can be seen not only in humans but also in animals.[12] Similarly, in his treatise on *The Cleverness of Animals* (Πότερα τῶν ζώων φρονιμώτερα or *De sollertia animalium*), Plutarch takes an example from animal behaviour as a token of the universal nature of human virtues. He describes the community of ants as an image of the human world in a drop of water:

Τὰς δὲ μυρμήκων οἰκονομίας καὶ παρασκευὰς ἐκφράσαι μὲν ἀκριβῶς ἀμήχανον, ὑπερβῆναι δὲ παντελῶς ὀλίγωρον· οὐδὲν γὰρ οὕτω μικρὸν ἡ φύσις ἔχει μειζόνων καὶ καλλιόνων κάτοπτρον, ἀλλ' ὥσπερ ἐν σταγόνι καθαρᾷ πάσης ἔνεστιν ἀρετῆς ἔμφασις· 'ἔνθ' ἔνι μὲν φιλότης' (Ξ 216) τὸ κοινωνικόν, ἔνι δ' ἀνδρείας εἰκὼν τὸ φιλόπονον, ἔνεστι δὲ πολλὰ μὲν ἐγκρατείας σπέρματα πολλὰ δὲ φρονήσεως καὶ δικαιοσύνης.

It is impossible to relate in full detail all the methods of production and storage practiced by ants, but it would be careless to omit them entirely. In fact, nowhere else does Nature have so small a mirror of greater and nobler enterprises. Just as you may see greater things reflected in a drop of clear water, so among ants there exists the image of every virtue. 'Love and affection are found' (Hom. *Il.* 14.216), namely their social life. You may also see the reflection of courage in their persistence in hard labor, and there are many seeds of self-control and many of good sense and justice.

(Trans. after Helmbold)

In this passage, the behaviour of ants is seen as a miniature image of the Platonic and Stoic cardinal human virtues: courage, self-control, prudence, and justice.[13] Plutarch is not the only example of such reasoning in antiquity. One thinks, for example, of Varro's and Vergil's anthropomorphic descriptions of the community of bees;[14] it is notable that Varro and Vergil also deliberately signpost their analogical reasoning (Varro: *apes... ut homines*, 'bees are as humans'; Vergil: *si parva licet componere magnis*, 'if one may compare small things with the great').[15] Plutarch's image of a small mirror, however, is more vivid, and perhaps triggers further associations in the mind of the modern reader, who may think of mirrors as parts of optical instruments that make small things visible, such as the microscope. Here it is worth pointing out with McCarty that mirrors in antiquity were often convex and thus produced smaller images of larger objects.[16] At any rate, the assumption that underlies Plutarch's image is that the nature of living beings works uniformly across the scale of magnitudes.

Conclusion

The examples above show that the phrase 'the mirror of nature' in Greek and Latin literature activates two images: that of a personified nature holding a mirror, and that of nature seen in a mirror as an optical instrument. The first image is consistent with typically Epicurean rhetoric, which often represents nature in anthropomorphic terms, gendered as female.[17] The second image can also be connected with Epicurean epistemology, and is suggestive of the modern notion of an optical instrument. The genealogy of this image can be explained as follows.

All Greek and Latin words for mirror – κάτοπτρον, ἔνοπτρον, εἴσοπτρον; *speculum* – are formed from roots that denote vision and visibility. The words κάτοπτρον, ἔνοπτρον, and εἴσοπτρον were formed from prepositions κατά-, ἐν-, and εἰς-, the root -ὀπ-, and the suffix -τρον.[18] The root ὀπ-, a very productive root in Greek,[19] denotes seeing. The suffix -τρον is used to denote instruments (as in, e.g., ἄροτρον, Lat. *aratrum* for 'plough'). A very similar etymological formation can be seen at work in Latin, where the word *speculum*, which translates Greek κάτοπτρον, is formed from the root *spec-*, which denotes seeing, and the suffix *-culum*, which denotes instruments (as in *poculum*, 'cup').[20] Etymologically, the main words for mirror in both Greek and Latin mean 'an instrument of seeing'. By way of contrast, in English, French, and German the words for mirror — 'mirror', 'miroir', and 'Spiegel' – are derived from remote Latin roots *mirari* and *speculum*, and their use does not immediately activate their etymology in the mind of the reader in the same way in which their Greek and Latin counterparts would have done.

Greek and Latin words for mirror thus primarily convey the ideas of seeing and visibility. In each of the instances of the phrase 'the mirror of nature,' one could easily replace the word 'mirror' with the phrase 'visible image.' The step from the idea of visibility to the notion of understanding is not difficult; as an optical instrument, a mirror comes to represent an instrument of understanding. Finally, it is seen as an emblem of the cognitive process of analogy; the word 'mirror' in the instances discussed above can also by rendered simply by the term 'analogy', as in 'an analogy provided by nature.' This meaning makes the idea of a mirror particularly well suited to the purposes of Epicurus, whose physics depends entirely on analogical reasoning and explains the parts and workings of the world that are not directly accessible to the senses by drawing analogies with those that are.

We cannot be sure whether it was Epicurus who coined the phrase or someone else. The first two passages discussed above seem to point to him; the remaining two show that the phrase was, or at some point became, a part of the philosophical koine, and that it could have been used by the followers of other philosophical schools as well. What is certain, however, is that Epicurus's epistemology stems from a principle that goes back to Anaxagoras, who held that 'the visible is an image of the invisible' (ὄψις γὰρ τῶν ἀδήλων τὰ φαινόμενα).[21] This principle contains the nucleus of the idea of the 'mirror of nature': the word ὄψις ('image') shares the root ὀπ- with the word κάτοπτρον ('mirror'), and in this instance the two words can be considered practically interchangeable. All the examples discussed above display the same logic: one segment of visible reality is used as a source from which the same set of principles is transferred to the other segment. The use of the word 'mirror' anticipates to some extent the prosthetic use of optical instruments in modern times.[22] As for the idea of nature as something seen in a mirror, it reflects the philosophical concept of the universe as a unified organism with its internal principles inscribed in each of its parts.[23]

CHAPTER 11
'THE UNSPOTTED *DIOPTRA* OF PROPHECY': A MIRROR METAPHOR IN BYZANTINE LITERATURE[1]

Eirini Afentoulidou

After having been defeated by the famous frontiersman Digenis Akrites in the homonymous Medieval Greek poem, the Amazon Maximoú proposes the following deal: since Digenis is the first one to defeat her, she shall be his wife and helper. Digenis responds that he already has a beautiful and noble wife. However, as Maximoú takes off her coat because of the heat and remains with a thin shift, Digenis has intercourse with her, having been overcome by her beauty:

> Maximou's shift was gossamer-thin,
> and it revealed her limbs as in a mirror
> and her breasts rising just a little above her chest.[2]

There is plenty to discuss in this episode in terms of gender relations. However, I wish to draw attention to one detail: the use of the mirror-simile. Indeed, the *tertium comparationis* between Maximoú's gown and a mirror is that they both allow the viewer to see through, revealing something which is normally concealed. This function of the mirror contradicts ancient and modern optics. Yet, the metaphor of mirror as means to revelation is found throughout the Eastern and Western Middle Ages and beyond.[3]

Mentions of actual mirrors were infrequent in Byzantine literature and usually had connotations of vanity and deception, mostly associated with women. Mirror metaphors, on the other hand, were quite common.[4] The terms used for mirrors were κάτοπτρον, ἔσοπτρον, and διόπτρα, the etymology of which is examined elsewhere in this volume (Bonati and Reggiani). The first two terms were interchangeable and were used both literally and metaphorically. The term διόπτρα on the other hand was much less common; it was used almost exclusively in metaphors in connection with visionary revelation. In the present chapter I will examine the mirror metaphor in the spectrum between notions of participation of the effigy in the original, representability of the original through the medium, and prophetic revelation, closing with the only instance of the mirror as title metaphor known from the Byzantine period.

I. *'The unspotted mirror of God's majesty'*: The original and its likeness

In praising the Wisdom of God the author of the *Book of Wisdom*, traditionally identified with King Solomon, writes: 'she (sc. the personified Wisdom of God) is the brightness of eternal light, and the unspotted mirror of God's majesty, and the image of his goodness'.[5] The Wisdom is God's emanation, and this relation is expressed as a relation between the mirror and the original. The *Book of Wisdom* enjoyed the status of a canonical Old Testament book throughout the Christian Middle Ages. The mirror metaphor, with or without explicit reference to this passage, was widely used by Byzantine theologians, whose thought was permeated by the platonic (or rather neoplatonic) concept of the supreme original and its manifold earthly manifestations.[6] In this section I will discuss selected texts, in which the mirror metaphor is employed to express the relation between two entities as a relation between original and reflection. These texts are dogmatic treatises pertaining to issues of Christology, i.e. the question of Christ as God and/or human and as one of the triune Divinity, of the validity of icon veneration, and of hesychasm, or they are moral exhortations and hagiographic works presenting a perfected human as mirror of God, or they elaborate on the theme of literature as mirror of a person, be it the author, be it the hero/heroine.

Christology

In Christian readings the personification of the *Book of Wisdom* goes a step further, so that the Wisdom is identified with the person of the Son of God Jesus Christ. Thus the author of the *Letter to the Hebrews*, in Christian tradition identified with the Apostle Paul, refers to Christ alluding to this passage but leaving the word ἔσοπτρον out: 'the brightness of his glory, and the express image of his person'.[7] Even if the 'unspotted mirror' is left out in the *Letter to the Hebrews*, the mirror analogy in allusion to the *Book of Wisdom* was occasionally used by Christian authors to define the relation between God the Father and God the Son. The seventh century author Anastasius of Sinai, for example, claims: 'In the Son, as in some divine mirror, we see the glory of the Father. So it is written: "He who has seen me, has seen the Father (John 14, 9)."'[8]

Few Byzantine authors, however, used the mirror analogy in trinitarian context, i.e. to define the relation between the divine persons of the Holy Trinity. The reason must be sought in its implications, which are incompatible with the consubstantiality dogma of the Nicean Creed (325 CE). According to this dogma, the three persons of the Holy Trinity are of the same substance. A mirror, on the other hand, is ontologically different from the original, even if it temporarily bears its reflection. Therefore, the mirror was rather used by theologians for relations, in which the hierarchy was uncontested. A not uncommon occasion was Christ's incarnation. For example we read in the *Physiologus*, a symbolic bestiary circulating in various versions since Late Antiquity (the following passage is a Byzantine interpolation): 'But God's Wisdom, i.e. our Lord Jesus Christ, descended from heaven and shone in the world through his flesh, which he took from the holy maiden and God-bearer Mary, as in a mirror.'[9] A mirror of Christ's divine power are also his works: 'From what the Son did before and after incarnation, his infinite power appears as in a mirror'.[10]

These examples are characteristic in as much as they demonstrate the emphasis Byzantine theologians put on the problem of the *perceptibility* of God. Indeed, the aim of the mirror analogy is to show how what we see (Christ, Christ's body, Christ's deeds) relates to what we cannot see (God the Father, Christ's divinity). The question of the perceptibility of the Divine culminated in the iconoclastic and hesychastic controversies, to which the mirror analogy almost lends itself.[11]

Icons

The eighth and ninth centuries in Byzantium witnessed a major controversy on representation, widely known as iconoclasm. The question was whether it is appropriate to venerate icons, despite the prohibition 'You shall not make for yourself a carved image, or any likeness' in the Ten Commandments.[12] As the winning party were eventually those in favour of icon veneration, the writings of those against are only transmitted in excerpts quoted by their opponents. However, we can reconstruct the main lines of the controversy. One argument brought against icons was that they could depict only the human nature of Christ, therefore venerating them is denying Christ's double nature as God and human. The iconophile answer was that the icon is a symbol referring to the original; as such, it essentially refers to the original as a whole, regardless its own nature and the deficiencies of the representation. John of Damascus (*ca.* 650–*ca.* 750), the most prominent theologian of the iconophile party, wrote quoting Paul's *Letter to the Corinthians*: 'As the divine apostle says, "We see now through a mirror in a riddle". The icon, too, is a mirror and a riddle, according to the denseness of our body'.[13] Similarly, Theodore the Studite (759–826), a leading personality in the second phase of the icon controversy, wrote in one of his letters:

> It seems to me that this fits with the example of the mirror; indeed, it is possible to say that the face of the viewer appears in the mirror, and yet the likeness remains outside the matter. Even if he thinks that he kisses his image there, he does not embrace the matter, because it is not for the matter that he comes close, but for the likeness represented in it. This likeness adheres to the material of the mirror. Anyway, as soon as he moves away from the mirror, gone is with him the image too, for it does not inhere in the material of the mirror. The same can be said then of the material of the icon: if the likeness that is seen in it and towards which the veneration is directed were to disappear, the material would remain without veneration, because it would have nothing in common with the likeness.[14]

After the victory of the iconophile party and the hence unquestioned veneration of icons in Byzantine culture, the mirror imagery became one of the literary topoi regarding icons. Thus, the epigram by Manuel Philes (*ca.* 1275–1345) on an icon commissioned by a certain Kallierges after he was healed miraculously, reads as follows: 'O stranger, observing clearly in the mirrors of the images / marvel at the picture of the miracle'.[15]

Hesychasm

One of the last major theological disputes of the Byzantine times was the hesychast controversy. It began as an attack on mystical practices, but soon became a dispute on the perceptibility of God. In 1336/1337 Barlaam the Calabrian mocked the practice of Byzantine monks, who called themselves 'hesychasts' (lit.: those keeping stillness), of praying constantly repeating the short phrase 'Lord Jesus Christ, Son of God, have mercy upon me the sinner' with the gaze fixed on their navel. This method of prayer should lead to seeing a light, which the hesychasts interpreted as the divine light manifested by Christ in his Transfiguration. Soon the dispute turned to whether this light was God: many Byzantine theologians argued that the hesychasts' claim to seeing the divine light contradicted the Christian belief that God is invisible and unfathomable. To answer these accusations the chief theorist of the hesychast party, Gregory Palamas, developed the teaching of God's *uncreated* energies as opposed to his substance: God's substance is unfathomable, but God's energies can be perceived. These energies, however, are not God's creation according to Palamas, but part of God himself. The latter was the main objection of anti-palamite theologians, who accused Palamas of introducing multiple deities. Palamas' theology was officially recognized by the Byzantine Church. As in the case of icons, also in the theory of the energies vs. substance the mirror analogy lends itself:

> Sight is formed from the manifold dispositions of colours and shapes, smell from odours, taste from flavours, hearing from sounds, touching from things rough or smooth according to position. The formations that occur in the senses arise from bodies that are not bodies though corporeal, for they do not arise from bodies in an absolute sense, but rather from the forms which are associated with bodies. They are not themselves the forms of bodies but the impressions left by the forms, like images inseparably separate from the forms associated with the bodies. This is more evident in the case of vision and especially in the case of objects seen in mirrors.[16]

The properties of a body, claims Palamas, are inseparable from the body itself, but it is the properties that one perceives, not the entire body. He explains the distinction between body and properties (representing substance and energy) by the mirror analogy: it is not the body, but its visual properties that are reflected.

Mirror of God as a state of perfection

The 'unspotted mirror' of the *Book of Wisdom* could also refer to humans mirroring God, as expressed in a passage from Paul's *Second Letter to the Corinthians*: 'As all of us reflect the glory of the Lord with unveiled faces, we are becoming more like him with ever-increasing glory by the Lord's Spirit'.[17] This has moral/ascetic repercussions: the cleaner the mirror, the more accurate the reflection; the more one has purged himself/herself from passions, the clearer he/she reflects God's glory. The mirror analogy was thus used in exhortations and catecheses, mostly monastic. 'You are, by Christ's grace, sober and vigilant, reflecting the glory of the Lord with unveiled face. For, since you took away from your eyes the rheum of the attachment to the world through your holy conduct of obedience, you see things clearly, I mean the vanity of life, the close succession of forceful impulses in every way of human whirling, and that there is only one stable and lovable, God,' writes the aforementioned Theodore the Studite in a catechesis addressed to the monks of his monastery.[18] It also became a literary topos in hagiographic literature – hymns, epigrams, encomia: the saint was praised for having become an unspotted mirror of the divinity. 'Your purest heart, martyr, is an unspotted mirror of the Holy Spirit, shining with mystic rays', writes John Mauropous (eleventh century) in a hymn for Saint Demetrios.[19]

Literature as mirror: Letters and encomia

The concept of accessing a remote original through a tangible token that participates in it permeated Byzantine thinking, also beyond theology, such as in epistolography. In Byzantine intellectual life letter writing was not only a way of communicating practicalities, but also a means of maintaining and strengthening interpersonal ties *in absentia*. Among the epistolographic topoi was that receiving and reading the letter was like seeing the sender in person through a mirror.[20] An early example is found in a letter by Basil of Caesarea (fourth century), whose correspondence, as well as his brother's Gregory of Nyssa and his friend's Gregory of Nazianz, were considered exemplary throughout the Byzantine period. Basil wrote to his friend Ascholius of Thessalonica that he was delighted to receive his letter, even though circumstances did not allow a personal encounter, 'since it was really possible to behold even your very soul, as it were, shining through a sort of mirror of words.'[21] Centuries later, between 1208 and 1217, Euthymios Tornikes wrote to his friend Michael Choniates: 'Dwelling on your most wise letters and fixing thereupon the insight of the mind, we illustrate in them as in good mirrors some divine apparitions of your angel-like sight.'[22] And in the fourteenth century Gregory Chioniades wrote: 'We already gladly got in our hand the marvelous mirror (διόπτραν) of your dear letter, best friend and best man, and floated it leisurely and with pleasure, and nonetheless we saw its gold-gleaming ray mirrored clearly, and (we saw mirrored) how you appropriate our affairs, honouring nothing at all more than spiritual friendship.'[23]

If in epistolographic topoi it is the author who is mirrored in his or her product, in encomiastic literature it is the object of the encomion that is mirrored. The text is a mirror, through which the listeners can contemplate on the object of praise. This is the background of the following passage on the biblical Abraham, originating in a homily falsely attributed to John Chrysostom (fourth century) and reproduced verbatim in a catechesis by Theodore the Studite. After bringing the example of painters, who spend several days observing their model, the text continues: 'As we are about to paint now, not a type of a bodily form, but the beauty of the soul and mental prettiness and flourishing conduct of the righteous, and the meekness, and the gentleness, and the magnanimity, and all the other virtuousness, it is necessary to indulge longer in this, so that, by the continuous mirroring (διοπτρίσεως) of the words, we do not miss the likeness of the archetype.'[24] The words of the encomium function as a mirror, through which the audience can observe Abraham. Thus, the author continues, one can deposit the image in their souls, so that they can carry it and find solace in it anywhere. Literature as mirror not of a person, but of deeds, is the idea beyond the mirror simile in a speech to the Emperor John the Comnenian, written in 1138 by Michael Italikos. The author praises the Emperor for his struggles in Syria, claiming that it is the deeds that make the words bright, not the other way round: 'For a splendid image of the glory is sparkling upon the words, reflecting from the struggles upon the words, since the deed is seen in it as if in a mirror.'[25]

II. 'Through a mirror in a riddle': Medium and revelation

In the passages discussed in the previous section the mirror analogy pertains to the relation between two ontologically different entities, namely the original and its reflection. The function of the mirror does not go beyond reflection. In other contexts, however, the mirror functioned as a means to seeing things otherwise concealed, whereas questions on the nature of the original and the image remained untouched. The mirror as medium to revelation is a common metaphor throughout the Middle Ages – including the description of Maximoú's gown at the beginning of this article. The background of this mirror metaphor in Antiquity and the Middle Ages was the belief that mirrors were means to prophecy and clairvoyance, manifested in the practice of catoptromancy, i.e. divination using a mirror, and its related forms – notably lecanomancy, i.e. divination using a bowl filled with a liquid.[26]

The mirror functions as medium in a much-quoted passage from 1 Corinthians 13, 12: 'we see now through a mirror in a riddle, and then face to face'.[27] There are two things to point out regarding the English translation of this passage. The first is the phrase 'δι' ἐσόπτρου', which I translated as 'through a mirror'. The King James Bible preserves the sense of the Greek preposition διὰ by translating '*through* a glass', whereas modern English translations have '*in* a mirror'. The ancient and medieval concept of the mirror as a medium, largely lost today, is preserved in further older European translations: in German, Martin Luther translated '*durch* einen Spiegel', whereas the modern German standard translation (Einheitsübersetzung) has '*in* einen Spiegel'; the standard French translation by Louis Segond (nineteenth century) has '*au moyen d*'un miroir'. The second point regards the literal translation of 'ἐν αἰνίγματι' to 'in a riddle'. English versions of the Bible usually translate 'obscurely' or, less often, 'darkly'. However, Byzantine authors, some of whom I will quote subsequently, wrote of riddles in allusion of this passage, therefore I opted for preserving the word 'riddle'.

The mirror in this Pauline passage is ambivalent: the view it allows is mediated, and therefore imperfect; on the other hand, it is still the best one can hope for in present life. The ambivalence towards the mirror as medium is retained throughout the Byzantine period. When this passage is quoted, then it is mostly with an emphasis to the temporary imperfection of the vision. Thus, it became a hagiographical topos to praise the saint not only for being a stainless mirror, but also for having overcome the mediation of mirrors after entering the Heavenly Kingdom. For example in a canon, a popular hymnographic genre with a highly formulaic structure, Saint Nicephorus, Patriarch of Constantinople, is thus praised: 'Now, father, you contemplate the Divine, not in a riddle, as the shadow and the mirrors are gone, but you enjoy Christ being full of divine light.'[28] Often, however, although without reference to 1 Corinthians 13, 12, the mirror as medium enables vision. The following passage from Gregory of Nyssa (fourth century) combines the simile of the mirror as a reflexion of the archetype examined in the previous section with that of the mirror as a means through which the spectators can reach higher knowledge:

> I remember having promised before to show you the picture of things about the Father and the Son as through a mirror (δι' ἐσόπτρου), because what concerns the divine nature is not subjected to human reason. [...] Although he was not human, he appeared as human, but was and still is God in nature, having circumscribed his unfathomable greatness in a body and shown us his whole greatness of God as if through a mirror (δι' ἐσόπτρου), so that we can use it as a mirror (διόπτρᾳ) and become spectators of the father too.[29]

The two functions of the mirror may be regarded as two aspects of one and the same. Notice, however, the different terms for mirror: whereas the mirror circumscribing God's greatness is called ἔσοπτρον, the mirror one uses to contemplate (shift to the spectator!) is called διόπτρα.

The literal meaning of the latter, *dioptra*, is see-through. It is most commonly used for an instrument to measure the distance between two distant objects, including celestial bodies.[30] The term is never used for actual mirrors – overall, actual mirrors are rare in Byzantine texts. The meaning 'mirror' for *dioptra* is listed after other surveying instruments in several Byzantine lexica.[31] It is precisely in this meaning, namely as a means to contemplate on things otherwise concealed, that διόπτρα is used in metaphors as an alternative to the two other words for mirror, κάτοπτρον and ἔσοπτρον. The function of the mirror as means to vision in Late Antique and Byzantine texts is twofold: it can be a see-through veil, which reduces the splendour of the object to such a degree that it can be viewed without destroying the viewer, or it can be a device, in which things present and future or distant are seen clearly in their true nature.

The see-through veil

Maximoú's thin gown at the beginning of this article was not the first revealing garment in a romance to be compared to a mirror. Already in the second century CE, Achilles Tatius wrote the erotic 'novel' *Leucippe and Clitophon*. In this the heroine's garments are thus described: 'the breasts (were) confined, as well as her tunic, by a girdle: and the tunic was a mirror (κάτοπτρον) of the body'.³² In most cases, however, the mirror as veil is revealing precisely because it is impossible to see with the bare eye, often by retaining the erotic connotations. For example, the emperor Theodore II Laskaris (*ca.* 1174–1221) writes to his friend George Akropolites in an allegorical narration that he was brought by the personified Virtue to a magnificent palace. Throned in this was a glorious king, who welcomed him and presented him with two women. At dusk the sun personally entered the palace. The narrator could not bear the brightness of the sun, so the two women 'drew some beautiful embroideries from inside their clothes, covered my eyes and ordered me to see as in/through a mirror (ὡς ἐσόπτρῳ), and they said that there is no other way to look at the sun except from this'.³³ Similar is the function of the mirror in the laudatory verses by the already mentioned poet Manuel Philes. The mirror enabling the viewer to see the dazzling beauty not of God, but of the praised person, are the words of a poem: 'I take the figure of the mirror (διόπτρα) of the words / and watch your beauty without blinking'.³⁴

The mirror as see-through veil is usually attested in metaphoric or allegoric usage, but sometimes it seems to be used literally. In the *Acts of Thomas*, a third century New Testament apocryphal, the Apostle Thomas is summoned by the Indian/Parthian king Gondophares to bless his newly-wed daughter and son-in-law. After that, in a passage echoing the encratitic origin of the text (i.e. from an early Christian sect preaching sexual abstinence and vegetarianism), Jesus himself persuades the couple to practice a celibate marriage. The next morning the bride turns up unveiled and explains to her baffled parents: 'I will no more veil myself, because the mirror (ἔσοπτρον) of shame is removed from me; and therefore am I no more ashamed or abashed, because the deed of shame and confusion is departed far from me.'³⁵ It is possible that the choice of the word ἔσοπτρον instead of more common words for veil was a hint to the readers to interpret the passage allegorically in a gnostic/encratite context: the veil prohibiting a direct view of higher things is a result of corporeality, sin and shame, whereas asceticism removes the veil and leads to higher levels of contemplation. It is worth noting that the modern editor of this text did not consider the interpretational possibilities of the ancient and medieval terms for mirror and suggested in the critical apparatus the emendation σκέπαστρον (cover/veil) in the place of ἔσοπτρον. In a similar sense, in a poem on the properties of animals Manuel Philes writes of animals who supposedly see while sleeping that 'the overcoat of their eyelids is wide open, since another softer shift guards their pupils like a mirror (διόπτρας)'.³⁶

What is noteworthy in all these passages, is that all three words for mirror, ἔσοπτρον, κάτοπτρον and διόπτρα are used in the sense of 'see-through veil'. This means that 'see-through veil' was not just a second meaning of one of these words. It rather points to the conceptual relation of mirrors and veils in the Medieval Greek mind.

Prophecy and clairvoyance

In another biblical apocryph, the *Acts of John*, originating in a gnostic milieu, Jesus sings the following song before his arrest, while his disciples form a circle around him holding hands and singing the refrain: 'A lamp am I to you [singular] who behold me. Amen. A mirror am I to you who perceive me. Amen. A door am I to you who knock at me. Amen. A way am I to you a wayfarer.'[37] The mirror metaphor is placed between the lamp, and the door and way metaphors – between illumination and passage. A hole allowing the only vision possible of the divine is likened to a mirror in the *Dispute against a Jew* by Nicholas of Otranto (D. 1235). Nicholas is referring to Exodus 33, 18–23, in which Moses asks God that he may see his glory. God answers: 'you cannot see my face; for man shall not see me and live'. Instead, he orders Moses to hide in a hole of a rock, which God will cover with his hand until he passes by; then God will remove his hand and Moses will see his back. This is for Nicholas an argument in favour of the Incarnation: God's back was seen 'by a mirror (ὑπὸ ἐσόπτρου), the hole of the rock, that is, the God-bearer Mary.'[38] Imagery with sexual connotations was not rare regarding Christ's birth.

The mirror is a means not only for theophany, but also for envisioning the affairs of this world in their true nature, without the constraints of space, time and visibility. This is what the simile in an account of miracles performed by Saint Hilarion implied. The author, the Cypriot hermit Neophytos the Recluse (*1134), recounts the story of a certain Italikos, whose horses participated in the hippodrome races. A godless rival put a charm on Italikos' horses and charioteers, and mocked his Christian faith. Fearing defeat, but also to save the honour of his faith, Italikos resorted to Saint Hilarion. The saint ordered Italikos to hold a cup full of water in his hands. 'And lo, he saw everything clearly in the water as if in a mirror, namely the horses and the horse stables and the charioteers and the chariots, all bound by the spells of the opponents.'[39] In the bowl Italikos saw not only things that were remote, but also the otherwise invisible bonds of the spells. Needless to say, Italikos won, after sprinkling all he had seen with the water of the bowl. Notice that lecanomancy, otherwise condemned by the Byzantine Church, is an acceptable process when performed by a saint.

As already indicated above, it is in connection with visionary revelation that the otherwise uncommon term διόπτρα as mirror is used. The Byzantine mystic Symeon the New Theologian (949–1022) claims in one of his poems that few holy individuals (including himself) receive the divine light, but that they are not recognized by the masses, just as Christ was not recognized as God by those who saw him only with their bodily eyes; he continues: 'only to those who have the eye of their soul cleared do we appear as in a mirror (διόπτρα); but by the impure, neither God nor ourselves are seen, nor are we believed to have become such (sc. holy) at all'.[40] At about the same time in the *Life of Saint Basil the Younger* the first-person narrator, Gregory, a disciple of Saint Basil, was granted a vision of the Last Judgement. After a lengthy description of the rewards and the punishments he recounts his awakening with the following words: 'When I awoke from that awesome and immeasurable astonishment and vision and considered the dioptra through which I had seen these things etc.'[41] The editors and translators chose to leave the word διόπτρα untranslated. In a similar sense a liturgical canon (hymn) in honour of the prophets says: The unstained mirror (διόπτρα) of prophecy, apprehending the future with foreseeing eyes, indicates it afore as present, and echoes the distant as near.[42] A praise for the Emperor by Manuel Philes includes the verse 'The dense intellect, the mirror (διόπτρα) of the words'.⁴³ But also the more common terms for mirror, ἔσοπτρον and κάτοπτρον, were used in connection with prophecy. In the fourteenth century Nicephoros Callistos Xanthopoulos wrote in his *Church History* about the fourth-century Egyptian hermit Anthony: 'He used to say that if someone strongly desires to foresee, he shall be pure in the soul, and seeing the future will follow, as God will show him the knowledge of future things in a mirror (ἐσόπτρου)'.⁴⁴ The aforementioned Neophytos the Recluse praises John Chrysostom (i.e. the gold-mouthed) as 'the all-golden mirror (ἔσοπτρον), revealing the unseen and hidden'.⁴⁵

For those who were not granted prophetic visions themselves, prophetic books could function as a mirror. 'Poor me!' wrote Michael Choniates in a poem on the Second Coming of Christ. 'My hair stands on end and my heart beats / as I see in written characters, as in a mirror, / what horrible punishments await us.'⁴⁶

III. Mirror as title metaphor: The *Dioptra*

Literature as a mirror was a topos in the multifarious functions of the mirror metaphor examined above: epistolographic literature as a mirror reflecting its author, encomiastic literature mirroring the praised, literature as a shade filtering the glare and thus enabling the view of the original, literature as medium to see future things. Stratis Papaioannou analysed the normative function of mirrors as metaphors for literature, notably in the *Book of Ceremonies*.⁴⁷ The book, commissioned by the Emperor Constantine VII Porphyrogenitus (905–959), is a compilation of material about imperial ceremonies, many of which were at that time in disuse. Its function was to represent an ideal, not the current state. The preface claims that the book shall be a 'transparent mirror (κάτοπτρον) [...], in which both what is appropriate to imperial authority and what is worthy of the senatorial body might be seen'.⁴⁸

Literature as mirror was a topos not only in Byzantine literature, but, even more, in Western European literature from the Middle Ages and beyond. From the twelfth century the mirror became a popular title metaphor for works written in Middle Latin (speculum) and in vernacular languages (miroir, myreur, mirour, mirouer, merour, specchio, Spiegel etc.). The innumerable works thus titled ranged from normative treatises that should lead to self-knowledge and self-improvement, to comprehensive descriptions, in which the reader could 'see', as if in a mirror, the world or part of it.⁴⁹

In Byzantium the mirror as title metaphor never became a trend. The only Byzantine work thus titled was the *Dioptra*, written in 1095 by the monk Philippos, usually referred to as Monotropos.⁵⁰ The *Dioptra* is written in over 7000 'political' verses, i.e. 15-syllable verses, a metre first recorded in the Middle Byzantine period that has become increasingly popular up to date. It is structured in five books: the first (or, in another version, fifth) is a 'catanyctic' poem of contrition addressed to the soul – a quite common form of poetic expression that should lead to mourning for one's sins and repenting.⁵¹ The other four books have the form of a dialogue between the body (Greek σάρξ, feminine) and the soul (Greek ψυχή, feminine), personified as maid and mistress respectively. The mistress poses questions on various theological and philosophical questions, ranging from 'What shall I do to achieve salvation?' to 'Why is the voice different from human to human?' or 'Why did God not create all humans at once, as he created the angels?' The answers are based on scriptural and patristic knowledge, as well as natural science interpreted within a Christian context. These were questions that occupied the mind of both a monastic and an urbane, averagely or above-averagely educated audience.[52] This, together with the simple language, the vivid metre and a touch of humour, lead to the considerable popularity of the *Dioptra*.

The title metaphor is not elaborated in any part of the book. The title of the Slavic translation, made in the fourteenth century, is the transliteration 'dioptra', which is subsequently interpreted as, depending on dialect, zъrcalo/zercalo, meaning mirror.[53] Other title metaphors in Late Antique and Medieval Greek literature have connotations of *anthology* – itself a metaphor, meaning a selection of various flowers: Στρωματεῖς means patchwork,[54] Κύκλος means circle,[55] Στέφανος means garland (made of various flowers),[56] Κλίμαξ means ladder (consisting of steps),[57] Μέλισσα means bee (collecting nectar from various flowers).[58] In the light of the connotations of the mirror metaphor in Byzantine literature, it is reasonable to assume that the title metaphor in the *Dioptra* is to be interpreted in a similar way to its Western equivalents: as a mirror, through which the readers can get a clear overview of things visible and invisible, present and future.

The eleventh-century work of the monk Philippos was not the first to be titled *Dioptra*. In the first century CE, Hero of Alexandria, who authored several treatises on various instruments (including mirrors), wrote a treatise on the homonymous instrument for measuring the distance between two distant objects.[59] A similar work titled *Geodesy* was known in Byzantium, too; this stands very close to the context of the Heronian *Dioptra* and is ascribed to a Hero or Hero of Byzantium (or Hero the younger).[60] It is therefore likely that Philippos knew of Hero's work. Indeed, he had a keen, if not profound, interest in science, which he liked to show off time and again. If this is the case, then the title metaphor of the *Dioptra* would include the connotations of mirrors as means to prophetic revelation, while nodding at Hellenistic scholarship – a combination typical of Philippos.

Conclusion

The mirror was a popular metaphor with multiple interpretational possibilities from the Antiquity to Eastern and Western Middle Ages and beyond. In this article I left out of my scope the normative function of the mirror as means to self-reflection. Instead, I concentrated on two different but related concepts, based mostly on philosophical/theological, but also secular texts. The first is reflection. A mirror could be Christ's body and deeds as a human, reflecting his divinity. It could be an icon, reflecting the depicted person. It could be God's perceivable works, reflecting his unperceivable substance. It could be a virtuous human, reflecting God. It could be a piece of literature, reflecting its author, or its subject. The second concept is vision aid. A mirror could be a shade, enabling vision by reducing the unbearable glare of the object. It could be a medium for clearer vision of things extant, but invisible to the bare eye. This medium could be a book. Thus, the mirror metaphor represents two major traits of Byzantine thought: that the unfathomable is reflected in the fathomable, and that the visible and invisible, past, present and future form an entity, concealed for the many but waiting to be revealed.

CHAPTER 12
MIRRORS AND MIRRORING IN DREAMS: SELF-REFLECTION AND LIMINALITY IN THE *ROMAN DE LA ROSE* AND IN THE *HYPNEROTOMACHIA POLIPHILI*[1]

Efthymia Priki

Oh, Kitty! how nice it would be if we could only get through into Looking-glass House! I'm sure it's got, oh! such beautiful things in it!

Let's pretend there's a way of getting through into it, somehow, Kitty. Let's pretend the glass has got all soft like gauze, so that we can get through. Why, it's turning into a sort of mist now, I declare! It'll be easy enough to get through —' She was up on the chimney-piece while she said this, though she hardly knew how she had got there. And certainly the glass was beginning to melt away, just like a bright silvery mist.

In another moment Alice was through the glass, and had jumped lightly down into the Looking-glass room.

Carroll 1871, 11–12

The curious tale of Alice and of her adventures in the dream world that she finds 'through the looking glass', written by Lewis Carroll in 1871, has fed childhood imaginations for generations. The inversion of reality, the liminality of a reflective surface, and the creative potential of a dream narrative, all central themes both in *Through the Looking Glass* and in *Alice in Wonderland*, have made these stories a constant source of inspiration in popular culture. These themes, however, are deeply rooted in literary traditions all over the world. Already in antiquity mirrors were constructing liminal spaces; the terms εἴδωλον in Ancient Greek or *simulacrum* in Latin, for example, were used to describe both the shades of dreams and the dead, as well as a mirror's reflections.[2] Moreover, there are numerous examples in world literature from the epic of Gilgamesh (e.g. Tablet 7, Enkidu's dream) to medieval romances and early modern fairy tales where the device of the dream narrative has been used providing authors with a blank space – similar to a blank canvas – where they have the creative liberty to construct their own imaginary worlds, to impersonate ideas, divine forces and other abstractions, to be sexually explicit, to make the impossible possible, and to orchestrate supernatural intervention in their characters' stories giving clues, prophecies, or consolation. This creativity is best exemplified in the construction of oneiric otherworlds, which often serve utopian or dystopian functions.[3]

Michel Foucault, in his 1967 essay 'Des espaces autres', proposed the term *heterotopias* in order to define those sites (*emplacements*) that 'are endowed with the curious property of being in relation with all the others, but in such a way as to suspend, neutralize, or invert the set of relationships designed, reflected or mirrored by themselves'.[4] Interestingly, Foucault categorizes mirrors as a site that provides a joint experience as both a utopia, being a placeless place, and a heterotopia, since the mirror is an object that exists in reality and counteracts with it. As I have argued elsewhere,[5] another sort of 'place' that could also be categorized as a heterotopia is dream space – we could perhaps call it *oneiric heterotopia* – which is, actually, often associated with mirrors or mirror metaphors.[6]

Taking the correlation of mirrors, dreams, and liminality, as well as Foucault's notion of heterotopia as starting points, in what follows I will examine two cases, one from thirteenth-century France and one from fifteenth-century Italy, where these themes converge in two narratives about a dreamer's initiation in love. In the Old French *Roman de la Rose* and the early printed prose romance *Hypnerotomachia Poliphili*, a first-person narrator takes the reader through his initiation, which is presented as a spatial progress towards the gods of love and towards the object of desire that is achieved through a series of threshold crossings, ritual gestures and instructive sessions. The dream frame of these first-person narratives has several implications on the use and function of space therein. Dream spaces and spatial objects can be designed to be as fluid and mutable as the dreamers' minds. Their ekphrastic descriptions express the subjective experience of an ever-changing and ever-expanding liminal space, which is intricately connected with the psychological state of the dreamers-narrators – a state which, just as the dream spaces, is constructed by the author. The liminality and subjectivity inherent in these oneiric heterotopias is particularly evident when the dreamers are confronted with mirrors and other reflective surfaces. In both texts, such spatial elements and artefacts may function as thresholds, particularly when accompanied with acts of self-reflection, often facilitating those transitions in the initiation process that carry the most tension and contradiction, because of their association with the realization of the dreamers' identity. Below, I will examine the use and function of mirrors and of other reflective surfaces in the two texts, focusing on their significance in the narrative and spatial structure of the dreams. Particular emphasis will be given on two crucial moments of the dreamers' initiations, namely, Amant's encounter with the fountain of Narcissus in the *Roman de la Rose* and Poliphilo's exploration of the triumphal portal in the *Hypnerotomachia*.

The *Roman de la Rose* is an allegorical verse romance, in which the poet introduces himself as the first-person narrator of a past dream, which takes place on a May morning and in which the dreamer discovers an enclosed garden where his initiation unfolds leading to his encounter with the Rose, his object of desire. The *Rose* survives in about 320 manuscripts and manuscript fragments with dates ranging from the thirteenth to the sixteenth century, as well as in many printed editions from the fifteenth and sixteenth centuries. Due to its continued popularity, it has exerted enormous influence on love poetry in later periods, both in France and abroad. Italy was no exception. Scholars have examined the *Rose*'s influence on *Il Fiore* and on Dante's *Commedia*, but few have ventured into a comparative examination with the *Hypnerotomachia,* possibly due to the fact that the texts (particularly the *Hypnerotomachia*) were not easily accessible, especially in terms of language. In 1910, Luigi Foscolo Benedetto, published a study examining Italian works influenced by the Rose, including among them the *Hypnerotomachia*. In his comparative analysis, Benedetto does not go in depth but rather briefly comments on some common plot elements, such as the direct or indirect intervention of Venus or the reserved character of Bel Accueil and Polia, to illustrate that there is indeed a point of contact between the two works. More recent comparative studies include an article by Gilles Polizzi (1990), where he focuses on a comparison of the gardens in the *Rose* with those in the *Songe de Poliphile*, the 1546 French edition of the *Hypnerotomachia*, demonstrating the development in the perceptions of the garden and the manifestation of a new style of garden design representative of renaissance gardens, as well as an article by Hester Lees-Jeffries (2006), in which she compares the fountains in the two texts and their narrative function. The present study aims to investigate the relationship between the two works a bit further, identifying some thematic and structural parallels relating to the scenes discussed.

The *Roman de la Rose* is comprised by two parts, written by two different poets: Guillaume de Lorris and Jean de Meun. Guillaume de Lorris' part, written between 1225 and 1230, comprises the first 4056 lines of the romance ending abruptly, without the story coming to a conclusion. The seemingly unfinished narrative was later continued by Jean de Meun who provides a lengthy narrative of about 17620 lines. The continuation dates between 1269 and 1278.[7] Here, I will only discuss the events in Guillaume's *Rose*, considering it in its own terms, especially given that the dreamer's initiation in love is more or less completed in the first 4000 lines and that the poem's unending is in itself an important parameter in the interpretation of Guillaume's text.[8]

A key element for understanding the spatial aesthetics of Guillaume's *Rose*, but also its allegorical significance, is the use of mirrors and of other reflective surfaces along with the dynamics of vision.[9] The narrative progresses with the dreamer penetrating a series of mental, metaphorical and spatial enclosures (the dream itself, the garden, Deduit's *carole*, the fountain, the rose-garden), which constitute the liminal points of his initiatory journey. Most of these threshold crossings are accomplished through the act of looking through a reflective surface, which is either metaphorical – i.e. the dream as a mirror, distorting or bending reality – or spatially defined, such as the mirror of Oiseuse and Narcissus' fountain.

Oiseuse, traditionally translated as Idleness, is the gatekeeper to Deduit's garden, which the dreamer discovers in his dream. She is portrayed as a beautiful young lady holding a comb and a mirror (Fig. 12.1). Oiseuse's beauty and her preoccupation with her appearance – evident in the possession of a mirror – sets her in direct opposition to the images of Vices on the wall of the garden, with their ugly and pale appearances. As Sarah Grace Heller argues, Oiseuse 'sets the tone for the work's standard of luminescent beauty and illustrates some important aspects of medieval colour perception. Oiseuse is instrumental in introducing the lover to beauty and, thereby, to love'.[10]

The allegorical meaning of Oiseuse and, especially, of her mirror as well as her significance as a gatekeeper have been an issue of rigorous debate,[11] which has generated

Fig. 12.1 Oiseuse with her attributes and the dreamer. Bibliothèque nationale de France, fr. 12593 (fourteenth century), f. 6r. Source: https://gallica.bnf.fr/ark:/12148/btv1b6000348j (accessed 18 November 2018).

various interpretations for her role in the *Rose* and her place in literary and artistic tradition. A compelling argument regarding the role of this character is offered by Marta Harley (1986) who connects Oiseuse with Ovid's Salmacis, a water nymph whose main attributes are also a comb and a mirror, providing thus an interpretative basis for Oiseuse's role and for her relationship with Amant and the fountain. In Book IV of Ovid's *Metamorphoses*, an evident subtext to the *Rose*, Salmacis forcibly merges with her object of desire, Hermaphroditus, into one body inside her fountain, which is then cursed to transform all who enter it into intersex beings. The supernatural entrapment of an object-of-desire/lover by a divine being at the site of a fountain with magical qualities and the merging of the lover with the beloved are elements occurring in Guillaume's *Rose* as well, as it will be shown further below.

Regarding the importance of Oiseuse's mirror in the crossing of this threshold, there are a couple of points to be made.[12] Firstly, this mirror foreshadows the mirror-like fountain of Narcissus[13] and, consequently, Oiseuse can be viewed as the dreamer's counter-image in the garden, mirroring his future actions as well as his present attitude towards pleasure; a pleasure that is mainly derived from looking at things.[14] Lewis also draws attention to the key with which Oiseuse unlocks the door – an element that is sometimes included in miniatures depicting the scene, replacing Oiseuse's other attributes – juxtaposing it to the key with which Amour locks Amant's heart.[15] Therefore, in her capacity as a gatekeeper, Oiseuse may be viewed as the dreamer's mirror-image through which he passes into the garden. From this perspective and taking into account the intertextual parallel between Oiseuse and Salmacis, the dreamer also resembles the Ovidian nymph in that he becomes infatuated at the location of a fountain with the Rose, with which his identity, as we shall see, momentarily merges. Secondly, Oiseuse's act of looking at her own reflection in her mirror accentuates the fact that this is an inward looking and exclusive garden, but more importantly it draws attention to the female body as a visual object,[16] thus, anticipating the sight of the rose, the desired object, in the fountain of Narcissus.

The 'jeu de miroir' in the *Rose*, as Stephen G. Nichols characterized it,[17] serves not only as a means to multiply perspectives, but it also alters the dreamer's perception of the world around him, thus, causing the transformation of the dream space.[18] There are two notable examples of such spatial transformations. The first is when the actual bedroom where the narrator has fallen asleep is substituted with an illusory image of that same bedroom, thus, deceiving the dreamer that the illusion is real. The second instance is when he gazes into the fountain of Narcissus and its magical crystals. By doing so, he discovers a new space, the enclosed rose-garden that does not seem to be a part of Deduit's garden, but rather a place inside the reflective surface of the fountain. Such an assumption is supported by the fact that its location within the garden is not specified and, in addition, by the dreamer's obscure displacement from the site of the fountain to that of the rose-garden, which gives the impression that the dreamer has passed through the perilous mirror of the fountain and has found himself in a new spatial context, an alternative version of the garden. But let us look more closely at this episode.

After exploring the entirety of Deduit's garden, the dreamer reaches a pleasing spot with a fountain under a pine tree, whose location within the garden is rather vague. Apart from a marble stone through which two water channels are gushing forth and which bears an inscription on its upper edge labelling the structure as the fountain of Narcissus, the fountain has no distinguishable artificial characteristics, its most remarkable feature being two crystals at its bottom that have marvellous properties. The fountain's crystals have puzzled scholars generating a plethora of different, sometimes complementary but often opposing, views. They have been interpreted as the eyes of the lady,[19] as the eyes of the dreamer,[20] or even as the eyes of both,[21] while some scholars propose completely different interpretations, viewing the fountain with its crystals as an allegory of vision,[22] as a rhetorical apparatus and an allegory of the allegorical dream vision,[23] or as an image of fiction.[24] The crucial element as regards the crystals and the fountain, in my opinion, is the emphasis on number two (two water channels, two crystals at its bottom), a duality which has significant implications for this pivotal point in the dreamer's initiation in love, pointing to a multiplicity of vision and of the self. In this respect, I tend to agree with Akbari's analysis:

> Simultaneously, the crystals mark a liminal moment in Guillaume's allegory of vision, for after the lover looks into them, he passes from the realm of reflected vision, intuitio, into that of refracted vision, detuitio or deduit. Just as the crystals, when struck by the sun, literally produce 'colors plus de cent' ('more than a hundred colours' 1544), so they allegorically produce a multiplication of the self: after his look into the fountain, the lover begins to encounter multiple redoubled images of himself in Amors, Amis, Dangiers, and Bel Acueil. The crystals simultaneously produce multiplication of what should have been a single object of desire: instead of a single rosebud, the lover comes to desire the young man who attends the rosebushes, Bel Acueil.[25]

It is at this point that the dreamer first encounters the desired object, but does so by looking at his own reflection and, thus, momentarily the Subject/Dreamer and the Other/Rose merge together, while also being separated from each other. This paradox is also expressed in the, probably deliberate, confusion between a plural (*.ij. pierres de cristal*; *cristaus*) and a singular form (*le cristal*) for the crystal(s),[26] which the dreamer discovers as soon as he finds the courage to approach the fountain (1535–1567):[27]

Ou fonz de la fontaine aval
Avoit **.ij. pierres de cristal**,
Qu'a grant entente remiré.
Mes une chose **vos** dire,
Qu'a mervoilles, ce cuit, tandroiz
Maintenant que vos l'entendroiz:
Quant li solaus qui tout aguete,
Ses rais en la fontaine gete,
Et la clartez aval descent,
Lors perent colors plus de .c.
Ou **cristal** qui par le soleil
Deviant jaunes, ynde, vermeil.
Si ot **le cristal** merveilleus
Itel force que touz li leus,
Arbres et flors et quanque orne
Li vergiers, i pert tout a orne.
Et por faire la chose entendre,
Un essemple vos vueil aprendre:
Ausis comme li mireors mostre
Les choses qui sont a l'ancontre
Et i veoit on sanz coverture
Et la color et la figure,
Trestout ausi vos di de voir,

> Que **li cristaus** sanz decevoir
> Tout l'estre dou vergier encuse
> **A ceaus qui dedanz l'eaue musent**
> Car tout jorz quell que part qu'il soient,
> L'une moitie dou vergier voient
> Et s'il se tornent maintenant,
> Puent veoir le remenant.
> Si n'i a si petite chose,
> tant soit repote ne enclose,
> Dont demostrance ne soit faite,
> Com s'ele ere ou cristal portraite.

> Down at the bottom of the spring were **two crystals**, which I gazed at most attentively. And I shall tell you something that will, I think, seem **marvellous** to you when you hear it. When the all-seeing sun sends down its rays into the spring, and light descends into its depths, more than a hundred colours appear in **the crystal**, which turns blue and yellow and red in the sunlight. **The crystal is so marvellous** and has such power that the whole place, with its trees and flowers and everything adorning the garden, is revealed there in due order. To help you understand the phenomenon I shall give you an illustration. **Just as things placed in front of a mirror are reflected in it,** and their appearance and colour are seen **quite plainly**, exactly so, I assure you, does **the crystal truly** disclose the whole of the garden **to those who gaze into the water**. For whichever side he is on, he can always see half of the garden, and by turning he is at once able to see the remainder. And so there is nothing so small, so secret, or so hidden that it is not displayed, as if it were etched in the crystal.[28]

A further point to be made in relation to the language of this passage is the use of the personal pronoun 'vos'. With this pronoun, the narrator refers to the readers, who are his implied audience, inviting them to penetrate his work of fiction. Furthermore, I would suggest that the reader is also invited to look into the fountain and its crystals and, from this point of view, the phrase '*A ceaus qui dedanz l'eaue musent*' (1559) is another reference to the readers. But how can the readers look into a fictional fountain? The answer is provided by understanding the crystals as a narrative device. Given that the fountain constitutes the narrative centre of the romance, its crystals, reflecting, on a spatial level, the two halves of the garden, could also reflect, on a narrative level, the two parts of the story: the first part where the dreamer enters the garden of Deduit and indulges in its pleasures and the second part, which is instigated by the episode at the Fountain of Narcissus, where the dreamer, now as Lover, strives to conquer his object of desire.[29] As it will be shown below, there is a significant shift at this point in the narrative: the dreamer becomes the Lover (Amant) and the garden of pleasure is transformed into a garden of love.[30] Therefore, the crystal(s) represent a liminal point with narrative, spatial and ritual ramifications. In what follows, I will examine closely at how this shift is achieved.

Mirrors and Mirroring

The dreamer, while being inside the garden, views the entire image of that garden by gazing into the fountain's crystal(s) and, at the same time, he is being stared at by a personification of the garden, Amour, the god of love. Therefore, not only does the fountain provide a more concentrated version of the garden, but there also seems to be a gradual narrowing of the dreamer's perception of space which anticipates his eventual entrapment by Amour.

Regarding the equation of the garden with the god of love, this is evident in Amour's first appearance as one of Deduit's companions in the *carole*. The dreamer describes Amour as being clothed in an almost indescribable robe, decorated with every imaginable flower of every possible colour, as well as with patterns of birds and beasts (lines 878–898). This description of his garment presents him as a concentrated version of the garden itself.[31] In other words, Amour encloses the concept of the garden and is himself enclosed by the garden. Considering the association of Amour with the garden, the fountain through the mirrored image of the garden, in which Amour/love is enclosed, becomes an emblem of the romance, and in extent, of fiction.

Moreover, if the crystals reveal everything within the garden, the dreamer would also come to the realization that he is being stalked like a prey by the god of love.[32] Even though the latter is not mentioned at this point, the dreamer characterizes the fountain as the '*mireors perilleus*' (1568), the perilous mirror and goes on to describe how Cupid set it as a trap to deceive and capture young men and women. Harley traces this cautionary remark about the fountain back to Ovid's *Metamorphoses*, not to the myth of Narcissus, but rather to the myth of Hermaphroditus, which is introduced with a comment on the contaminating waters of Salmacis' pool, which has a transformative power over the men who bathe therein (4.286–4.287).[33] It is interesting to note that the narrator now refers to the fountain as a '*fontaine d'amors*' (1594) whose properties are a '*mistere*' (1599) to be explained.

The scene reaches its climax when the dreamer, lured by the beauty of the fountain and the crystal(s), finally looks at his own reflection in the mirror-like fountain, realizing that it has also deceived him: he has fallen into Cupid's trap by falling in love with the rose. Thus, the mirror is perilous, because it activates the dreamer's erotic desire directed towards the Rose, at which moment Amour attacks with his five arrows and demands the dreamer's submission to him. By being entrapped by Amour and by swearing allegiance to him, he now becomes Amant, the lover.

There seems to be a superimposition of the act of actually approaching the rose-garden on the act of looking into the mirror and seeing the rose-garden (1612–1615, 1622–1626):

Ou mireor entre mil choses
Quenui rosiers chargez de roses
Qui estoient en un destor
D'une haie clos tout entor

I perceived in the mirror, among a thousand other things, rose-bushes laden with roses in a secluded place completely enclosed by a hedge.[34]

Vers le rosier tantost me tres
Et sachiez bien, quant je fui pres,
L'odors de la rose savoree
M'antra jusqu'an mi la coree
Que por noiant fuse embaumez.

I at once approached the rose-bushes, and I assure you that when I drew near, the sweet scent of the roses penetrated my very entrails and I was all but filled with their fragrance.[35]

And in another passage, when Amour shoots the dreamer with his arrows, the latter describes how he attempts to approach his chosen rose after each consecutive blow, until finally he makes 'a great effort to walk towards the little rose to which his heart was drawn':[36] *Et m'esforçai mout de marchier (…) Vers le rosier ou mes cuers tent* (1792–1794). Interestingly, the first arrow that strikes the dreamer (Beauty) penetrates his heart through the eye. Thus, the overlapping of the episode at the fountain and of his attempt to approach the rose creates a spatial confusion that may be resolved by understanding this liminal point in terms of an alteration in the dreamer's visual perception of the dream space caused by the refracted vision that the crystals provide and by Amour's supernatural interjection (first arrow) (Figs 12.2 and 12.3). At the end of this episode,

Fig. 12.2 Amant discovers the rose-garden. Bibliothèque nationale de France, fr. 1558 (early fourteenth century), f. 13v. Source: https://gallica.bnf.fr/ark:/12148/btv1b6000316k (accessed 18 November 2018).

Fig. 12.3 Amant is shot in the eye by Amour's arrow. Bibliothèque nationale de France, fr. 1558 (early fourteenth century), f. 14r. Source: https://gallica.bnf.fr/ark:/12148/btv1b6000316k (accessed 18 November 2018).

Amant is alone – Amour has mysteriously disappeared – lingering outside the enclosed rose-garden in the vicinity of which there is another structure, Raison's tower. Deduit's secluded space and the characters that the dreamer encountered there are never mentioned again, at least not in Guillaume's *Rose*. Therefore, while being inside a garden, suddenly Amant finds himself outside another garden, 'un jardin dans le jardin' as Marie Francoise Notz characterized it,[37] wanting to penetrate it as well. The rose-garden becomes the new focal point of the narrative, replacing the fountain which, simultaneously, encloses it. However, this garden is not as accessible as the garden of Deduit, especially not after being further enclosed by a fortified castle constructed by Jalousie in order to prevent and discourage Amant's advances on the Rose and on Bel Acueil, the figure who represents it.

The obstacles that prevent Amant from passing this final threshold are insurmountable and Guillaume's Amant never surpasses them. In this manner, the mirror-fountain, the enclosed rose-garden and the Castle of Jalousie become symbols of the unattainability of the lover's desire, which is deferred indefinitely by the poem's un-ending – Guillame's dreamer never wakes up.

Turning now to the *Hypnerotomachia Poliphili*, we venture into a completely different oneiric heterotopia in terms of scale, structure and aesthetics:[38] a humanistic heterotopia, which nevertheless draws heavily upon the medieval tradition and has both implicit and explicit references to the *Roman de la Rose*. *Hypnerotomachia* is an early printed book published in 1499 by Aldus Manutius in Venice. Despite being initially a business failure (Lowry, 1979, 124), the luxurious Aldine edition with its 172 woodcuts quickly became a *desideratum* for collectors, while it also exerted considerable influence on artistic and literary production in subsequent centuries. Part of its allure was the deliberate anonymity of its author, its strange, difficult to understand, macaronic language, and its enigmatic illustrations, whose meaning is attainable only through the reader's exploration of the text/image interactions within the book. The central plot revolves around Poliphilo as first-person narrator, and is, essentially, a lover's oneiric journey to find and retrieve his beloved Polia, who is revealed to be dead at the end of the book.

Poliphilo's dream is dominated by contradiction and paradox as he is torn between hope and despair, curiosity and fear, awe and terror, sexual urges and idealized desire, life and death. Such contradictions are particularly intense in the first stages of his initiatory dream journey. His movement from the calm and silent shore to the ruined city can be seen as a gradual development of these contradictions, which reach their climax in Poliphilo's encounter with the dragon. The hostile forces that haunt Poliphilo from the immense dark forest to the narrow dark labyrinth seem to be transformations of the same thing: the externalization of Poliphilo's emotional fears.[39]

The example examined here concerns Poliphilo's exploratory stroll in the ruined city dominated by the great pyramid. The entire pyramid complex in the ruined city is described in exhaustive detail with a long *ekphrasis* that begins with the exterior and interior of the great pyramid and then follows Poliphilo's gaze and movement within the piazza next to the pyramid, which includes the statue of a horse, a male colossus, and an elephant bearing an obelisk, before it finally concludes with a thorough exploration of the great portal (*porta triumphante*) of the pyramid.

The male colossus draws Poliphilo's attention by the groaning sound that the wind produces passing through its body. The interior of this gigantic statue is accessible through his mouth and all of its organs are designated with trilingual inscriptions in Chaldaean, Greek and Latin. By exploring it, Poliphilo is offered a lesson in human anatomy, but, on another level, this is also a self-reflective experience, since the male colossus is a spatial manifestation of Poliphilo himself. Consequently, when he reaches the heart, Poliphilo's emotions are intensified:

Et quando al core applicai, vidi legendo come d'amore si genera li sospiritti, et dove amore gravemente offende. Et quivi tutto commoto, dal profundo dil mio core subtraxi uno mugente suspiro, polia invocando. In tanto che tuta la erea machina risonare cum non poco horrore sentiti.[40]

And when I approached the heart, I saw by reading, how from love are generated the little spirits' sighs, and where love gravely strikes and hurts, and hereupon altogether moved, from the depth of my own heart I heaved a roaring sigh, calling upon Polia so much that I heard, with no little horror, all the bronze mechanism resonate.[41]

Mirrors and Mirroring

Coming out of the colossal human body, Poliphilo notices the forehead of the colossus' female counterpart, barely visible as it was buried beneath the ruins. Evidently, this female colossus is a spatial manifestation of Polia, who, even in this form, is still unattainable and remains unexplored. The fact that it is buried may be seen as a subtle reference to Polia's dead body.

However, for Poliphilo, the most captivating marvel in the ruined city is the triumphal portal, where he rushes with great desire after his exploration of the piazza monuments to contemplate its proportions and its decorations. This is the only full functioning element in this dream space and it serves as the sole threshold to be found in this enclosed valley: 'no one could exit, return, or enter except by this open portal' (*che niuno valeva d'indi uscire, overo indrieto ritornare, o intrare per questa patula porta*).[42]

The bas-reliefs with which the portal is decorated depict mythological scenes relating, particularly, to Aphrodite and her son, Eros. One of these scenes shows a boy-child being delivered to a man for instruction, demonstrating Poliphilo's need for education in the art of love. However, without the proper guidance such an education is incomplete; Poliphilo contemplates the scenes but remains, at this point, ignorant to their mythological significance.

As with the other structures in this space, the portal has a double effect on the dreamer. Poliphilo is fascinated by it, but, at the same time, he hesitates to enter it because it leads to darkness. Poliphilo's reluctance to pass through the portal, even though he is curious as to what this venture might offer him, may be seen as a neophyte's difficulty of passing from one stage of his initiation to another. The only way to move forward at this stage is by force and this is what the dragon's surprise attack achieves (Fig. 12.4).

The sounds of the dragon's arrival remind Poliphilo of the dark forest, while the timing of the dragon's appearance brings to mind the Lover's entrapment in the *Rose*. Poliphilo has just looked into a mirror-like black surface:[43]

> Quivi al dextro et sinistro lato, di expolitissimi marmori era il tabulato pariete. Dil quale nella mediana parte dil alamento era impacta una grande rotonditate, inclaustrata di circuitione d'una frondosa gioia cum egregia associatione di caelatura. Il quale (simile all'altro per opposito) era di petra nigerrima, al duro ferro contentibile di nitore speculabile. Tra gli quali (di essi disaveduto) facendo transito, **fui dilla propria imagine da repentino timore invaso.**

> There on the right and left sides was panelled walling of highly polished marble, in the central part of the surface of which was impacted a great roundel hemmed about the circumference by a leafy carnouse or garland, with outstanding accompaniment of carving: each – like the other one straight opposite – was of blackest stone, that could contend with hard iron, mirror-like in sheen. Between them – unaware of them – making my way through, I was assailed with sudden alarm by my own image.

Mirrors and Mirroring in Dreams

Fig. 12.4 The dragon attacks Poliphilo at the triumphal portal. Sp Coll Hunterian Bh.2.14, f. d3v: *Hypnerotomachia Poliphili* (1499). By permission of the University of Glasgow Library, Special Collections.

His self-reflection causes him sudden fright, while he gets unexpected pleasure by looking at all the beautiful scenes reflected in that same surface (*da uno inopinato piacere fui retemperato*).[44] The captivating power of the marvellous sights entraps him within the threshold of the portal: the dragon advances from the ruins and Poliphilo can only escape by plunging into the darkness ahead. In order to rediscover light and escape the terrible labyrinth he has to remember his desire of Polia and set on a quest to find her. Praying to the omnipotent gods, he is finally able to see a source of light, which leads him to a holy altar of Aphrodite. This sacred subterranean space ascribes a chthonic quality to the goddess of love, thus, hinting at her association with nature and fertility. Through such an association, Poliphilo appears to be in the womb of Mother Nature, about to be reborn by coming out of the labyrinth.

When he eventually manages to exit the labyrinth from a narrow opening, Poliphilo finds himself in a paradisiacal landscape, the realm of Queen Eleuterylida. As he emerges through the exit portal and enters the forested mountains surrounding this realm, he essentially undergoes a second birth. His gradual movement from the mountain to the meadow through the forest of chestnuts marks his gradual acculturation to this new space; it is a progress from darkness to pleasant shade to light. As he progresses in this new space, he eventually encounters five nymphs representing the five senses. In the accompanying woodcut (Fig. 12.5), a large tree separates a timid Poliphilo on the left side of the image from the five nymphs on the right side. We can identify each of the senses

Fig. 12.5 Poliphilo encounters the Five Senses. Sp Coll Hunterian Bh.2.14, f. e2v: *Hypnerotomachia Poliphili* (1499). By permission of the University of Glasgow Library, Special Collections.

through their attributes and gestures: Aphea extending her hand to Poliphilo and slightly bending as a welcoming gesture is followed by Osfressia (background) holding what seems to be a cloth – Carl Nordenfalk argues that it is a '(presumably) fragrant bathing-towel'[45] – and Achoe (foreground) holding a stringed instrument, who are followed by Orassia (background) holding a mirror and Geussia (foreground) carrying a drinking vessel.

This is an important moment in the dream and this is further justified by its inclusion in the visual narrative of the book. It is the first time Poliphilo meets inhabitants of the dream world and the first time that they meet him. Through this social interaction, during which Poliphilo is being observed, he is given an opportunity for self-reflection. Given that these nymphs could be considered as allegorical manifestations of his own senses, it is as if he looks into a mirror and the mirror looks back, inquisitively. Interestingly, in the woodcut Orassia (Sight) is not depicted looking into the mirror she is holding – as it often happens with depictions of Oiseuse in illuminated manuscripts of the *Rose* – but rather she is holding a round mirror in front of her chest with the reflective surface of her mirror looking in the direction of Poliphilo. I would argue that this imagery and its narrative context point to the fact that Poliphilo, having overcome his initial fears and willing to embark on his love-quest with new determination, is now in need of instruction, contemplation and self-reflection in order to decide on his next step: the choice of path at the three portals. Moreover, his interaction with the Five Senses is an opportunity for self-realization. When the nymphs ask him to identify himself, Poliphilo, speaking for the first time in his dream, hesitantly defines himself as an unhappy lover who has no knowledge of this space. Sympathizing with him, the nymphs invite him to the bath, where they provide him with information on this new region, which is characterized by perpetual leisure, much like the garden of Deduit in the *Roman de la Rose*. The nymphs are also responsible for his sensual and sexual awakening. In the octagonal bath of the five nymphs, Poliphilo receives his first bath, at which point he names himself to the nymphs, and later anoints himself with an ointment that has an aphrodisiac effect on him. The events in the bath-building, along with the octagonal shape of the building – mostly associated with baptisteries, especially in the early Christian period[46] – allude to the rite of baptism. The dreamer is reborn as a lover and the discussion on his name defines him as the lover of Polia.

Following the self-reflective experience at the octagonal bath and the activation of Poliphilo's sensory capacities, the Five Senses lead the dreamer through the three entry thresholds of the palace of Queen Eleuterylida guarded by the nymphs Cinosia, Indalomena, and Mnemosyna, whose names and attributes (embroidered curtains) are heavy with signification. The ritual crossing through the three curtains serves as an allegory of the process of cogitation,[47] therefore, mirroring the activation of the dreamer's mental capacities. Having activated both his sensory and mental capacities, Poliphilo is on the path to self-realization and, thus, ready to encounter Queen Eleuterylida (Freedom or Free Will) and her court, as well as to receive more advanced instruction by nymphs Logistica (Reason) and Thelemia (Desire). Overall, the time spent in the realm of Queen Eleuterylida constitutes a formative stage of Poliphilo's initiation, preparing him for the next step: the choice of a path in the realm of Queen Telosia (Aim). Given his self-realization as a lover, Poliphilo chooses the middle portal – the path of love – leading him to his union with Polia in the realm of Materamoris.

To conclude, this chapter aimed to show the similar ways in which mirrors and mirror-like surfaces are used in the two texts to signal crucial moments in the narrative and in the characters' development. In the *Roman de la Rose*, mirrors and other reflective surfaces, literal or metaphorical, are used throughout the dream narrative not only to denote the turning points in the initiation process, but also as allegories of the fiction of the dream. Amant's territorial passage from one dream space to the next is at the same time a visual passage relating to alterations in visual perception, e.g. when entering the dream narrative and when looking into the fountain, or to an exchange of gazes and reflections, e.g. when entering Deduit's garden and later the rose-garden. Moreover, as the dreamer moves forward in his dream, there is a gradual narrowing of his visual perception of the dream space, signalling his eventual entrapment to love; in other words, the development of the dreamer's visual perception traces his progress in his initiation in love. Similarly, in the *Hypnerotomachia*, there is a gradual narrowing of space as the hero moves forward in the first part of his journey: from a vast plain to a dark forest to the ruined city and, finally, to the dark labyrinth, where he is called to question the purpose of his journey as well as his identity. Resurfacing in the realm of Queen Eleuterylida, he is born anew, his purpose clear, a lover in search of his beloved. The act of self-reflection is the cause behind his progression in this first part of his journey, as well as the catalyst for his initiation in the realm of Queen Eleuterylida. Finally, the analysis has shown that

Mirrors and Mirroring

reflective surfaces in these dream narratives are used to point out, on the one hand, the disruptive effects of self-reflection (materialized in the dreams as attacks from the god of love and from the dragon, but ultimately pointing at the dreamers' inner struggles), and on the other hand, the illusory and transformative effects of such reflective surfaces on the dreamers' visual, or rather mental, perception of the dream space.

PART IV
MIMETIC MIRROR

CHAPTER 13
PLANE AND CURVED MIRRORS IN CLASSICAL ANTIQUITY
Maria Gerolemou

Introduction

The fascination with catoptrical illusions has a long history. In antiquity they are described as the product of perceptual misjudgement or the effect of imaging technologies. In the first case, optical illusions are either the result of an 'error' by the perceiver or a 'flaw' in the reflected object; thus, they appear to depend on the quality of the visual faculty of the perceiver, the physical circumstances under which they are seen, as well as on the visibility of the object itself, i.e. its corporeity, colour, brightness, size, shape, location (e.g. if it is situated far away from the viewer), whether it is in motion or at rest. In the second case, optical illusions are due to an 'error' of the reflecting medium itself; although they also depend on, for instance, the position of the perceiver's eyes in respect to the object, they are more determined by the quality of the reflecting surface: its material, whether it is clear or shining, plane or spherical (convex/concave), and the number of reflecting surfaces involved in the process.[1]

In the best-case scenario, the product of a plane mirror can be a virtual image, a perfect replica that could be mistaken for the reflected object itself;[2] this is particularly true in cases of humans acting as reflected objects. In classical antiquity, a faultless image replicating a human being was used: a. for self-improvement, as a means of acknowledging human imperfection – as in the case of the didactic mirror (see e.g. Diogenes Laertius, *Vitae Philosophorum* 2.5; Plato *Apol.* 15.8–15); or b. as a means of replicating, in the sense of displaying, an ideal/perfect image worthy of imitating (see e.g. Sen. *Clem.* pro.1.1),[3] or a seductive passive similitude (see e.g. the story of Narcissus). Nevertheless, the most common catoptrical experience in antiquity is the one coming from a non-shining spherical mirror made out of metal.[4] This type of mirror provides dim, warped images, distorted in size, shape and colour, inversed, displaced or even deleted. Deformed catoptric images are often depicted by ancient authors either as examples of misusing mirror-technology, which highlights the moral decadence of the user, or as evidences of the metaphysical power of mirrors, which help the viewer to transcend the medium's physical boundaries and, for instance, gaze upon the unseen divine;[5] in both cases the mirror does not passively show an image determined by the form of the real object. Finally, due to the ability to actually replicate, and thus replace, and deform or delete the reflected object, mirrors, both plane and spherical, are often associated with the uncanny that can terrify, astound or entertain a certain audience.[6]

Mirrors and Mirroring

The usual association of mirror images, and mirrors generally, with didacticism, deceit or the supernatural, disassociates them from their technical properties and potentials; this is precisely what catoptrical texts in antiquity mainly attempt to revise by focusing on one instance: the bending of the visual ray at the reflecting surface.[7] By underlining the capacities of mirrors and by associating them with the technical production of an image (rather with conceit or deceit), the idea of the mirror as an imaging device gains impetus: mirrors, for example, unlike other imaging technologies, are able to produce an image with accuracy, ease and swiftness; moreover, they can multiply and delete images or create entirely new ones. Thus, they reduce the search for resemblance or realism which haunts traditional media of mimesis, particularly with regard to relative size, shape, position and form of the mimetic object. In other words, what the study of mirrors in general seems to implie, is that the change from naturalism to a more abstract way of viewing images, which Elsner famously describes in his book *Art and the Roman Viewer* (1995), is rooted not merely in the viewer and his social/cultural milieu but also in the medium of image-production itself.

This chapter restricts itself to two observations, the first relating to plane mirrors (as the least curved mirrors) that can produce virtual images, and the second to curved mirrors with the ability to deform reality. As I argue, plane mirrors are associated with the representational mode of mimesis. I will try to prove this point by concentrating on the treatment of the mirror analogy in Plato's *Respublica* and Apuleius' *Apologia*. On the other hand, the exploration of curved mirrors in antiquity is associated with cases of deformation of images and the production of new ones, and thus to what I label catoptric animism (in this case the images give the impression that they enjoy a certain freedom of action, in deviation from the original). Catoptric animism is further associated with the notion of creative *phantasia*, which is a representational medium more forceful and more accurate than mimesis, as it is able to also reproduce what is not seen through the physical eyes; and though creative *phantasia* is not particularly related with spherical mirrors, it is included in this second part of the chapter as a process analogous to that achieved by spherical mirrors. This part of the chapter will focus mostly on ps. Hero's description of mirror's mode of operation in his *De Speculis*.[8]

Plane mirrors and catoptric mimesis

In Plato's *Respublica*, Socrates, in his attempt to minimize the value of mimesis, discusses, along with other imaging, delusive technologies such as poetry and painting, the properties of reflecting surfaces (water and mirrors).[9] According to Socrates, if you are willing to carry a mirror, you can act as a *thaumastos anêr*, a miracle worker, having the ability to rapidly imitate/reproduce almost everything, e.g. plants and animals, humans, the sun, earth and heaven, the gods and the underworld (596d–e); in this context, a mirror image is signified as something quickly captured from an imaging device, a mirror, that can be transported; moreover, the mirror is promoted as something that can capture everything, even things that cannot be seen with human eyes, like the divine or the underworld (cf. Plat. *Criti*.107c–d).

As Halliwell points out in relation to the above passage, Plato uses the mirror analogy to provocatively relate pictorial arts to an aesthetic of perfect, sterile mimesis.[10] However, the ancient mirror, as we have already mentioned in the introduction, though trying to simulate the world, cannot be its objective reflector, as it is usually metal and curved; thus, the images it produces are reversed and, to a degree, dimmed. That is to say, even if we assume that Plato has in mind a plane, shiny mirror, able to produce real images, such a mirror would still reproduce something far from reality, reversed and, furthermore, disassociated from its wider context, i.e. fragmented;[11] to elaborate on the latter point, due to the fact that mirrors in this period were small,[12] all they could offer was merely a series of partial views of reality, captured by a constantly shifted mirror. In other words, the mirror analogy in the *Republic* cannot be seen as an exaggeration of the likeness skills of the painter. Plato merely appears to be invoking reflections as carbon copies that display the world as it actually is. In actuality, by considering mirrors to be an imaging technology, he describes, though in a preliminary fashion, their role specifically (and that of the artistic *medium* in general) in challenging reality and visual perception.

On another level, just as an *agathos zôgraphos*, a brilliant painter (*R* 598c), has found, through the art of *sciagraphia*, a way to solve the problem of depicting form in relatively real terms (598c, 602c–d, see also *R*. 523b, *Soph*. 235e–36a, *Tht*. 208e, *Parm*. 165c, Pliny the Elder *HN* 35.60–62[13]), mirrors represent an easy solution to art's *amêchania* before real motion, precisely due to their ability to capture motion, thereby representing the world as a moving target and as being 'alive'. Hence, though mirroring does not produce anything but φαινόμενα, by stressing the iconopoetic effectiveness of mirrors Plato, probably unwittingly, opens a window onto a wider discussion (that will be fully developed in later centuries) on what can determine aesthetic value: this shift, which intersects with other forms of *technai*, illuminates the role of the medium, the artist or the materials in art production and frees art and artistic value from their *prosaic* obsession with the produced images.

Later on, the mathematical school of Euclid, Hero and Ptolemy discharges the medium of the mirror from the 'guilt' of the illusory likeness or, to borrow Smith's wording, they 'save' the dignity of images, and, by rationalizing them through the principle of the visual ray, they create such conditions that the viewer finds himself prepared even in front of unprecedented images and, thus, against a differentiated reality.[14] The perceiver of catoptric images is, then, aware of the fact that different kinds of realities may be produced by mirrors depending on the type of catoptric surface used. Thus mirror-images in contrast to images produced by traditional arts, do not insult the intelligence of the spectator who, despite being captivated by the illusion of lifelikeness, is aware of how this is created and the way it works; this allows him to praise the medium for offering new possibilities for capturing reality and, at the same time, for producing a different perceptual experience.

In light of this beneficial reconsideration of mirrors and their products, Apuleius, in his *Apologia* (13.5–16.6), can defend himself against his enemies who accuse him for using such a medium. Specifically, they chastise him for being vain and also disapprove of the mirror's effects. In response to these accusations, Apuleius lists the virtues of the medium.[15] The mirror, as he argues, in following nature's paradigm (14),[16] not only offers a reliable picture of reality, if it is plane, but, if spherical, can also provide a different spectacle, precisely by having the ability to warp reality (16). In this instance, Apuleius seems to borrow concepts from the mirror analogy in the *Respublica* examined above, particularly emphasizing the ability of the mirror to reproduce things quickly and easily, and also to capture motion; unavoidably, its virtues are highlighted further through its contrast to traditional imaging technologies such as sculpture. What is new in Apuleius' statement, compared to Plato, is the fact that art-making and its media are being tied to working with materials and their physical properties. Specifically, in the case of reflections, these are pictured as standing beyond the limitations of matter without losing accuracy,[17] something unavoidable in artistic productions made by human hands.[18] This argument does not merely point to accurate representation (i.e. a likeness in the expected sense) as the basic art-critical term, but, as Jeffrey Ulrich argues, to the ability of good art to represent not simply motion, but rather change, *flux* (14).[19] As Apuleius points out, the most convincing element in likeness is motion, *motus*,[20] and this cannot be reproduced through clay, which is deprived of life, through marble, which is colourless, or through painting, which lacks solidity (Apuleius, 14). Here, the meaning of motion differs from the aforementioned platonic one (in the *Respublica*) in that it is not sensed in a direct way. Motion here rather points to the constancy of the body's natural transformation and to metabolic change in general (see e.g. Heraclitus B12, Plato *Leges* 893b, Ar. *Physica* 201a 10–11, 27–29, 201b 4–5). This becomes obvious shortly thereafter, when Apuleius, who desires a commemorative medium to capture his image, chooses a mirror image instead of an immobile statue or a painting (14f.) based on the assumption that other artistic materials affect, or rather limit, the mimetic procedure and its outcome (clay, bronze, stone, wax, paint, 14).[21]

The restricted capacities of artistic materials to reproduce reality are also noted by Plutarch in *De Pythiae oraculis* 404c. Here, Plutarch, referring to the properties of various materials (wax, gold, silver and copper) used in artistic mimesis, bemoans the fact that each of these materials eventually forms the likeness of an object in terms of its distinct properties (404c–d). He thus praises the mirror as far superior to all art media/material because of its ability to produce truthful representations. Moreover, he praises the moon as the best mirror surface, though in his *De facie* the surface of moon is uneven and rugged, producing fractured and deflected rays and, consequently, deformed images (930d).[22] Likewise, Dio Chrysostom in *Or.* 12 discusses, *inter alia*, the limitations of plastic arts because of their material bounds – though not compared to mirrors but to poetry (69–71[23]) – which make creation stagnant (ἀκίνητον καὶ μένον), laborious and slow (ἐπίπονον καὶ βραδύ; cf. Horace *Ars P.* 294. Plut. *Mor.* 636c; see further Lucian *Somn.* 9),[24] whereas poetry, like reflections (which are also deprived of physical, material existence), can escape the single pose of the image to which plastic arts are restricted (ἓν σχῆμα ἑκάστης εἰκόνος).[25]

Particularly remarkable, however, is that the above texts do not discuss the fact that mirrors provide the possibility of transmitting and processing data without requiring a craftsman, due to the fact that reflections are, to borrow Byzantine term, *acheiropoiêtoi*.[26] This opposes the very idea of art as a slow and laborious process (though the swift production of images by mirrors is noted by both Plato and Apuleius) and, consequently, the connection of image production with the artist's skills in mastering his material.[27] The benefit arising from the absence of the artist in mirroring is best highlighted by the phenomenon of the simultaneous production of multiple images, mainly described in texts on catoptrics (see also Pliny *NH* 33.45 and Lucretius *DRN* 4.302–310): ps. Hero of Alexandria, for instance, in his attempt to demonstrate the ability of mirrors to clarify and disclose things, among them motion (*De Speculis* 18.1, motum ... apparere; see also 2; 3 and 4), refers to the example of the *polytheoros* mirror.[28] This kind of mirror can multiply faces or fingers, producing, for example, a Zeus with three heads. In paragraph 23 of the *De Speculis* ps. Hero describes a five-mirror installation with the same effect. How does this function? The mirror surfaces reflect the same subject from different angles, effectively multiplying it five or more times. In a similar vein, Euclid, in proposition 14 of his *De Speculis*, gives instructions on how to make a polygon of mirrors in which various images can appear simultaneously (see also pr. 13 and 15). The phenomenon of the simultaneous formation of images is also discussed by Ptolemy: specifically, he depicts the projection of multiple images by a composite of plane mirrors, either arranged in relation to the viewer (*Optica* 4.155, 171–173) or placed inclined towards one another in various combinations (4.175–182; see also Plutarch *De facie* 930a–c). By exhibiting the possibility of multiple images, mirrors once again problematize the divide between fabrication/copy and truth/original.

To produce readymade, time-based catoptric artworks *en masse*, without hard labour or skill/expert knowledge, and thus quickly, means to substitute multiple copies for a unique artwork and, at the same time, to reduce the viewer of art to a simple user/consumer.[29] This is best reflected in the ps. Heronian doctrine: in mirrors one can see whatever he wishes to (*De Speculis* 24). Usership breaks down the binary relation between the production and reception of an artwork; this becomes more obvious if we take into consideration the fact that perceivers of reflections have a stake in the images appearing in front of them: Moreover, to put it differently, the artist is not the hand of the craftsman but the eye of the observer,[30] catoptric images cease to be once the reflected object is removed.[31] In this way, for instance, the beneficial estrangement that the didactic speculum could offer to the viewer when he sees his own image in the mirror becomes a matter determined by the taste of each consumer, or, according to Taylor,[32] by his passive or active stance towards the mirror. In short, with the acknowledgement of mirrors as imaging technologies, a gap opens between a mode of using a mirror and looking at a mirror image that is paired with self-knowledge, and *other* ways of using mirrors and looking at images. For Seneca, for instance, mirrors, while they were initially created to provide knowledge, were eventually misused (*NQ.* 1.17. 4–10). He grounds his claim in an example of bad usership: Hostius, who, in order to satisfy his sexual phantasies and increase his erotic pleasure, uses the mirror to magnify his genitals when having sex (1.16.4–5, 8–9, cf. 1.13.1, 1.15.8, 1.16.2).[33]

A different side of catoptrical images is to be found in cases where reflected subjects are not merely replicated through mirrors but reveal a side of the original object otherwise unseen (in nature or in divine sphere); in this light, they could deform the reflected subject or, even worse, make it completely disappear from the spectrum or/and replace it with an alien image. This is the second point I wish to turn to.

Curved mirrors and catoptric animism

While usually in antiquity the original artwork preserves its full authority over the copy (see e.g. Dion. Hal. *Is.* 20.25), this does not seem to apply to a catoptrical reproduction of images. A reflection goes beyond the area of origins, proving to be more powerful than a mere imitation of the original. Moreover, by departing under certain conditions from the target of naturalistic verisimilitude, catoptric reproduction deforms or replaces the original and highlights aspects of it which are accessible only through the right curvature or a combination of mirrors. The anti-naturalistic conception of reality that mainly spherical mirrors offer stands in contrast to the paradigm of the didactic plane mirror which is meant to reproduce an almost identical picture of the sensed object.[34] Studies of the former type of mirror occur from the Hellenistic period onwards, when the audience's artistic taste shifts from naturalism to a more abstract way of both producing and viewing images.[35] Although, the passage from Apuleius' *Apologia* and the episode of Hostius in Seneca's *NQ*, examined above, refer only briefly to the mirror's ability to disfigure images (16), this aspect is fully explored in the catoptric treatises, which explain how mirrors, and especially spherical mirrors, distort the form of an object's image in terms of size, shape and colour or make it appear nearer or farther away than it ought to look (Ptolemy *Optica* 3.117–120). Thus, apart from the usual catoptric reversion of right and left[36] according to these texts, images produced by spherical mirrors may appear larger or smaller than the real object.[37] Furthermore, the curvature of the spherical mirror affects the shape of the image; for example, according to Euclid's *De Speculis*, convex mirrors produce convex images (23), whereas concave mirrors produce concave images (28–29).[38]

By playing with the idea that spherical mirrors might deform the reflected subject and, thus, exert an artistic appeal ps. Hero notes that mirrors can create a wonderful setup (*De Speculis* 2.4, admirabilem speculationem), as they can show people and things in an unreal and funny way, for instance upside down, or as if they have three eyes and two noses, and with facial expressions like those during mourning (2.6). Distorted images are basically a parody of reality that can provoke laughter, as the description of the mirror in passage 19 of Hero's text suggests. This convex mirror is here called μωκός, the mocker (19.1, *mokeion*).[39] The more one inclines towards this mirror, the more one's image stretches, appearing elongated.[40] In another case, at 17, the spectator sees images, including her/his own, deformed in all possible ways. For better results, Hero proposes to rotate the whole mirror structure along a horizontal axis so that the user can see every possible aspect of the image, which sometimes appears upright and sometimes inverted; e.g., when the mirror is rotated, the viewer's head appears over the heels. At paragraph 21 a mirror compilation reveals to the viewer her/his own self-floating image; while standing on the ground, the viewer sees her-/himself flying, or as Jones puts it, 'like a flying god'.[41] The observer has the impression that either the world has turned upside down, or that he has overcome the world.[42]

Even more effective is the ability of mirrors to persuasively represent all that is hidden from the eye and which is marvellous and/or supernatural. Although this case is not explicitly described as related to the spherical type of mirror, it is nevertheless included in this section as it underlines too an idea which is mainly linked with spherical mirrors, namely that they are able to show things detached from sensed reality.[43] As mirrors can enhance sight, they are largely used not only to 'restore' the true dimensions of subjects (see the mirror's ability to represent motion discussed above) but also to reveal the sight of hidden things, such as those of everyday life, nature or the divine.[44] Philo of Alexandria, the first century AD Jewish philosopher who uses the mirror metaphor quite frequently, while acknowledging the fact that mirrors can deceive the senses (*De specialibus legibus*, 1.26), discusses *phantasia*'s potential to perceive the supersensory, i.e. things going beyond everyday experience, what could not be otherwise seen, through an analogy to a mirror reflection: as he puts it, the mind can imagine (φαντασιοῦται) the creation, functioning and management of the whole universe in the same way a mirror is able to capture its surroundings (*De Decalogo* 105; cf. *De Opificio mundi* 77, *Migr.* 190). Here, *phantasia* refers to what Anne Sheppard[45] calls creative *phantasia* which is evoked by the intellect (see further Synesius *On Dreams* 4. 134b and 149c–d and Iamblichus *De Mysteriis* 2.10, on *phantasmata* and mirror analogy).[46] This kind of *phantasia*, which can fashion what cannot be seen, is described in Philostratus' *Life of Apollonius of Tyana* as coming in contrast to mimesis, which imitates only what can be seen with one's eyes (6.19).[47] This creative *phantasia* is implied first, *mirabile dictu*, in Plato's *Timaeus* 71a–d, where the liver is described as a kind of an imaginative mirror where divination, offering images, warnings, etc. for the future, is located (catoptromancy).[48] The association of mirroring with *phantasia*, though in this next case a purely sensorial activity, becomes more obvious in Aristotle's *On Dreams* 459b28–30, explaining how one, through *phantasia*, receives sensory impressions in dreams (459a, *phantasmata*):[49] in the same way as *phantasia*, then, a clean, new mirror is able to capture even the smallest fleck (in this case a blood fleck in the woman's eye[50]), which is not visible to the naked eye.[51] An example of mirrors disclosing things which are not in our field of view is described by ps. Hero; in *De Speculis*, he refers to a mirror on the ceiling of a room reflecting, through a tube that penetrates the wall of a building, the view of the street.[52] The resident of this building is able to see, without being seen, the movement of passers-by outside (22). In other words, while inside the house, the mirror gives the perceiver the opportunity to see how many people are outside in the streets and what they are doing (or who is standing behind him, 2.6). Why bother going outside if this can be achieved inside?

Finally, the ability of mirrors to delete images is often related to the divine sphere, probably because it could serve so well the notion of divine epiphany.[53] This assumption is best exemplified in Pausanias' description of a mirror on a wall of the temple of Demeter and Kore in Lycosura, Arcadia. When a believer looks at this mirror, he sees himself very dimly, or not at all (his reflection is deleted); in the latter case, the mirror shows the images of cult statues instead (8.37.7). A scene from a Lucanian nestoris of the early fourth century (Naples, No. 1984) can perhaps, though serving another context (Dionysian mirror of *metamorphosis*), prove further this case: here, Orestes looks in a mirror held by a Maenad, but sees Clytemnestra's picture instead of seeing his own face.[54] Euclid verifies this phenomenon by studying convex and concave mirrors that delete images when the surface of the mirror where the visual ray bounces is covered (*De Speculis* Assumptions 4 and 5; see also ps. Hero *De spec.* 10).[55]

Nevertheless, the 'irrational' way a spherical mirror interrupts the reality of its visual field and the disproportion of shape and size, or the awkwardness of the reflection's form, are not threatening to its receiver; any changes or deletions that images suffer from spherical mirrors are temporary and only within the mirror's reality (away from the contextual reality). To offer a conclusion, generally, the discussion of mirrors and reflections in the ancient world from the fourth century BC onward seems to focus on three major questions also related to other imaging technologies: (a) to what extent are images separable from their media, (b) to what extent are images influenced by the properties of their media, and (c) when we deal with an image, are we referring to something mimetic or to the result of *phantasia*?

CHAPTER 14
REFLECTIONS ON LUCIAN'S LUNAR MIRROR: *SPECULUM LUNAE* AND AN ANCIENT TELESCOPIC FANTASY[1]

Karen ní Mheallaigh

In *True Histories* (*VH*), a Greek prose fiction from the second century CE, Lucian, the protagonist, flies to the Moon. There he encounters Endymion, the King of the Moon, joins in a cosmic battle between the forces of the Moon and the Sun, and describes in detail the marvellous customs and possessions of the men (for it is exclusively men) who live there. The climax of lunar wonders is the great lunar mirror, propped above a well, that enables the visitor to see the Earth below, magnified up close:

> καὶ μὴν καὶ ἄλλο θαῦμα ἐν τοῖς βασιλείοις ἐθεασάμην· κάτοπτρον μέγιστον κεῖται ὑπὲρ φρέατος οὐ πάνυ βαθέος. ἂν μὲν οὖν εἰς τὸ φρέαρ καταβῇ τις, ἀκούει πάντων τῶν παρ' ἡμῖν ἐν τῇ γῇ λεγομένων, ἐὰν δὲ εἰς τὸ κάτοπτρον ἀποβλέψῃ, πάσας μὲν πόλεις, πάντα δὲ ἔθνη ὁρᾷ ὥσπερ ἐφεστὼς ἑκάστοις· τότε καὶ τοὺς οἰκείους ἐγὼ ἐθεασάμην καὶ πᾶσαν τὴν πατρίδα, εἰ δὲ κἀκεῖνοι ἐμὲ ἑώρων, οὐκέτι ἔχω τὸ ἀσφαλὲς εἰπεῖν. ὅστις δὲ ταῦτα μὴ πιστεύει οὕτως ἔχειν, ἄν ποτε καὶ αὐτὸς ἐκεῖσε ἀφίκηται, εἴσεται ὡς ἀληθῆ λέγω.

> Furthermore, I beheld another marvel in the palace: an enormous mirror is positioned above a well that is not very deep. Now if one goes down into the well, one hears everything that is being said by our people on the earth, and if one looks into the mirror, one sees all the cities and all the peoples, just as if one were standing over them. On that occasion I observed my family and my entire homeland, but I cannot now tell for sure if they saw me. Whoever does not believe that this is so, if ever he reaches that place himself, he will know that I am telling the truth.[2]

Of all of the intriguing artefacts from the story-world of *True Histories*, the lunar mirror has commanded the most fascination among Lucian's readers. A powerful symbol of Lucianic satire and a *mise en abyme* of *True Histories* itself,[3] this object seems to leap out of its antique context and reach across time to optical instruments – real and imagined – far in the future: to Boccalini's *lentes*, Galileo's telescope and Borges' *Aleph*.[4] Usually, such connections are made tentatively in footnotes, or framed with a more sober comment about the exuberance of Lucian's fancy and the impossibility that his lunar mirror should have any serious scientific heft. But here, I wish to push the margins of our usual interpretation and argue that this artefact is not pure whimsy or literary symbol, but that it has serious scientific heft in terms of ancient theories about both the Moon and of mirrors (for the two are connected, as we shall see), and that it provides us with a striking insight into the ancient scientific imagination.

In one sense, this great lunar marvel constitutes the ultimate historiographical instrument. In his essay *On how to write history*, Lucian counsels the would-be historian to cultivate a perspective that is unclouded by bias or literary decoration: the historian's mind should operate *like a mirror* that reflects the world in undistorted pellucidity (as if any such mirror existed). The historian should also, Lucian continues, strive to achieve an overview of events, like Zeus observing the world from above.[5] Here on the Moon, Lucian's audio-visual apparatus – the shallow well with mirror suspended above – offers the visitor the supreme opportunity for *autopsia* (eye-witness) and *akoē* (hearing), those twin pillars on which the edifice on historiographical authority is built. That this historiographical contraption should be embedded in a narrative of flagrant lies is a master-stroke of Lucianic irony.

Lucian's fantastical view from above also strikes more strictly literary and philosophical chords. It plays, for example, with the motif of *kataskopia* or 'view from above' that was characteristic of Menippean Satire. This genre was avowedly one of the ingredients of Lucian's own literary invention, the comic dialogue, and one that influenced the *VH* as well.[6] I have suggested the term *selēnoskopia* for this distinctive variation on the theme, which takes in the Earth from the Moon. This is one of Lucian's trademarks, for we encounter it in *Icaromenippus*, where (the pointedly named) Menippus gains a satirical panorama of the people of Earth from the platform of the Moon.[7] Lucian's *selēnoskopia* also plays on the cosmic viewpoint of ancient and contemporary philosophy – that exercise of mental and emotional detachment that was so beloved of the Stoics and of the Emperor Marcus Aurelius himself, in whose reign Lucian lived and worked.[8] Here in the *VH*, however, the emphasis is less on *what* Lucian sees, and more on *how* he achieves the vision: through a mirror suspended above a well. By unpacking some of the thinking behind Lucian's catoptric device, I will show how it offers us deep access to ancient thought about the Moon and its relation to our world.

The early catoptric Moon: Heliophotism and the witch

We find our first explicit association between the Moon and mirror in Aristophanes' comedy *Clouds* in the late fifth century BCE. Here the curmudgeonly Strepsiades visits the *phrontistērion* to consult with Socrates about how to get rid of his debt. Among the more ludicrous plans he evolves is the idea to employ a Thessalian witch to pull down the Moon:

Στ. γυναῖκα φαρμακίδ᾽ εἰ πριάμενος Θετταλὴν
καθέλοιμι νύκτωρ τὴν σελήνην, εἶτα δὴ
αὐτὴν καθείρξαιμ᾽ εἰς λοφεῖον στρογγύλον,
ὥσπερ κάτροπτον, κᾆτα τηροίην ἔχων –

Σω. τί δῆτα τοῦτ' ἂν ὠφελήσειέν σ';
Στ. ὅ τι;
εἰ μηκέτ' ἀνατέλλοι σελήνη μηδαμοῦ,
οὐκ ἂν ἀποδοίην τοὺς τόκους.
Σω. ὁτιὴ τί δή;
Στ. ὁτιὴ κατὰ μῆνα τἀργύριον δανείζεται.

St: If I were to hire a Thessalian witch-woman
and draw down the Moon in the night,
then lock it up in a circular case,
like a mirror, and then keep guard over it –
Soc: How on earth would this help you?
St: How? If a Moon were never to rise anymore,
I would not pay interest.
Soc: How's that?
St: Because money is loaned by the month![9]

We know that in Classical Athens interest was calculated and debts collected at the New Moon.[10] Strepsiades believes Thessalian witches have the power to draw the Moon down from the sky – the so-called 'Thessalian trick.'[11] He is naive enough to think that – if he could arrange this – the calendar would simply come to a stop, thus freezing the monthly interest on his debt. The scholiast explains the allusion in verse 752 to locking the Moon away in a box 'like a mirror' with reference to the similar shape of mirror and Moon: 'for the circle of the Moon is curved/round just like mirrors' (ὁ γὰρ τῆς σελήνης κύκλος στρογγυλοειδής, καθάπερ καὶ τὰ ἔσοπτρα). But Strepsiades' reference could allude in a more concrete way to the apparatus actually used by those in antiquity who performed this feat. This seems to be depicted on the so-called 'Hamilton vase' which was found in southern Italy and made part of Sir William Hamilton's collection. The vase itself is now lost, but the image survives in an engraving made by Tischbein, which was published in 1795.[12] In it, two women have cast a rope around the Moon, which appears trapped in a mirror. The women brandish a sword and a stick, heightening the atmosphere of coercion, and an inscription which appears to address the Moon hovers overhead. We also know from Hippolytus, Roman bishop of the second to the third century CE, that magicians in the imperial period used mirrors to perform other illusions involving the Moon, such as conjuring the Moon to appear indoors.[13]

Strepsiades, therefore, could well be evoking such magical practices. But Aristophanes is also poking fun at *philosophers* in this play, and the allusion to locking the Moon away *like a mirror* could represent Strepsiades' garbling of the philosophical theory that the Moon *was like a mirror* – a 'mirror-like body' (κατοπτροειδὲς σῶμα) – in yet another demonstration of his difficulties with conceptual thinking.[14] This theory, which was ascribed to Pythagoras in the later doxographical tradition, is evidently related to the revolutionary theory that the Moon *reflected* light from the Sun, the principle of 'heliophotism' whose discovery is ascribed to Parmenides in the early parts of the fifth century BCE.[15] There are, therefore, clear links between the Moon and mirrors in the thought-worlds of magic and philosophy going back as far as the fifth century BCE.

Historical heuristics and analogical drift

I would like to propose here a new, additional link between the mirror and the Moon – one that emerges from the use of mirrors as a heuristic tool to enhance understanding of the Moon.[16] This takes us into the realm of science in the imperial period. The following two passages evoke simple experiments that were designed to explain the Moon's light and variations thereof. The first is from Plutarch's dialogue *On the Face of the Moon* (or *De facie*), which is dated to the late first century CE.[17] Here the speaker is refuting Stoic objections to the theory that the Moon, as an opaque body, reflects the Sun's light like a mirror. If the Moon really were a mirror (the argument goes), then we should expect to see the Sun itself reflected in its surface, just as we would see on the surface of water. The fact that we do *not* see the Sun reflected in the Moon thus is presented as an obstacle to the mirror-theory and the principle of heliophotism itself:

> ὅταν γὰρ αὐγῆς ἀφ' ὕδατος πρὸς τοῖχον ἁλλομένης ὄψις ἐν αὐτῷ τῷ πεφωτισμένῳ κατὰ τὴν ἀνάκλασιν τόπῳ γένηται, τὰ τρία καθορᾷ, τήν τ' ἀνακλωμένην αὐγὴν καὶ τὸ ποιοῦν ὕδωρ τὴν ἀνάκλασιν καὶ τὸν ἥλιον αὐτόν, ἀφ' οὗ τὸ φῶς τῷ ὕδατι προσπίπτον ἀνακέκλασται. τούτων δ' ὁμολογουμένων καὶ φαινομένων κελεύουσι τοὺς ἀνακλάσει φωτίζεσθαι τὴν γῆν ὑπὸ τῆς σελήνης ἀξιοῦντας ἐπιδεικνύναι νύκτωρ ἐμφαινόμενον τῇ σελήνῃ τὸν ἥλιον, ὥσπερ ἐμφαίνεται τῷ ὕδατι μεθ' ἡμέραν, ὅταν ἀνάκλασις ἀπ' αὐτοῦ γένηται.

> For whenever a ray of light bounces from water against a wall, and our vision falls on the area that is illuminated by the reflection, it observes the three components: the ray that is being reflected, the water that is making the reflection, and the Sun itself, the source of the light that is reflected as it falls on the water. On the basis of these agreed and evident facts, they (i.e. the Stoics) bid those who claim that the Earth is illuminated by the Moon by reflection to show that the Sun appears in the Moon at night, just as it appears in the water by day whenever reflection from it takes place.[18]

In this simple demonstration, the image of sunlight ricocheting off the surface of water is offered as an analogy for the Sun's light reflecting off the surface of the Moon. The catoptric interaction of light and the water's reflective surface illustrates the principle of heliophotism, and the Moon is equated with the mirror-like water.

Achilles Tatius, an astronomical writer from the third century CE, uses the mirror heuristically as well, this time to illustrate how the Moon's phases work:

> ὥσπερ γὰρ εἰ κάτοπτρον λαβών τις ἐθέλοι τὴν ἀπ' αὐτοῦ ἀντανάκλασιν τοῦ εἰδώλου θεάσασθαι, ἐξ ἐναντίας τοῦ προσώπου αὐτοῦ τὴν θέσιν τοῦ κατόπτρου

ποιήσεται... εἰ δὲ πλαγιάσειε τὸ κάτοπτρον, πρὸς τὸν πλαγιασμὸν καὶ τὴν ἔγκλισιν τοῦ κατόπτρου ἢ τὸ δίμοιρον ἢ τὸ ἥμισυ ἢ βραχύ τι μέρος τούτου θεάσεται ἀντανακλώμενον τοῦ κατόπτρου ἐγκλινομένου, οὕτω καὶ ἐπὶ τῆς σελήνης.

It is as if one took a mirror and wanted to observe the reflection of the image from it: one will position the mirror directly opposite one's face.... But if one were to slant the mirror, then following the mirror's slant and incline, one will observe either two-thirds or half or a tiny fraction of this image reflected back as the mirror is turned away, and it is just so with the Moon.[19]

In this experiment, as he invites us to imagine the Moon waning from full to gibbous to half-moon, Achilles Tatius evokes the common experience of observing one's own face in a mirror. Observed fully frontal, the mirror, and one's face in it, appears round (the shape of most Greek and Roman mirrors was indeed round),[20] but little by little, as it slants away, its circle diminishes to half and eventually a sliver.

Demonstrations like these would have reinforced the Moon's identification with mirrors in an example of the general tendency that Colin Webster has called 'analogical drift,' meaning the slippage between the *literal* tools which theorists use, and the ways in which they then conceptualize the object of their scrutiny.[21] Basically: the mirror (or mirror action) is used to explain the Moon – and the Moon, in return, becomes re-interpreted in terms of the mirror.

Speculum lunae: The great cosmic mirror

Parmenides' discovery that the Moon reflects light from the Sun created a watershed in the understanding of the Moon's physical nature by revealing that it must be an opaque, solid body rather than an airy or fiery, impermanent one, as previously believed.[22] Another crucial consequence of heliophotism – albeit one less frequently remarked upon – is that it locked the Earth, Sun and Moon into a triangular relationship, with the Moon as a vital mediating agent between the other two. The Moon's agency played out in both directions. The more apparent function was its role as a mirror-like agent that reflected the Sun's light and heat down towards the Earth, tempering the violent solar heat and light to a more moderate quality as it went. The newly discovered principle of heliophotism was clearly germane to this idea, but it was also buttressed by older traditional beliefs about the Moon's cooling and moisturizing influence on the Earth.[23] Its agency in the opposite direction was less obvious but equally important, for the Moon was also believed to mediate nourishing exhalations from Earth up towards the Sun. This process was believed to be vital for sustaining the Sun's energy, and the Moon played a crucial role in purifying these terrestrial fumes and perfecting them for solar consumption.

The correlation between these two functions of the Moon emerges beautifully in the following passage from Plutarch's *De facie*, where the speaker describes the workings of the cosmos in terms of a mighty organism:

ἀλλὰ τοῦ κατὰ λόγον κρατοῦντος οἱ μὲν ὥσπερ 'ὄμματα φωσφόρα' τῷ προσώπῳ τοῦ παντὸς ἐνδεδεμένοι περιπολοῦσιν, ἥλιος δὲ καρδίας ἔχων δύναμιν ὥσπερ αἷμα καὶ πνεῦμα διαπέμπει καὶ διασκεδάννυσιν ἐξ ἑαυτοῦ θερμότητα καὶ φῶς, γῇ δὲ καὶ θαλάσσῃ χρῆται κατὰ φύσιν ὁ κόσμος, ὅσα κοιλίᾳ καὶ κύστει ζῷον. σελήνη δ' ἡλίου μεταξὺ καὶ γῆς ὥσπερ καρδίας καὶ κοιλίας ἧπαρ ἤ τι μαλθακὸν ἄλλο σπλάγχνον ἐγκειμένη τήν τ' ἄνωθεν ἀλέαν ἐνταῦθα διαπέμπει καὶ τὰς ἐντεῦθεν ἀναθυμιάσεις πέψει τινὶ καὶ καθάρσει λεπτύνουσα περὶ ἑαυτὴν ἀναδίδωσιν.

On the contrary, the rational principle is in control; and that is why the stars revolve fixed like 'radiant eyes' in the countenance of the universe, the sun in the heart's capacity transmits and disperses out of himself heat and light as it were blood and breath, and earth and sea 'naturally' serve the cosmos to the ends that bowels and bladder do an animal. The moon, situated between sun and earth as the liver or another of the soft viscera is between heart and bowels, transmits hither the warmth from above and sends upwards the exhalations from our region, refining them in herself by a kind of concoction and purification.'[24]

Here the Sun, a fiery body situated high up in the heavens, is aligned with the heart, the organ that was believed to dispense heat and energy to the rest of the body. In contrast, the Earth, a place of murky, heavy elements which was believed to be situated low down in the centre of the cosmos, was identified with the bowels that are low down in the body and filled with impure bodily dregs and vapours. The Moon, which was located in between the two and which mediated between the upper and lower parts – cooling the Sun's rays and purifying the Earth's bowelish decoctions – is identified explicitly with a soft organ in the middle of the body such as the spleen or liver. This idea of the liver-Moon constitutes a perfect analogue for the mirror-Moon for, as Ava Shirazi argues in this volume, the liver itself had catoptric associations in Plato's *Timaeus* as well as in ancient thought more generally.[25]

These mirror-like functions are reflected, in turn, in the Moon's role as a metaphysical junction in the cosmos, mediating between the mortal realm below (on Earth) and the immortal realm in the changeless heavens above. Xenocrates, who was associated with the Old Academy, seems to have established the influential idea that the Moon was the abode of that quintessentially intermediate race of beings, the *daemones*, and the doctrine is expounded at length in the myth of Plutarch's *De facie*.[26] The Moon's catoptric associations also fit well with its daemonic nature, particularly through the widely held belief – on which the practice of catoptromancy was founded – that mirrors offered the viewer a portal to what Rabun Taylor has called 'the dorsal spirit world'.[27]

To move away from the realm of metaphor, we find the Moon *literally* conceptualized in terms of a mirror in the tradition of the *speculum lunae* or 'mirror-moon'. In Plutarch's *De facie*, the theory is ascribed to the Peripatetic philosopher Clearchus of Soli:

λέγει γὰρ ἀνὴρ εἰκόνας ἐσοπτρικὰς εἶναι καὶ εἴδωλα τῆς μεγάλης θαλάσσης ἐμφαινόμενα τῇ σελήνῃ τὸ καλούμενον πρόσωπον... ἥ τε πανσέληνος αὐτὴ πάντων ἐσόπτρων ὁμαλότητι καὶ στιλπνότητι κάλλιστόν ἐστι καὶ καθαρώτατον.

The man says that the so-called face is actually mirror-images and reflections of the great sea that appear in the Moon… and the full Moon itself is the finest and clearest of all mirrors in terms of its smoothness and brightness.[28]

Hegesianax of Alexandria Troas, a poet of the third century BCE, attests directly to the idea. In one of the fragments of Hegesianax's astronomical poem *Phaenomena*, quoted in the same passage of the *De facie*, he evokes the markings on the lunar disk as a mirror-image of the Earth's ocean below:

ἢ πόντου μέγα κῦμα καταντία κυμαίνοντος
δείκελον ἰνδάλλοιτο πυριφλεγέθοντος ἐσόπτρου.

or a great wave of ocean surging forward
would appear as a reflection of a mirror that blazes like fire.[29]

In *Icaromenippus* 20, among the litany of complaints relayed to Menippus by the personified Moon there is the philosophers' slanderous claim that she 'hangs over the sea like a mirror' (κατόπτρου δίκην ἐπικρέμασθαι τῇ θαλάττῃ).

Aëtius, who dates to the second century CE, provides a more sober version of Lucian's lunatic doxography. He devotes seven chapters to the Moon, collating scholarly opinion on its substance, size, shape, the source of its light, the nature of lunar eclipse, its earth-like appearance and its distance from the Sun and Earth.[30] One of these chapters (2.30) treats precisely the theme that is germane to Plutarch's *De facie*: the markings on the lunar surface that impart to the Moon its earth-like appearance. Aëtius provides his usual bullet-point summary of different opinions on the matter: Philolaus and some Pythagoreans, he reports, explain the Moon's earth-like appearance by proposing that it is, in fact, a parallel earth, inhabited like our own.[31] Others – Aëtius must mean other *Pythagoreans* in this context – declare that the image in the lunar disk is a reflection (*anaklasis*) of the sea that lies beyond the torrid zone of our inhabited world (ἄλλοι δὲ τὴν ἐν τῇ σελήνῃ ἔμφασιν ἀνάκλασιν εἶναι τῆς πέραν τοῦ διακεκαυμένου κύκλου τῆς οἰκουμένης ὑφ' ἡμῶν θαλάττης). This is clearly related to the Pythagorean doctrine that the Moon is a 'mirror-like body.'[32] But Aëtius' expanded version provides us with an ancient attestation to the so-called tradition of the *speculum lunae* that viewed the Moon as a cartographical instrument or 'catoptrical machine,' mirroring back to us parts of our world that were as yet unexplored.[33] As Mario Neve has shown, the perceived mirror-images of our world in the Moon were crucial to cartographers in the medieval and early modern period.[34] In fact, this catoptric relationship that was believed to exist between Moon and Earth worked in both directions: it also prompted the earliest attempts to map the *Moon*. Glimmers of a pre-modern tradition of lunar cartography that was based on the assumption that the Moon mirrors the Earth can be discovered in Plutarch and (in a more fully developed account) in the Byzantine treatise *On the Black Figure in the Moon*

Mirrors and Mirroring

by Demetrius Triclinius (*ca.* 1300 CE).[35] Even in the early modern period, it is notable that Hevelius' original nomenclature for the features of the lunar topography still cast the Moon as the mirror-image of our world: in 1647 there was a *Pontus Euxinus* on the Moon, along with a lunar Mediterranean.[36] For the ancient earth-bound viewer, whose perspective is restricted by physical location and geographical obstacles, the Moon functioned as an 'encyclopedic mirror', a transcendental device that reflected back to him images of things that lay beyond his normal sight: a sort of prosthetic eye that extended the natural range of vision.[37] This property of mirrors (particularly convex mirrors) was well-known to ancient technical writers.[38]

The *speculum lunae* tradition, in which *we* view the Moon in miniature from the Earth below, represents an inverse of the tradition of *selēnoskopia* with which we started out. From the lunar platform in *selēnoskopia*, the imaginary eye could survey with supreme detachment our world in its entirety, compressed into one convenient eyeshot. On the other hand, when viewed from Earth below in the *speculum lunae* tradition, the Moon appears to reflect our whole world back to us in a miniature mirrory map. Either way, the Moon becomes the ultimate *mise en abyme*: a fantasy archival space, which offers us sensory command of the whole world, and a catoptric *précis* of all our knowledge and existence.[39] In this sense, it becomes symbolic both of the limits of human knowledge and of the imperializing desire to control the world of knowledge, which Jason König and Tim Whitmarsh have explored.[40]

Lucian's lunar observatory

This leads us back to the catoptric device that is located on Lucian's Moon, for through it, the Moon offers the viewer a condensed view of the whole earth – a distant avatar of *Blue marble*, the paradigm-shifting photograph of 1972 – and a version of the *speculum lunae* theory, which was known to Lucian, as we have seen.[41] Wälchli, the scholar who has devoted the most attention to the technological dimensions of Lucian's apparatus, identifies this mirror as a panoramic surveillance device on the basis of similarities with the use of trick-mirrors in temples, or similar surveillance-mirrors described in Hero's *Catoptrica*.[42] He even speculates – rather fancifully, perhaps – that, since Lucian himself held an administrative position in Egypt, he may have observed such panoramic installations, perhaps even Hero's original itself, if one existed.[43] However, Lucian's mirror is a technological fantasy. It offers a perspective that is simultaneously condensed *and* magnified, for the viewer sees in its surface an absolute panorama of the Earth (*all* the cities and *all* the peoples: πάσας μὲν πόλεις, πάντα δὲ ἔθνη ὁρᾷ) that is also revealed in minute detail ('as if he were standing over each one': ὥσπερ ἐφεστὼς ἑκάστοις). In it, he sees his own family and his whole country as well (τότε καὶ τοὺς οἰκείους ἐγὼ ἐθεασάμην καὶ πᾶσαν τὴν πατρίδα). The lunar mirror therefore seems to combine – impossibly – the effects that were known to be achieved by the convex mirror (condensation) *and* the concave (magnification).[44] The experience is similar to the combined telescopy and microscopy in the magical *selēnoskopia* of *Icaromenippus*, where Menippus sees all the peoples of the world at the same time as observing each individual engaged in his or her own affairs. There, Menippus emphasizes the bewildering chaos of his disconcerting vision (*Icar.* 16–17). But here, in the presence of the mirror, Lucian has a different concern: whether or not those on whom he is spying *can see him in return* (εἰ δὲ κἀκεῖνοι ἐμὲ ἑώρων, οὐκέτι ἔχω τὸ ἀσφαλὲς εἰπεῖν). This plays on mirrors' tricky ability to refract the visual ray in ways that can conceal or alternatively expose what lies hidden – a quality that Maria Gerolemou has explored more fully in this volume. Lucian avowedly cannot see his own image in the lunar mirror – but perhaps it is being reflected to viewers on the world below, a great face peering down at them from the Moon. Perhaps, in answer to the momentous question of Plutarch's *De facie*, we are invited to imagine that the 'Man in the Moon' is – Lucian himself.

The combination of the mirror with the *well* on the Moon is more challenging to interpret. Fusillo compares the lunar well with the prayer-holes in *Icaromenippus* 25, through which voices from the world below can infiltrate the realm of the gods.[45] It is true that the well on the Moon amplifies sounds from the Earth below. Others cite as a parallel the catoptromantic oracle at the shrine of Demeter in Patrae, which juxtaposes a mirror and a spring (*pēgē*): according to Pausanias (7.21.12), a mirror was lowered down into the spring in order to receive an oracular response.[46] But we should be cautious: Lucian's mirror is a purely optical instrument, not a divinatory one, and there is no mention of *water* in his well, so the analogy is not as close as one might wish. Wälchli argues strenuously for the relevance of a passage in Plutarch's essay *On the daemon of Socrates* where the transmission of prayers to spirits is compared to the method of transmitting sounds telephonically through the use of shields.[47] As he points out, shields were associated with mirrors in antiquity, which might have suggested to Lucian his audio-visual configuration of well and mirror. But in this case the analogy, albeit intriguing, seems even more tenuous to my mind: shields are not wells.

Wälchli's thesis that Lucian's imaginary object was rooted in the technological realities of his own time is surely right, however. That wells amplify sound is commonplace and self-evident, and we do not need to resort to shields to justify the well's acoustic role here. Instead – in addition to this acoustic function – I suspect that Lucian had in mind the *dioptra*, the 'seeing tube' that was principally used in land surveying in antiquity, and also to aid astronomical observation.[48] One form of the *dioptra* was a simple hollow tube which the viewer could hold up to his eye whilst observing the sky. It should not be confused with the telescope, since it did not contain a lens and did not magnify vision in any way; it simply aided observation by focusing the line of vision on a specific segment of the sky and blocking out ambient light. Aristotle explains that it is similar to the effect achieved by shading one's eyes with one's hands: it works by channelling the visual ray directly to or from the eye, rather than allowing it to dissipate. It is for this reason, he claims, that animals with sunken eyes have keener distance-vision than those whose eyes are prominent.[49] In antiquity, this *dioptra*-effect could also be achieved by digging a pit or well: the viewer descended into the well and looked upwards at the sky from the bottom, using its rim as an artificial horizon:

ὁ γὰρ αὐτὸς ἐπηλυγασάμενος τὴν χεῖρα ἢ δι' αὐλοῦ βλέπων τὰς μὲν διαφορὰς οὐθὲν μᾶλλον οὐδ' ἧττον κρινεῖ τῶν χρωμάτων, ὄψεται δὲ πορρώτερον· οἱ γοῦν ἐκ τῶν ὀρυγμάτων καὶ φρεάτων ἐνίοτε καὶ ἀστέρας ὁρῶσιν.

For the man who shades his eyes with his hand or looks through a tube will not distinguish differences of colour any better or worse, but he will see farther; at any rate, people sometimes see stars from pits and wells.[50]

Aristotle's incidental remark about people *seeing stars* from the bottom of such pits and *wells* is of great moment for understanding Lucian's device. It has been suggested that the idea lurks beneath the well-known anecdote about Thales falling into a well whilst he gazed at the stars: on this reading, the astronomer was in the well by design, not accident, and his strange predicament was actually misunderstood by the girl in the anecdote who pokes fun at him; it turns out, therefore, that the last laugh may be on *her*, and not the absent-minded philosopher, after all.[51]

If we now return to Lucian's lunar well – and add his great magnifying mirror into the picture – we can see that what he offers us is not just some outlandish fantasy, not a purely literary symbol, nor even simply a play on the ubiquitous theories and demonstrations that associated the Moon with mirrors in antiquity, as I have tried to explain here. It *is* all of these things, of course, but it is also more. Lucian has invented a fantastical *proto-telescope*, for he has welded together with imaginative ingenuity the disparate apparatus of ancient astronomical observation. His device combines: elevated platform (the Moon – better than any of the common spots used by ancient astronomers for surveying the cosmos, such as a terrestrial roof or mountain-top);[52] a well (a full-body immersive *dioptra*, which happens to amplify sound as well as enhance observation); and – Lucian's uncanny innovation and the *coup de grâce* – a giant mirror to compress and magnify vision. This is a super, multi-sensory observatory on the Moon. Whether or not this telescope was actually *functional* is a separate question and one, I suspect, that did not really interest Lucian at all. The *True Histories* is not the place to find the nuts and bolts of real-world machinery, and if there is a device of any sort in this story-world, we should expect it to be both paradoxical and marvellous. But it is the presence of any sort of optical technology *at all* that is compelling, in my view; after all, the *selēnoskopia* of the *Icaromenippus* is achieved through purely magical means, and Lucian could have done the same here, but chose otherwise. For this reason, if no other, the presence of the mirror and the well is pointed, demanding our admiration (it is a θαῦμα, after all) and scrutiny.

Conclusion

Lucian's evocation of a magnifying mirror for the observation of a distant world (albeit our own) is a boldly imaginative move that seems to reach forward and anticipate – as an *idea* – Galileo's telescope from 1609. I do not wish to ascribe to him (or to the Greeks more generally) the invention of telescopic technology *avant la lettre*, though claims of this nature have, of course, been ventured, both seriously and in the spirit of the hoax.[53]

Nevertheless, though it is an imaginary device, it deserves an important place in the history of science, for it tells us much about ancient ideas relating to the Moon, about ancient anxieties and excitement concerning mirrors, and about the long history of telescopic aspiration in the pre-modern world.

I have, therefore, presented a case here for regarding Lucian's lunar mirror as an emblem of what we might call the ancient scientific imagination for the way in which it amalgamates diverse strands of thought that associated the Moon with mirrors in magic, philosophy and scientific practice. I have also argued that Lucian's telescopic fantasy draws on the realities of contemporary technology and astronomical observation in more complex ways than has previously been realized. Some of the resonances with Lucian's contemporary technological culture are difficult for modern ears to detect, but it is important for us to consider what these would have meant to ancient readers. Would Lucian's lunar mirror have provoked their suspicion? Quite possibly: mirrors were slippery devices, associated with deception and lies; in order to fend off charges of sorcery, Apuleius famously had to justify owning one. Would his lunar observatory have imbued his fiction with an air of awe-inspiring exactitude and scientific method? Quite possibly too: this was, after all, the era of Hero and Ptolemy. The point is that it would surely have elicited a mixture of feelings: wonder, confidence and mistrust. How better to enhance a work of lies, not one of which is to be believed?

CHAPTER 15
MIRRORING THE FACE OF GOD: THE CHALLENGE OF THE 'INVISIBLE FACE' AND THE METROPOLITAN CRUCIFIXION IVORY[1]

Kallirroe Linardou

To the unspoiled gaze of my students

Κ ά τ ο π τ ρ ο ν οὖν μᾶλλον ἄν τις εἴποι τὸ τοῦ ὀφθαλμοῦ·

Hermias, *In Platonis Phaedrum scholia*

The headlights of a car may look to us like a pair of glowing eyes, and we may even call them so. The artist may use this similarity to work his magic of transformation. Picasso did precisely that when he created his wonderful bronze baboon with his youth ... The artist's discovery of an unexpected use for the car has a twofold effect on us. We follow him not only in seeing a particular car as a baboon's head but learn in the process a new way of articulating the world, a new metaphor, and when we are in the mood we may suddenly find the cars that block our way looking at us with that apish grin that is due to Picasso's classification.

Gombrich, 1996, 89

A similar 'unexpected use' for a renowned Byzantine image struck me in the classroom years ago, when a young student-artist in the audience projected an alternative visual classification upon the familiar configuration of the picture on the screen; instead of a representation of the Crucifixion (Fig. 15.1), he discerned an ubiquitous holy face emerging as a ghost from the shadowy contours of the projected image (Figs 15.2 and 15.3). Sadly my first reaction was to politely dismiss the comment as irrelevant to our discussion and stick to the safe scholarly identification of the object: it was a renowned minute carved ivory plaque of the Crucifixion, a master-piece of the so-called Macedonian renaissance, dated to the middle of the tenth century on stylistic grounds, and today housed in the medieval collection of the Metropolitan Museum of Art.[2]

Yet this familiar, albeit unregistered and unclassified holy face on the Metropolitan Crucifixion, once firmly sighted could never escape visual memory. As a matter of fact, there is no doubt in my mind that the young artist was right, and I can instantly discern the elusive face of the dead Christ and not the Crucifixion. Even so, reflexive circumspection persistently undermines the fresh and unspoiled gaze of the uninitiated – this 'new way of articulating the world' and by extension the world of representation – in favour of pictorial sense and familiar vision. In the end, one must decide either to follow this alternative gaze or to dismiss it.

Fig. 15.1 Crucifixion ivory, mid-tenth century, Constantinople. The Metropolitan Museum of Art.

For the purposes of my chapter in this volume dedicated to *Mirrors and Mirroring* I had to reconcile two principal concepts that at first may appear irreconcilable: mirrors and mirroring in conjunction with the acheiropoietic icon, a medieval manipulation of ancient beliefs and practises that eventually would be superseded by the luminous acheiropoietic impressions of photography.[3]

On the one hand and at a purely pragmatic level, a looking-glass or any reflective surface is commonly perceived as a medium facilitating self-examination, self-knowledge and even self-fashioning. By extension, mirrors also became the springboard of a metaphor for the mimetic accuracy and often illusory nature of vision and artistic representation, and a simile for sight and vision.[4] For Hermias, the fifth-century Alexandrian Neo-Platonist philosopher and commentator of Plato, the eye is like a mirror.[5] In a Christian context,[6] St Paul's renowned aphorism on mirrors as an analogy to indirect and therefore incomplete knowledge of God in 1 Corinthians 13:12 – *Now we see but a poor reflection as in a mirror; then we shall see face to face* – was particularly relevant to the historical circumstances of the epistle's addressees, since the Corinthians

Fig. 15.2 Drawing of the Crucifixion ivory by the artist Athanasios Yiotakis (pencil on paper, 2017). By the permission of the artist.

were famous as the producers of some of the finest bronze mirrors in antiquity.[7] In Byzantium – a premodern society – mirrors were rare and precious objects and thus an aristocratic luxury,[8] while mirror-gazing was an ambiguous, even negative activity, principally associated with the feminine imperfection, sensuality and self-deception.[9] Perhaps this is the reason why Byzantine mirrors and mirror-gazing are hardly represented in any surviving material works.[10] In Byzantine texts mirrors are predominantly employed as metaphors that enable their viewers to contemplate a better self, a superior moral exemplar and, by extension images of the anticipated divine order; they tend to constitute prescribed 'models for imitation rather than likeness of their viewers'.[11] According to Stratis Papaioannou, 'Mirroring surfaces include such things as the scriptures (or similar texts such as saint's lives), icons, holy men, and souls purified by virtue, and none are represented as enabling self-reflection'.[12]

On the other hand, and by definition, the *acheiropoietos* image is a faithful reproduction of a certain likeness wrought with no interference of human hands; it is a reflection, an

Fig. 15.3 Drawing of the Crucifixion ivory by the artist Ioannis Efthimiou (coal on paper, 2018). By the permission of the artist.

eidolon that escapes the catoptrical illusion of shadows and is materialized. It is an iconic paradox 'trespassing' on the realm of representation and ensuring access to a perfect manifestation of the divine. It thus reconciles the status of an accurate reflected image with the idea of a representation paradoxically formed without human agency. By inversion of the argument, any catoptrical reflection can be seen as an acheiropoietic, immaterial and faithful image caught upon the mirroring surface;[13] its visibility and perception depend solely upon the visual faculties of the beholder and not the art of representation. In this circular schema I believe we can risk the inclusion of a further category of images: cryptomorphs, i.e. hidden or ambiguous images. Acheiropoietic in essence,[14] and certainly dependent upon visual perception and the imaginative gaze, they maintain an ambivalent status and occasionally constitute 'an act of terrorism against pictorial sense'.[15] They constantly challenge any attempt to tame individual encounters with images and the process of viewing itself: 'What is the flesh of an image and what is it that is formed in the gaze that we cast upon it?'[16]

In what follows I wish primarily to demonstrate that the elusive face of the dead Christ on the Metropolitan Crucifixion ivory was a meaningful cryptomorph, an image hidden within an image, whose decipherment and visuality depended upon the responsive gaze of the medieval viewer. Secondly, I wish to demonstrate that this hidden portrait was meant as a mental indirect reflection and alternative visual interpretation of the renowned *acheiropoietos* icon/touch-relic of Christ's face – the Image of Edessa, better known as the *Mandylion* – that arrived in Constantinople in 944. It, thus, provides us with an excellent opportunity to contemplate a mirror-image of a faithful acheiropoietic reproduction of the divine as if we were looking at Christ's face through multiple looking-glasses.

The distinctive iconography and supreme craftsmanship of the Metropolitan Crucifixion ivory have dominated scholarly discussion since an early date, primarily in an attempt to trace earlier iconographical models and literary sources that may have triggered its design as such.[17] The main theme of the composition unfolds with no surprises and in a lively narrative style: the mourning Virgin and John on either side of crucified Christ, two angels on top and the three Roman soldiers dividing Christ's garments at the foot of the cross. The unique and unprecedented iconographical feature is the bearded half-naked reclining man stabbed in the stomach by the cross of Christ. The inscription above him identifies him as the personification of Hades and he is most certainly inspired by early patristic literature and Romanos's the Melodist hymnography. Hades' inclusion is believed to have produced a dramatic effect on the overall impression by accentuating the epic victory of Christ over death and the triumph of the cross. So far, no sufficient explanation has been provided as to why the representation was not repeated in any other period or medium. It therefore remains an iconographical *hapax* among surviving Byzantine examples of the Crucifixion.[18]

As already stated, the Metropolitan ivory plaque is of minute dimensions;[19] it measures 15.1 × 8.9 × 0.8 cm and thus it can comfortably rest on a small palm. This microscopic icon is thought to have originally served as the centre-piece of a triptych designed for private devotion.[20] Sometimes, when it is reproduced in books and scholarly publications, this essential material feature, its small scale, is overlooked, and as a result the viewer is misled to believe that the object is much bigger than in reality.[21] An obvious and understandable explanation for such a concession is the visibility of tiny iconographical details and the particulars of stylistic rendering as well as the legibility of inscriptions and *nomina sacra*. 'Yet, even more than other foundational constructs such as color, line, or shape, scale directs attention towards the capacity of an artwork to respond to a specific location and place, while simultaneously calling into question the role of the viewer. Scale foregrounds the relation between materiality and meaning by its very refusal of arbitrariness; things are not a particular size for their own sake but are scaled according to some predetermined rule or standard of judgement'.[22] Nothing is made by chance, least of all sumptuous ivory carvings where 'value lay in the material, not in the price of labour and probably not even in the relative competence of the craftsman'.[23]

Mirrors and Mirroring

Apparently, the iconographical particularities and technical details of the artwork in our case were prioritized and therefore monopolized scholarly attention at the expense of the total visual effect – an important aspect easily eluding our reflexive viewing if we disregard the object's original scale. Then again, what if we conform to the functional requirements and constructional prerequisites predetermined by the creators of the object: a petite deeply and deftly carved ivory plaque meant to be viewed not only closely but also from the distance we would normally hold a book? In other words, what if this object was designed to function meaningfully both on close inspection and distant contemplation? What if it was upon the beholder to either zoom-in or zoom-out the image? The point I am trying to articulate is that we have left out of our sight and scholarly consideration the zoom-out option and this is precisely what I intend to focus my attention on.

In the concluding chapter of the authoritative monograph dedicated to the art of Byzantine ivory, Anthony Cutler regrets the paucity of written sources that would hopefully give us a comprehensive glimpse on the viewer's response to the qualities of ivory carving and the impact of its viewing under specifically staged circumstances that might have altered its appearance.[24] In my mind, it is no coincidence that in order to demonstrate his point and test his thesis, he exclusively employed the Metropolitan Crucifixion ivory. In a hypothetical setting where candles would be lit not in front of the artwork but instead behind it, the heavy shadows cast upon the ground-plane of the composition – a distinctive and essential aesthetic feature of this particular ivory plaque – would vanish miraculously. As a result all figures would be dramatically animated as if set within a three-dimensional scenic platform.[25] According to my reading, we should spare the heavy shadows and let them perform their magic, precisely because their inclusion was part of the original compositional design and in all probability their purpose and visuality was meaningful. If we leave aside for a moment the fleshed out figures and follow the shadowy contours formed by the deeply carved canopy, the bended arms and legs of crucified Christ, the suppedium of the cross and the three soldiers on its base, our eye will inevitably discern the familiar countenance of the dead Christ crowned with what should be perceived as the wreath of thorns. Mary and John on his side form the outline of his skinny cheeks (Fig. 15.4). The beholder contemplating this tiny icon privately and from the distance he/she would normally address his/her prayer to an icon in a room illuminated with candles or oil-lamps, would be able to observe simultaneously Christ's Crucifixion as well as a close-up of the Saviour's tormented face. This petite icon would instantly render visible the figure of death and the principal of eternal life through subjugation of death.

Does the elusive-face-scenario have any validity and, if so, how can it fit into the historical circumstances that may have prompted the ivory's design and creation in such a particular way? Above all, was this acheiropoietic face-impression an intentional and meaningful choice of the creators; was it originally meant as a cryptomorph, i.e. an image that harbours another image,[26] or was it instead a conditional phenomenon, an accidental schema, a whim? If the answer is affirmative on the side of intention and meaningfulness, then how is it to be understood and interpreted?

Fig. 15.4 The Metropolitan Crucifixion ivory as exhibited in the Museum show-case. Photo by the author.

The history of ambiguous and puzzling images that presupposed an active and responsive viewer to subtle visual stimuli was already old in tenth-century Byzantium. Specifically after Iconoclasm, Byzantine discourses on vision and sight employed a series of metaphors 'that in reality were describing cognition and the mental process of perception ... the mind's grasp and apprehension, not the literal grasp of the eyes'. In this process the faculty of imagination was especially critical for the collection and collation of fragmented sensory data obtained through the operation of all five senses.[27] Moreover and as demonstrated by John Onians, the shift away from naturalism towards stylization and abstraction in Late Antiquity signals a major turning point for the operation of visual faculties.[28] The growing emphasis invested upon the active role of the sophisticated viewer and his/her imaginative engagement with, even fulfilment of, art was the result of a century-long training into a theoretical framework promoted by rhetorical education that favoured the development of visual imagination and a viewer that would see more into something than it was actually there.[29] The ingeniously book-matched marble revetments in Hagia Sophia in Constantinople and other Byzantine churches exemplify precisely this kind of art demanding imaginative viewing in order to be fully appreciated.[30] Finally, Gilbert Dagron in his masterly article on *Holy Images and Likeness* traces the evolution of the beholder's predisposition towards the holy icon.[31] An object of worship with its own raison d'être, it depended for its identification as such neither on literal likeness nor on the artist's imagination and the craft of mimesis but instead on the collective imagination and cultural consensus. As it appears early medieval viewers were encouraged to endorse spiritual vision,[32] and therefore they were better acquainted with manipulating and amending works of art mentally to uncover hidden images.[33]

On 15 August 944, the feast-day of the *Koimesis*, Constantinople received in jubilation and public celebrations one of the most precious Christian relics, the *acheiropoietos* icon of Christ's face, commonly known as the *Mandylion*, enshrined for centuries in the Syrian city of Edessa – modern-day Urfa in south-eastern Turkey.[34] This touch-relic of Christ was submitted to the Byzantine general John Kourkouas as part of a pact made with the local authorities of Edessa during the siege of the city by the imperial army. The capture of the icon and its transfer to Constantinople are historically attributed to the initiative of Romanos I Lecapenos (920–944), a usurper to the throne of the lawful Macedonian dynasty.[35] Unsurprisingly, and immediately after the relic's arrival to the Queen City, Romanos's co-emperor and legitimate successor Constantine VII Porphyrogennetos (913–959) would 'cash in' the symbolic capital of this newly-appropriated asset; his ascension to the throne was miraculously foreseen and foretold by the agency of the holy icon itself.[36] The reception of the relic marked the sad downfall of the Lecapini and the restoration to power of the popular Macedonians in December 944.[37] According to Averil Cameron, 'The kudos for Constantine was as great as that won by Heraclius with the recovery of the True Cross.'[38]

After a long and adventurous journey from Edessa, the relic was escorted in a solemn procession into Constantinople. A detailed account of the ceremonials and public festivities that followed its reception, the *Narratio de Imagine Edessena*, was later written under the auspices of the reinstalled Constantine.[39] The final resting place of the legendary relic was the palatine chapel of the Virgin of Pharos,[40] although it is debated whether this was the initial plan of Romanos. According to a different interpretation, the *Mandylion* was to be accommodated in the small chapel of Christ Saviour that was erected by Romanos above the *Chalke* Gate, the official entrance to the imperial palace, precisely for the enshrinement of this precious relic.[41] Indeed, it might have been placed there initially only to be subsequently removed under the initiative of Constantine in order to join the imperial collection of Christ's Passion relics deposited in the Pharos chapel.

In my mind this debate over the relic's custody and sacred contextualization was not only a matter of claim upon its glory, prestige and authority but also a matter of interpretation and eventually of its symbolic and ideological investment. According to Sysse Engberg the logical place to install this particular relic would have been the ceremonial gate to the imperial palace; thus, it would continue a long tradition that had elevated the *Mandylion* to the status of a palladium invested with apotropaic qualities.[42] This hypothesis is corroborated by the subsequent use of its reproduction in monumental painting; it has been pointed out that the frequent appearance of the *Mandylion* in depictions above main entrances or at the summit of the arch leading into the sanctuary of Byzantine churches may have been a reflection of its original position at Edessa above the main entrance to the city as a protective image.[43] In all probability, Romanus's initiative aimed at precisely this kind of exploitation of the newly acquired asset.

In contrast, Constantine must have favoured an alternative interpretation and use for the *Mandylion* and not necessarily to suppress or diminish its significance and importance as it has been proposed.[44] His primary concern was to expropriate the relic and its symbolic value from his predecessor and appropriate it for himself by erasing any record of its initial installation over the *Chalke* Gate, and secondly to promote and publicize a new symbolic meaning and function for it that would immediately place it under absolute imperial control and jurisdiction. He therefore transported the relic to the imperial chapel of Pharos where it would be viewed as part of a very particular sacred context: the True Cross, the Crown of thorns, the cane and the sponge, the lance, and the nails, i.e. in the company of the instruments of Christ's passion. Thus, from a palladium meant to safeguard the security of the city and its citizens, it would automatically be transformed into a material testimony of Christ's kingship extended upon the power and authority of the earthly ruler. In addition to this and as a result, the Passion relics and the *Mandylion* would be equated to symbols of Christ's human flesh and therefore as tokens of his sufferings. It is precisely this concept of imperial use that would appeal to the Norman rulers of Sicily in the twelfth century in order to incorporate the depiction of the *Mandylion* and the *Hetoimasia* throne in the Pantocrator programme of the Monreale dome as it has been pointed out by Ernst Kitzinger.[45] Another visual reverberation of this equation and interpretation can be found in the twelfth-century bilateral Novgorodian icon today housed in the Tretyakov Gallery in Moscow that combines a representation of the *Mandylion* with the Adoration of the True Cross and the instruments of Christ's Passion on its reverse.[46]

The telling of the *Mandylion* story was long, extremely complex and diachronically amended and augmented in order to serve a series of different ideological and theological purposes.[47] By the time of its arrival in Constantinople in 944 the mainstream version stated that it was created in Christ's lifetime as an authentic token of his likeness and at the request of King Abgar, ruler of Edessa, who suffered by a grave illness.[48] Christ handed over to the king's messenger a towel that he had pressed upon his moist face. This piece of cloth would retain an impression of his facial features. The king was miraculously healed by the acheiropoietic icon, which remained in the city even after its conquest by the Arabs.

But there was a secondary and subordinate literary tradition that connected the relic to Christ's Passion. In the *Narratio de Imagine Edessena*,[49] the official account composed in Constantinople after the relic's arrival, it is reported briefly that the image was produced willingly by Christ but not upon Abgar's request. During the Agony and his prayer in the Garden of Gethsemane (Luke 22.44) Christ's sweat was 'like drops of blood trickling down to the ground'. A disciple was said to have handed him a cloth on which Christ left an impression of his face. The image of Edessa was purported to be this cloth, sent to king Abgar after Christ had ascended to heaven.

This subordinate literary tradition that linked the *acheiropoietos* icon with Christ's Passion would become the predominant version in a different textual account, the homily of Gregory the Referendarius (§ 11–12, 16, 25–26). The text survives in a single manuscript kept in the Vatican and dated to the eleventh century.[50] Specifically in § 26–27 it is stated explicitly that the image was formed miraculously by the drops of sweat from Christ's face and the finger of God. Gregory juxtaposes meaningfully the sweat on Christ's face and the impression that resulted from it with the water and blood poured out from the wound on his side during the Crucifixion.[51] This deliberate attempt to reinforce a connection of the *Mandylion* to Christ's final hours and his Crucifixion and by extension to the relics of his Passion must have had a very specific aim: smoothing the path for the relic's *translatio* to its final resting place, the Pharos chapel. Seen under this light the placement of the *Mandylion* within the imperial collection of relics would seem only appropriate and natural.

Gregory the Referendarius was a contemporary of Constantine, an archdeacon of the Great Church and by office an intermediate between the Patriarch and the Emperor. A legitimate speculation would be that his sermon was composed at the instigation of the emperor but not for the celebration of the relic's reception on 944 as has been suggested.[52] To state the obvious, I can hardly imagine the public performance of a festal homily celebrating an event of paramount significance that would conspicuously omit any reference to the reigning senior co-emperor at the time, namely Romanos, and his sons. According to my understanding the sermon must have been composed and performed a year later during the first anniversary of the *Mandylion* feast-day on 16 August 945 and for the purposes of its new *translatio* from the *Chalke* to the Pharos chapel while Constantine was the sole reigning Emperor. The whole discourse is that of a panegyric and not a detailed historical account of the relic's reception. In § 18–19 the homilist recounts a solemn procession the whereabouts and details of which remain unclear.[53] A beloved anonymous emperor emphatically likened to King David,[54] an officiating patriarch, numerous priests and a crowd of people followed on foot the ark containing the holy relic. At the head of the procession a chanting chorus was leading the way. The final destination is described only metonymically. The homilist does not specify straightforwardly the imperial chapel of the Virgin of Pharos but instead he enumerates the principal relics of Christ's Passion kept there; with these the *Mandylion* would be eventually reunited. According to my reading there is nothing in this particular sermon to confirm that this procession should be seen as part of the public festivities that marked the entrance of the *Mandylion* into Constantinople in August 944.

My interpretation of the circumstances of the sermon's delivery may be only conjectural but there remains the fact that in Constantinople of the middle of the tenth century circulated a tradition that explicitly linked the Crucifixion and Christ's passion to the acheiropoietic icon of Christ's face that arrived from Edessa. Constantine VII Porphyrogennetos must have been the instigator of this story precisely because he was eager to authenticate the relic's ideological appropriation and its re-contextualization.

Studied against this historical backdrop the cryptomorph of Christ's tormented face upon the Metropolitan Crucifixion is perfectly understandable. Therefore, it is my contention that the acheiropoietic hidden image of Christ's face was a meaningful and purposeful choice inspired by this secondary literary tradition that precisely linked the Mandylion to Christ's passion. I would even risk its identification as the first Veronica, the first true icon (*vera icona*) and faithful reflection of God's face.[55] This supreme specimen of Constantinopolitan ivory carving dated to the middle of the tenth century and intended for private devotion can fit perfectly into the historical setting of its creation.

As to its intended audience – the responsive and imaginative viewer – we can safely speculate. Constantine is reported to have been a particularly attentive and active viewer of puzzling images. Upon the *Mandylion*'s arrival to the Byzantine capital, Constantine and Romanos's two sons were summoned to see the faint impression of Christ's countenance on the fragile piece of cloth brought from Syria.[56] 'It was said that Romanos's sons could only see a blurred countenance on the picture, but the Porphyrogennetos clearly distinguished the features – a portent that the holy monk Sergios interpreted very unfavourably for the former.'[57] According to his words and the Psalm of David (Psalms 33.15), 'The eyes of the Lord are over the righteous and his ears are open to their prayer; but the face of the Lord is against them that do evil, to destroy their memorial from the earth'. The discernment of the image did not depend solely upon the visual faculties of the viewers but on their inherent spiritual qualities and their trained imaginative gaze. Constantine, a sophisticated viewer trained in the art of visual manipulation,[58] is a fitting candidate that would certainly appreciate the puzzling image on the Metropolitan Crucifixion ivory. Christ's elusive face, an accurate mental reflection of the divine countenance, stands as a metaphorical mirroring surface upon which the elect viewer would eventually gaze the perfection of God, the ultimate moral exemplar/mirror for self-fashioning.

CHAPTER 16
TECHNOLOGIES 'MADE IN GREECE': KONSTANTINOS SIMONIDES' STEAMPUNK INVENTIONS THROUGH THE LOOKING-GLASS
Lilia Diamantopoulou

'The mirror's fascination lies in its ambiguous relation to truth.'[1] This is how Nikolas Calas introduces his *Mirrors of the Mind* (1975). In this essay he reflects on mirrors, prisms, self-reflections, narcissism, mechanical reproductions such as photography, and illusions as a part of reality from a philosophical, psychological and artistic perspective, taking into consideration examples that range from byzantine icons to Van Eyck and Picasso. Calas had already been preoccupied with mirrors in *Confound the Wise*; more than thirty years earlier he wrote: 'Just as much as fire or steam or electric light or the camera, the mirror is a machine, machine meaning nothing else, as its Greek origin indicates, than invention'.[2] Taking Calas' thoughts as a starting point, my chapter deals with the relationship of mirrors and reflections to truth and reality, as well as illusion and deception in the work of Konstantinos Simonides, who vehemently advocated the Greek origin of several crucial European technological inventions of the nineteenth century.

In 1849, Konstantinos Simonides, who is now known as a great forger, publishes the *Symais*, which is claimed by the editor to be a work of the Byzantine monk Meletios of Chios, dated back to the thirteenth century. Its subject is the 'History of the Apollonian School of the Island of Symi'. The book is furnished with a detailed preface, footnotes and references in scientific form, as well as a glossary. Already on the title page Simonides appears as the sole editor, publishing the manuscript for the first time 'unchanged with addition of notes and Prolegomena'.[3] The text is a mélange of real and invented sources: historical characters like Stephanos Byzantios, Strabo, Eustatius of Thessalonica and Diodorus are mixed with imaginary authors and their treatises such as Eulyros and his 'Εθνικά [National]', or Laostefos and his 'Ποικίλη Ιστορία [Varied History]'. As may have been expected, Simonides was preparing the way for future editions of these fictitious texts, which he announced in the footnotes and from which he had already published extracts in newspapers. The *Symais* is prefaced by a brief letter from the monk Meletios of Chios to his colleague Methodios. In the letter Meletios states that he now pursues his desire to provide informations about the most important painters of the Holy Mountain. The work ends with the wood print of the signature of Meletios, a note specifying that the work was completed in 1236. On page 61 we find an extended list of all teachers, pupils and inventors of the school of Symi, enriched with brief biographical information.[4]

The invented authorial persona of Meletios did not want to confine himself to the icon-painters of Mount Athos, and therefore he resolved to go back to the description of the Apollonian School founded in 377 AD on Symi, from which the first major school of icon-painting emerged.[5] This kind of listing important painters and artists and their works is strongly reminiscent of Pliny's *Historia Naturalis* (book 35) and Vasari's *Vite* and may well have been inspired by them.

According to Meletios, the High School of Symi was a miraculous site: it had already anticipated all the great inventions and technological achievements of modern times, since Late Antiquity and the early Greek Middle Ages. Among other things, the printing press, copper engraving (p. 16), the paper (p. 17), the fire cannon (pp. 20–23; 140–145), the telescope (p. 19) and the diving bell were invented there. Mirrors, glasses and polished silver plates play an important role as technical components of these inventions. As for Simonides, to detect and publicize these achievements constitutes a patriotic act. He writes in his comments to *Symais*:

> A new time dawns in Greece today. Thanks to Meletios from Chios. The invention of the telescope is considered a new thing, and is attributed to the German Jansen. If Germany boasted of Jansen and his puny telescope, how well must Greece [brag] to have the much wiser, much older, the great Sevastos who has not just invented the telescope, which is described as much more important than anything ever preceeding, but also oil painting, engraving, stone and wood printing, papermaking and more or less also the divine typography for which our contemporaries brag as inventors.
>
> Above all, however, is the mercury underwater boat (as it is described) that the Europeans have yet to invent, no matter how hard the wisest and most imaginative brains in Western Europe might ever try, persistently and pointlessly investing time. The Europeans boast of it, and with them, unfortunately, many of us who have become their advocates. But let the gentlemen know that compared to our immortal, glorious ancestors, whose fame we share as their true descendants, they are merely infants. And how many more superior inventions come from this school and bring forth the greatness of the Greeks, but remain buried or unknown because the written testimonies are lost.[6]

With the case of the telescope, Simonides consciously selects a prestigious object of first-class scientific value. The telescope is connected to the scientific revolution of the sixteenth/seventeenth centuries and is associated with names like Galileo Galilei, Tycho Brahe or Johannes Kepler.[7] Certainly, Simonides had his 'sources of inspiration' and it might be presumed that he extracts his information from contemporary newspapers and reports on the current technological developments of his time in order to project them to the past as alleged technological achievements of ancient and medieval Greece. The description of the diving bell, that consisted of mirrors among other things, is a good example to illustrate this point:

Anastasios Nikolaou dived to the bottom of the sea and rode around, wearing an asbestos suit and sitting in an iron bell and an iron ship constructed by concave mirrors and skins in the middle. Before diving, he made a coal fire in the iron bell, added mercury, moved the copper machines through fire and mercury, dived, and flames and steam shot out of the pipes.[8]

Actually, Simonides describes methods of immersion which are reminiscent of the technological developments of his own time. The anachronistic projection of the diving bell to a distant past is not unique, unusual or unprecedented, especially if seen against the background of literary traditions. Consider, for example, the numerous representations of Alexander the Great in the miniatures of illuminated manuscripts of Alexander's romance, depicting the Hellenistic monarch in a diving bell.[9]

Finally, it is not uncommon for contemporary scientific works to seek prestigious origin for new inventions in (Greek and Roman) antiquity or in myth. This can be further illustrated by the example of the burning glass (Fig. 16.1). Wilhelm Benjamin Busch (1804: 195–206) discusses the origins of concave mirrors, beginning with Hebenstreits' theory mentioned in *De speculis* (1727), according to which Prometheus, presented as a Caucasian prince, was the first to use burning glasses.[10] As further sources of evidence for the knowledge of fire-making mirrors Busch recalls Plutarch and Pliny and deals with the question of the destruction of Marcellus' Roman fleet by Archimedes with the help of such mirrors.[11] The sources usually cited in the contemporary technological debate are ranging from Galen, Lucian, Anthemius of Tralles ('Περί παραδόξων μηχανημάτων [Concerning Wondrus Machines]', fragment printed by Dupuy in 1777), and far beyond this Zonaras (who cites the burning of Vitalianus' fleet during the siege of Constantinople as a parallel example), to Tzetztes and Eustathios of Thessalonike; the latter refers to the writings of Diodorus of Sicily, Dio Cassius, Hero, Philo and many more,[12] whose complete works, however, are lost (they survived either in fragments or in Arabic or Latin translations) and therefore their historical credibility is called into question.[13]

Athanasius Kircher (1602–1680) was one of the most famous scientists who tested such reports through experiments.[14] After him other scientists and artists tried to manufacture burning glasses and prove that wood, stone, metals and even the almost indestructible diamond could be burned or melted by bundled sunlight. In this way, more or less authentic sources triggered a scientific Renaissance and modern scholars came up with their own inventions through practical examination of ancient sources.

Seen under this light Simonides appears to be a man of his time, doing nothing less than his contemporaries by adding another (albeit fictional) incident to this series of reported inventions and inventors that anticipated modern developments. More specifically he reported that the Symian inventor Evdoupos managed to scare away Arab pirates by using burning mirrors from on top of the mountains of Symi.[15] Moreover, Simonides also used texts generally accepted as real sources. He refers, for example, to the above mentioned Anthemius of Tralles (*ca.* 474–558), best known as one of the architects of the Hagia Sophia in Constantinople, and presents him – as it might have

Fig. 16.1 Front page of the Latin edition of Alhazen's *Book of Optics* (ed. Friedrich Risner, 1572) showing the use of burning mirrors, distorted images caused by refraction in water, rainbows and other optical effects.

been expected – as a student of the school of Symi.[16] In a long footnote where Anthemius is praised as the inventor of steam power, he refers to his main sources *Byzantida* and *Konstandiada*, which are both fictitious works. The passage concludes with an anecdote extracted from Agathias Scholastikos Kyrinaios in the edition of Niebuhr.[17] Simonides cites it with bibliographic accuracy.[18] According to this (apparently real) source, Anthemius was in dispute with his neighbour Zenon, who had built his house too high. Since Anthemius did not achieve anything by legal means, he contrived other ways to annoy Zeno: he virtually engineered a minor earthquake by sending steam through leather tubes he had fixed around Zeno's house and by simulating thunder and lightning into Zeno's eyes from a slightly hollowed mirror. In Anthemius' treatise 'On Burning Glasses', the ancient sage intended to construct a kind of surface that would reflect sunlight to a single point, thus trying to recreate the mirror construction of Archimedes, with which the ancient Greek engineer was said to have set fire to Roman ships at the Battle of Syracuse. Unluckily, Anthemius failed. Apparently inspired by this (seemingly very imaginative) passage, Simonides reports of (the fictitious) Sevastos, who experimented with burning glasses in a similar way, inventing also a two weeks lasting 'luminous ball [φωτοβόλος σφαίρα]' and leaving behind ten books entitled 'Michanikon'.[19] Sevastos's end, Simonides claimed, was tragic as he was hit and burned by his own invention: a jet of fire produced by a 'huge mirror [μέγα κάτοπτρον]' (p. 22).

The significance of the reflected image, mirrors and optics is also crucial in order to comprehend another invention, the 'heliotypia', a forerunner of photography. As expected, Simonides attributes this invention to the Greeks. Simonides repeats the attribution of the heliotypia to the Greek legendary Athonite monk/painter Manuel Panselinos in his forged version of the 'Painter's Manual'.[20] In Simonides' version of the Manual we are dealing with several forms of textual counterfeiting. It should first be noted that the basis was provided by a manuscript which is not suggested as fiction. Simonides' source, the 'Painter's Manual', is supposed to have been written between 1723 and 1733 by Dionysius of Phourna (*ca.* 1670–1745), an Athonite monk, based on presumed older manuals. The Manual contained instructions for the production of pigments and provided instruction and iconographic guidance for the illustration of individual figures and complex compositions. Moreover, it introduced the reader to the world of the 'anthivola' (preparatory drawings on paper), their production and the technologies of their use for the faithful reproduction of standard iconographic types of saints and scenes either on murals or on icons. The Manual had and still has a wide circulation among painters but became public only after a French translation was edited by Adolph Didron and Paul Durand in 1845. They discovered the book in 1839, during a journey on Mount Athos.[21] Konstantinos Simonides, who visited Mount Athos at about the same time as the French travellers, made a copy of his own from the original manuscript around 1840, which he later offered to the Frenchmen.[22] The main concern of the Simonideian version was to falsely date the manuscript back to the year 1458. Both, title page and incorporated text, should indicate this year.[23] Simonides had intended to imitate a linguistically older style by means of corrections; however, Alexandros Rangavis (1851, 553), Papadopoulos-Kerameus (1909) and Stefanos Koumanoudis unmasked it as a forgery.[24] Simonides announced in the newspapers that he had in his possession a more complete and more accurate version of the 'Painter's Manual', and thus presented it to a circle of Greek scholars in Athens. The Ministry of Education of the 'Bavarocracy' appointed a specialized examination-committee in order to investigate the authenticity of Simonides' manuscript, which was declared an original. Nevertheless, several scholars, such as Rangavis, remained sceptical.[25] Simonides' manuscript was finally edited in 1853 and it evidently contained fake passages that are not found in any other version of the 'Painters' Manual'.[26]

The most outstanding fake passage is the one referring to Manouel Panselinos. There the legendary painter is declared not only the greater Greek painter of all but also the inventor of heliotypia, a precursor of (colour!) photography.[27] The procedure is described as follows:

How to raise houses, trees, animals, people, and whatever else you desire, into the sunlight.

> First set out to construct a telescope of walnut wood that can be unscrewed in the middle; then fix two rounded pieces of glass to either side. These pieces of glass are made in Constantinople by the famous Joasaph of Polycarp, whose workshop is near the church of the Three Hierarchs. Then build a stand upon which to place it. [...] Then take red powder, the kind that goldsmiths use for cleaning silver and gold, and sugarstone, which you must first burn in the oven and then rub until it becomes white like flour. In this powder you must add the juice from wild celery root, after having boiled it well and kneaded it, and once it dries you must rub it again. [...] Then [...] you must polish the panel [...] until it shines. [...] You must then take your instrument and point it at what you wish to bring into the light, and once you have managed to project the outlines of the objects on the back glass clearly, you must carefully place the panel in its place, and quickly uncover the piece of glass at the front, but only until you can count to ten. [...]. And even you will be amazed; for not only will the forms be unaltered, but the natural colours will also be the same, and I dare say, they will appear even more beautiful.[28]

This section did not find its way into the French edition of the *Encheiridion* by Didron and Durand.[29] Simonides explained the omission as either an indication of the incompleteness of the manuscript used by Didron and Durand, or an indication of their malicious intentions.[30] At the same time, his description is intended to challenge the invention of photography as a French invention and to present it as a Greek invention instead. At any rate, Manouel Gedeon and Konstantinos Oikonomos were the first to accept the thesis that Panselinos was the inventor of photography, although they themselves noted that Simonides' description of the heliotypia clearly had parallels with Daguerre's (1787–1851) *Manual of Photography*, while the name 'heliotypia' itself goes back to Joseph Nicéphore Niépces' (1765–1833) 'heliography'.[31]

In the description quoted above, chemicals that could not have existed in the sixteenth century were replaced by Simonides with natural 'juice of wild celery' or 'crushed shellfish', thus making out of Simonides an early representative of steampunk.[32]

The whole procedure of observing through a hole in the window the mirror-inverted projection of an image onto the opposite wall, as set out in the further course of the Simonideian painter's manual, is much reminiscent of the techniques used by of the camera obscura (Fig. 16.2):

> I made this discovery as follows: one day I slept until noon, when I stayed in the monastic Skete of Saint Demetrios; suddenly I woke up from a terrible dream and I saw on the wall of my room various trees, animals, monks and similar things. First, I became ecstatic and I watched for one hour, then it went off. Then I observed that the window of my room had a hole in the size of a Konstantinato-coin, and opposite it a wall with a window, and between them was a large glass [...] and on that glass was drawn shadowy everything I saw, and I was amazed.[33]

Most probably Simonides knew about it through his education as a painter and engraver as well as via foreign travellers who were using the camera obscura frequently.[34] Furthermore, it should be noted that the first photo studios of the newly established Greek state, shortly after the invention of the new medium, beside Athens, were set up on Mount Athos.[35] Simonides himself, being a person who visited several libraries worldwide and resided in the monasteries of Mount Athos and at Saint Catherine's on Sinai – both places claiming to possess the largest reservoir of manuscripts and early printed books – he could have easily accessed fundamental sources containing theories of optics, vision, light and colour as for example basic works like *The Book of Optics* (printed in 1572 by Friedrich Risner, see Fig. 16.1) by the medieval Arab scholar known as Alhazen (965–1039/40) or the popular *Magiae Naturalis* (1558) by Giambattista della Porta (*ca.* 1535–1615). All these treatises were accessible in various editions, and they all contained similar descriptions of burning mirrors and camerae obscurae (Fig. 16.2).

The attempt to cast images of the real world by optical aids led to the development of technical innovations regarding the projection, reflection and fixation of the image on a surface, either by copying the image with the technique of traditional anthivola, with the help of a camera obscura, camera lucida or with curved mirrors, or later on by capturing it with chemical photography.[36]

Fig. 16.2 Ink drawing of a camera obscura from an early seventeenth century illustrated *Sketchbook on military art, including geometry, fortifications, artillery, mechanics, and pyrotechnics* (Rosenwald Coll. ms. no. 27, p. 249; Library of Congress, Rare Books and Special Collections Division).

According to my understanding, Simonides is trying meticulously to sneak in the idea of a Renaissance back in Byzantine time. For the Greeks, the return to the classical principles of image-making was not a re-discovery, but a continuation process that preserved the ancient Greeks' achievements through Byzantium. Moreover, he underlines the significance of the Byzantine link for the transmission of knowledge to the West and the development of sciences and the arts. In cases where the sources do not attest to his theoretical schema, he allows himself to help a little.

In this context Simonides goes another step further in his mystification of the painter Panselinos: he publishes an engraving of the Evangelist Matthew's portrait, a facsimile of a fresco painting allegedly preserved on Mount Athos and made by Hierotheus in the fifth century. The latter was a disciple of Manouel Panselinos (Simonides 1861 and 1862, frontispiece). The painting bears no similarities to any other painting by Panselinos or his disciples and is rendered in a clearly western, naturalistic style, which comes to confirm Didron's declaration of Panselinos to be 'le Raphaèl ou plutót le Giotto de l'école byzantine'.[37] In a commentary to the painting, which eventually develops into a concise treatise on Byzantine art in general, Simonides concludes that garments and ornaments in this painting 'denote the affinity between Grecian and Byzantine art'.[38] It is again Rangavis who reveals the fraud: he confirms that he himself saw Simonides in the library for hours, copying an image from a large book.

If we now summarize Simonides' balancing act between fact and fiction according to what has been said above, we reach the following conclusion: his presumed philological editions are meticulously made to look like scientific editions. In an age when philology as a scientific field flourished, Simonides emulated the characteristics of widely circulating philological editions by imitating the printed image, adding footnotes and annotations, transcriptions, illustrations, engravings and facsimiles. In the footnotes, he clearly differentiates between his own words ('editor's notes') and quotes (source references). In my mind, what is striking is his constant concern to advertise and confirm the originality and authenticity of the presented text. To forestall critics, Simonides denies his authorship in his editions, arguing that he never could have that much imagination.

But when it comes to credibility and originality, why is the text so easily debunked as a fake? Simonides is – like almost every other counterfeiter – an incorrigible narcissist; in the end, he does not want to be remembered as the mere publisher of the discovered texts, but as their author. And if it were not for his conspicuous (in some cases unethical and criminal) intention to deceive, Simonides would have earned poetic laurels.

Disillusionment leads above all to the fact that the quoted sources and names of persons, places and writers cannot be verified by other sources as they do not appear anywhere else. According to Rangavis (1851, 595), it is also the similarities in style in all discovered manuscripts that convict him as a forger.

In addition to the personal motivations that drive each counterfeiter – Anthony Grafton cites social or professional ambitions, fun or hatred[39] – Simonides clearly has also ideological reasons. His forgeries, as has been shown, have mainly socio-political intentions: through his 'discoveries' he tries to shape the image of Greece outside its tight borders, and therefore he makes an earnest effort to contribute to the process of nation-building. At the same time, he takes advantage of the zeal of the Europeans – mostly German and French travellers and scholars – who demonstrated an increasing interest in the late antique and medieval culture of the Greek-speaking world.

In Greece, the Simonides phenomenon became a national affair: the newspapers took sides either in favour or against him. In the end a committee of experts was formed to decide on the authenticity of the manuscripts, and whether the publication of his works, which would be deemed a national treasure if their authenticity was proven, should be promoted by the state or not. The committee of experts under the 'Bavarian Reign', resolved that a large part of the Simonideian corpus should be genuine.

Patriotic motivation still plays a fundamental role in the ongoing recognition of his work. This is evident in a hitherto unpublished poetic reception of Simonides' *Symais* by Kalodoukas N. Kyramarios (also Kyramaridis Polynikou Simaiou, 1862–1945). The poem, which relates the history of the island of Syme from the year 1885,[40] lists the inventors and their inventions mentioned in *Symais* and praises Simonides himself as the 'wise man who best told the story of the island of Syme'.

Simonides' nationalist-patriotic counterfeiting activities are undoubtedly an extreme and dazzling case. Despite this, it highlights and illuminates the interrelated processes of nineteenth-century nation-building and how the education of the nation is involved with fictional narratives. Early research on nationalism was in constant use of concepts such as 'invented traditions' (Eric Hobsbawm) or 'imagined communities' (Benedict Anderson). Simonides provides us with an idealistic and almost stereotypical example of the temptations of fiction for national narratives.[41]

If we come back to the subject of mirrors and mirroring we can summarize their usage in art (painting, photography) and science (technological inventions) by projecting on two figures: Narcissus and Prometheus. Although they seem to be very different figures, Narcissus and Prometheus have one thing in common: the mirror. Nikolas Calas, who was mentioned at the beginning of this chapter, had outlined the relation between Narcissus and Prometheus in an inspirational way. We can conclude with his words: 'The doctrine of art for art's sake makes of art the mirror of art and of Narcissus the opposite of Prometheus. The dichotomy must be overcome. Fire is produced by holding a mirror to the sun' (Calas 1975, 9). One could argue that Simonides himself bears characteristics of both Narcissus and Prometheus: on the one hand, he possesses narcissistic self-admiration, on the other hand he displays creative ambitions. Simonides is not writing for himself; his works are not meant to be just *belles lettres*. His actions are aiming at a wider audience, pursuing highly ambitious cultural-changing goals.

NOTES

Introduction

1. Calas 1975, 6.
2. Ibid.
3. See Beretta 2009, 26–40 on glass mirrors in antiquity and Pendergrast 2003, 15; see also MacFarlane and Martin 2002, 5, 16 and ch. 3 and ch. 4, esp. 62–78, ch. 5.
4. This occurred in the fifteenth century, when the Venetians invented mirrors made of a layer of a liquid mercury and tin, see Melchior-Bonnet 2001, 30–31 and Pendergrast 2003, 119f, also Pendergrast 2008, 3.
5. See e.g. Walter Benjamin's *Arcades Project*, where he explores the role of mirrors in changing visual perception in urban life in nineteenth-century Paris; see further the PhD thesis of Etheridge 2016.
6. See Lindberg 1975, 1976, 1983; Simon 1988; Lejeune 1989; Gilson 2001, ch. 1; Smith 2014.
7. See e.g. Webster 2014, esp. 132–140: ancient mirrors were part of the experience of sight.
8. See Gongdon 1981; Jonsson 1995, 36–42; see further de Grummond and Hoff 1982; Balensiefen 1990; DePuma 2013.
9. Hockney and Falco 2000 and Hockney 2001.
10. On mirror-spectacles and -perspectivists, see Ilardi 2007; Edgerton 2009; Carman 2014.
11. For ancient catoptromancy see Addey 2007; for early modern examples Gessmann 1905, 180. For catoptromancy and other forms of divination in Byzantium see Koukoules 1957, 155–226. On the role of mirrors in popular belief see Politis 1975, 23–27; for the dissemination of the fairy tale of Snow White in which the mirror is sometimes swapped with the sun see Aggelopoulou-Mprouskou 1994, 133–154. For the occurrence of mirrors in the household during Ottoman rule, see Dimitropoulos 1996, 37–62.
12. Papaioannou 2010, 82. For the use of mirrors in Byzantium see also Afendoulidou and Linardou in this volume.
13. Byzantine mirrors were rather small, made of glass, polished silver or other metals; see Koukoules 1952, vol. 4, 370.
14. See Schulte 1999; Stacey 2007; Reinle and Winkel 2011; for Byzantine examples see Papaioannou 2010, 81–101. One of the most striking examples from early modern Greece is Kaisarios Dapontes' *Καθρέπτης γυναικών* [*Mirror of Women*] (1766); for further reading see Kaplanis 2001.
15. See on mirror metaphor Grabes 1982 and Nolan 1990; cf. further Abrams 1971.
16. Foucault 1986. For further details see also Priki in this volume.
17. See Calas 1942, 209, 'The evolution of the idea of simultaneity produced the belief that mirrors revealed the past and the future'.
18. Mabille 1938, 14–18, 66 and 1940.

Notes to pp. 3–11

19. Eco 1993, 27 (see also chapter 7 in Eco 1984, 202–227). For Lacan's mirror-stage and Eco's studies on mirrors see also Nolan 1990, 275–282.
20. For the term 'Selfie Generation' see Eler 2017 and Gojny, Kürzinger, Schwarz 2016. For an analysis of the mirror-function of selfies see ibid. pp. 15–24 as well as Fausing 2015. The artist Douglas Coupland's statement that 'selfies are mirrors we can freeze' is telling (2015, 24).
21. See in relation to ancient Greek and Roman mirrors e.g. McCarty 1989; Vernant and Frontisi-Ducroux 1997; Bartsch 2006; Taylor 2008, 20f.; Ulrich 2016.
22. See, however, Melchior-Bonnet 2001; Pendergrast 2003; Anderson 2007; Frelick 2016.
23. Werness 1999, 7, 4; Etheridge 2016, esp. pp. 37f. and ch. 3 and 4.
24. This was supported by the Faculty of Historical and Cultural Studies and the Austrian Society of Modern Greek Studies (ÖGNS).
25. 'Les miroirs feraient bien de réfléchir un peu plus avant de renvoyer les images', *The Blood of a Poet [Le Sang d'un poète]* (1930). See Cocteau 1999, 52.

Chapter 1

1. *Tim.* 71b and once again at 72c.
2. *Rep.* 431a–444e and *Tim.* 69c–72d.
3. For a general comparison of the tripartite soul in the *Timaeus* and the *Republic*, see Taylor 1928, 496–499. For a comparison of the theory of body and soul in the *Timaeus*, the *Republic*, and the *Phaedo*, see Johansen 2004, 137–159. On the embodiment of the appetite in both the *Republic* and the *Timaeus*, see Lorenz 2006, 1–95. On the medical significance of the tripartite physiology, see Nutton 2004, 115–124, esp. 117–118.
4. *Tim.* 70e. In *Rep.* IX, 588c7–e2, Plato likens both the spirit and the appetite to a brute animal. He suggests, nonetheless, that the spirit resembles reason in a way that the appetite does not.
5. *Tim.* 71a.
6. I.e. as a plot against the powers (the *eidōla* and *phantasmata*) that enchant – *psychagōgien* – the appetite. Cornford (1937, 286–287 n.2) takes the doubtful phrase 'τούτῳ δὴ θεὸς ἐπιβουλεύσας αὐτῷ' as 'designing to gain this very influence'. Following similar formulations such as 'ἐπιβουλεύειν τυραννίδι,' he suggests that the 'τούτῳ αὐτῷ' indicates what the gods also want to exercise: i.e., ψυχαγωγία, the last thing mentioned.
7. *Timaeus* 71a–d.
8. Lorenz 2006, 55.
9. 71d–72b.
10. Hepatoscopy is generally thought to be the most important form of divination next to the Delphic Oracle (Collins 2008, 320). But there is little evidence on how hepatoscopy was exactly practiced by the Greeks. Scholars have generally looked for answers in in Mesopotamia, from where the practice is thought to have moved west towards Greece (see Burket 1992, 46–53; Collins 2008, 320; see Bachavora 2012, for a re-evaluation of this general consensus).

    For an overview on Greek hepatoscopy, see Halliday 1913, 163–204; For a detailed analysis and attempted reconstruction of the practice through extant evidence, see Collins 2008. On the connection between the liver and the divine more broadly see Jastrow 1907, 121–131.
11. See Collins 2008, 325.

12. Bronze mirrors were produced as early as the Mycenaean period and continued to be the predominant reflective surface until approximately the start of the common era. Approximately sometime after the twelfth century BCE, however (perhaps with the fall of the Mycenaean palaces), mirrors seem to disappear only to reemerge during the early seventh (possibly eighth) century BCE in both Greece and Etruria. This gap is quite evident in both the material and literary evidence: with a few exceptions, the bulk of extant bronze mirrors date to the beginning of the archaic period, and furthermore there are no iconographical representations or literary mentions of mirrors until the mid-late sixth century. For overviews of mirror production in the Greek and Roman world see Charbonneaux 1958; Lamb 1969; and Congdon 1985.

13. The well-known Piacenza bronze liver (*ca.* 100 BCE), however, was found close by in Etruria (Musei Civici di Palazzo Farnese). Modelled after a sheep's entrails, the Piacenza liver represents the regions of the Etruscan cosmos on its surface and is believed to have been used as a guide for the interpretation of the visual qualities of an actual animal liver, in particular its colour and texture in the favourable and unfavourable regions. For a comprehensive study of the Piacenza liver, see Thulin 1906 and Van der Meer 1987. See also Collins 2008, 326f.; Nutton 2004, 159 (for a medical perspective); G. E. R. Lloyd 1987, 45; and Bachvarova 2012, 148–153.

    Perhaps it is also significant that the Piacenza liver is made of bronze – the only material out of which Greeks made mirrors in the archaic and classical period. When polished, moreover, the bronze model would have had something in common with the actual animal organ: a shiny surface.

14. Collins 2008, 321 has argued that the Greeks system of reading livers was never quite as developed as the Near-Eastern, Etruscan and Roman cultures. He contends that the Greek practice of hepatoscopy was fundamentally based on a binary system, i.e. the divinatory interpretation ultimately yielded a yes or a no answer to a question posed by a *mantis* or a *haruspex*. Nonetheless, he suggests that the arrival at the favourable or unfavourable conclusion was a complex and sophisticated process.

15. See, for example, Black-Figure, Neck Amphora. 550–500 BCE. Florence 3856. Attributed to Antimenes by Unknown. Beazley Vase Number 19409.

16. For a comprehensive list and discussion of all the images see Durand and Lissarrague, 1979.

17. See Black-Figure, Neck Amphora. 550–500 BCE. Florence 3856. Attributed to Antimenes by Unknown. Beazley Vase Number 19409.

18. See for example Red-Figure Neck Amphora. 525–475 BCE. Attributed to Kleophrades by Beazley and Hartwig. Wurzburg L507. Beazley Vase Number 201654.

    All of my interpretations of such images above and below closely follow those of Durand & Lissarrague 1979, 99–106.

19. See Aesch. *PB*, 493–495; Eur. *El.* 826–829.

20. Collins 2008, 33.

21. Cf. Philostr. *VA*, 8.7.15; see Collins 2008, 332–336.

22. The liver's ability to make the invisible visible can also be extended to Greek discourses on the liver as the seat of emotions: see Cornford 1937, 286; Onians 1998, 84–92; Loraux 1987, 54; Collins 2008, 327–328; Shirazi 2017, 230–250.

23. See Etruscan Bronze Mirror. Fourth-century BCE. Vatican Museum. 12240.
    On the relationship between Etruscan hand-held mirrors and their Greek counterparts, see Shirazi 2017, 42–48. On the efforts to harmonize Etruscan and Greek divinatory practices, see Collins 2008, 325–326.

24. See also Grummond 2002, 70f.

25. See, for example, Red-Figure Amphoriskos. 450–400 BCE. Oxford, Ashmolean Museum, V537. Attributed to Eretria Painter by Beazley. Beazley Vase Number 216946.
26. As Frontisi-Ducroux (1997, 82) argues of the mirror, its presence in the woman's hand establishes 'réflexivité,' through a parallelism with the eyes. We see a similar kind of parallelism between the liver and eyes in the images depicting hepatoscopy (such as the Attic vase paintings and the image of Calchas discussed above).
27. That what Calchas is seeing or what the viewer of the mirror will see is 'lucky' (i.e. a good omen) is possible but debatable. There are no clear indications that mirrors and reflections indicated good luck in either the literary or visual evidence (though we should note that many mirrors are found as grave goods in burials). One example of mirrors as good omens is perhaps the 'apotropaic' image of Medusa on the back of a Greek (South-Italian) mirror (Getty 96.AC.109). Though mirrors, like the liver, seem to have been associated with numinous images, e.g. Lucanian nestoris. Naples. Museo Nazionale. 82124 (see also discussion below).
28. On the visual characteristics of the bronze mirror, such as light, colour, and texture, see Shirazi 2017.
29. Aristotle, *de insomniis* 459b23; the passage examines why the surface of a bronze mirror changes in colour and texture – a process which, of course, is really a result of the corrosion of its polish. Aristotle, however, ties this material change to the mechanism of sight, in particular the stream of a menstruating woman's vision. See Kazantzidis in this volume.
30. As argued elsewhere (Shirazi 2017, esp. 9–89) bronze mirrors would have produced what I term 'dynamic' visual experiences and reflections, characterized by the emission of light, contrast in colour, change in texture, and variations in perspective. Reflection therefore was a far more complex phenomenon than that of simple and straightforward representation, and the mirror was an object whose visual purpose went far beyond the reflection of the self.
31. See Lucanian nestoris. Naples. Museo Nazionale. 82124.
32. See *Timaeus* 70b–d.
33. Lorenz 2006, 55.
34. This is what Lorenz 2006, 57 identifies as the 'Timaeus Problem', namely that 'Plato's psychological theory requires that reason can affect and influence appetite by communicating with it; but that it conceives of appetite as being unable to understand, or anyhow as being such as not to care about, the predicational structures that constitute the discourse of reason'. Lorenz, however, does not think that the passage is successful at solving the problem. Rather he suggests that it foreshadows an important development in Plato's psychological theory: namely that 'the sensory imagination can play a mediating role that enables reason to affect and influence appetite by communicating with it'. Lorenz then argues that the closeness in the language and conception between the *Timaeus* and the *Philebus* (cf. 38 E 12–40 C 6) suggests that the latter is a resolution of the *Timaeus* problem (99–110).
35. τούτῳ δὴ θεὸς ἐπιβουλεύσας αὐτῷ (71a).
36. We should note that even the word for 'structure', ἰδέα, is visual, indicating shape, form, outward appearance.
37. As Cornford (1937, 287) notes γλυκύς here in the *Timaeus* seems to refer to both a quality already in the liver and a quality of the influence of reason, much like the bitterness.
38. To complicate the matter further, there are two different phrases for what Timaeus uses to refer to Reason: i) the 'power' (δύναμις) of the thoughts (τῶν διανοημάτων) that are coming from the mind (νοῦς) and ii) the 'breath' (ἐπίπνοια) of gentleness from intelligence (διάνοια).

It may be that *dunamis* is a physical pressure (as though pressing a finger onto the mirror and leaving discolouration – while *epinoia* is more like breathing on a mirror, leaving a fog on its surface. In both these instances, the analogy is much more material than it may first appear. For similar conceptions of speech as a 'breath on the mirror' in Mayan folklore, see Tedlock 1993.

And while the exact definition of each of these formulations is not the main interest of my analysis, the variety of verbal constructions for what we can in short think of as *logos* points to the complexity of the psychic powers of the rational part of the soul that are all acting upon – touching, bending, moving, producing images on – the primary organ of the appetite, the liver.

39. The juxtaposition of mirroring and painting in the *Timaeus* should bring to mind Book X of the *Republic* where Socrates famously compares all creators to mere mirror holders in order to undermine the value of the mimetic arts such as painting (10.596c–597e). For re-evaluation of the mirror in this passage of the *Republic*, see Cain 2012. For a comparison between the mirror in the *Timaeus* and the *Republic*, see Shirazi 2017, 273–297.

40. See also *Tim.* 45b–46a, where Timaeus explains the phenomenon of dreams via the mirroring qualities of the eyes. This discussion of vision as reflection seems to inspire an excursion on catoptrics more broadly at 46a–b. Similar to the liver-mirror passage, here Plato closely connects *phantasmata* and *eidolopoiia* with the mirror, suggesting once again the significance of the mirror as a tool with which to conceptualize visualization and the ways in which its image-producing powers further connect it with the power of the liver in the tradition of hepatoscopy.

41. Relevant to this discussion is also Plato's use of the verb *psychagōgein* to describe how the appetite reacts to *eidōla* and *phantasmata*. The verb is particularly appropriate in the context of the *Timaeus* since it literally means 'to lead the soul' – and here it is a specific part of the soul that is in fact being influenced. On the more numinous sense of the verb, cf. Plat. *Laws* 909b and see Asmis 1986, 156 and Taylor 1928, 510–511.

42. As Sheppard 2003, 204, has argued, this strange account of the liver has had considerable influence on later Platonist accounts of the imagination, in particular the link between the imagination, dreams, and prophecy.

43. This is evident in the doxographical tradition. See also Simon 1998; Netz and Squire 2016; Rudolph 2016; Shirazi 2017, 179–192.

44. Cf. *Phaedrus* 247c–d on the visual qualities of the Forms: ... ἀχρώματός τε καὶ ἀσχημάτιστος καὶ ἀναφὴς ... μόνῳ θεατὴ νῷ.

45. Cf. Plat. *Sym.* 211e–212a, where the form of Beauty is also presented as pure and unmixed (καθαρόν, ἄμικτον), without the flesh and colour belonging to mankind or mortal trash (ἀλλὰ μὴ ἀνάπλεως σαρκῶν τε ἀνθρωπίνων καὶ χρωμάτων καὶ ἄλλης πολλῆς φλυαρίας θνητῆς).

Chapter 2

1. The research for this article was funded by Riksbankens jubileumsfond, Sweden, as part of the programme *Representation and Reality* (2013–2019), hosted by the University of Gothenburg (http://representationandreality.gu.se).

2. See, for instance, Casati 2012. I would like to thank Michalis Filippou for his helpful advice about the contemporary discussions on this issue.

3. See Berryman 2012.

4. On the *Mantissa* and the identity of its author, see the introductions in Sharples' edition 2008 and translation 2004a, as well as Sharples 2004b.

5. πῶς δὲ εἰδώλου ὄντος τοῦ ἐν τῷ κατόπτρῳ εἴδωλα πάλιν ἀπορρεῖ τοσαῦτα, καὶ διὰ τί τὰ ἐν τοῖς κατόπτροις εἴδωλα παχύτερα, ὡς τοσαύτην ἀπ' αὐτῶν ἀπορροὴν γίνεσθαι; διὰ τί δὲ καὶ μένει ταῦτα καὶ οὐ κινεῖται; διὰ τί δὲ καὶ μένοντα οὐχὶ καὶ ἀπελθόντος τοῦ ὁρῶντος αὐτὰ κἂν ἐπ' ὀλίγον μένει; διὰ τί δὲ οὐκ ἐπὶ τῆς ἐπιφανείας τῶν κατόπτρων τὰ εἴδωλα, ἀλλὰ ἐν βάθει;

6. For a detailed discussion on the identity of Alexander's opponents in this section of the *Mantissa*, see Ierodiakonou (forthcoming).

7. ἔτι πῶς μετὰ τὴν κλάσιν ἤτοι τὴν ἀπὸ τοῦ κατόπτρου ἢ τὴν ἀπὸ τῶν διαφανῶν ἔτι τὸ τῆς ἐπερείσεως σώζεται; οὐδὲ γὰρ ἐπὶ βακτηρίας τοῦτο δυνατόν· πάντα γὰρ τὰ κεκλασμένα, ὥσπερ τὰ πηρὰ σώματα πρὸς τὰς ἐνεργείας, κἀκεῖνα πρὸς τὰς ἐπερείσεις ἐκλύεται.

8. On the Epicurean theory of vision, see Lee 1978; Hahm 1978.

9. On the Stoic theory of vision, see Sambursky 1959: 22–27; Ingenkamp 1971; Todd 1974; Hahm 1978; Løkke 2008, 37–39; Ierodiakonou (forthcoming).

10. In Avotins' view (1980, 452–453), for instance, Alexander attributes to the atomists a theory of mirroring different from what we find in Lucretius' *De rerum natura* (4.98–109), where it is said that the effluences from the external objects bounce back by the mirror and do not remain in it. Lucretius' account, according to Avotins, is in better agreement with the other testimonies on the Epicurean teachings.

11. ἐναργὴς δὲ φαντασία λέγεται ποτὲ μὲν ἥ τε ἀληθὴς καὶ σφοδρά (τουτέστιν ἡ καταληπτική), ποτὲ δὲ ἡ σφοδρὰ μόνον ἡ τῇ ἀμυδρᾷ ἀντιτιθεμένη. ἕπεται δὲ τῇ σφοδρᾷ φαντασίᾳ συγκατάθεσις, εἰ μὴ εἴη δι' ἄλλων τινῶν πεφωραμένη ψευδὴς οὖσα, ὡς ἐπὶ τῆς φαντασίας τῆς τοῦ μὴ κινεῖσθαι τοὺς ἀστέρας πάσχομεν, καὶ ἐπὶ τῶν γραφῶν κατὰ τὰς εἰσοχάς τε καὶ ἐξοχάς, καὶ ἐπὶ τῶν ἐμφαινομένων τοῖς κατόπτροις. οὐ γὰρ διότι μή εἰσι σφοδραὶ ἀπιστοῦμεν αὐταῖς, ἀλλ' ὅτι διαβέβληται δι' ἄλλων· καὶ γὰρ ἀληθέσι τισὶ καὶ σφοδραῖς πολλάκις ἀπιστοῦμεν, ἂν ὦμεν προδιαβεβλημένοι.

12. ἄλλως δέ ἐστι ψευδῆ ταῦτα, ὅσα ἔστι μὲν ὄντα [ψευδῆ], ἔστι δὲ ψευδῆ ἡ ἀπ' αὐτῶν φαντασία τῷ φαίνεσθαι ταῦτα ἢ μὴ οἷά ἐστιν ἢ ἃ μὴ ἔστιν. ἄλλως δέ ἐστι ψευδῆ ταῦτα παρὰ τὸν προειρημένον τρόπον· ὧν γὰρ ψευδής ἐστιν ἡ φαντασία, ταῦτα οὐκ ἔστι ψευδῆ, ὡς ἦν τὰ προειρημένα. ἔστι μὲν γὰρ ταῦτά τινα, οὐ μὴν οἷα φαίνεται. τοιαῦτά ἐστι τά τε ἐν ταῖς γραφαῖς καὶ ἐν ταῖς σκιαγραφίαις, ἃ ἔστι μέν τινα, οὐ μὴν ἃ φαίνεται ἔστιν· φαίνεται γὰρ ζῷα οὐκ ὄντα ζῷα, καί τινα ἄλλα ὧν ἂν καὶ ἡ σκιαγραφία ᾖ. ὁμοίως καὶ τὰ ἐν τοῖς ὕπνοις φαντάσματα ἔστι μέν τινα (κινήματα γάρ τινα γίνεται τοῖς ὁρῶσι τὰ ἐνύπνια), οὐ μὴν τοιαῦτά ἐστιν οἷα φαίνεται. φαίνεται γὰρ βαδίζειν τι ἢ διαλέγεσθαι, οὐ μέντοι οὕτως ἔχει. τοιαῦτα καὶ οὕτω ψευδῆ καὶ τὰ ἐμφαινόμενα τοῖς κατόπτροις· ἔστι μὲν γάρ τι καὶ αὐτά, ἀλλ' οὐχ ὃ φαίνεται.

13. γίνεται δὲ τὸ χρῶμα ἐν τῷ πεφωτισμένῳ τε καὶ φωτὶ οὕτως ὡς καὶ τὸ φῶς ἐν τῷ διαφανεῖ, οὔτε κατὰ ἀπόρροιάν τινα, οὔτε ὡς ὕλης ἢ τοῦ διαφανοῦς δεχομένου τὸ φῶς ἢ τοῦ φωτὸς τὸ χρῶμα (ἀπελθόντων γοῦν τῶν ταῦτα ἐμποιούντων εὐθὺς συναπέρχεται τὸ μὲν χρῶμα ἐκ τοῦ φωτός, εἰ τὰ χρωννύντα αὐτὸ ἀπέλθοι, τὸ δὲ φῶς ἐκ τοῦ διαφανοῦς, εἰ τὸ φωτίζον αὐτὸ μὴ παρείη), ἀλλ' ἔστι τις ἡ ἀπ' ἀμφοτέρων κίνησις ἐν τοῖς δεχομένοις αὐτὰ γινομένη κατὰ παρουσίαν τε καὶ ποιὰν σχέσιν, ὡς γίνεται καὶ ἐν τοῖς κατόπτροις τὰ ἐν αὐτοῖς ὁρώμενα ... γίνεται δὲ τόδε τὸ φῶς ἐν τῷ διαφανεῖ παρουσίᾳ πυρὸς ἢ τοῦ θείου σώματος. κατὰ σχέσιν γὰρ τοῦ φωτίζειν δυναμένου πρὸς τὰ φωτίζεσθαι πεφυκότα τὸ φῶς. οὐ γὰρ σῶμα τὸ φῶς. διὸ καὶ ἀχρόνως γίνεται.

14. τὸ δὲ ἀπελθόντων τῶν ὁρωμένων ἔτι τινὰ δοκεῖν καταλείπεσθαι τῶν χρωμάτων ἐν τοῖς ὀφθαλμοῖς τοῖς ἰδοῦσιν οὐκ ἔστιν σημεῖον ἀλλοιώσεως. τοῦτο γὰρ οὐχ ᾗ διαφανές ἐστι πάσχει, ἀλλ' ᾗ ἔμψυχόν τε καὶ φαντασιοῦσθαι δυνάμενον. διὰ γὰρ τοῦτο δύναται φυλάττειν μέχρι τινὸς τὰς γενομένας κινήσεις ἔτι ἀπὸ τῶν ἔξωθεν ἐν τοῖς αἰσθητηρίοις. καὶ γὰρ καὶ ἐν ὑστέρῳ χρόνῳ πρὸ ὀμμάτων τίθεσθαι τὰ ἔμψυχα δυνατά ἐστιν τὰ γενόμενα αὐτοῖς φαντάσματα. τὰ γοῦν κάτοπτρα καίτοι λεῖα ὄντα καὶ διαυγῆ οὐδὲν ἐν αὐτοῖς φυλάττει τῶν ἐμφαινομένων

χρωμάτων ἤτοι τοῦ φωτὸς ἀπελθόντος ἢ τῶν φωτιζόντων ἢ τῶν ὁρατῶν, ὅτι μήτε πάσχει μήτε ἐστὶν ἔμψυχα.

15. On this debate, see Sorabji 1992, 2001; Burnyeat 1992, 1995. Also, for recent alternative interpretations, see Caston 2005; Lorenz 2007.

16. See Sorabji 1991. For a literalist interpretation of Alexander's theory of visual perception, see Crampton 2016.

17. ἀλλ' οὐδ' εἰ μέλας καὶ λευκὸς ἀλλήλους ὁρῷεν, κεκώλυται ὁ μεταξὺ ἀὴρ ἀμφοτέροις αὐτοῖς ἅμα διακονεῖσθαι τῷ μὴ παθητικῶς μηδὲ ὡς ὕλη γινόμενος αὐτῶν ὑπ' αὐτῶν κινεῖσθαι. οὐδὲ τὰ ἐν τοῖς κατόπτροις δὲ ἢ ἐν τοῖς ὕδασιν ἐμφαινόμενα χρώματα τοιαῦτα αὐτὰ ποιεῖ ὁποῖά ἐστιν αὐτά. συμπαύεται γοῦν ἑκάστου τούτων ἡ ἀπὸ τοῦ αἰσθητοῦ κίνησις ἐν αὐτοῖς γινομένη, ὅταν μηκέτι ᾖ παρὸν τὸ αἰσθητόν.

18. εἰ δὲ λέγοιεν φῶς τὸ ἐκπεμπόμενον εἶναι, δεικτέον αὐτοῖς ὅτι τε ἀσώματον καὶ οὐχ οἷόν τε ἐκπέμπεσθαι καὶ προχεῖσθαι, ὥς φασι. γίνεται γὰρ κατὰ σχέσιν τοῦ φωτίζεσθαι πεφυκότος πρὸς τὸ φωτίζειν δυνάμενον· διὸ οὐδὲ κίνησις φωτός ἐστιν. ἅμα γοῦν ὁρῶμεν καὶ τὰ ἐγγὺς καὶ τὰ πόρρω τοῦ φωτίζειν πεφυκότος φωτιζόμενα, ὅσα ἀπὸ τοῦ αὐτοῦ διαστήματος οἷά τε φωτίζεσθαι ὑπ' αὐτοῦ· ὃ ἦν ἂν ἀδύνατον, εἰ ἦν τὸ φῶς σῶμα. ὅτι δὲ σχέσις τις καὶ κατὰ σχέσιν τοῦ φωτίζοντος πρὸς τὸ φωτιζόμενον καὶ μὴ οὐσία τις καὶ σῶμα τὸ φῶς, δῆλον καὶ ἐκ τοῦ μηδ' ἐπ' ὀλίγον ὑπομένειν αὐτὸ τοῦ φωτίζοντος παρενεχθέντος.

19. Ὅτι δὲ ἐν σχέσει τὸ φῶς, ἀλλ' οὐκ ἐν ἀλλοιώσει, δῆλον ἀπὸ τοῦ τὰ μὲν ἀλλοιούμενα οὐκ εὐθὺ τῷ τὸ ἀλλοιοῦν ἀπελθεῖν πεπαῦσθαι τοῦ ἐγγενομένου πάθους ἐν αὐτοῖς ὑπ' αὐτοῦ (οὐ γὰρ τοῦ θερμαίνοντος ἀπελθόντος εὐθὺς καὶ τὸ θερμαινόμενον ὑπ' αὐτοῦ τῆς ἐγγενομένης ὑπ' ἐκείνου θερμότητος αὐτῷ παύεται), τὰ δὲ κατὰ τὴν πρός τι σχέσιν ὄντα τοιαῦτα, ἀπελθόντος τοῦ πρὸς ὃ ἡ σχέσις, συμπαύεσθαι καὶ ταῦτα τοῦ ἔτι εἶναι ἐν τῇ πρὸς ἐκεῖνο σχέσει· υἱοῦ γὰρ ἀποθανόντος πέπαυται καὶ ὁ πατὴρ πατὴρ ὤν, καὶ τοῦ ἀριστεροῦ ἀπελθόντος ὁ δεξιὸς οὐκέτι δεξιός ἐστιν. οὕτω δὲ ἔχει καὶ τὸ φῶς· συναπέρχεται γὰρ ἀθρόον τῷ φωτίζειν πεφυκότι.

20. ἔστι δὲ οὐ τοιαύτη ἡ ἐν τῷ ἀέρι καὶ τῷ διαφανεῖ τῷ κατὰ δύναμιν ὑπό τε τοῦ πυρὸς καὶ τῶν χρωμάτων τροπή, ὁποίαν φαμὲν ἐν τοῖς ἀλλοιουμένοις γίνεσθαι. ἡ μὲν γὰρ ἀλλοίωσις κίνησίς ἐστιν καὶ ἐν χρόνῳ γίνεται καὶ κατὰ μεταβολήν, τὸ δὲ διαφανὲς οὐχ οὕτως τὸ φῶς καὶ τὰ χρώματα δέχεται, ὡς ἠλλοιῶσθαι καὶ ταῦτα, ἀλλ' ἔστιν οὕτως λεγόμενον πάσχειν τὸ διαφανές, ὡς εἰ καὶ τὸν δεξιὸν γενόμενόν τινος πεπονθέναι λέγοι τις μήτε κινηθέντα αὐτὸν μήτε τι πάθος ἀναδεξάμενον ἐν αὐτῷ. τοιαύτη γὰρ καὶ ἡ τοῦ διαφανοῦς τροπὴ κατά τε τὸ φῶς καὶ τὰ χρώματα· τῇ γὰρ τοῦ φωτίζοντος ἢ κεχρωσμένου παρουσίᾳ τοιοῦτον τὸ διαφανὲς γίνεται, ὡς καὶ τῇ τοῦ ἐξ ἀριστερῶν παραστάντος σχέσει ὁ δεξιός· σημεῖον δὲ τοῦ τοῦτον ἔχειν τὸν τρόπον, ὅτι ὡς ὁ δεξιὸς παύεται δεξιὸς ὢν μεταστάντος τοῦ ἀριστεροῦ, οὕτως καὶ τὸ φῶς παύεται μεταστάντος τοῦ φωτίζοντος, ὁμοίως δὲ καὶ τοῦ ὁρᾶσθαι πεφυκότος παύεται τοιοῦτον εἶναι ὡς οὐδὲν πάθος ἀναδεξάμενον κατὰ τὴν ἐν αὐτῷ μεταβολήν, ἀλλὰ γενομένης αὐτῷ τῆς δοκούσης ἀλλοιώσεως κατὰ σχέσιν.

21. The noun 'schesis', which derives from the verb 'echein', is used extremely seldom by Plato, and only in contexts unrelated to the subject of relatives. It refers to a temporary condition, often in opposition to a more permanent state denoted by 'hexis', a noun also derived from 'echein'; for instance, both in the fifth book of the *Republic* (452C) and in the *Timaeus* (24B), 'schesis' is used to talk about citizens bearing arms (see Mugler 1957). It is probable that 'schesis' acquired the more technical sense of a relation with the Stoics (e.g. Plotinus, *Enneads* 6.1.30; Simplicius, *in Cat.* 166.22; 28).

22. Note the way Alexander introduces this suggestion, that is, with the connective particle 'ἤ', translated as 'or better', 'alternatively', which suggests that this may be the position Alexander himself endorses.

23. ἢ δεῖται μὲν τὸ ὁρᾶν σχέσεώς τινος, οὐ μὴν ἐν τῇ σχέσει τὸ ὁρᾶν (τὸ δὲ δεξιὸν ἐν τῇ σχέσει)· ἀλλὰ καὶ δύναμίν τινα εἶναι τὴν ἀντιληπτικὴν τῶν ὁρωμένων· ἄνευ γὰρ ταύτης οὐδὲν ὄφελος πρὸς τὸ ὁρᾶν τῆς σχέσεως. διὸ τὸ μὲν ἐν τῷ διαφαίνειν καὶ κατὰ σχέσιν, τὸ δὲ ὁρᾶν οὐκέτι κατὰ σχέσιν.

24. The term 'mere Cambridge change' was coined by Peter Geach (*God and the Soul*, London 1969, 71–72), in order to describe this kind of change that was discussed at the time among several Cambridge philosophers.

25. Aristotle, too, has been interpreted as being aware of cases of merely Cambridge change. In particular, it has been argued that his two definitions of a relative in the *Categories* (ch.7, 6a36–b4; 8a29–35) reflect his attempt to take into consideration such cases (see Sedely 2002). For the relatives of the first definition are soft relatives, in the sense that they are characterized principally by an internal condition (for example, knowledge), whereas the relatives of the second definition are hard relatives, in the sense that their very being consists in their relation to something else and their relational attribute is thus subject to merely Cambridge change (for example, double). But not all scholars agree that Aristotle's two definitions reflect two degrees of relativity (see Harari 2011; Duncombe 2015).

26. See Sharples 2005, 346, note 6; Caston 2012, 156, note 376. For a different view, see Crampton 2016, 109–145.

27. For a systematic discussion of Aristotle's and Alexander's account of colour in terms of the transparency that characterizes all bodies, see Ierodiakonou 2018.

Chapter 3

1. I would like to thank Lilia Diamantopoulou and Maria Gerolemou for the invitation to participate in the workshop and for inducing me to accept the challenge of going back over Epicurean catoptrology and reconsidering questions that have been tantalizing me, ever since I first read this passage many years ago and readily dismissed it as particularly impenetrable. I am grateful to Professor Alexander Jones and Dr Crystal Addey for kindly sending to me their valuable contributions on the subject. Lucretius' text and translations are quoted from Rouse 1924, rev. by Smith 1992; of Seneca's *Naturales Quaestiones* from Hine 2010; of Diogenes of Oinoanda from Smith 1993; of Apuleius' *Pro se magia (Apologia)* from Jones 2017.

2. Koenen 1996, 826. Accounts are found in Ps.-Plutarch *Epit.* 4.14 and Stobaeus *Ecl.* I. 52 [44] [both under Aëtius 4.14.2 p. 405 Diels *Dox. Gr.*] as well as Ps.-Galen *Hist. Philos.* 95 [p. 636–637 Diels *Dox. Gr.*]. Cf. also Avotins (1980, 452), who notes that 'When dealing with mirrors Alexander appears to be attributing to the atomists a theory which disagrees with information found in Lucretius. In the *Mantissa* 135.27–30 he assumes that, when an object is seen in the mirror, vision occurs because an idol of the object remains stationed in the mirror and emits other idols. Lucretius, of course, explains mirrors differently. According to him idols, when hitting a shiny surface, are bounced back by it undeformed (4.98–109).'

3. Addey 2007. Cf. Odgen 2001, 195–196: 'Catoptromancy was divination from images in the glittering or distorted reflections of mirrors. It is first attested in Greek culture by Aristophanes, whose Lamachus, on seeing Dicaeopolis reflected in his polished and oiled bronze shield, "sees" an old man who will be charged with cowardice. [. . .] It is possible that some sort of necromantic catoptromancy underlies the obscure tale that Pythagoras' "mirror-game", in which he wrote letters in blood on a mirror, which was then used – somehow – to reflect them onto a full moon, from which they were read by an assistant.' Cf. Scholiast Aristophanes *Clouds* 752 (Holwerda) and Suda s.v. *Thettale gyne*; Delatte 1932, 149.

4. De Grummond 2002, 73–75. See also Seaford 1981, 62–64; Addey 2007, 37–39; Dillon 2017, 268–271.

5. Apuleius *Apology* 13–16 with Hunink 1997, 57–67.

6. Taylor 2008, 7.

7. Cf. *mirabile*, 2.1028; *mirantur*, 6.59; *mirari*, 6.654.

8. See also Lucretius' metaphorical use of a mirror, already in *DRN* 3.974–5: personified Nature admonishes the man who cannot bear the thought of dying, holding up a mirror of *futurum tempus* which is blank, because there is nothing at all to be seen (*hoc igitur speculum nobis natura futuri | temporis exponit post mortem denique nostrum*. 'This therefore is a mirror which nature holds up to us, showing the time to come after we at length shall die.'). See Kenney 2014 *ad loc.*

9. McCarty 1989, 170.

10. See also *DRN* 4.311–317 (Why is it that the reflection of right as left and left as right does not take place in the case of concave mirrors?) with Koenen 1996; *DRN* 4.318–23 (Why, when we walk in front of the mirror, does our image in the mirror move along with us?) with Algra 1999. For Lucretius' passages that I discuss see also Bailey 1947 *ad loc.*; Císar 2001; Godwin 1986 *ad loc.*; Munro 1893 *ad loc.*

11. Sharples 2002.

12. Clay 1983, 48. Cf. *DRN* 1.478 *perspicere*, 1.949 *perspicis*, 1.956 *pervideamus*, 1.1114 *pernosces*, 1.1117 *pervideas*, 2.90 *pervideas*, 3.181 *pernoscere*, 4.25 *persentis*, 6.380 *perspicere*.

13. Garani 2007, 119–120. Cf. e.g. *DRN* 5.637–649, 6.137–141, 6.552–556.

14. Avotins 1980.

15. Fowler 2002, 386.

16. In connection with Lucretius' description, scholars point to Hero's of Alexandria *Catoptrica* (plausibly a first-century AD treatise, known only through a thirteenth-century Latin translation of an abridgment, produced by William of Moerbeke probably in 1269). See Jones (2001) who doubted the attribution to Hero. See also Tybjerg 2003 and 2005. The second part of this treatise deals with instructions about how to construct mirrors with useful or entertaining purposes. Among other instructions, we read about a catoptrical device for tracking foot-traffic on a street from within a closed building (*Catopt.* 22 Jones). However, when comparing it to Lucretius' poem, there is a great difference in style: what predominates in Hero is the geometrical vocabulary – resounding Euclid's accounts – a style of demonstration that would be alien within the framework of Lucretius' philosophical poem. What is even more, one can easily take notice of a *reversal regarding the point of view*: whereas Hero's periscopic mirrors allow an observer who is situated within the house to watch on the passers-by in the street and thus *bring in* their image, in the other way round, Lucretius aims at *eliciting* the image for the sake of someone who is standing outside. In more general terms, in a way similar to Lucretius, the emphasis in Hero's account is laid upon the idea that knowledge of the principles of optics is what will prevent the investigator from suspension of judgement. See Lloyd 1982, 160–161. However, unlike Lucretius, Hero does not banish astonishment from his account; in fact, he believes that the subject of catoptrics is a source both of useful devices and of devices designed to *create wonder*. To quote Tybjerg (2005, 450): 'Hero shows that wonder forms a continuum with utility and wonder and utility cannot be meaningfully separated.'

17. Lucretius draws the same antithesis between light and darkness in connection with Heraclitus (*DRN* 1.635–704), when he rejects the latter's obscure style (*DRN* 1.639 *clarus ob obscuram linguam*). About the principle of clarity see also Marković 2008, 87–90 and *passim*.

Notes to pp. 41–47

18. Garani 2007, 24–25.
19. Garani 2007, 100–102.
20. A characteristic example is to be found in *DRN* 6.108–115, when Lucretius explains one of the possible causes of thunder, by comparing clouds buffeted by winds with awnings of a theatre and then with paper and clothes hung up to dry. For discussion see Garani 2007, 102–103.

Chapter 4

1. For a list of the treatises and bibliographical information, see Lindberg 1975, 1–58. One finds a good general overview of the theories of vision in antiquity in the following authors: van Hoorn 1972, 42–71; Lindberg 1976; Simon 1988, 21–56; Smith 2015; Thibodeau 2016, 130–144. One can encounter more information about particular ancient theories of colour in Hahm 1978, 60–95; Ierodiakonou 1999, 123–141; Burnyeat 2005, 35–53; Ierodiakonou 2005, 1–37; Ierodiakonou 2015, 227–250; Kalderon 2015; Rudolph 2015, 36–53. For an extended bibliography on the topic, see Smith 2015, 430–453; Squire 2015, 264–305.
2. Cf. Heiberg 1895.
3. Cf. Lejeune 1989.
4. For more information about geometrical optics in antiquity, see Jones 1994, 47–76; Netz-Squire 2015, 68–84.
5. Cf. Aët. 4.13.1 (Stob.) = A29; Teophr. *Sens.* 50 = A135; concerning the application of the theory to the concept of reflection, see Aët. 4.14.2 = A31.
6. Cf. Lucr. 4.217.
7. Aetius (IV 21 = *SVF* 2.836) defines the ruling principle as 'the soul's highest part, which produces impressions, assents, perceptions, and impulses', Long-Sedley 1987, 315. The Stoics posited the ruling faculty in the heart (*SVF* 2.837–9, 843).
8. According to some reports, the visual *pneuma* increases the tension of the air, cf. *SVF* 2.868. For more on the effect produced on the air by the visual *pneuma*, see Hahm 1978, 60–95.
9. Alexander describes this affection as a cone's base being 'imprinted' by the object, see *SVF* 2.864.
10. λαμπρόν, κάθαρον, αὐγοειδής – *SVF* 2.860, p. 232.
11. De Lacy 2005, 460–461.
12. Remarkably, Galen mentions the reflections in the mirrors himself in *PHP* 7.5.39–41. There he reports on the 'geometers' who 'offer proofs that we see in straight lines and that vision, when it falls on something completely smooth and bright, is reflected at the same angle as the angle of incidence'; see De Lacy 2005, 460–461. Galen also notes that he discusses this topic in more detail in the lost treatise *On Demonstration*.
13. Bjørnbo-Vogl 1912, 82.
14. Melchior-Bonnet 2014, 10.
15. Bjørnbo, A. A. and Vogl, S. (1912), *Alkindi, Tideus und Pseudo-Euklid*, Leipzig/Berlin. Here, I translate the passages on pages 73–80 of this edition.
16. Bjørnbo supports this suggestion: ,'Schon im Titel spürt man übrigens die Übersetzung aus dem Arabischen und noch mehr im Texte mit den vielen aus dem Arabischen herkommenden sprachlichen Schwerfälligkeiten'; Bjørnbo-Vogl 1912, 152.

17. Burnett 2001, 249–288. The work is listed as 'Liber Tidei de speculo tractatus'.
18. Bjørnbo-Vogl 1912, 152: ,'Wie in Akindis Optik werden mit Vorliebe die Wörter *sermo*, *forma*, *dispositio* und *cadere supra* (oder *super*) benutzt <...>. Wörter wie *diuersificare*, *exemplificare*, *ratiocinare* und Wendungen wie *res non est*, *sicut*; *et illud est*, *quoniam*; *et haec est res, quae*; *et propter illud fit, quod*; *et illud est, quoniam*; *ergo tunc*; *similiter iterum*; *et ex hoc modo fit*, gehören auch ganz der wortgetreuen Übersetzungsweise des Gerard v. Cremona zu <...>'
19. Meyerhof 1928.
20. It is quite illustrative that in *Ten Treatises* 109.15–25 Ibn Ishaq provides an argument about the reflection in the mirrors, which one does not find in Tideus. Of course, this still leaves open the possibility that Tideus might have read Ibn Ishaq but chose to ignore him. However, Ibn Ishaq generally tends to elaborate on the key arguments borrowed from Galen's *PHP*, whereas Tideus' explication of these arguments does not resemble Ibn Ishaq's. For instance, Ibn Ishaq inserts an original digression about the nature of nerves (107.1–108.10) which elaborates on Galen's analogy between the nerve and the air, in relation to the brain and the eye; this passage is absent in *De Speculis*, although Tideus borrows Galen's original claim. Another example is the way Ibn Ishaq frames the question whether something enters the eye or emanates from it. Although Tideus also discusses this topic in *De Speculis*, Ibn Ishaq formulates it in a considerably more sophisticated way than Galen. Moreover, Tideus' argument resembles Galen's one, but not Ibn Ishaq's.
21. The name varies in the MSS.: Regoiu (P), or Ruegoui (A) (apparently, in abl.).
22. This seems plausible, especially if we keep in mind that a prominent medical school developed in Southern Italy, above all Salerno, from the ninth century onwards. If Tideus' hometown was indeed Reggio di Calabria, then the later development of medicine in southern Italy might well harmonize with Tideus' suggested job as a physician. On the flourishing of the medical schools in southern Italy, see Haskins 1928, 273.
23. I do not include the translation of this passage in the present publication.
24. Of the suggested identifications of Tideus, the one with Diocles seems to be worth mentioning, being supported by at least three scholars: Leclerc (in Leclerc 1876, 413), Steinschneider (in Steinschneider 1886, 81–110) and Burnett (in Burnett 2001, 249–288). Diocles was a Greek mathematician active between 200 and 70 BCE, who wrote a treatise *On Burning Mirrors*. The English translation of the treatise (see Toomer 1976) clearly demonstrates the differences in approach and elaboration between the two authors. Lindberg also objects to such identification in Lindberg 1975, 77.
25. Lindberg 1996.
26. 'Since you desire to stir and dispose yourself and others worthy of wisdom to a knowledge of *perspectiva*, you should know that many authors treat this science. But some do so too briefly, as Euclid, Jacob Alkindi, and Tideus; <...>' (the alternative beginning of *Persp.* I.1.1, 'based on the collation of seven manuscripts') Lindberg 1996, 336–337, 391.
27. *Persp.* I.7.2,73–78; see the citation in the footnote to the translation below.
28. Lindberg 1975, 76–77.
29. For the list of MSS. used for the critical edition, see Bjørnbo-Vogl 1912, 163–164. One can find the description of the manuscripts in Bjørnbo-Vogl 1912, 123–147.
30. *Cod. Digbean.* 168 ascribes the work to the mathematician Theudius, who is presumably Theudius of Magnesia, an author of a pre-Euclidian *Elements*.
31. Both treatises are present in at least six currently available MSS.: *Codex Ambrosianus* (A), *Codex Basilensis* (B), *Cod. Crakov.* 569 (K), *Cod. Digbean.* 40 (Q), *Cod. Coll. Rom. H.C.* 93, *Cod. Vatic.* 2975.

32. Six MSS. containing both works: A, B, *Cod. Amplon.* Q. 385, Q, *Cod. Coll. Rom. H.C.* 93, *Cod. Vatic.* 2975.

33. Both works are found in at last five MSS.: A, B, K, Q, *Cod. Coll. Rom. H.C.* 93, *Cod. Vatic.* 2975.

34. For instance, Roger Bacon mentions Tideus as being on a par with Euclid (apparently, Bacon means the author known to us as Pseudo-Euclid), and Al-Kindi. This might be the evidence that Bacon had access to one of the six MSS., containing all the treatises; it might well have been *Cod. Digbean.* 40, which stems from the thirteenth century.

35. Brown 1981, 81–82.

36. Particularly misleading is the fact that Vogl inconsistently translates *superius* and *inferius* with *Nähe* and *Entfernung vom Spiegel* in the key passages on pages 78–79; the same is true about the translation of *quantitas* with *Quantität* instead of *Größe* throughout the whole treatise.

37. Abbreviations follow *Oxford Classical Dictionary*, fourth edition where possible.

38. Tideus seems to have in mind the reaction of calcium with vinegar. We encounter references to this reaction already in the Latin literature of the Imperial period, so the reaction must have been well known by his own time. For instance, a relevant passage is found in Plin. *HN* XXIII 27.54.1–3; possibly, Pliny means soil, enriched with calcium. He maintains that the vine, along with its products, was thought to have the power of cooling. At the same time, this power must have been associated with a capacity to shatter frozen objects. For a parallel, see Pedanius Dioscorides, *De Mat. Med.* V.27. See the full list with relevant citations in Bjørnbo-Vogl 1912, 83–85.

39. Cf. Gal. *PHP* 7.5.1.1–2: 'A person would be most convinced that this happens when he has learned the probable account of how we see'; De Lacy 2005, 452–453.

40. Cf. Ptol. *Opt.* III.13; V.22.

41. For similar arguments that alteration happens instantaneously, especially in the propagation of light, see: *Arist. Sens.* 446b28–447a7; *Alex. Mantissa* 143.30–34; Al-Kindi, *de Asp.* 9. Compare this against *PHP* 7.5.1.3–2.2: 'A body that is seen does one of two things: either it sends something from itself to us and thereby gives an indication of its peculiar character, if it does not itself send something, it waits for some sensory power to come to it from us. Which of these alternatives is the more correct may best be judged in the following way <...>'; De Lacy 2005, 452–453. Cf. Ibn-Ishaq, *Ten Treatises* 3.103, 20–29.

42. Cf. *PHP* 7.5.5.1–3: 'We are left, then, with the view that at the time when we look at something, the surrounding air becomes for us the kind of instrument that the nerve in the body is at all times'; De Lacy 2005, 454–455. See also: Damianus, *Optik*, p. 24.7–12. Interestingly, Nemesius of Emesa frames Galen's theory in similar terms, and he also shifts the stress from the visual *pneuma*. See Nemesius, *De natura hominis* 7 180,21–181,10.

43. Cf. *PHP* 7.5.46.1–4; cf.: 'If then the sight alone of the senses, when it perceives the sense-object that moves it, uses air as a medium, not as a kind of walking stick, but as a homogeneous part that forms one body with itself <...>'; De Lacy 2005, 460–461. Cf. Ibn-Ishaq, *Ten Treatises*, 3.109,1ff. For the reports about the Stoic source of this analogy, see *SVF* 2.864, 865, 867

44. Compare *PHP* 7.5.7.3–7: '<...> and when it [i.e., the light] strikes the surrounding air it produces by its first impact an alteration that is transmitted to the furthest distance — the surrounding air being, of course, a continuum, so that in a moment of time the alteration spreads to the whole of it'; De Lacy 2005, 454–455. Cf. Al-Kindi, *de Asp.* 7.

45. Compare the parallel in Galen's *PHP* 7.5.49.1–3: 'For we do in fact perceive by the more earthy of the sense organs, touch, the earthy nature in objects of sense, and by the most luminous, sight, the luminous nature <...>'; De Lacy 2005, 462–463. Cf. Galen, *Usu Part.* 8.6

vol. 3, p. 639 = *SVF* 2.860; Ibn-Ishaq, *Ten Treatises*, 3.108, 24–34. According to Tideus, the air takes on the colours of the object, and then communicates these colours to the eye, thus causing the corresponding alterations in the moistures within the eye. This is supposed to establish a correspondence between certain kinds of alteration in the air, and certain alterations in the eye, which would be associated with a colour. Tideus explains the possibility of such co-alteration, implicitly referring to the principle of 'like to like' (cf. Empedocles, A 20).

46. Cf. Arist. *Mete*. 3.2 372a32–b6.

47. Roger Bacon refers to this passage in *Persp.* 1.7.2, 73–78: 'And Tideus, in his *Book on Vision*, affirms this and advances the argument that sight would never [be able to] certify the distance between itself and the visible object, nor the size of the visible object, nor its location and orientation, if visual rays did not proceed from the eye to the object, rest on it, grasp its surface, and embrace its extremities'; Lindberg 1996, 101–102. Cf. Ibn Ishaq, *Ten Treatises* 3.104, 6–11.

48. Cf. Phlp. *in de An*. 296.25–297.10.

49. Compare this to Galen's language in *PHP* 7.4.25.1–5: 'Thus it is likely that in this way the pneuma coming into the eyes is united at the first impact with the surrounding air and alters the air to its own peculiar nature but does not itself extend out to the furthest distance'; De Lacy 2005, 452–453. Cf. Ibn-Ishaq, *Ten Treatises* 3.110, 3–7.

50. The parallels in Galen's *PHP* are, for instance: (i) *PHP* 7.5.6.1–3: 'It seems that the effect produced on the air around us by the emission of the pneuma is of the same sort as the effect produced on it by the light of the sun'; De Lacy 2005, 454–455; (ii) *PHP* 7.4.24.1–25.1: 'For it was stated that what people call a transmission of power is a transfer of qualitative change, such as occurs also in the air by the agency of sunlight'; De Lacy 2005, 452–453. Cf. Ibn-Ishaq, *Ten Treatises* 3.105, 7–15; 3.103, 8–10; 3.111, 1ff. We encounter a similar idea in Damianus, *Opt*. 13, 1–8, Schöne 1897, 14–17.

51. As Vogl notes in Bjørnbo-Vogl 1912, 89, the theory of the four elements stems from Empedocles (cf. DK B23). A similar argument is found in Ibn-Ishaq, *Ten Treatises*, 3.110, 8–18.

52. In the translation of this sentence, I follow MS. K (*Cod. Crakov. Bibl. Jagiellońska*, MS. 569, pp. 261–262. XIV century): '<...> *diversificatur lumen cuiusque eorum a suo compare per quantitatem diversitatis, quae est inter ipsum et ipsum, propter quod diversificantur lumina*'.

53. Tideus most probably means Plato here, cf. *Tim*. 45b–d; also see *Arist. Sens.* 439b14–18, 439a18–21, and Arist. *De an*. 418b9–20. For discussion about the corporeality of light in late antiquity, see John Philoponus, *in de An*. 326, 38–329, 2; 330, 28–331, 1.

54. See the similar argument in Galen's *PHP* 7.4.11.1–12.1: 'That a pneuma is carried through these passages to the eyes you learn from the structure and also from the fact that when one of the eyes is closed the pupil of the other is enlarged, and when it is reopened, the pupil of the other quickly returns to its natural size'; De Lacy 2005, 450–451. Cf. Ibn Ishaq, *Ten Treatises*, 3.100, 23ff.

55. It should also mean that the base surface of the cone or the frustum embracing the reflected object is wider than the diameter of the mirror, i.e. that we are not dealing with a cylinder.

56. Cf. Pl. *Tht*. 191c–d, 194c, *Phlb*. 39a–b; Arist. *De an*. 424 a 17 ff., 425 b 23, 434 a 29; *Mem*. 450a30; the Stoics, *SVF* 2.53, 55, 56, Cicero, *De oratore*, II, 87.360; Al-Kindi, *de asp*. 7; Thomas Aquinas, *In De anima*, Lectio 24 on Book II, par. 553–4. On this subject, see Burkert 1977, 97–109; Carruthers 2008, 18–55.

57. Cf. Plot. *Enn*. IV.5 23–28.

Notes to pp. 54–61

58. Cf. Plotinus, *Enn.* II.8 4–9.
59. Tideus seems to mean that the angle at the top of the light cone issued from the mirror is a constant.
60. Cf. Al-Kindi, de asp., 22.37,6–12; Bjørnbo-Vogl 1912, 37.
61. *Liurellus*, a diminutive from *lura*, or *lorum*. The primary meaning is 'a leathern thong or strap' (cf. Pompeius Festus' *De Verborum Significatione*, 10.86.25-7, in Lindsay 1913, 107). However, in the passage in question, *liurellus* rather means the thong holding the mouth of a small leathern bag, and so, figuratively, the whole leathern bag or sack.

Chapter 5

1. The introduction as well as Parts 1a/b and 2 are authored by I. Bonati and were written during her Post-Doctoral Fellowship at the North-West University in Potchefstroom, South Africa; Part 1c is authored by N. Reggiani and develops some thoughts already presented in Reggiani 2018b.
2. See Chantraine 1968: 811 s.v. ὄπωπα and Frisk 1970, 407 s.v. ὄπωπα.
3. On the myth of Narcissus, its ancient sources and modern reception, see Bettini-Pellizer 2003. See also, e.g., McCarty 1989, 161–95; Pellizer 1984, 21–35 and 1991, 13–29; Frontisi-Ducroux-Vernant 1997, 200–241.
4. See Tmosis 1999, 160–161.
5. See Milne 1907, 150–152. Cf. also the diminutive διόπτριον applied to a small rectal speculum in Leonid. *ap.* Paul. Aeg. VI 78, 4,5 (CMG IX 2, 122,27 Heiberg) = Orib. XLIV 20, 66,5 (VI 2,1, 141,1 Raeder).
6. Only the verb ἐνοπτρίζω, 'to reflect', 'to see / be seen as in a mirror' is attested, cf. P.Pommersf. 1,478 (second half of the VI cent. AD, ?) and P.Oxy. XXXI 2603 (III–IV AD), a Christian letter of commendation in which it appears interestingly in a figurative sense, vd. ll.3–4 τῶι ἔσοπτρον κτησαμένωι ἢ ἄλλο τι τοιοῦτο ἐν | χειρὶ ἔχοντι ἐν οἷς τὰ πρόσωπα ἐνοπτρίζεται ('a man who has acquired a mirror, or holds in his hand something else of that sort, in which faces are seen represented . . .').
7. See Russo 2006, 191–193.
8. Both the presence and the meaning of the adjective κασιωτικός are uncertain. The term is translated as 'inlaid' in the *ed.pr.* (p. 195), but the author remarks that 'Casiotic joinery is surprising in an object so small as a mirror' (p. 196). It is possible that the letters before the lacuna may be the beginning of a new word rather than an adjective referring to κάτοπτρον. In such a case, a comma should be inserted in the transcription: κάτοπτρον δίπτυχ(ον), κασιω[τικόν]. An alternative reading, as the editor rightly observes, is καδιω[, perhaps hiding a new attestation of κάδιον, a type of container that has several occurrences in marriage contracts and papyrus documents linked to feminine world. See Bonati 2016, 59–85 (esp. pp. 69–70), and Russo 2005, 215 and 218–219. However, the presence of δ or σ cannot be decided with certainty. In case of σ, see the proposal κασιωτικὰ ἱμάτια ('Casiotic garments') by Mitthof 2005, 260.
9. See *ed.pr.* p. 77 and Russo 1999, 44–46, in particular: 'quale che fosse lo scopo finale di questo frammentario elenco di beni (forse rubati?), ci sembra molto improbabile che si trattasse di beni dotali. Da un'analisi dettagliata di questi oggetti, sembrerebbe, piuttosto, che essi appartenessero ad un artista' (p. 44), probably a woman or an effeminate man, for instance a *kynaidos*. Other hypotheses on the possible nature of the fragment in McGing 1987, 73–74.

10. Russo 1999a, 45 and 2005, 226 and n. 59 also suggests the possibility that the word in l.6 is κάμπτρον, 'chest', hence 'a chest with an inscription'. For this word, cf. P.Coll.Youtie I 7,9-10 discussed *infra*. However, checking the printed image of the papyrus (see McGing 1987, 72), the scanty traces of the letters in lacuna seem to be more compatible with the reading κ]ᾀτ̣ο̣πτρου. It is for this reason that P.Dubl. 14 has been included among the *testimonia* of the word.

11. See Russo 1999b, 87-105.

12. The nature and the scope of this list are uncertain, but the typology of the goods, such as jewels, garments and cosmetic products, points to a female context. It is not excluded that these objects were part of a dowry. See Russo 1999a, 124-125 and 2005, 226.

13. Another two papyrological attestations of κάτοπτρον, dating back to the first century BC, do not belong to a documentary but to a philosophical context, since they are found in two carbonized papyri discovered in the Roman 'Villa dei Papiri' at Herculaneum: P.Herc. 152 fr.88b, col.9 sup., 5-6 containing fragments of the work *De dis* III by Philodemus of Gadara (τὰ το[ῦ] κατόπτρου καὶ τῆς ἐμφάσεως, τοῦ μὲν κα|τόπτρου τελέως μικροῦ φαινομένου) and P.Herc. 1506 fr.17, col.4, 11 containing fragments of another work by Philodemus, *De rhetorica* III (καὶ τὰν|[δρο]μήκη κάτο[πτ]ρα κατεσ|[κε]υακέ[γ]αι]).

14. As to κάμπτρα, see e.g. BGU III 717,13 (AD 149, Arsinoites); SB XIV 12024,6 (II AD, Tebtynis); P.Cair.Masp. I 67006r,89 (*ca.* 567, Antinoopolis) and III 67340r,79 (*ca.* 566-573, Antinoopolis).

15. Cf. col.II, ll.24-8 δύο καὶ χάλκωμα γυγαικεῖ|ον πρὸς (δραχμὰς) η· Ἀλεξάνδρας | ἐγχειρίδιον πρὸς (δραχμὴν) α καὶ κόγ|δυα χαλκᾶ δύο καὶ κύαθος | οἰνηρός, ἔσοπτρον πρὸς (δραχμὰς) η.

16. See Russo 2005, 217 n. 10.

17. See Russo 2005, 234-236.

18. On this text and the image of the mirror, see Harrop 1962, 132-140 (esp. pp. 139-140). Cf. ll.3-7 τῶι ἔσοπτρον κτησαμένωι ἢ ἄλλο τι τοιοῦτο ἐν | χειρὶ ἔχοντι ἐν οἷς τὰ πρόσωπα ἐνοπτρίζεται | 5οὐ χρεία ἐστιν τοῦ λέγοντος ἢ μαρτυροῦντος | περὶ τοῦ αὐτῶι ἐπικειμένου χαρακτῆρος | καὶ τῆς χροίας καὶ τοῦ εἴδους ὅπ\ως/ [[. π̣ο̣]]ὑπάρχει ('a man who has acquired a mirror, holds in his hand something else of that sort, in which faces are seen represented, has no one to tell him, or testify about the character that lies upon him, and his complexion, and appearance, how it is'); ll.12-6 οὐ γὰρ κατὰ τοὺς ἄλ|λους ὑπάρχει τοὺς ἐν ἀγνοίαι ὄντας | καὶ τοῦ ἐσόπτρου πόρρω καθεστῶ|τας τοῦ τὰς πάντων ὁμοιώσεις ἐπιδεί|ξαντος ('for he is not like the rest who are in ignorance, and standing far from mirror that displays the likeness of all'); ll.17-9 καὶ γὰρ ὡς δι ἐσ[ό]πτρου κα|τίδες (*l.* κα|τεῖδες) τὴν πρὸς σέ μου ἔ[μ]φυτον | στοργὴν καὶ ἀγάπην τὴν ἀεὶ νέαν ('for as through a mirror you have seen my implanted affection and love for you ever fresh').

19. See Russo 1999a, 175-176 and 2006, 193-195.

20. The letter is indeed written by a certain Dionysos to his sister and he informs her that she would have received the items from their father Chaeremon: ll.1-4 Διονύσι[ος] Τ[ca.9 τῇ] | ἀδελφῇ χαίρ[ειν], | κόμισαι παρὰ τοῦ πατρὸς Χαι|ρήμονος ὀσυπτρον καὶ κτλ.

21. The *editores principes*, B. P. Grenfell and A. S. Hunt, transcribe the word as οσοπτρον, that is unparalleled, but it is just an editorial mistake. The digital image of the papyrus clearly confirms that the third letter is υ and not ο, hence ὄσυπτρον. For a re-edition of this text, see Bonati 2016, 235-249.

22. A detailed analysis of this document, its sociolinguistic context and its vocabulary has been conducted by Leiwo–Halla-Aho 2002, 560-580.

23. On the sealing practice in Graeco-Roman papyri, see in particular Vandorpe 1997, 231-291, but also the following webpage for an extensive bibliography on the subject: https://www.trismegistos.org/seals/biblio.html.

Notes to pp. 64–66

24. See Bonati 2016, 247.
25. Cf. BL II 2, 32, with bibliography. See also Scholl 1990, 955.
26. See at the address http://www.papyrology.uw.edu.pl/papyri/pberlin11780.jpg.
27. See already Preisendanz 1932, 231.
28. Cf. also the compound οσυπυρομαντιον (*pap.*) in a magical papyrus, PGM II 13,752 (346 AD), corrected as εἰσοπτρομαντιῶν by the editor of the text, K. Preisendanz. Yet, it may rather be interpreted as an incorrect form of ὀσυπτρομαντιῶν. See Gignac 1976, 292 n. 5.
29. As already pointed out, ὄσυπτρον is attested 10 times in 9 papyri, whereas ἔσοπτρον occurs 8 times in 6 papyri and κάτοπτρον 11 times in 10 papyri (plus one if we consider the possibility of reading κάτοπτρον in P.Coll.Youtie I 7,9–10, see *supra*).
30. See Bonati 2016, 246–248.
31. Cf. e.g. ὸν for ἐν in P.Med. I 33,4, (126–125 BC, Lykopolis); τὸ πλῆρος for πλῆρες in P.Oxy. XIV 1670,13 (III AD); ἀβαρός for ἀβαρές in P.Oxy. XIV 1757,14 and 18 (II AD). See Gignac 1976, 290–292.
32. Cf. e.g. ὑπότε for ὁπότε in P.Mich. V 276,30 (AD 47, Tebtynis) and ὑπώρε for ὀπώρα in P.Oxy. II 298,38 (I AD). See Gignac 1976, 293–294.
33. See respectively S. Eitrem and L. Amundsen in the *ed.pr.* of P.Oslo II 46, p. 113 *ad l.*: 'ὄσυπτρον, i.e. ὄσιπτρον for ἴσυπτρον, εἴσοπτρον – a very interesting instance of the metathesis of vowels in successive syllables', and D.S. Crawford in the *ed.pr.* of P.FuadUniv. 8, p. 12: 'a phonetic (spooneristic) transposition of the vowels. [...] It is more likely to be a phonetic rendering of a common mispronunciation than a mere clerical error'. See also Leiwo–Halla-Aho 2002, 572–573: 'the phoneme /i/ was written with a <υ>, though the actual sound change /y/ > /i/ [...] seems to have been completed much later. The metathesis is likely to have happened first [isoptron] > [osiptron], after which the variable (i) preceded by a round /o/ in the previous syllable could have easily rounded towards [y] in speech. The Latin form, then, emerges simply from orthographic interference ὄσυπτρον > *osyptum*, the Greek <υ> transliterated as <y> in Latin'.
34. Cf. e.g. ἐκθίσται for ἐκθέσθαι in P.Mich. V 347,1 (AD 21, Tebtynis) and μέρισι for μέρεσι in P.Flor. I 50, 91 (AD 269, Hermopolis). See Gignac 1976, 249–251.
35. Cf. Ch.L.A. XXV 783 (I–II AD, ?), Ch.L.A. V 295 (II AD, Caesarea) and P.Mich. VII 444 (end of the II AD, ?).
36. See Leiwo–Halla-Aho 2002, 576–580.
37. http://papyri.info; see Reggiani 2017, 222 ff.
38. The digital environment certainly requires that careful attention be paid to all relevant papyrological features, which have to be formalized and standardized at levels that have never been reached in the traditional paper editions.
39. Quite paradigmatic is the edition of P.Stras. IV 237, where the further spelling variant ὄσιπτρον (exhibiting an apparent change υ > ι, see Gignac 1976, 267–268) occurs and the editor thinks that it is a 'métathèse par inadvertence' from εἴσοπτρον.
40. Daris 1968 s.vv.
41. See Evans 2010a and 2010b.
42. If one is not aware of the spelling ὄσυπτρον and wants to search for mirrors in the papyri, then (s)he should perform at least two searches, one for εἴσοπτρον and one ἔσοπτρον (or one search involving a complex set of regular expressions), and (s)he would then be misled by the occurrences of εἴσοπτρον, which appear in the apparatuses only.

43. See Reggiani 2018a, 26–29 and Stolk 2018, where such a markup strategy is analysed and critically discussed.
44. A fitting precedent is represented by the treatment of iotacism, the phonetic interchange between ει and ι, which becomes such a 'standard' feature of the language of the papyri that it is very often left unregularized in both printed and digital editions (see Depauw-Stolk 2015, 213–214; Reggiani 2018b).
45. See Reggiani 2018a.
46. See Reggiani 2017, 255–270; Reggiani 2018, 47–54; Reggiani 2019.
47. See Russo 2005, 215.
48. On mirrors as a 'distinctly feminine attribute' in Ancient Greece, see Lee 2015, 165–167. See also Ead. 2017, 143–168.
49. The dowry (φερνή) of a bride in Graeco-Roman Egypt included the παράφερνα, literally the 'goods additional to the dowry', which represented the separate property owned by a married woman. These items, such as jewellery and clothing, remaining the wife's property, were entirely free from the control of her husband. See in particular Yiftach-Firanko 2003 with bibliography and Russo 2005, 213–241.
50. See Carpino 2010, 445.
51. See de Grummond 1981, 56; Carpino 2010, 445; Lee 2015, 166.
52. See Russo 2005, 217. On the temple lists on papyrus, see Grassi 1926 (pp. 31–32 for the mirrors).
53. Carpino 2010, 444.
54. Lee 2015, 166.
55. For an in-depth discussion of the ideological association between women and mirrors in the Greek world, see Frontisi-Ducroux–Vernant 1997, 53–250.
56. McCarty 1989, 170. See also Grabes 1982, 43; de Grummond-Hoff 1982, 32; Schefold 1940, 16; Lee 2015, 166.
57. This has been demonstrated by a modern experiment undertaken by Gisela Richter at the Metropolitan Museum of Art of New York, see Richter 1938, 341.
58. See LSJ^9 436 s.v.
59. The only two exceptions are BGU I 326r, col. II,15 (AD 194, Karanis) κωδικίλλων διπτύχων and P.Cair.Masp. III 67340,29 (VI AD, Antinoopolis) ἐνώτιον δίπτυχον ἕν, where the adjective defines a *codex* and an earring respectively.
60. On mirrors in Ancient Egypt, see Derriks 2001, 419–422.
61. On the history of Greek mirrors and their typologies, see Wunderlich 1951, 4; Cooney 1973, 215; Congdon 1985, 19–24; Schwarzmeier 1993, 355; Carpino 2010, 444; Lee 2015, 166. See also A. Netoliczka in RE X.1 [1921], 29–45 s.v. κάτοπτρον.
62. See Congdon 1981.
63. See de Grummond 1981, 57–58 and 1985, 27–29.
64. For some other exemplars, see Wunderlich 1951, 4–6; Cooney 1973, 215–21; Congdon 1985, 22–23; Schwarzmeier 1993, 354–357.
65. Hand mirrors with ivory handles were already in use in Greece during the archaic period and seem to have descended from a similar Mycenean type. See Merker 2003: 129–135 with bibliography. An exemplar, dating back to 1250–1050 BC and preserved in the British Museum, can be seen at the following address: https://www.britishmuseum.org/research/collection_online/collection_object_details.aspx?objectId=464482&partId=1&images=true.

66. See LSJ⁹ 1822 s.v.

67. See Merker 2003, 129: 'the hand mirrors were sometimes made entirely of bronze, the handle either cast separately in one piece with the mirror disc or cast separately in one or more part and assembled'.

68. A remarkable example is represented by a second-third century AD Greek inscription on a Roman lead mirror acquired by the Antikensammlung Staatlichen der Museen zu Berlin in 1910. Unfortunately, the object is lost, but a drawing in the inventory remains. According to the archaeologist Giulia Baratta (see Baratta 2014, 709-713) the inscription should be read: τῇ καλῇ τὰ καλὰ κυρίᾳ ἀγορᾶς ὄν με δηναρίου ('To the beautiful lady of the market the beautiful things, [a gift offered] with a denarius'). A new transcription has been proposed by Litinas 2015, 158: τῇ καλῇ τὰ καλά. κυρία, ἀγόρασόν με δηναρίου ('To the beautiful lady the beautiful things. Lady, buy me with a denarius'). By taking αγορας with ον to form the imperative ἀγόρασον, the writing can be understood as an inscription to the potential buyer urging her to buy the mirror for the price of one denarius. This interpretation demonstrates that the mirrors with inscriptions were not produced only for votive purposes, but they could be found also in household contexts related to women.

69. See ll.16 πε[ριδέξι]ᾳ παιδικ(ὰ) ι καὶ παιδικ(ὸς) δακτύλ(ιος) α ('10 armlets for a child and 1 ring for a child') and 18 ψέλιο(ν) ἀργ(υροῦν) παιδι[κ(όν)] ('a silver bracelet for a child').

70. See LSJ⁹ 1172-1173 s.v.: 'younger', 'more recent'.

71. See LSJ⁹ 1172 s.v.: 'youthful'.

72. An even less convincing interpretation is found in Grassi 1926, 31-32.

73. For theories and a bibliography on the topic, see Bonner–Darby Nock 1948, 213-215; Darby Nock 1953, 283-296; Bookidis–Stroud 1997, 365-366 and 436-437; Lee 2000, 31-32; Økland 2004, 82-83; Mastrocinque 2012, 105-118; Concannon 2017, 168 e nn. 44-45.

74. See Budenz 1858, 4-32; Debrunner 1917, 197-200; Chantraine 1933, 385-393.

75. See LSJ⁹ 837 s.v. Ἰσιακός: 'of or for Isis'.

76. See LSJ⁹ 258 s.v. Ἀσκληπιός.

Chapter 6

1. One year after his passing I would like to dedicate this small contribution to the memory of my Maestro, Professor Giovannangelo Camporeale. I discussed this subject with him over a long period of time, and his suggestions were always invaluable to me. We treasure his legacy, his great affection for his students, his passion for study, his scientific rigour, which was always the foundation for his research, but his absence is a daily unbridgeable gap

    I must thank Professor Nicole Cuddeback for correcting my English and reviewing this article and the editors of this book for the opportunity to publish this short study. A special thank goes to Dr Claudia Noferi who read the first draft of this work.

2. Flames on the extension of the *recto* of Etruscan Hellenistic bronze mirrors: from left to right: 1 – ex Collection Gorga, Museo delle Antichità Etrusche e Italiche, Sapienza, Università di Roma, Inv. BG662, third century BC (Ambrosini 2012, 89, n. 91, fig. 91a-f); 2 – Morlanwelz, Musée Royal de Mariemont, inv. Ac. 206 B, first half of the third century BC (Lambrechts 1987, 47-49, n 27, fig. 27a-d); 3 – Città del Vaticano, Museo Profano della Biblioteca Apostolica Vaticana, inv. 6552, third century BC (*CSE* Vaticano 1, 38-39, n. 18, fig. 18a-d); 4 – Città del Vaticano, Museo Profano della Biblioteca Apostolica Vaticana, inv. 6553, third century BC (CSE Vaticano 1, 39-40, n. 18, fig. 18a-d).

3. According to Mavleev 1990, 351, nn. F. 25, 26, 31 (and not 253 as reported in Mangani 2002, 37, footnote 50).

4. Wiman 1990, 201 ff.; Gilotta 2007, 96–97, n. 38; about the interpretation of the decoration in favour of the flame see Mangani 2002, 37, with indications about the production area in association with the 'tongue' specimens (a linguetta) in the context of a Volterra workshop. See also Mangani 1985, 21–40 for mirrors' workshops in northern Etruria.

5. For a general overview see Ambrosini 2012, 31, n. 1, fig. 1a–f.

6. Rebuffat-Emmanuel 1984, 215 ff. All the specimens are of the kind with disk cast with shaft. About possible dating of mirrors with Lasas (Etruscan female daemons) and Dioscuri see Cateni 2002, 41–57. For the presence of the Dioscuri on Etruscan mirrors see also De Puma 1973, 59–170; De Puma 1982, 89–90; De Grummond 1991, 10–31; and Carpino 2009, 182–197.

7. Mangani 2002, 35 ff. For the 'Maestro di Cacu' see Mansuelli 1943, 487–521.

8. Szilágyi 1994, 169 with a list of the known specimens attributed to the Master in *CSE* Hongrie-Tchécoslovaquie, n. 21 with additions in CSE U.S.A. 3, nn. 4, 11, 17 e CSE Italia, 4, nn. 6, 28, dated between the end of the third and the beginning of the second century BC. These specimens often show the presence of two characters interpretable as the Dioscuri, and the flame seems to have a connection with them.

9. For the list of these specimens see the appendix.

10. According to a statistical work performed by P. Moscati the motif of the Dioscuri (not only in relation to the flame under examination) appeared on 29.3 per cent of the known specimens at the time of calculation (Moscati 1986, 150–155).

11. On the epiphanies of the Dioscuri see Platt 2018, 229–256, with a wide anthology of sources and bibliography. Concerning Etruria see Colonna 1996 (with modifications in Colonna 2005) and Guarducci 1984, for an Italic overview.

12. '... *O Castor and Polydeuces, who go on swift-footed horses over broad earth and all the sea, and do so easily save men from lamentable death by leaping to the high-top of benched barks, there to sit far-seen upon the forestays, and so lighting the midnight path of the black ship*' (Alcaeus, Ox. Pap. 1233.4, Edmonds 1922, pp. 328–331, with reference to St. Elmo's fire. For this phenomenon and its connection with the Dioscuri see further and footnotes 42 and 43).

13. '*Do draw both ship and despairing shipmen from out of hell*' (Theocritus, Id. XXII, vv. 17 ff., Edmonds 1912, pp. 256–257).

14. '... *Demetrius, later on, when he sent back to the Romans what pirates he had captured, said that, although he was doing the Romans the favour of sending back the captives because of the kinship between the Romans and the Greeks, he did not deem it right for men to be sending out bands of pirates at the same time that they where in command of Italy, or to build in their Forum a temple in honour of the Dioscuri, and to worship them, whom all call Saviours, and yet at the same time send to Greece people who would plunder the native land of the Dioscuri*' (Strabo, Geog., V, 3. 5, Jones 1923, 390–393).

15. About the difference between public monument and private object, in particular with reference to the connected decoration, see Gilotta 1992, 77–84 about the so-called 'Cista del Trionfatore'.

16. For this inscription on a bronze foil, found next to an altar and about the introduction of the Dioscuri's worship in Italy, see Castagnoli 1959, 109–117; Castagnoli 1983, 3–12.

17. See on this exceptional document Colonna 1996, 174 e ff., recently revised in Colonna 2005.

18. Colonna 1996, 174 e ff.; about the inscription see recently also Facchetti 2015, 141–182.

Notes to pp. 75–76

19. For an examination of the presence of the Dioscuri in Etruria, see Colonna 2005, 2101 ff. About the 'Tomba del Letto Funebre' however, conflicting opinions have been expressed. The cult of the divine twins would be evoked by the presence on the funeral bed of two *piloi*, interpreted by G. Colonna as symbols of the Dioscuri, while M. Torelli aims to interpret them as a representation of the marital couple (Torelli 1997, 138).
20. Colonna 2005, 2101 ff.
21. Sassatelli 1993, 49-51 (also for two 'knights' preceding the deceased on Etruscan steles); Colonna 2005, 2107. For the Homeric Hymn see Evelyn-White 1914, 463 and Càssola 1975, 453-457.
22. According to Colonna 2005, 2107.
23. See for this Guarducci 1984, 144 with references to the iconography of the Dioscuri on votive *pinakes* or the so-called 'dischi sacri' (holy disks) and in particular 151 for the influences on the Etruscan world.
24. Della Fina 2002, 57.
25. Od. XI, 303; Alcm. fr. 7 Page. Later tradition in Pind. *Pyth*. XI, 61-64, *Nem*. X, 55-57.
26. Later tradition in Pind. *Pyth*. XI, 61-64, *Nem*. X, 55-57.
27. Colonna 2005, 2099-2101 with bibliography.
28. See Van der Meer 2001, 79 ff.
29. Overviews on the subject have already been made in *CSE* Hongrie-Tchécoslovaquie, 33 by J. G. Szilàgyi and in *CSE*, Italia, 4, by M. S. Pacetti.
30. In particular, three possibilities can be assumed, not only linked to the material use of the object but also to Etruscan religion: 1– that some mirrors were used during everyday life or particular moments (cult and religion) and then placed in the tomb; 2 – that some mirrors were especially produced for the afterlife; 3 – that both uses could coexist. We will come back to these concepts later on, but we can consider how the presence of an object, decorated with scenes connected to the myth or divinity inside the funerary kit, could be an indication of particular religious beliefs, and not just a decoration favoured by a workshop. For the role of mirrors in Etruscan Art and society, especially concerning those with Dioscuri and Lasas see also De Puma 2013, 1041-1067.
31. Cristofani 1985a, 14, considers the images on the mirrors as *exempla* of the conceptual ethical system underlying and functional to the ideology of those purchasing the mirrors; Cristofani 1985b, 2-12.
32. Maggiani 2002, 7-22. The scholar, considering a mirror from Civita Castellana, now in the Metropolitan Museum of New York, interpreted the embrace between Admetus and Alcestis not as the sacrifice of the wife for her husband but rather as a wedding scene presided over by Hymenaios, a divinity who leads the wedding procession. A. Maggiani proposed for the mirror a function as wedding gift that underlines the bride's good virtues.
33. On the presence of the Dioscuri on Etruscan mirrors as patrons of athleticism and warfare, see Izzett 1998, pp. 218-223.
34. For this interpretation see Massa Pairault 1985, 109 ff.
35. See *supra*.
36. Paus. V, 19, 2-3.
37. See Colonna 2005, 2101, with bibliography.
38. For a commentary on the episode see Platt 2018, 249; Paus. III, 16. 1-3. It could be the same plant that appears on some Etruscan mirrors, see for example: *CSE* Italia, 6.2, n. 95.

39. Plut. *Thes.* 32.2; Plut. *Lys*, 12.1; Plut. Mor. 426c. For a commentary see Platt 2018, 245.
40. On which also Diod. IV, 43, 2.
41. Platt 2018, 246.
42. See *supra* footnotes 12 and 37.
43. Platt 2018, 231 ff. The effect bears the name of sailors' patron, Saint Elmo or Saint Erasmo, and the blue lights were considered a symbol of his presence. A famous description of this phenomenon appears in *Moby Dick* by Herman Melville (ed. 2017 by Jovian Press): "'Look aloft!' cried Starbuck. 'The corpusants! The corpusants!' All the yard-arms were tipped with a pallid fire; and touched at each tri-pointed lightning-rod-end with three tapering white flames, each of the three tall masts were silently burning in the sulphurous air, like three gigantic wax tapers before an altar."
44. See *CSE* USA 1, n. 8, where they are separated by a dot; USA 2, n. 39, with a four-pointed star in the middle; *CSE* DDR 2, n. 4, where a four-pointed star is decorated with five points. We could think that dots could be a sort of stylized stars, maybe an allusion to the deities' epiphanies in the form of stars or flames on the tops of the ships' masts, as sources tell.
45. For this 'funerary' aspect see M. S. Pacetti, in *CSE*, Italia 4, 19 ff.
46. Naso 2003, 117, 120–122, nn. 171, 172 fig. 52a–b, 53 a–b, pl. 61; M. S. Pacetti, in *CSE*, Italia 4, 19 ff.
47. It seems interesting to quote, *mutatis mutandis*, the case of the Christian crucifix, which many believers wear around their necks, symbol of adherence to Christian religious precepts, and that very often, like a wedding ring, symbol of marriage, remains on the body of the deceased. On the contrary the same ring sometimes can be worn by the living spouse and therefore be absent on the body of the deceased.
48. Naso 2003, 117, 120–122, nn. 171, 172 fig. 52-a-b, 53 a–b, pl. 61; M. S. Pacetti, in *CSE*, Italia, 4, 19 ff.
49. Thus identifying the flame itself with a religious symbol.
50. See *CSE* BRD, 2, n. 1; *CSE* Italia, 1.1., n. 34; *CSE* Italia, 3.1., n. 26; *CSE* Italia, 5, n. 25; *CSE* USA, 1, n. 10. About Lasas see, for example, Rallo 1974.
51. Even if we have to consider that this flame mostly appears on specimens with the Dioscuri, and that probably mirrors with Lasas and those with Dioscuri were sometimes made in the same workshops. Furthermore, Dioscuri and Lasas seem to share common descriptive characters sometimes. A connection with the Dioscuri cannot anyway be excluded. See Mangani 1985, 21–40 and Cateni 2002, 41–57. About Lasas see Rallo 1974.
52. The presence of a light source could be necessary for functional reasons but for religious purposes too. The connection of the flame with Dioscuri and Lasas could be an indicator of peculiar cults or rites.
53. Plin. *N.H.* XXV, 120, (Aragosti et al. 1985, 688–689. My translation from Italian).

    The Greeks call *verbascum* the *phlomon*. There are two main varieties: white that is considered male, and black that would be female. A third variety is found only in the woods. It has leaves wider than those of cabbage, and hairy; the straight stem, higher than one cubit. The seed is black and useless for illumination, the root is single, the thickness of a finger. These plants grow in the plains. The wild type has leaves like sage's, with tall, woody branches. There are also two varieties of *phlomis*: they are hairy, low and have rounded leaves. A third variety is called *lychnitis* (others called it *thryallis*): it has three or four fat, thick leaves, suitable for making lamp wicks.

    Isid. *Etym.* XVII, 73 (from Valastro Canale 2004, my translation from Italian).

> *Phlomos,* i.e. the verbascum, is called by the Latins '*herba lucernaris*' because you can make wicks and small lamps with it. It is also known as *lucubros*, as it illuminates areas of shade.
>
> Isid. Etym. XVII 94.
>
> *Phlomos.* The herb called *verbascum* by the Latins. There are two kinds: a masculine, with whitish narrow leaves, and feminine, with wider black leaves.

54. Plin. *N.H.* XXV, 120, '*Herba lucernaris*'.
55. For Dioscorides see Beck 2005, 227–228, 291–292.
56. Paus. I, 26, 6; Aristoph. *Vesp.* 251; Athen. *Deipn.* 700e, where θρυαλλὶς stands for wick.
57. See *supra*.
58. Diosc. IV, 103.
59. Diosc. IV, 103. It is significant how both Pliny and Dioscorides connect the etymology of the *thryallis* variety to the fact that the leaves had three lobes. The term can be linked to the Greek word θρυαλλίς with which we identify the wick in Aristoph. *Vesp.* 251, and in Paus. I, 26, 6.
60. Our representation could even carry a particular semantic value unknown to us.
61. Herod. II, 62, from Godley 1920, 348–349.

> 'When they assemble at Sais, on the night of the sacrifice, they keep lamps burning, in the open air round about their houses. These lamps are saucers (ἐμβάφια) full of salt and oil, the wick floating thereon, and burning all night. This is called the Feast of Lamps. Egyptians who do not come to this assemblage are careful on the night of sacrifice to keep their own lamps burning, and so they are alight not only at Sais but throughout all Egypt. A sacred tale is told showing why this night is thus lit up and honoured.'

62. We should keep in mind that the event's description may depend either on Herodotus' little knowledge of Egyptian lighting techniques or how much it may derive from his knowledge of Greek lighting techniques.
63. Moullou 2011, 55, fig. 12 I–II; Fileni 2015, 118, footnote 51.
64. For the use of the plant for wicks in Greece see Moullou 2011, 51, with reference to the denominations of the plant as *loumini, lyhnaraki, fitilaki*. For the *Ballota* you can consult the record at the web address: http://www.actaplantarum.org/flora/flora_info.php?id=1137&pid=-1&p=1
65. Romeo 1937, 155–159. The technique of mixing water and oil keeps the wick from burning when the oil runs out without leaving traces of burning on the vessel, allowing the floral wick to be reused.

Chapter 7

1. According to Rebold 2009, 'glass mirrors, so common today, were unknown during the Middle Ages (as in Antiquity) when mirrors were made of polished metal' (p. 114). However, Pendergast 2003 and Sand 2011, 532 argue for the existence of glass medieval mirrors.
2. The term was coined by Greenblatt 2012.
3. Adlin 2013, in fact, argues that 'the origins of the term "toilette" (or toilet) can be traced to the Middle Ages, when men and women began spreading on a table a *toile* (French for cloth), or *toilettes*, as they became known, when the table was to be used for serving meals, correspondence, and game playing as well as applying cosmetics' (p. 5).
4. Paris term '*amour courtois*' is the provençal expression *fin' amor*, or 'elegant love'.

5. For further information about this topic, see Le Goff 1988.
6. Stewart 2017, n.pag.
7. See further on mirrors in *Le Roman de la Rose*, Priki in this volume.
8. Another interesting case is giving and accepting padlocks as a gift, which were common love tokens in courtly spaces. Their keyholes and the small size reinforce the topic of the secret of love.
9. 'Some [mirrors] were pierced so that they could be hung on a wall' (Sand 2011, 532).
10. I am referring to the letter of 18 July from *The sorrows of the Young Werther*, when he compares his servant with that stone, because of his contact with Charlotte: 'It is said that the Bologna stone, when placed in the sun, absorbs the sun's rays and is luminous for a while in the dark. I felt the same with the boy. The consciousness that her eyes had rested on his face, his cheeks, the buttons of his jacket and the collar of his overcoat, made all these sacred and precious to me' (p. 48).
11. See Priki in this volume, especially the link between the key to the reading of '*jeu de miroir*', which articulates with other reflecting surfaces – literal or metaphorical ones – and the subsequent sight allegories that are displayed throughout *Roman de la Rose*. In fact, Priki analyses certain passages in which Amour attacks certain characters with arrows that go through their hearts after passing through their eyes.
12. Adlin 2013, 4.
13. According to Boucher 2009, women were inspired by '*romances*, taking ideas for the purchase of shoes or embroidered girdles' (142).
14. Smith 2017, 84.
15. Mirrors, books and jewels, due to their size, beauty and memory character, have many features in common. Günther explains that medieval prayer books 'seem likely that [they were] intended to be worn, serving both as devotional aid and as jewelry; it could have been hung around the neck or, more probably, from the girdle of its owner' (n.pag).
16. As Silver 2017, n.pag, notes: 'Eye miniatures, also known as lover's eyes, were a subgenre of jewelry that became the height of fashion in the Georgian era. For centuries, tiny personal portraits of one's beloved had been common adornments, but depictions of that person's eyes alone were something pretty new'.
17. For further information about the authorship of *Le Roman de la Rose* and the discontinuity between the two parts see Root, 2011.
18. We must remember that the fountain as mirror is a strong image in the first part, when the Lover saw Narcissus looking at himself into the water.
19. The quotes come from the edition and translation of Horgan 1990.
20. See Priki in this volume, in particular the author's reflection around Oiseuse's mirror as artefact that adorns Narcissus' fountain, as a reflection of his attitude towards pleasure (especially if this pleasure derives from the admiration of certain things and if it is an attribute that makes his own body a visual object).
21. Rimell 2006, 59.
22. Pendergrast 2003, 122.
23. 'Medieval culture was a gift culture' (Camille 1998, 53).
24. In Spanish, there is a wonderful word that means at once garment and token: *prenda* ('guarantee'): from the Latin *pignora*, *prenda* can be applied to fashion (*prenda de vestir*, 'piece of clothing') and love (*prenda de amor*, 'love token').

Chapter 8

1. Wilde 2010, 50.
2. Frankel 2011, 239.
3. This is not a new concept; the connection of knowledge with mirroring goes back into Plato and Seneca the Younger.
4. See mostly Dickson 1983, Cohen 1986, Nunokawa 1992, 1995 and Bruhm 1995, 2001. Novak (2008) performs an interesting reading of the text emphasizing its use of pictures/photographs and their connection to identity, especially in terms of realism, in nineteenth-century fiction.
5. For the way Narcissus, and in effect the homosexual subject, disappears from Lacan's story see Butler 2013, 194–197.
6. This has led to a number of problematic readings of Narcissus in both ancient and modern texts. See Vinge 1967, 3–41.
7. For the connections of the Ovidian myth with Plato's *Phaedrus* see Bartsch 2006, 84–114. For a survey of the overall influence of Ovid's Narcissus in Western literature and culture, see Vinge 1967 and, more recently, Bettini and Pellizer 2003. In regards to 'The conception of Narcissism' in early psychoanalysis see Ellis 1929.
8. Ellis 1929: 348–349 and Vinge 1967.
9. See Bartsch 2006, 84–96.
10. From Classical Hollywood cinema (see Lawrence 1991) to Queer Aesthetics (see Bruhm 2001).
11. Ellis 1929, 351. There is a number of very interesting re-incarnations of Narcissus in literature (Petrarch, Rousseau, Milton etc.), painting (Poussin, Waterhouse, Caravaggio etc.) and science. For more on these see indicatively Vinge 1967.
12. Ellis 1929, 365. For more see Freud 1957, 67–102.
13. Ellis 1929, 370.
14. Sadger 1921, 148. Cf. Ellis 1929, 364.
15. Ellis 1929, 369.
16. For more on this, see Kosofsky Sedgwick 1990, esp. 182–212.
17. Cavafy 1983, 36.
18. Kosofsky Sedgwick 1990, 48.
19. Frankel 2011, 6.
20. This was not the case with the 'anonymous' *Green Carnation* (1894) that scandalously described the sexual relationships of two men, Esmé Amarinth (considered to be Oscar Wilde) and Lord Reginal Hastings (considered to be Lord Alfred Douglas). Many believed that the book's author was Oscar Wilde – the book was used against him in court – but it was later proven that its author was Robert Hichens. The book was withdrawn in 1895.

Notes to pp. 95–100

21. See further Bredbeck 1994; Bruhm 1995; Cohen 1987; Dickson 1983; Dollimore 1987; Frankel 2011; Janes 2014; Manny 2017; Marcovitch 2010; McCormack 1997; Novak 2008, 118–145; Nunokawa 1995 and 1992; Riquelme 2000; Walker 2007, 91–115.
22. Regarding their relationship, see at least Nunokawa 1992.
23. Frankel 2011, 58.
24. Ibid.
25. Frankel 2011, 61.
26. Bruhm (1995, 62) claims that the link of Narcissus with creativity goes as far back as Shegel.
27. This happened especially in regards to the two antithetical myths he associates with art: Minerva and Narcissus. For a comparison between the two, and relevant bibliography, see indicatively Carman 2014, 25–54.
28. Spencer 1966, 64; Sinisgalli 2006, 161–162.
29. McMahon 1956, I:49, par.72.
30. Van Alphen 2005, 36–37.
31. BIII 432–433. All ovidian translations, unless otherwise indicated, are taken by Melville in Kenney 2009.
32. BIII 360–363.
33. BIII 389.
34. BIII 390.
35. BIII 391–401.
36. Frankel 2011, 59.
37. Lacan 1977, 2.
38. Frankel 2011, 67.
39. Ibid.
40. BIII 431.
41. Bonnefoy 1991, 493.
42. BIII 436–438.
43. Cohen 1987, 806.
44. Frankel 2011, 144–145.
45. Lacan 1977, 2.
46. Ibid.
47. Frankel 2011, 182.
48. Frankel 2011, 185.
49. Lacan 1977, 4.
50. Frankel 2011, 188.
51. The passage can be found in the Penguin Classics' edition of *The Picture of Dorian Gray* (2000: 110), which reproduces the 1891 edition. The 1891 version is an edited and enriched version of the 1890 version that appeared in the Philadelphian *Lippincott's Monthly Magazine*. For more information regarding publication history see Frankel 2011, 35–54 and Mighall 2000, ix–xxix.
52. Frankel 2011, 185. Dorian reacts in the same way as Narcissus did when Echo tried to touch him.

53. Remember the line 'Sin is a thing that writes itself across a man's face. It cannot be concealed' (Frankel 2011, 183).
54. Frankel 2011, 188–189.
55. Ibid.
56. Ibid.
57. Frankel 2011, 190.
58. Frankel 2011, 207–209.
59. Frankel 2011, 159.
60. This difference between imaging technologies, the mirror, and pictorial arts, the former able to capture time, is already noted in antiquity. For more see Gerolemou in this volume.
61. Frankel 2011, 216.
62. Ibid.
63. Ibid.
64. BIII 349–350.
65. Frankel 2011, 189.
66. See also Bruhm 1995, 178.
67. Hart Davis 1962, 352.
68. Ibid.

Chapter 9

1. I am grateful to Maria and Lilia for organizing the conference, and I would like to extend warm thanks also to Professor Robin Osborne, Dr Rebecca Flemming and Daniel Hanigan who all read, commented on, and discussed the chapter with me at length. Infelicities that remain are my own.
2. Except where mentioned otherwise, translations are from the Loeb Classical Library with slight modifications.
3. On the 'problem of presence', a phrase originally coined by anthropologist Webb Keane 1997, 51, see the work of Mathew Engelke especially 2007, 2010. For the same theme in art see van Eck, van Gastel and van Kessel 2014; van Eck 2015.
4. On divine mediation and media see, as a start, Derrida 1996; de Vries 2001; Stolow 2005; Meyer 2006; Meyer and Verrips 2008; Morgan 2008; Eisenlohr 2012. See, too, Robbins 2017 on divine *distance*.
5. I use the term 'technology' to describe objects, processes and knowledge following Bijker, Hughes and Pinch 1987, 4.
6. Various examples of Mesoamerican obsidian mirrors are preserved including ones housed in the British Museum (inv. 1966,1001.1) and in the Museo de América in Madrid (inv. 09996).
7. This is true not only of mirrors, but of other (iridescent) objects, too. See Magaloni Kerpel 2015 on this quality in feathers, for example.
8. Houston and Taube 2000, 284–285.
9. The codex, now in the Medicea Laurenziana Library in Florence was written by Fray Bernardino de Sahagún. It is bilingual in Spanish and the local Nahua language and shows

a keen interest in indigenous religion. On the impact of the conquest on indigenous conceptions of materiality (and specifically shininess) see Saunders 1998, 2001, 2003; Russo, Wolf and Fane 2015.

10. Sahagún 11.221–231.
11. Both the *Śiva Purāṇa* and the Hindu epic *Mahābhārata* describe how the Goddess Pārvatī covering the Great God Śiva's eyes with her hands plunges the whole universe into darkness: *Śiva* 2.5.42.14–22; *MhB* XIII, Appendix I, No. 15, 280–305.
12. Babb 1981; Eck 1985. See also Gell 1998, 118.
13. Cort 2001, 79.
14. Eck 1985, 10. On seeing as a form of tactile contact between objects and rays in Greek thought (though not in Greek religion) see Smith 1996, 23–24 with Ptolemy *Optics* 2.13, 2.67; Smith 2015, 29–33; Platt and Squire 2018, 81.
15. The bibliography on the topic in general is immense. For the way in which the mirror fits into Plato's theory of the Forms and *mimesis* see especially Halliwell 2002, 37–118; Cain 2012; Capra 2017.
16. Iambl. *Myst.* 3.14 (*phōtagōgia*).
17. Iambl. *Myst.* 2.10.93–94. For more on the relation between images and the divine in Iamblichus, see Shaw 1995, 162–178; on Neoplatonic abstractions of the Dionysian mirror see Seaford 1998, 141–143; on Plotinus' theory of visual perception Smith 2015, 134–142; on the mirror, the real and the perceived in Plotinus see Clark 2016, 83–90; more generally on the divine double from Plato to early Christianity, Manichaeism and Neoplatonism see Stang 2016 with especially 185–230 on Plotinus.
18. Alc. Fr. 333.
19. My depiction of these myths is necessarily, but lamentably, brief and there is more to say on how these two myths work together in both art and text. See, for example, Bartsch 2006, 84–102; Elsner 2007, 132–176; van Eck 2015, 45–49; Grethlein 2016, 96–100 as well as, on the mirror in ancient art more generally, Balensiefen 1990; Taylor 2008.
20. Plato *Resp.* 10.596e.
21. Plut. *Dem* 11.2=850e. For more on the mirror's connection with the self: Bartsch 2006.
22. E.g. McCarty 1989; Too 1996; Frontisi-Ducroux and Vernant 1997; Balensiefen 1990; Bartsch 2006; Taylor 2008; Sinisgalli 2012.
23. See especially Frontisi-Ducroux and Vernant 1997, 155–176 on the paradoxes of the mirror.
24. Mechanical authors are explicitly excluded from the discussion by Frontisi-Ducroux 1997, 133: '... je n'ai nullement l'intention de revenir sur ces textes difficiles, et pas davantage sur les traités d'optique.' See, however, Bartsch 2006, 38, 62.
25. On vision and visuality Foster 1988, ix.
26. In this, I disagree with the analysis undertaken by Netz and Squire 2016. The authors argue for the 'weakness of mathematical optics' (80) in contributing in any significant way to culture or to philosophy.
27. Magnification: Pseudo-Hero *Cat.* 15. Cf. Euclid *Cat.* 5 which it closely follows. Distortion: Pseudo-Hero *Cat.* 17. Cf. Ptolemy, *Optics* 4.161; Anthemius, *On Burning Mirrors* 5. Multiplication: Pseudo-Hero *Cat.* 20; 23. A version of Euc. *Cat.* 14. Omission: Pseudo-Hero *Cat.* 10. A model inspired from Euc. *Cat.* 4 (5 and 6 create the same effect off concave and convex surfaces). See, too, Gerolemou in this volume.
28. Especially Gell, 1992. See also Gell 1998, 68–71.

29. I will refer to the author of this text as Pseudo-Hero though the reader may variously find it attributed to Pseudo-Ptolemy (e.g. Jones), Hero of Alexandria (e.g. Schmidt, Smith), or even Ptolemy in older scholarship. The dubious authorship and messy manuscript tradition are the first hurdles to overcome when dealing with this work. The original Greek version has been lost and the text comes down to us only in a Latin version translated in the thirteenth century by William of Moerbeke in the *Ottobonianus lat.* 1850 (**O**). Wilhelm Schmidt's 1976 Teubner edition relies on a later, corrected and subsequently lost manuscript, and for this reason I here follow Jones' 2001 edition, modifying his translation in places (though the diagrams in Schmidt are often more useful than Jones'). The manuscript **O** is not without its own problems, however, first and foremost the gaps where William of Moerbeke was struggling with translation from Greek to Latin. The work is attributed to Ptolemy in the **O** manuscript, but scholars are unanimous that this is mistaken, and that the work is certainly earlier. The frivolous tone, philosophical meanderings, and cosmology of the opening are all inconsistent with Ptolemy's extant work. The most convincing alternatives are that this is either an abridged version of Hero of Alexandria's now lost work *Catoptrica* (to which reference is preserved in Damianus), or, slightly more cautiously, perhaps simply the work of someone of the same school as Hero. For a more detailed explanation than the summary I offer see Jones 2001, 145–151. For the dating of Hero see Neugebauer 1938, 21–24; Souffrin 2000; Sidoli 2005, 2011; Masià 2015.

30. Pseudo-Hero *Cat.* 2.4.

31. On mirrors enhancing vision cf. Plut. *De Pyth. or.* 21=404d and McCarty 1989, 166.

32. Cf. Hero *Aut.* 1.1

> Τῆς αὐτοματοποιητικῆς πραγματείας ὑπὸ τῶν πρότερον ἀποδοχῆς ἠξιωμένης διά τε τὸ ποικίλον τῆς ἐν αὐτῇ δημιουργίας καὶ διὰ τὸ ἔκπληκτον τῆς θεωρίας.
>
> The study of automaton-making has been considered by our predecessors worthy of acceptance both because of the ingenuity of the craftsmanship involved and because of the stunning nature of the spectacle.

33. Pseudo-Hero *Cat.* 2.5.

34. And it is about epistemology from the word go. Pseudo-Hero opens with the assertion that there are two senses which lead to knowledge: sight and sound (1.1).

35. Pseudo-Hero *Cat.* 2.5–11 with Pseudo-Hero *Cat.* 17 and 22.

36. Pseudo-Hero *Cat.* 17.

37. Cf. Tybjerg 2003 and Garani in this volume.

38. This is the case, too, with Hero's *On Automata* and *Pneumatics,* see Bur 2016.

39. Aristophanes *Ach.* 1128–1131. Cf. Schol. Aristophanes *Ach.* 1128a and Suda K 867 which explain the mantic parody.

40. Delatte 1932, 134: 'l'éblouissement favorise la divination'.

41. Pseudo-Hero *Cat.* 5.4–7.

42. One can relate this to the way verbal ambiguity works in oracular pronouncements Bowden 2005, 49–51; Kindt 2006.

43. This is one way in which the various forms of divination by gazing (collectively termed lecanomancy) might be theologically united. Individual techniques merit their own investigation though I suspect that image and distortion were paramount in all lecanomantic contexts. Delatte 1932 sees catoptromancy and hydromancy as working separately; Addey 2008 interprets them together. On children and gazing rituals Johnston 2001.

44. Paus. 7.21.12.

45. Paus. 7.21.11–13.
46. Catoptric potential not lost on Pseudo-Hero himself, see Pseudo-Hero *Cat.* 5.9–11.
47. Lucian *Ver. Hist.* 1.26.
48. Pseudo-Hero *Cat.* 18.1.
49. Schmidt 1976, 412; cf. Jones 2001, 160.
50. Pseudo-Hero *Cat.* 18.1–2. With Schmidt 1976, 412 on lacunae.
51. Pseudo-Hero *Cat.* 18.4–7.
52. Pliny *HN* 33.129.
53. Anthemius *On Burning Mirrors* 5–7.
54. Pseudo-Hero *Cat.* 24.
55. Cf. Hero *Aut.* 4.4–5 with Bur 2016, 43–44.
56. Pseudo-Hero *Cat.* 24.26.
57. Pseudo-Hero *Cat.* 24. Versions of this arrangement are given in Euclid, Anthemius, and Witelo (Jones 1987, 8–11).
58. Pausanias 8.37.7.
59. Platt 2011, 222–223 also focuses on the phenomenological potential of the mirror but sees the 'optical paradox' as creating a clearer apprehension of the divine by tensions of presence and absence. See also Platt 2015 on sight and the gods more generally.
60. On mysteries as ecstatic experiences, Bowden 2010. For further on mirrors and reflection in Dionysiac cult see Seaford 1987, 1998; Taylor 2008, 90–136.
61. Mudie-Cooke 1913, 167–169 (plate XI) first interpreted it as a scene of divination and is followed by Delatte 1932, 189–190; de Grummond 2002, 73–74. Nilsson 1957, 75 interprets it as a drinking scene. Gazda 2000, 1 believes it depicts the epiphany in the initiation process; the reading of Taylor 2008, 129–133 places emphasis on the mirror as a tool for possession and metamorphosis.
62. For the Roman architectural interest in harnessing the problematics of reflection (especially using the mirror of Aphrodite) see Hales 2008, 243–248.
63. On the visual in Biblical studies see Heath 2013, 13–37.
64. E.g. 2 Cor. 3:18; James 1:23-25. On the image of God in man see Burghardt 1961.
65. As explored in, for example, Nasrallah 2010, 171–295; Heath 2013 esp. 215–225; Heath 2016; Stang 2016.
66. Clem. Al. *Strom.* 7.3.13; Clem. Al. *Protr.* 2.18.1.

Chapter 10

1. In her taxonomy of the metaphorical use of mirroring, McCarty 1989 touches upon two of my examples (Cicero and Plutarch). See McCarty 1989, 164–165 and 170.
2. E.g., Taylor 2008, Bartsch 2006.
3. E.g., Stang 2016, Frontisi-Ducroux/Vernant 1997.
4. Lucr. 3.830–842.
5. For a brief survey of the section and its sources, see Reinhardt 2002, 294–298. Reinhardt's analysis begins at 3.931 and stops at 3.971, leaving out the lines discussed here. Wallach 1976,

82–83 sees in these lines, as elsewhere in this section of Lucretius's poem, the influence of Cynic-Stoic diatribe. As Reinhardt points out, this does not mean that the poet's goals are not distinctively Epicurean.

6. Analogical reasoning as one of the two main methods of explanation in Greek philosophy is studied by Lloyd 1966, 172–420. For analogical reasoning and Epicurean epistemology, see Sedley and Long 1987, 78–97, and Asmis 1999. In a way, this passage could be interpreted, broadly speaking, as a 'diachronic analogy' (for the term see Schiesaro 1990, 91–139).
7. Lucr. 2.112–124.
8. Plin. *NH* 7.188–191.
9. Plin. *NH* 7.190.
10. Cic. *Fin.* 5. 48 and 55.
11. Cic. *Fin.* 5.55, trans. Woolf. Gigon and Straume-Zimmermann 1988, 555–556 note that this method can easily be attributed to the Epicureans and the Stoics, but not to Aristotle (e.g., *Eth. Nic.* 1100a1–4 and *Pol.* 1260a31–33); it was probably adopted by Theophrastus.
12. Cic. *Fin.* 5.55.
13. See Plat. *Resp.* 435b; Zeno in Plut. *Moral.* 1034c.
14. Varro *Rust.* 3.16.1–38, and Verg. *G.* 4.149–227.
15. Varro *Rust.* 3.16.4, Verg. *G.* 4.176.
16. McCarty 1989, 167 and 170–171.
17. Cf. Kennedy 2002, 90–93, and Marković 2008, 131–132.
18. See further Bonati and Reggiani in this volume.
19. E.g., ὄπωπα 'I have seen'; ὄψομαι, 'I will see'; ὀπτός, 'seen' or 'visible'; ὄψ or ὤψ, 'face'; ὀφθαλμός, 'eye'.
20. Ernout-Meillet 1980⁴, s.v.
21. B 21a Diels and Kranz. The thought became a popular maxim in classical literature (see Marković 2008, 84 n. 4).
22. For mirrors as prostheses, or extensions of our eyes, see Eco 1986, 208–210.
23. For the sense of the word in Hellenistic philosophy, see Pellicer 1966, 29–32; for *natura* as a synonym of 'the universe', see ibid. 242–252.

Chapter 11

1. Much of the material for this article was gathered in the framework of the now finished project 'Dioptra. Edition der griechischen Version', financed by the Austrian Science Fund (FWF) (Einzelprojekte P21811). I wish once again to thank Wolfram Hörandner for the long inspiring discussions on the subject.
2. Καὶ ὁ χιτὼν τῆς Μαξιμοῦς ὑπῆρχεν ἀραχνώδης·/ πάντα καθάπερ ἔσοπτρον ἐνέφαινε τὰ μέλη/ καὶ τοὺς μαστοὺς προκύπτοντας μικρὸν ἄρτι τῶν στέρνων. Edited and trans. by Jeffreys 1998, Grottaferrata Version 6, 783. The Grottaferrata version is dated into the twelfth century.
3. See for example Anderson 2007.
4. See Papaioannou 2010, 81–101.

5. Ἀπαύγασμα γάρ ἐστιν φωτὸς ἀιδίου καὶ ἔσοπτρον ἀκηλίδωτον τῆς τοῦ θεοῦ ἐνεργείας καὶ εἰκὼν τῆς ἀγαθότητος αὐτοῦ. Sapientia 7, 26, Douay–Rheims translation.
6. See Tatiana Bur's contribution in the present volume; also Benakis 1982, 75–86.
7. Ὃς ὢν ἀπαύγασμα τῆς δόξης καὶ χαρακτὴρ τῆς ὑποστάσεως αὐτοῦ. Hebrews 1, 3. Trans.: King James Version.
8. Ἐν τῷ Υἱῷ ὡς ἐν ἐσόπτρῳ θείῳ τινὶ ὁρῶμεν τὴν δόξαν τοῦ Πατρὸς κατὰ τό· Ὁ ἑωρακὼς ἐμὲ ἑώρακε τὸν Πατέρα. Ed. and trans. by Kuehn and Baggarly 2007, II 140–142.
9. Ἀλλ' ἡ σοφία τοῦ Θεοῦ, ἤγουν ὁ Κύριος ἡμῶν Ἰησοῦς Χριστός, κατελθὼν ἐκ τῶν οὐρανῶν καὶ ὡς ἐν ἐσόπτρῳ διὰ σαρκὸς λάμψας ἐν κόσμῳ, ἣν ἔλαβεν ἐκ τῆς ἁγίας θεόπαιδος καὶ θεοτόκου Μαρίας. Ed. by Sbordone 1936, Appendix, p. 316, 30–33. The translation is mine.
10. Ἐξ ὧν πεποίηκεν ὁ υἱὸς καὶ πρὸ σαρκώσεως καὶ μετὰ σάρκωσιν, φαίνεται κατὰ νοῦν ὡς «ἐν ἐσόπτρῳ» ἡ ἄπειρος αὐτοῦ ἰσχύς. Reuss 1966, Fragment 485 (attributed to Ammonius). The translation is mine.
11. Avenarius 1998, English translation 2005.
12. Exodus 20, 4. Trans.: English Standard Version.
13. Φησιν ὁ θεῖος ἀπόστολος· «Ἐν ἐσόπτρῳ καὶ ἐν αἰνίγματι νῦν βλέπομεν» (1 Corinthians 13, 12). Καὶ ἡ εἰκὼν δὲ ἔσοπτρόν ἐστι καὶ αἴνιγμα ἁρμόζον τῇ τοῦ σώματος ἡμῶν παχύτητι. *Contra imaginum calumniators orationes tres.* In: Kotter 1975, II 5, 11–13, p. 72. My translation is based on Allies 1898.
14. Καί μοι δοκεῖ τῷ ἐν κατόπτρῳ παραδείγματι ἐοικέναι· κἀκεῖ γὰρ οἱονεὶ διαγράφεται τοῦ ὁρῶντος τὸ πρόσωπον καὶ μένει ἔξω τῆς ὕλης τὸ ὁμοίωμα. κἂν δόξειεν ἀσπάσασθαι τὴν ἑαυτοῦ ἐκεῖσε εἰκόνα, οὐ τὴν ὕλην προσεπτύξατο, ὅτι μηδὲ δι' αὐτὴν πρόσεισιν, ἀλλὰ τὸ ἐν αὐτῇ ἀπεικονισθὲν αὐτοῦ ὁμοίωμα, δι' ὃ καὶ προσέφυ τῇ ὕλῃ. ἀμέλει μεταστάντος αὐτοῦ τοῦ ἐσόπτρου συναπέστη αὐτῷ ἅμα καὶ τὸ ἴνδαλμα, ὡς μὴ κοινωνοῦντι τῇ τοῦ ἐσόπτρου ὕλῃ, ὥσπερ οὖν καὶ ἐπὶ τῆς εἰκονικῆς ὕλης, ὅτι ἀφανισθέντος τοῦ ἐν αὐτῇ ὁρωμένου ὁμοιώματος, ἐφ' ᾧ ἡ προσκύνησις, ἔμεινεν ἡ ὕλη ἀπροσκύνητος, ὡς μηδὲν κοινωνοῦσα τῷ ὁμοιώματι. Fatouros 1992, Letter 57, vol. I, p. 167, 91–101. My translation is based on Cattoi 2015, 138.
15. Τρανῶς ἐνιδὼν τοῖς ἐσόπτροις τῶν τύπων/ Τεραστίου θαύμασον εἰκόνα, ξένε. Miller 1855–1857, Codex Parisinus, poem XI 1–2. For comments and translation see Talbot 1994.
16. Ἐκ τῶν χρωμάτων καὶ τῶν σχημάτων πολυειδῶς διακειμένων μορφοῦται ἡ ὄψις, ἡ δὲ ὄσφρησις ἐκ τῶν ἀτμῶν, γεῦσις δὲ ἐκ τῶν χυμῶν, ἐκ δὲ τῶν ψόφων ἡ ἀκοή, ἡ δὲ ἁφὴ ἐκ τῶν τραχέων ἢ λείων κατὰ τὴν θέσιν. αἱ δὲ κατὰ τὰς αἰσθήσεις ἐγγινόμεναι μορφώσεις ἐκ σωμάτων μέν εἰσιν, ἀλλ' οὐ σώματά εἰσιν, εἰ καὶ σωματικαί· οὐ γὰρ ἁπλῶς ἐκ σωμάτων εἰσίν, ἀλλ' ἐκ τῶν κατὰ τὰ σώματα εἰδῶν. ἀλλ' οὐδ' αὐτά εἰσι τὰ τῶν σωμάτων εἴδη, ἀλλὰ τὰ ἐκτυπώματα αὐτῶν καὶ οἷόν τινες εἰκόνες ἀχωρίστως χωριζόμεναι τῶν κατὰ τὰ σώματα εἰδῶν. καὶ τοῦτο δῆλον μᾶλλον ἐκ τῆς ὄψεως καὶ μάλιστα ἐκ τῶν δι' ἐσόπτρων ὁρωμένων. Ed. and trans. by Sinkewicz 1988, 98–99.
17. Ἡμεῖς δὲ πάντες ἀνακεκαλυμμένῳ προσώπῳ τὴν δόξαν κυρίου κατοπτριζόμενοι τὴν αὐτὴν εἰκόνα μεταμορφούμεθα ἀπὸ δόξης εἰς δόξαν. 2 Corinthians 3, 18. Transl.: International Standard Version.
18. Ἐστὲ γὰρ χάριτι Χριστοῦ νήφοντές τε καὶ γρηγοροῦντες, ἀνακεκαλυμμένῳ προσώπῳ τὴν δόξαν κυρίου κατοπτριζόμενοι. ἐπὰν γὰρ τὴν λήμην τῆς τοῦ κόσμου προσπαθείας περιήρατε ἐκ τῶν τῆς ψυχῆς ὀφθαλμῶν ὑμῶν διὰ τῆς κατὰ τὴν ὑποταγὴν ἱερᾶς πολιτείας ὑμῶν, καὶ καθαρῶς βλέπετε τὰ πράγματα, τὴν τοῦ βίου λέγω ματαιότητα, τὴν ἐπάλληλον φορὰν ἐν πᾶσι τρόποις τῆς ἀνθρωπίνης περιδονήσεως, καὶ ὅτι ἓν μόνον ἐστὶ στάσιμον καὶ ἀγαπητὸν καὶ ἐραστόν, ὁ θεός. Papadopoulos-Kerameus 1904, 713.12–714.9. The translation is mine.

Notes to pp. 131–134

19. Ἀκηλίδωτον ἔσοπτρον ἡ καθαρωτάτη, μάρτυς, καρδία σου τοῦ ἁγίου ὤφθη Πνεύματος, μυστικὰς ἀκτῖνας ἀποστίλβουσα. D' Aiuto 1994, Canon 3 l. 46–50. The translation is mine.
20. See Karlsson 1962, 96.
21. Καὶ γὰρ ἦν τῷ ὄντι καὶ αὐτήν σου καθορᾶν τὴν ψυχὴν οἷον δι' ἐσόπτρου τινὸς τῶν λόγων διαφαινομένην. Courtonne 1961, Epistle 165, 12–13. Trans. by Way 1951, 326.
22. Τοῖς σοφωτάτοις ἐναδολεσχοῦντες σου γράμμασι καὶ τὸ τοῦ νοὸς διορατικὸν τούτοις προσεπερείδοντες, ὡς ἐν καλοῖς τούτοις ἐσόπτροις θείας τινὰς ἐμφάσεις τῆς ἀγγελοπρεποῦς σου θέας παρυφιστῶντες. Kolovou 1995, 67, 18–20. The translation is mine.
23. Τὴν τῆς σῆς ἤδη φίλης ἐπιστολῆς θαυμασίαν διόπτραν, ὦ φίλων ἄριστε καὶ ἀνδρῶν, εἰς χεῖρας ἀσμένως ἀπειληφότες καὶ ταύτην ἠρέμ' ἀπηωρηκότες καὶ ἤδιστα τὴν χρυσαυγῆ ταύτης οὐδὲν ἧττον ἀκτῖνα κατωπτρισάμεθα ἐναργῶς καὶ ὅπως γε τὰ καθ' ἡμᾶς ὑπὸ σαυτῷ ἰδιοποιῇ μηδὲν τῆς πνευματικῆς ἑταιρείας προτιμώμενος τὸ παράπαν, οἷα λόγου σύντροφος καὶ παιδείας. Papadopoulos 1927, Epistle 13. The translation is mine.
24. Ἐπεὶ οὖν καὶ ἡμῖν ζωγραφῆσαι πρόκειται νῦν, οὐχὶ τύπον μορφῆς σωματικῆς, ἀλλὰ ψυχῆς κάλλος, καὶ νοητὴν εὐμορφίαν, καὶ πολιτείαν ἀκμάζουσαν τοῦ δικαίου, καὶ τὸ πρᾶον, καὶ ἥμερον, καὶ μεγαλόψυχον, καὶ τὴν ἄλλην ἅπασαν αὐτοῦ ἀρετήν, δέον πλείονα τὴν διατριβὴν πρὸς τοῦτον ποιήσασθαι, ἵνα τῇ συνεχείᾳ τῆς τοῦ λόγου διοπτρίσεως τῆς τοῦ ἀρχετύπου ὁμοιότητος μὴ διαμάρτωμεν. Iohannes Chrysostomus, *Contra theatra*. In: Patrologia Graeca 56, col. 544, and Pignani 2007, l. 887–894. When referring to the Patrologia Graeca, I give the volume instead of the year. The translation is mine.
25. Καὶ γὰρ πῶς τοῖς λόγοις ἐμμαρμαίρει τι δόξης ἀγλαὸν εἴδωλον, ἀνακλώμενον ἀπὸ τῶν ἀγώνων ἐπὶ τοὺς λόγους, ὥσπερ ἐν ἐσόπτροις αὐτοῖς ἐμφαινομένης τῆς πράξεως. Gautier 1972, 246, 2–5. The translation is mine.
26. See Tatiana Bur's contribution to the presenst volume.
27. Βλέπομεν γὰρ ἄρτι δι' ἐσόπτρου ἐν αἰνίγματι, τότε δὲ πρόσωπον πρὸς πρόσωπον. See also Cain 2016, Hugede 1957 and Seaford 1984.
28. Νῦν οὐκ αἰνίγματι, πάτερ,* κατοπτεύεις τὰ θεῖα,* παρηγμένης τῆς σκιᾶς καὶ τῶν ἐσόπτρων,* ἀλλὰ πλήρης θείου φωτὸς ἀπολαύεις Χριστοῦ. Spanos 2010, 169, 120–122. The translation is mine.
29. Μέμνημαι δὲ ὑποσχόμενος ἔμπροσθεν ὥσπερ δι' ἐσόπτρου δείξειν ὑμῖν τὴν εἰκόνα τῶν περὶ τὸν πατέρα καὶ τὸν υἱόν, ἐπείπερ ἀνθρωπίνῳ λόγῳ τὰ κατὰ τὴν θείαν φύσιν οὐχ ὑποτέτακται. [...] οὐκ ὢν ἄνθρωπος πέφηνεν μὲν ἄνθρωπος, κατὰ φύσιν δὲ θεὸς ἦν τε καὶ ἔστι τὸ ἀπερίληπτον μέγεθος αὐτοῦ σώματι περιγράψας καὶ δι' ἑαυτοῦ ὥσπερ δι' ἐσόπτρου τὸ ὅλον ἡμῖν μέγεθος τοῦ θεοῦ παραφήνας, ἵν' ὥσπερ διόπτρᾳ τούτῳ χρησάμενοι καὶ τοῦ πατρὸς θεαταὶ γενώμεθα. Adversus Arium et Sabellium de patre et filio. In: Müller 1958, 73. The translation is mine.
30. Lewis 2001.
31. Latte 1966, No. 1843, p. 447, *s.v.* κάτοπτρα; De Stefani 1920, 367, 20–21, *s.v.* διόπτρα; Tittmann 1808, 521, *s.v.* διόπτρα.
32. Ἡ συνάγουσα ζώνη τὸν χιτῶνα καὶ τοὺς μαζοὺς ἔκλειε, καὶ ἐγίνετο τοῦ σώματος κάτοπτρον ὁ χιτών. Vilborg 1955, I 1, 11. Translation based on Gaselee 1917. I omitted Gaselee's interpretative additions '*a kind of* mirror of *the shape of* her body'.
33. Κεστοὺς ὡραίους τινὰς ἐκ τῶν ἔνδοθεν ἐνδυμάτων ἐξάξασαι, τοὺς ὀφθαλμούς μου περιεκάλυπτον, καὶ ὡς ἐσόπτρῳ ὁρᾶν με ἐκέλευον, καὶ οὐκ ἂν ἄλλως ὁρᾶν τινα τὸν ἥλιον δύνασθαι, ἢ οὕτως, ἔλεγον. Festa 1898, 67–71. The translation is mine.
34. Τὸ σχῆμα λαβὼν τῆς διόπτρας τῶν λόγων/ Ἀσκαρδαμυκτὶ πρὸς τὸ σὸν κάλλος βλέπω. Miller (1855–1857), Codex Parisinus CCVII, 5–6. The translation is mine.

35. Οὐκέτι σκεπάσομαι, ἐπειδὴ τὸ ἔσοπτρον τῆς αἰσχύνης ἀπ' ἐμοῦ ἀφῄρηται· καὶ οὐκέτι αἰσχύνομαι ἢ αἰδοῦμαι, ἐπειδὴ τὸ ἔργον τῆς αἰσχύνης καὶ τῆς αἰδοῦς ἐξ ἐμοῦ μακρὰν ἀπέστη. Bonnet 1903, 120, 2–5. Trans. by James 1924, who provides the explanation '(veil)' after 'mirror'.
36. Ἐκπέπταται γὰρ ἡ χλανὶς τῶν ὀμμάτων/ ἄλλου τινὸς χιτῶνος ἁπαλωτέρου/ φρουροῦντος αὐτοῖς, ὡς διόπτρας, τὰς κόρας. Caramico 2006, v. 1252–1254. The translation is mine.
37. Λύχνος εἰμί σοι τῷ βλέποντί με. Ἀμήν. Ἔσοπτρόν εἰμί σοι τῷ νοοῦντί με. Ἀμήν. Θύρα εἰμί σοι κρούοντί με. Ἀμήν. Ὁδός εἰμί σοι παροδίτῃ. Bonnet 1898, 198, 11–13. Trans. based on James 1924; I tacitly modernized the grammar.
38. Ὑπὸ ἐσόπτρου (τῆς ἐκ τῆς πέτρας ὀπῆς, ἤτοι τῆς θεοτόκου Μαρίας). Chronz 2009, 33, 9–10. The translation is mine.
39. Καὶ ἰδοὺ ὡς «ἐν ἐσόπτρῳ» ἐν τῷ ὕδατι καθαρῶς ἔβλεπε πάντα ὁμοῦ, ἤτοι τοὺς ἵππους καὶ τὸν ἱππῶνα τούς τε ἡνιόχους καὶ τὰ ἅρματα δεδεμένους πάντας γοητείᾳ τῶν ἐναντίων. Giagkou and Papatriantafyllou-Theodoridi 1999, 291, 177–180. The translation is mine.
40. Μόνοις δ' οἷς ὄμμα ψυχῆς κεκαθαρμένον/ πρόσεστι φαινόμεθα ὡς ἐν διόπτρᾳ,/ τοῖς δ' ἀκαθάρτοις οὐ θεὸς οὐδ' ἡμεῖς γε/ οὔθ' ὁρώμεθα οὔθ' ὅλως γεγενῆσθαι/ τοιοῦτοί ποτε πιστευόμεθα πάντως. Kambylis 1976 and Koder 1969.1971.1973, Hymn 50, 207–217. The translation is mine.
41. Ἐλθόντος μου οὖν εἰς ἑαυτὸν ἀπὸ τῆς φρικτῆς ἐκείνης καὶ ἀμετρήτου ἐκστάσεως καὶ θεωρίας καὶ τὴν διόπτραν τῶν θεαθέντων μοι ἀναλογιζομένου etc. Ed. and trans. by Sullivan, Talbot and McGrath 2014, VI 1.2.
42. Ἡ ἀκηλίδωτος τῆς προφητείας διόπτρα προβλεπτικοῖς τοῖς ὄμμασι κατανοοῦσα τὸ μέλλον προϋπογράφει ὡς παρόν, ὑποφωνεῖ καὶ τὸ πόρρω ὡς ἐγγίζον. Schirò 1976, 17th December, Canon 29, l. 17–20. The translation is mine.
43. Ὁ νοῦς ὁ πυκνός, ἡ διόπτρα τῶν λόγων. Miller (1855–1857), Codex Parisinus, poem LV 16. The same poet praises the Emperor's nephew, saying that his eyes are a 'mirror (διόπτρα) of hopes'. Cod. Escur. XCI, 12. The translation is mine.
44. Εἰ δέ τῳ ἔρως καὶ τοῦ προειδέναι ἐνέσκηψε, καθαρὸς εἴη ψυχήν, ἔλεγε· καὶ τὸ διορᾶν τὸ μέλλον ἕψεται, τοῦ Θεοῦ διά τινος ἐσόπτρου τὴν τῶν ἐσομένων γνῶσιν παραδεικνύοντος. Nicephorus Callistus Xanthopulus, Historia ecclesiastica. In: Patrologia Graeca 146, col. 153 D–156 A. The translation is mine.
45. Τὸ παγχρυσότατον ἔσοπτρον τῶν ἀφανῶν καὶ ἀδήλων τὴν δήλωσιν ἐκκαλύπτον. Giagkou and Papatriantafyllou-Theodoridi 1999, 311, 244–246. The translation is mine.
46. Τάλας ἐγώ, τρίχες ὀρθαί μοι, κραδίη δὲ πατάσσει/ ὀσσομένου γραπτοῖσι τύποισιν, ὁποῖ' ἐν ἐσόπτρῳ,/ ὅσσαι τλήμονας ἡμέας ἐκδέξονται ποιναί. Lampros 1880, 391–392, l. 45–47. The translation is mine.
47. Papaioannou 2010.
48. Vogt 1935, 2. The passage was brought to my attention by Papaioannou 2010. The translation is based on Papaioanou's translation.
49. See for example Grabes 1973; Bradley 1954.
50. Afentoulidou, 2019. The hitherto sole, although non-critical, printed edition is Spyridon Lavriotes 1920. This edition was republished in Prochorov, Bil'djug, Miklas and Fuchsbauer 2008. The Klauthmoi were edited in Auvray 1875. A modern critical edition of the *Dioptra* is being prepared by the author of this article.
51. Giannouli 2013.
52. Afentoulidou 2012.

Notes to pp. 137–143

53. See the Introduction of the recent edition of part of the Slavonic translation of the *Dioptra*, Miklas and Fuchsbauer 2013, 41–44.
54. Stählin and Früchtel 1960 and Stählin, Früchtel and Treu 1970.
55. See Cameron 1970, 12–29.
56. See Gutzwiller 1998.
57. Iohannes Climacus, Scala Paradisi, Patrologia Graeca 88, col. 632–1164.
58. Patrologia Graeca 136, col. 765–1244.
59. Schöne 1903, 188–314 (Dioptra); Nix and Schmidt 1900, 368–372 (Catoptrica). See Coulton 2002.
60. On the anonymous Byzantine 'Geodesy' see Lewis 2001, 56–58 and 289–298, as well as Dain 1933.

Chapter 12

1. This chapter is based on material from my unpublished doctoral thesis (Priki, *Dream Narratives and Initiation Processes: A Comparative Study of the Tale of Livistros and Rodamne, the Roman de la Rose, and the Hypnerotomachia Poliphili*, 2015).
2. See also: McCarty 1989; Bartsch 2006; Anderson 2007; Taylor 2008.
3. On the term 'utopian function' see: Lochrie 2006.
4. Foucault 1984, 1574.
5. Priki 2015, 115–117.
6. On the connection between dreams with mirrors, see also: Preus 1968; Clay 1980; Nolan 1990; Kruger 1992, 136–140.
7. Strubel 1992, 5–7.
8. For references to mirrors in Jean de Meun's part of the *Roman de la Rose*, see Casanueva Reyes in this volume.
9. A thorough examination of optics and optical allegory in the Rose has been conducted by Akbari 2004. See also: Baig 1982 and Fleming 1986.
10. Heller 2001, 938–939.
11. See, for example: Fleming 1984; Richards 1982.
12. Oiseuse and her mirror are also discussed by Casanueva Reyes in this volume, where Oiseuse is associated with Luxuria and the mirror is discussed as a garment and as an instrument of beauty.
13. See also: Nouvet 2000, 364–365.
14. See also: Akbari 2004, 52; Lewis 1992, 218.
15. Lewis 1992, 218.
16. Lewis 1992, 218; Blamires and Holian 2002, 65.
17. Nichols 2003, 97.
18. The idea that these alterations in visual perception through mirrors signal liminal points in the dream is also discussed by Akbari 2004, 50.
19. Lewis 1958, 125; Frappier 1959, 151; Köhler 1963, 99; Louis 1974, 55–56.

20. Robertson 1962, 95; Fleming 1986.
21. Harley 1986, 326, where the crystals are seen as a reference to the Ovidian myth of Salmacis and Hermaphroditus pointing to the indivisibility of lover and rose; Peklar 2017, 92.
22. Agamben 1981, 139; Knoespel 1985, 80, 84–85; Akbari 2004, 55–66. Akbari, in particular, associates the crystals with refracted vision and a multiplicity of the self.
23. Nouvet 2000, 360–368.
24. Lewis 1992, 222; Lees-Jeffries 2006, 5; Hult 1981, 72; Hult 1986, 283–291. Also, see Root 2011, on a discussion of the fountain and the crystals in relation to the narrative discontinuities in Guillaume's romance.
25. Akbari 2004, 66.
26. This issue has been addressed by Hult (1986, 279), where he argues that 'the transference from two crystals to a single one presents a physical parallel to the two types of perception that are being highlighted in the poem'. Harley (1986, 325–326) offers a slightly different interpretation by pointing out the similarities between the description of the eyes of Salmacis in Ovid's *Metamorphoses* (4.347–349) and the description of the crystals in the Rose.
27. The text is cited from Strubel's edition (1992). Numbers in parenthesis refer to lines.
28. Horgan 1994, 24–25, with minor adjustments.
29. Lees-Jeffries (2006, 5) argues that the Fountain of Adonis in the *Hypnerotomachia Poliphili* has a similar function, reflecting 'both halves of the narrative, the erotic dream landscape of Poliphilus's quest and the proto-magic realism of Polia's Treviso, making no clear distinction between "real" and "unreal"'.
30. A similar argument associating the fountain with its crystals with a transformation and shaping of the self has been made by Peklar 2017, 100.
31. Huot 2010, 17. For a different interpretation of the robe as indicative of the individual's life force and potential for love, see: Grace-Heller 2000, 190; Grace-Heller 2001, 947.
32. On the association between Amour's gaze and the reflecting surface of the crystals in this scene, see also: Nouvet 2000, 370–374.
33. Harley 1986, 326.
34. Horgan 1994, 25.
35. Horgan 1994, 26.
36. Horgan 1994, 28.
37. Notz 1978, 470.
38. On the oneiric architecture of *Hypnerotomachia*, see indicatively: Polizzi 1987; Lefaivre 1997; Stewering 1996; Winton 2002; Pérez-Gómez 2006; Priki 2015, 179–222.
39. See also: Fierz-David (1987, 64): 'Everything is the same, yet not the same. The varying forms of the figures do not signify a difference of essence, but a difference of experience'.
40. Pozzi and Ciapponi 1980, 28.
41. I would like to thank Mr. Ian White for providing me with a copy of his yet unpublished English translation of the *Hypnerotomachia*, from which all translated passages are quoted.
42. Pozzi and Ciapponi 1980, 15.
43. Pozzi and Ciapponi 1980, 51.
44. Pozzi and Ciapponi 1980, 51.

Notes to pp. 152–159

45. Nordenfalk 1985, 15.
46. Some indicative examples of such baptisteries in Italy are the Battisterio Lateranense in Rome (fifth century) and the the Battistero di San Giovanni in Florence (early Christian but rebuilt in the eleventh and twelfth centuries). On baptisteries, see also: Bowersock et al. 1999, 332–334; Brandt 2006; Jensen 2011, 178–229.
47. For the interpretation of the three nymphs as the faculties of the human brain, see: Pozzi and Ciapponi, 1980, vol. 2, 105–106; Ariani and Gabriele, 1998, vol. 2, 695–697; Trippe, 2004, 245–249.

Chapter 13

1. On the archaeology of mirrors see Jonsson 1995, 36–42; see de Grummond and Hoff 1982; de Grummond 2002; Balensiefen 1990; DePuma 2013.
2. Though, even in cases of plane mirrors, images are not real; they are remote from the real object and reverse right and left.
3. For the mirror as self-improvement-device reflecting moral model-images see Mette 1983; Bartsch 2006, ch. 1; McCarty 1989; Lada Richards 2005; Hulkes 2007; Taylor 2008, 20–21; Ulrich 2016, ch. 1.
4. Gongdon 1981, 22–24. Even if we take into consideration the few sources that refer to the existence of glass mirrors in classical antiquity (on that see Beretta 2009, 26–40 and below fn. 21), we should acknowledge the fact that these, being costly, could not have been widespread.
5. Kauntze 2007, 60–61. Cf. the ancient Chinese magic mirror's ability to unmask the invisible; see on that Hirth 1907; on Chinese 'magic' mirrors, see Goldberg 1985, ch. 3. On Eurasian mirrors of the Iron Age in general, see Moyer 2012.
6. Taylor 2008, 246.
7. For a survey of ancient catoptrical texts, see Lejeune 1948, 1957; Knorr 1983, 1985; Simon 1988, 17–42; 2003; Takahashi 1992; Smith 1996; 2014, 1–180; Jones 2001.
8. While the properties esp. of concave mirrors have been studied since the time of Euclid, only ps. Hero seems to explore their use and utility. But, see further, among others, Diocles (*De speculis comburentibus*) and Anthemius of Tralles (*Concerning Wondrous Machines*) studying the case of burning mirrors and Huxley 1959 and Toomer 1976; see further on the utility of mirrors in ancient medicine Bliquez 2015, 15, 18, 48–50, 53f., 249–55.
9. On this see Halliwell 2002, ch. 4; Cain 2012; Capra 2017.
10. 2002, 136. Optical fidelity of images, according to Halliwell, is what Plato calls in the *Sophist eicastic* image making, while the *phantastike* category, in which most mimetic arts are placed, highlights as the artistic criterion for a representation a less mirrorlike replication of the world (430a–d, 432a–d). See further Halliwell 2002, 45f., 126–129 referring to *Cratylus* 430a–431d on the notion of perfect imitation (cf. *Laws* 2.656–657 and 7.799a–b). See also Steiner 2001, 45–56, 68–74.
11. Mirrors can minimize (*Alcibiades* i 132e–133b), reverse right and left (*Theaetetus* 193c–d, *Timaeus* 45 b–c), and inverse reality (*Laws* 905b).
12. See e.g. Seneca *NQ* 1.17, Apuleius *Ap.* 13, Juvenal *Satires* 2, on full-length mirrors and MacFarlane and Martin 2002, 16.

Notes to pp. 159–161

13. With Rouveret 1989, 24–26, 50–59 and Halliwell 2002, 58, 125. On *sciagraphia* see also Trimpi 1978. On *scenographia* as cognate with *sciagraphia*, see Vitruvius 7 praef. 11, 1.2.2, Polybius 12.28a 1.4-2-1, Dionysius of Halicarnassus *Isaeus* 4; on *scenographia* and optics see Proclus *Euclid* I 40, Geminus in Hero *Definitiones* 135; Rouveret 1989, 65–127; Camerota 2000; Hub 2008, 249–253; Sinisgalli 2012, 36–39; Small 2013. Generally, on perspective see Simon 1988, 50–64.

14. Smith 2014, 54.

15. On Apuleius' mirror in the *Apology* see Hunink 1997, 57–67; McCarty 1989, 167ff.; Bartsch 2006, 18–41; Taylor 2008, 86–88; Too 1996, 142–143; Libby 2011, 308–310; Ulrich 2016, ch. 1.

16. Cf. Vitruvius, *De arch.* 10.1.1–6, who also describes machinery as developed according to nature; Greene 2008, 801.

17. On *akribeia* see Pollitt 1974, 117–125, 351–357; Tanner 2006, 169. See also Plato's Philebus 56c–58e, where *technai* are differentiated according to *akribeia*, and the *Sophist* 235d–e on accurate proportions; see further Pliny *NH* 34.58.

18. Cf. the connection between *acheiropoiêtoi* images and photography made by Barthes 1981, 82 and Bazin 2004, 13. On *acheiropoiêtoi* images in antiquity, see Platt 2001, 96–100, 122f.

19. 'deest enim et luto vigor et saxo color et picturae rigor et motus omnibus, qui praecipua fide similitudinem repraesentat, cum in eo visitur imago mire relata, ut similis, ita mobilis et ad omnem nutum hominis sui morigera'. On that see the excellent dissertation by Ulrich 2016, ch. 1, esp. 90, 140f.

20. Ulrich 2016, ch. 1, esp. 132–136; see further Too 1996.

21. The connection was already established by Pliny the Elder in his description of stone and metal technology in *NH* 34–36. On the role of the construction material in the mimesis process and reproduction, though the topic deserves a study of its own, see Pliny *NH* 34–36, esp. on mirrors made of various metals which influence the outcome, see 33.45 on obsidian, transparent volcanic rock which reveals the shadow of objects rather the objects themselves, and 36.67 on glass mirrors; see also Seneca *QN* 1.17. In the *Apotelesmata* of ps. Apollonius of Tyana, a work of unknown date, guidelines are given on how to construct a mirror in order to see the mysteries in all parts of the earth and in heaven. The text instructs us to make a mirror of various metals and glass (bronze, quicksilver, silver, gold, tin), place it in a small silver plate, write names like Bisarakh, Sarsatzie, Murde, Biarag and Galga, place a strip of gold leaf on the face of the mirror and insert seven precious stones, and carve on each one this mystery, in sequence: Ankhour, Zazekhar, Samps, Epras, Magtes, Sakartes and Zakgram. If one wishes to see things happening below the earth, he shall look at the bottom part of the mirror, or, if he wishes to see things in heaven, he must look at the top part of the mirror. See on materials in antiquity, among others, Lapatin 2014.

22. On the connection between mirrors and the moon see Karen ní Mheallaigh in this volume.

23. With Porter 2010, 408.

24. Cf. Cicero *De Or.* 2.90.5 urges imitators not to select what is easy (*facilia*) or obvious (*insignia*) from a model, with Perry 2002, 159.

25. Ulrich 2016, 122.

26. On this term in relation to mirror images, see also Linardou in this volume. In their dematerialized status, mirrors resemble dream images and shadows. Lucretius at *DRN*

364–369 talks about shadows in the same way he talks about mirror images, underlining the fact that both, as imitating technologies, are able to capture motion. On this see Hardie 2010, 76; and Stoichita 1997, 11–20. On the connection between dream images and catoptric images see Plato's *Timaeus* 46a1ff., 71a–b and Aristotle's *De divinatione per somnia* 464b5 where he compares dreams with reflections in water, with Platt 2011, 258, fn. 22 and 23, p. 283 and Alexander, in *Met.* 432.11–22. On dream images and reflections see further Priki in this volume.

27. See on the *craftsmanly* nature of art, Porter 2010, 264–275.
28. Cf. Anthemius *De Speculis Ignigenis* 5–7. On the polytheoros mirror in a religious context see further Bur in this volume.
29. On the reduction of the art viewer to a mere user, cf. Walter Benjamin's essay 'L'œuvre d'art à l'époque de sa reproduction mécanisée' (1936).
30. Cf. Pliny *NH* 35.36; the painted curtain of Parrhasius has no existence without Zeuxis' real gesture to open it. See on this Maurice Benayoun 1999, media artist, http://benayoun.com/moben/1999/11/11/lart-coupable-mais-toujours-libre/.
31. See on that Plotinus VI.4.10; III.6.13; IV.5.7; VI.2.22; III.6.14, though in another context, i.e. as an analogy to matter as receptacle; generally, on the mirror analogy in Plotinus see Clark 2016, 83–90 and Cain 2016, 233–246. See further Alexander, *Mantissa* 135.27–32 and Grabes 1982, 113.
32. 2008, 21.
33. Jonsson 1995, 32–36; Frontisi-Ducroux/Vernant 1997, 177–181; Bartsch 2006, 106–114; Taylor 2008, 19; Myerowitz 1992, 149f. On ambiguous use of mirrors, see further the case of Pentheus in Euripides' *Bacchae*: he sees two suns and two Thebes, and the god, Dionysus, as a bull; the double vision of Pentheus produced, according to Seaford (1987), by a Dionysian mirror helps to disorientate and humiliate the young prince.
34. Cf. on non-natural art Vitruvius *De arch.* 7.5 and esp. 7.5.3: '<Nam pinguntur> tectoriis monstra potius quam ex rebus finitis imagines certae', and Elsner 1995, 16, 53f. and passim.
35. Elsner 1995 discussing the latter (viewing images) positions the shift later, during the Imperial era.
36. Euclid *De Speculis* pr. 20–23, 29 (ed. Takahashi); Ptolemy *Optica* 3.91–96 (Lejeune, 1956) (for plane mirror), 4.142–155.
37. Euclid *De Speculis* 21, 22; Ptolemy *Optica* 4.120–129 (concave mirrors). On reversion of heights, depths and lengths in mirrors see Euclid *De Speculis* 7 (plane mirrors), 8 (convex mirrors), 11, 12 (concave mirrors).
38. See also Ptolemy *Optica* 3.121–123, on convex mirrors distorting the shape of straight and convex objects; 3. 124–126, on convex mirrors distorting the shape of concave objects; 4.130-141, shape distortion according to the position of the image.
39. Jones 2001, 184.
40. See also Ptol. *Optica* 4.158–160: mirrors composed of a straight and convex section can produce images compressed along their length. See further Ptol. *Optica* 4.159f., mirrors composed of a concave and straight section can fashion images distended along their width; see also 4.161f. on mirrors composed of a concave and a convex section can produce both compressed and distended images.
41. Jones 2001, 184. For the experience of a floating image through the use of magnets see Pliny *NH* 34.148.

Notes to pp. 163–165

42. For images floating behind or in front of the mirror see also Ptolemy *Optica* 4.109–119; 4.69f.
43. Cf. mirror and imagination in the Renaissance: Melchior-Bonnet 2001, 195–197.
44. See Lucretius *DRN* 4.98–109, and Garani in this volume.
45. 2015, 361f.; Sheppard 2003.
46. Sheppard 2014, 83–85; Sheppard 2015, 360f. See also Elsner 1995, 26f.
47. See Platt 2009 for discussion and bibliography. Further see Watson 1988, ch. 4; Sheppard 2014, 80f. and Sheppard 2015.
48. Watson 1988, 12f.; Sheppard 2003 and 2014, 50–52, 78, 84 and Shirazi in this volume; see further on *phantasia* and mirror analogy, Plotinus *Ennead* 4.3. 30.1–11; 1.4.10–6–21; Proclus, *In Euc.* 121.2–7.
49. On the notion of the Aristotelean *phantasia* as producing images/visualization process see, among many, Watson 1988, ch. 2; Frede 1992; Scheiter 2012; Johansen 2012, ch. 10; Sheppard 2014, 6–10, 2015; against this opinion see Nussbaum 1978; Schofield 1992. On the Aristotelian notion of *phantasia* in the *De Somniis*, see Wedin 1988, 39–45; Nussbaum 1978, 234, 248; Scheiter 2012.
50. See also in Pliny *NH* 7.15, 28.23; Solinus, *Collectanea rerum memorabilium*, i. 58; Proclus, *In Platonis Rem publicam commentarii*, xii. I. 290.
51. On this passage with further bibliography, see van der Eijk 1994, 169–193.
52. Cf. the case of a sighting tube that concentrates the visual ray – either towards or from the eye – and doesn't let it scatter, which improves vision and enables the viewer to see farther; on that see Aristotle, *De Generatione Animalium* 780 b, 18–22, 781a 9–12. On the similar case of the dioptrical tube see mainly Hero's *Dioptra* and Lewis 2001, ch. 2 and ch. 3; Coulton 2002.
53. See among others Platt 2011 and Petridou 2016.
54. On that see Balensiefen, 1990, 34–36, 168–173, 223; Frontisi-Ducroux and Vernant 1997, 190, 238 and Taylor 2008, 103 with further bibliography. Cf. the similar case of the Apulian bell-krater in Zurich of the same period discussed by Balensiefen 1990, 217f. and Seaford 1998, 130f. See further the Pompeian fresco of the first century CE from the House of Loreius Tiburtinus, Pompeii. Here Narcissus is portrayed looking at a reflection in the water; however, the reflection does not resemble himself but Gorgo; on that see Grethlein 2017, 238.
55. See also Aristotle's *Meteorologica* 342b, 372a–b, 373a–b, 377b, where he argues that small reflecting particles can only reflect the colour, but not the form, of an object.

Chapter 14

1. This article expands on material that will be published in ní Mheallaigh forthcoming, esp. chapter 5. Translations are my own, unless otherwise stated.
2. Lucian, *VH* 1.26
3. All interpretations play with these one (or both) of these ideas: Koppenfels 1981, 30–31; Georgiadou and Larmour 1998, *ad loc.*; Fusillo 1999; von Möllendorff 2000, 182–188 and 566–569; ní Mheallaigh 2014, 216–227.

4. Boccalini, *I ragguagli di Parnasso* IV 2r. The connection with Boccalini and Galileo is noted by Fusillo 1999, 327. On Boccalini's fascinating exploitation of sixteenth century optical technology, see García Santo-Thomás 2017, 98–105. For the 'aleph,' a panoptic device, see Borges 1945/1970, 26–27, and for its connection with Lucian, see ní Mheallaigh 2019.
5. *Hist. co.* 49–50, with Georgiadou and Larmour 1994. On Lucian's use of the mirror-metaphor in *De salt.*81, see Lada-Richards 2005.
6. *Bis Acc.* 33. On Menippean satire and the *VH*, see Fusillo 1999.
7. *Icar.* 11–19, with ní Mheallaigh forthcoming, chapter 6.
8. Marcus Aurelius, *Med.* 7.47–48; 9.30; 11.1–2. For further Stoic advocacy of this mental exercise, cf. Seneca *Natural Questions*, preface 7–11, with discussion, including the passage of *Icaromenippus*, in Hadot 1995, 238–250. More generally, see Williams 2012.
9. *Clouds* ll. 749–756.
10. For the calculation of interest and collection of debts at the New Moon, see Aristophanes *Clouds* 16–17; Demosthenes 37.4–5, with Gainsford 2012, 11 n. 27.
11. Hill 1973.
12. Hamilton and Tischbein 1795, 72–74, Pl. 44.
13. *Ref.* 4.37–38.
14. Aëtius 2.25.15 (p. 357 *DG*).
15. DK 28 B14 and 15, with Graham 2013, 85–108.
16. For another heuristic deployment of mirrors – as a cognitive tool to enhance the understanding of the atomic world – see Garani in this volume.
17. On the *De facie*, see Görgemanns 1970, Taub 2008 and ní Mheallaigh forthcoming, chapter 4.
18. *De facie* 936c. For Aristotle's school, the Moon, which consisted of aether, exuded its own light.
19. Achilles Tatius, *Isagoge* p. 21 37–45 Maass.
20. Congdon 1985.
21. Webster 2014, 115–171.
22. On this 'lunar revolution', see Graham 2013, 85–136.
23. Attestations to these beliefs are assembled in Préaux 1973.
24. *De fac.* 928b–c, with translation by Cherniss 1957.
25. For Plato's liver-mirror, see *Tim.* 71b and 72c with Shirazi in this volume.
26. fr. 133 IP (= Aëtius, I 7, 30, p. 304 Diels); cf. Plutarch *On the obsolesence of oracles* 416c–d. On Xenocrates' daemonology, see Schibli 1993, 147–159, with further references, and Dillon 2003, 89–155 on Xenocrates' life and doctrines more generally. Other key passages relating similar theories include [Philip of Opus] *Epinomis* 984d–985c; Ocellus, *On the Nature of the Universe* p. 130.4–10 Thesleff. A detailed exposition of the lunar metaphysics of the Old Academy and Pythagoreans is beyond my present scope; for a fuller exploration of this complex topic, see Chapter 4 of ní Mheallaigh forthcoming.
27. Taylor 2008, 109–111.
28. Plutarch *De facie* 920f–921a.
29. Hegesianax fr. 467 *SH*, quoted at *De fac.* 921b.
30. See Aëtius 2.25–31, with Mansfeld and Runia 2009, 572–643.

31. For discussion of ancient ideas concerning life on the Moon, see ní Mheallaigh forthcoming, chapter 3.
32. Aëtius 2.25.15.
33. For the Moon as 'catoptrical machine', see Baltrusaitis 1978, 47.
34. Neve 2004, 296–304.
35. See Triclinius, *On the black figure in the Moon* ll. 101–108 Wasserstein. The treatise was supported by a diagram of the 'Man in the Moon'; see ní Mheallaigh forthcoming, chapter 6. For hints at lunar mapping in Plutarch, see *De facie* 944b–c.
36. On the complex traditions of lunar mapping, see Whitaker 1999. Hevelius' system (1647) was rapidly superseded by the toponyms proposed by Giovanni Battista Riccioli (1651), on which our modern nomenclature is based.
37. See McCarty 1989, 170 with n. 21 and Grabes 1982, 42–43.
38. See examples discussed by Gerolemou in this volume.
39. Dällenbach (1989, 10–15) compares the transcendental power of the mirror in art, with that of the *mise en abyme* in literature: both have the ability to actualize realities that lie 'outside' themselves. The most famous example in art is the role of the mirror in Velázquez's *Las Meninas*.
40. See König and Whitmarsh 2007, esp. 14.
41. For a synkrisis of fantastical and photographic views of our world from the Moon, see ní Mheallaigh 2019.
42. Wälchli discusses Lucian's lunar device at 2003, 185–199. As parallels, he adduces Pausanias 8.37.7 (the shrine of The Lady (Despoina) in Arcadia, where a mirror suspended on a temple-wall reflects not the viewer himself, but statues of the gods instead); Hero *Catoptrics* 16 and 18. On these and other 'trick' mirrors, see Gerolemou in this volume.
43. Wälchli 2003, 192–193.
44. That convex mirrors produce *reduced* images, see Euclid, *Cat.* 21–22; on the *magnifying* effect of concave mirrors, see Apuleius, *Apol.* 16.2; for further examples, see discussion by Gerolemou in this volume.
45. Fusillo 1999, 372 n. 49.
46. On the Demeter-oracle and catoptromancy, see Delatte 1932, 135–139; Frontisi-Ducroux and Vernant 1997, 194–195; Addey 2007; Taylor 2008, 102–104; also Gerolemou in this volume. Delatte (1932, 139) suggests that Lucian's mirror-and-well parodies the catoptromantic ritual at Patrae, whilst acknowledging the different role of the mirror in each passage; see also von Möllendorff 2000, 183, with Wälchli 2003, 186–187.
47. Wälchli 2003, 195–199. The passage in question is Plutarch *On the daemon of Socrates* 589c–d. This method is also described by Herodotus 4.200.2–3 and Aeneas Tacticus 37.6–7 (who imitates the Herodotean passage). Delatte (1932, 139) rather wishfully suggests that the auditory experience of the well may reflect *conchyliomancy* – divination through listening to spirit-voices inside shells – though he finds no evidence for this practice in antiquity.
48. On its use for measuring distances between stars and planets, see Hero, *Dioptra* 32 and cf. *Anonymus Byzantinus* (also known as 'Hero of Byzantium'), *Geodesy* 1. On the *dioptra* in its different forms, its applications, and the sources that describe it, see Lewis 2001; Coulton 2002.
49. Aristotle, *On the generation of animals* 781a1–12.

50. *On the generation of animals* 780b18–22. On the ancient 'observation well', see Sayili 2007.
51. Couprie 2011, 22, citing Eisler 1949, 324 n. 13. The anecdote is preserved in Plato, *Theaetetus* 174a4–b6 (DK 11 A9 = G7); cf. also Aesop, *Fab.* 40 'Astrologos,' in relation to an anonymous astronomer.
52. According to Posidonius, the astronomer Eudoxus of Cnidos used the roof-top of his house in Cnidos as his observatory (σκοπή); Strabo reports that he also had observatories in the city of Kerkesoura in Libya (Strabo 2.5.14; 17.1.30, with Huxley 1963). Mount Ida, a tall mountain in the Troad (modern Kaz Dağları, in Turkey) was the site for astronomical observations by the sixth century philosopher Xenophanes and Cleostratus of Tenedos. On Cleostratus, see Theophrastus, *De signis* 4 and Diels 1920, 5–6. A number of the *doxographica* for Xenophanes imply a connection between his explanation of the sunrise with observation at Mt. Ida; see Keyser 1992.
53. On Konstantinos Simonides' Byzantine forgery, see Diamontopoulou in this volume. Temple (2000, 121–195) presents a vigorous, if occasionally rebarbative, argument in support of the existence of the telescope in antiquity; Plantzos (1997) presents a more sober and sceptical view.

Chapter 15

1. My most sincere thanks are due to the editors of the volume for inviting me to contribute to it and to my colleague Andreas Ioannidis for sharing my enthusiasm on this topic. My thanks are equally extended to the young artists Ioannis Efthimiou and Athanasios Yiotakis for their drawings. Without their generous contribution this chapter would not have been the same.
2. Goldschmidt and Weitzmann (1934), cat. no. 6, p. 26, pl. II; Frazer (1974), 153–161, where also older bibliography; O'Neill, ed. (1987), 49, fig. 41; Howard (1994), cat. no. 17, p. 378; Evans and Wixon, eds (1997), cat. no. 97, pp. 151–152; Evans, Holcomb and Hallman (Spring 2001), 46; Stein (2016), cat. no. 32, pp. 114–115.
3. The word *acheiropoietos* first appears in Marc 14.58 and refers to the spiritual Temple that Christ would erect after his death and resurrection in order to replace the material Temple in Jerusalem. It was intended as a meaningful metaphor juxtaposing the Old to the New Law, the material to the immaterial and the palpable to the mental. See Dobschutz 1899, vol. 1, 118*. See also Belting 1994, 55–56; Mondzain 2005, 192–208.
4. Frelick, ed. 2016, 1–24.
5. Couvreur, ed. 1901, 255D, p. 202, line 9. For the most recent edition and translations see Lucarini and Moreschini, eds (2012); Bernard, trans. (1997); Baltzly and Share, trans. (2018), 10–20. On the eye-mirror analogy in Antiquity see Webster 2018, 132–140.
6. Goldin 1967, 3, where it is stated that the mirror appears in the writing of nearly every author of the middle ages.
7. Fee 1987, 647–648, note 45; Seaford (1984); Cain (2016) and Afentoulidou in this volume.
8. Pictorial examples representing female mirror-gazing are admittedly rare and mostly early-dated; see the fourth-century Projecta casket in the British Museum, London and the fifth-century mosaic from Sibi Ghrib, Tunisia, Bardo Museum, Tunis: Kalavrezou et al., eds 2003, 233–239, esp. figs. 20–21. See also Elsner 2003, 22–36, esp. 30–32.

9. Papaioannou 2010, 81–101, esp. 82. For a cultural history of mirrors and mirroring see Melchior-Bonnet 2001, esp. 1–6.
10. Papaioannou 2010, 85–90, notes 24–25.
11. Papaioannou 2010, 85. See further Afentoulidou in this volume.
12. Ibid, 85.
13. On the acheiropoietos status of reflections see further Gerolemou in this volume.
14. On puzzling images and cryptomorphs in particular see Elkins 1999, 142–190, esp. 145.
15. Elkins 1999, 167.
16. Mondzain 2005, 175.
17. Goldschimdt and Weitzmann 1934, 26; Frazer 1974, 153–161; Cutler 1994, 77, 157, 172, 244–245, 249.
18. Frazer 1974, 161.
19. On the availability of ivory and how circulation may have affected the size and quality of ivory carvings see Cutler 1985, 29–30.
20. Goldschimdt and Weitzmann 1934, 26; Evans and Wixon, eds 1997, 151–152.
21. The small scale of the ivory plaque is overlooked in Frazer 1974, 154; Cutler 1994, pl. V; O'Neill, ed. 1987, 49, fig. 41, and Stein 2016, cat. no. 32, p. 115. The following publications reproduce the ivory plaque in smaller scale: Goldschimdt and Weitzmann 1934, no. 6, pl. II; Evans and Wixon, eds 1997, 151; Howard 1994, cat. no. 17, 378, and Evans, Holcomb and Hallman 2001, 46.
22. Kee 2012, 499–501, quote in 499.
23. Cutler 1994, 248.
24. Ibid, 251.
25. Ibid, pl. V.
26. Elkins 1999, 142.
27. For the latest thorough discussion on the eclectic nature of Byzantine notions on sight and vision see Betancourt 2018, 6–7 and especially chapter 6, 142–155, where also older literature on the matter.
28. Onians 1980, 1–24.
29. James and Webb 1991, 1–17; Webb 2007, 13–32.
30. Onians 1980, 8–12; Tronzo 2018, 23–42, esp. 29–31.
31. Dagron 1991, 23–33.
32. Constas 1997, 114–125.
33. Trilling 1998, 109–127; Tilghman 2011, 292–308, esp. 300.
34. The bibliography on the *Mandylion* is extensive and it steadily grows bigger. Suffice it to mention here only a few titles: Dobschutz 1899, vol. 1: 102–196, 158*–249*; vol. 2: 29**–129**; Grabar 1931; Weitzmann 1960, 163–184; Cameron 1983, 80–94; Belting 1994, 49–57; Cormack 1997, 89–132; Kessler and Wolf, eds 1998; Engberg 2004, 123–142; Wolf et al., eds. 2004; Cuscin 2009.
35. Runciman 1929, 229–230; Cameron 1983, 93; *De Imagine Edessena*: cols. 424–454, esp. 444–448.
36. *De Imagine Edessena*: 448D; Runciman 1929, 230.
37. Runciman 1929, 232–237.

38. Cameron 1983, 93.
39. *De Imagine Edessena*: 424-454. See also Dobschutz 1899, vol. 2: 29**-129**; Cuscin 2009, 8-69; Magdalino 2013, 187-209, esp. 191.
40. For the Virgin of Pharos see Magdalino 2004, 15-30, esp. 24.
41. Engberg 2004, 130, 136-139; Magdalino 2004, 24.
42. Engberg 2004, 127-129.
43. Ibid. 127 and note 18. See also Cuscin 2009, 193-200.
44. Engberg 2004, 136.
45. Kitzinger 1995, 575-590.
46. Kitzinger 2003, 1175-1176, notes 67-68; Alpatov 1978, 17, pl. 38; Lazarev 1976, 10-11, pls 8-9.
47. Cameron 1983, 80-94; Cuscin 2009, 141-164.
48. *De Imagine Edessena*: 429-432; Dobschutz 1899, vol. 2: 49**-51**.
49. *De Imagine Edessena*: 433; Dobschutz 1899, vol. 2: 53**-54**.
50. Dubable 1997, 5-51; Cuscin 2009, 70-87.
51. Dubable 1997, 29; Cuscin 2009, 84.
52. Engberg 2004, 135-136.
53. Dubable 1997, 25.
54. The allusion to King David would have been particularly pertinent to Constantine. In the Paris Psalter (Paris, BnF Ms. gr. 139), a deluxe illustrated psalter of the second half of the tenth century that has been associated with the Porphyrogennetos, King David is presented in the guise of the ideal ruler and in accordance with contemporary notions of imperial ideology. See Evans and Wixon, eds 1997, cat. no. 163, 240-242.
55. A piece of cloth (*sudarium*) with the holy face imprinted on it and described as the Veronica would start its career in the West from the twelfth century onwards. It is recorded as being in Rome circa 1160. See Ragusa 1991, 97-106; Belting 1994, 215-224; Wolf 1998, 153-179.
56. Bekker, ed. 1838, 52D, p. 750; Engberg 2009, 133.
57. Runciman 1929, 230.
58. According to Kurt Weitzmann, the famous Sinai icon reproducing the reception of the *Mandylion* by King Abgar and dated to the second half of the tenth century represents Constantine in the guise of the ruler of Edessa as the new recipient of the legendary relic. It was thus visually manipulated with the explicit intention to disseminate the idea of Constantine as the pious and righteous emperor. See Weitzmann 1960, 182-184.

Chapter 16

1. The poet and art historian Nikolas Calas (1907-1988) is well-known as a key figure in the development of Surrealism in Greece, but what is less known is that he was also a great admirer of mirrors. The booklet *Mirrors of the Mind* accompanied a portfolio of prints and objects by renowned artists like Vincenzo Agnetti, Arakawa, Joseph Beuys, Marcel Broodthaers, Richard Hamilton, Roy Lichtenstein, Bruce Nauman, Meret Oppenheim,

Robert Rauschenberg, Man Ray and James Rosenquist and was presented in a number of international exhibitions (USA, Italy, Mexico, Greece) curated and compiled by himself in the years 1975–1977.

2. Calas 1942, 200.
3. Simonides 1849, frontpage.
4. The section closes again with the wood print of the signature of Meletios (p. 174) and his testament (175–178) and is followed by the biography of Eulyros written by a certain Nikephoros Daidalou from Corfu (pp. 178–180).
5. Simonides 1849, 3 Fn. 1; 61 (source in Greek).
6. Simonides 1849, 19.
7. For further reading see Van Helden/Dupré/Van Gent 2010, Edgerton 2009 and Willach 2008.
8. Simonides 1849, 93 (source in Greek).
9. This is for example the case in a miniature in a manuscript from the thirteenth century (No. 11040, Burgundy Library Brussels) printed in Beebe 1938, Fig. 6.
10. Busch 1804, 196.
11. For a thorough examination of the Archimedean mirror legend, see Simms 1977, 1–24.
12. To the list of sources mentioned by Busch Diocles should be added; see Toomer 1976. For burning glasses in Greek antiquity in general Knorr 1983 and Acerbi, 2011.
13. The Archimedian invention is discussed in Dutens 1775. Cf. also Donndorf 'Metallspiegel', 'Brennspiegel', Donndorf, 1818, 76; both could be Simonides' sources.
14. See *Ars magna lucis et umbrae*, Rome 1646, 888, Tab. XXXI.
15. Simonides 1849, 104–105.
16. See Simonides 1849, 20 footnote. For more information about Anthemius see Huxley 1959.
17. Niebuhr 1828, Book E, pp. 291–294.
18. Simonides may have known the 'Fragments' of Anthemius through the edition of Westermann's Παραδοξογράφοι *[Marvel Writers]* whose work may generally have been a source of inspiration for Simonides. Cf. specifically for mirrors and their typology in Anthemius, Westermann 1839, 149–158.
19. Simonides notes in a footnote to this invention: 'What can one say about this ball of light? Physicists should comment on this' (p. 23, fn. 1).
20. According to recent research, the painter Panselinos became legendary, so that the question has now been raised if he was 'man or metaphor'; on that see Milliner 2016.
21. Didron 1845, XXI, XXIII–XXVI and Kakavas 2008, 10. Brockhaus 1891, 160 fn. 3 mentions two manuals he saw in Karyes. Kakavas 2008, 267–301 lists 69 manuscripts of the 'Painters' Manual', four of which he attributes to Simonides. See also Hetherington's list on pp. 113–115. The publication contains many comments and has a long introduction. It is interesting that Didron dedicated it to the writer Victor Hugo, 'the immortal author of the Notre Dame de Paris [L'immortel auteur de Notre-Dame de Paris]', Didron 1845, frontpage. The manual was printed at the expense of the French government, see Unger 1870, 292.
22. See Omont 1888, 367, No. 38 and Kakavas 2008, 11. According to Omont 1888, 367, 38 and 39 and ibid. 1890, 432–433, there were two manuscripts in the Municipal Library in Chartres that came from Paul Durand to the library. Durand No. 827 (in Omont No. 38) is a copy made by Simonides at Athos around 1840 (Pap. 268 fol. P.); Durand 828 (in Omont No. 39) is a copy made by Durand (Pap. 409 fol. P). However, the former was destroyed during a bombing in 1944, see Hetherington 1974, V Fn. 7 and Kakavas 2008, 270–271. The manuscript

contained a note written by Durand (Hetherington 1974, v. 7) stating it was purchased from Simonides in 1847. There was a note from Simonides, that he had found it on Mount Athos on 15 March 1840 and copied it (Omont, 1888, 3, 367, no. 38). See also Papadopoulos-Kerameus 1909, ε', footnote 3 and Kakavas 2008, 11 footnote 23. For further headings of the manuscripts related to Simonides see Papadopoulos-Kerameus 1909, ιγ'-ιε', Fn. 1.

23. Papadopoulos-Kerameus 1909, ε'-η', ιδ'-κε' and Kakavas 2008, 11.

24. See Lykourgos 1856, 45ff. Brockhaus 1891: 158–161 deals extensively with the question of the linguistic differences between the manuscripts. Sathas 1868, 99–100, on the other hand, is deceived by Simonides and sees in the modern Greek of the manual an important example for the vernacular of the fifteenth century, its alleged time of writing.

25. For more details on this case see Mitsou and Diamantopoulou in Müller/Diamantopoulou/Gastgeber/Katsiakiori-Rankl 2017, 71–86 and 27–53.

26. See Kakavas 2008, 12.

27. Simonides dates the life of the inventor of the heliotype Manouil Panselinos to the sixth century and specifically in 518 AD. In the *Symais* a second painter called Panselinos is mentioned, who acted around 1032–1085. In his work Νικολάου επισκόπου Μεθώνης, Λόγος προς τους Λατίνους [Speech of Nikolaos, bishop of Methoni, to the Latins] (Simonides 1858) he mentions three other painters of the same name.

28. Simonides 1853, § 64, 40–41 (source in Greek).

29. For a detailed discussion of this omission and a comparison of the French and the Simonideian editions, see Rangavis 1851, 554–555.

30. 'Ατέλειαν του εκγαλλισθέντος χειρογράφου, ή εις κακοβουλίαν του μεταφραστού' (Simonides, *Αμάλθεια* Nr. 508, quoted after Rangavis 1851, 554). Rangavis points out the problems of this argument and says that such a 'malicious concealment' is a 'patriotism that transcends that of Curtius, or is incredible stupidity' (Rangavis 1851, 554).

31. Oikonomos refers to the manuscript as antique ('χειρόγραφον αρχαίον σώζεται' Oikonomos 1849, 4, 218, Fn. α) and recognizes in the heliotype a form of iconography which he compares to the daguerrotype. See also Papadopoulos-Kerameus 1909, στ'-ζ', Rangavis 1851, 553 Fn. β and Brockhaus 1891, 160 Fn. 4. Manouil Gedeon names Panselinos as the first inventor of photography: 'πρώτος εφευρέτης της φωτογραφίας, γράψας μάλιστα, κατά την παράδοσιν, και βιβλίον περί αυτής', Gedeon 1876, 53–54. See also Vasilaki 1999, 45.

32. The connection of Simonides' anachronistic technologies with the term 'steampunk' was first formulated by Siniosoglou 2016, 315.

33. Simonides 1853, § 64, 43 (source in Greek). In Hero of Alexandrias *De Speculis*, 22 occurs a similar description: Hero refers to a mirror on the ceiling of a room reflecting the view of the street through a tube that penetrates the wall of a certain building. The resident of this building was able to see, without being seen, the movement of passers-by outside. For further reading on mirrors and reflected images in Hero see Gerolemou and Bur in this volume.

34. For further reading on the camera obscura in art and science see Lefèvre (2007). For the early steps of photography in Greece see Xanthakis 1981.

35. For example, the work of the Russian art collector, amateur archaeologist and photographer Piotr Sevastianov (1811–1867) is well-known. He toured Athos at an early age, around 1851, 1852, and later more extensively from 1857–1860, and not only painted copious icons with several major Russian missions and other treasures, but also made numerous photographs; see Pyatnitsky 2011.

36. According to a theory advocated by the artist David Hockney and the physicist Charles M. Falco, art itself was revolutionized by the use of optical instruments, rather than solely due to

the development of artistic skills *per se*. In his book *Secret Knowledge* (2001) Hockney presented rich visual evidence to prove his theory, followed by an anthology of textual sources about vision and optics and the transcription of letters exchanged between various academics and himself during his research. It also includes pictures of Hockney's *Great Wall* (2000), which organizes printed images of art history; remarkably it begins with an Italo-Byzantine mosaic of the twelfth century from Norman Sicily. Obviously, the main concern of the artist is to visualize the abrupt shift towards a more naturalistic style during the Italian Renaissance, which Hockney explains by the use of lenses and mirrors – the two basic elements of the modern camera – in painting.

37. Didron 1845, 7.
38. Simonides 1864, 51.
39. Grafton 1991, 45–47.
40. See Kladaki-Vratsanou 2009 and 2010. The manuscript is owned by his grandson Loukas Kyramarios, who made it accessible online http://kyramarios.blogspot.com (accessed 15 December 2018).
41. This aspect of counterfeiting activities (also fake news, forged letters and documents) during the first years of the Independence War and in the early Greek State is the subject of a project I am leading at the University of Hamburg, financed by the German Ministry of Education and Research (BMBF).

BIBLIOGRAPHY

Introduction

Abrams, M. H. (1971), *The Mirror and the Lamp: Romantic Theory and the Critical Tradition*, Oxford.
Addey, C. J. (2007), 'Mirrors and Divination: Catoptromancy, Oracles and Earth Goddesses in Antiquity', in M. Anderson (ed.), *The Book of the Mirror: An Interdisciplinary Collection Exploring the Cultural Story of the Mirror*, Newcastle, 32–46.
Aggelopoulou, A. and Mprouskou, A. (1994), *Επεξεργασία παραμυθιακών τύπων και παραλλαγών AT 700-749*, Athens.
Anderson, M. (ed.) (2008), *The Book of the Mirror: An Interdisciplinary Collection Exploring the Cultural Story of the Mirror*, Newcastle.
Bartsch, S. (2006), *The Mirror of the Self: Sexuality, Self-Knowledge, and the Gaze in the Early Roman Empire*, Chicago.
Baudrillard, J. (1973), *Le miroir de la production ou l'illusion critique du matérialisme historique*, Paris.
Baudrillard, J. (1981), *Simulacres et simulation*, Paris.
Baudrillard, J. (2012), 'Structures of Interior Design: Mirrors and Portraits', in K. Mezei, Kathy and Ch. Briganti (eds), *The Domestic Space Reader*, Toronto, 210–14.
Beretta, M. (2009), *The Alchemy of Glass: Counterfeit, Imitation, and Transmutation in Ancient Glassmaking*, Sagamore Beach, MA.
Carman, Ch. H. (2014), *Leon Battista Alberti and Nicholas Cusanus: Towards an Epistemology of Vision for Italian Renaissance Art and Culture*. Visual Culture in Early Modernity, Farnham.
Cocteau, J. (1999), *Le sang d'un poète*, Lincoln, NE [reprint].
Congdon, L. O. K. (1981), *Caryatid Mirrors of Ancient Greece: Technical, Stylistic and Historical Considerations of an Archaic and Early Classical Bronze series*, Mainz.
Coupland, D. (2015), Die 2 ½ste Dimension. Notizen zu Selfies, in A. Bieber and D. Coupland (eds), *Ego Update – Die Zukunft der digitalen Identität*, Düsseldorf, 22–29.
De Grummond, N. T. and Hoff, M. (1982), 'Mirrors of the Mediterranean', in N. T. De Grummond, *A Guide to Etruscan Mirrors*, Tallahassee, 52–58.
De Puma, R. D. (2013), 'Mirrors in art and society', in J. M. Turfa (ed.), *The Etruscan World*, London and New York, 1041–1067.
Dimitropoulos, D. (1996), 'Στοιχεία για τον οικιακό εξοπλισμό στα χρόνια της οθωμανικής κυριαρχίας: η περίπτωση του καθρέφτη', *Τα ιστορικά* 13, No. 24–35, 37–62.
Eco, U. (1984), *Semiotics and the Philosophy of Language*, Indianapolis.
Eco, U. (1993), *Über Spiegel und andere Phänomene*, Munich.
Edgerton, S. Y. (2009), *The Mirror, the Window, and the Telescope. How Renaissance Linear Perspective Changed Our Vision of the Universe*, Ithaca, NY.
Eler, A. (2017), *The Selfie Generation*, New York.
Etheridge, K. (2016), *Dynamic Reflections: Mirrors in the Poetic and Visual Culture of Paris from 1850 to 1900*, Lincoln College, PhD Thesis.
Fausing, B. (2015), 'Self-media: The self, the face, the media and the selfies', *Triade* 3(1): 100–119.
Foucault, P. M. (1986), 'Of other spaces', *Diacritics* 16(1): 22–27 (English translation of 'Des espaces autres').

Bibliography

Frelick, N. M. (ed.) (2016), *The Mirror in Medieval and Early Modern Culture: Specular Reflections*, Turnhout.
Gessmann, G. (1905), *Katechismus der Wahrsagerkünste*, Berlin.
Gilson, S. A. (2000), *Medieval Optics and Theories of Light in the Works of Dante*, Lewiston, NY.
Gojny, T., Kürzinger, K. and Schwarz, S. (eds) (2016), *Selfie – I Like It: Anthropologische und ethische Implikationen digitaler Selbstinszenierung*, Stuttgart.
Grabes, H. (1982), *The Mutable Glass: Mirror-Imagery in Titles and Texts of the Middle Ages and the English Renaissance*, Cambridge and New York.
Hockney, D. (2001), *Secret Knowledge: Rediscovering the Lost Techniques of the Old Masters*, London.
Hockney, D. and Falco, Ch. M. (2000), 'Optical insights into Renaissance art', *Optics and Photonics News* 11: 52–59.
Ilardi, V. (2007), *Renaissance Vision from Spectacles to Telescopes*, Philadelphia, PA.
Jonsson, F. M. (1995), *Le Miroir, naissance d'un genre littéraire*, Paris.
Kaplanis, T. (2001), 'Women in the looking-glass, The philogynous Dapontes (1713–1784) within the misogynous tradition of the Middle Ages', *Comparaison* 12: 48–70.
Koukoules, Ph. (1952), *Βυζαντινῶν Βίος καὶ πολιτισμός*, Vols 4 and 5, Athens.
Koukoules, Ph. (1957), *Βυζαντινῶν Βίος*, Vol. AII, Athens, 155–226.
Lacan, J. (1966), 'Le stade du miroir comme formateur de la fonction du Je telle qu'elle nous est révélée dans l'expérience psychanalytique', in J. Lacan, *Écrits*, Paris, 93–100.
Lejeune, A. (1957), *Recherches sur la catoptrique grecque*, Mémoires de l'Académie Royale de Belgique: Classe des lettres et des sciences morales et politiques 52.2, Brussels.
Lindberg, D. C. (1975), *A Catalogue of Medieval and Renaissance Optical Manuscripts*, Toronto.
Lindberg, D. C. (1976), *Theories of Vision from al-Kindi to Kepler*, London.
Lindberg, D. C. (1983), *Studies in the History of Medieval Optics*, London.
Mabille, P. (1938), 'Miroirs', *Minotaure* 11: 14–18, 66.
Mabille, P. (1940), *Le miroir du merveilleux*, Paris.
MacFarlane, A. and Martin, G. (2002), *Glass: A World History*, Chicago.
McCarty, W. (1989), 'The shape of the mirror: Metaphorical catoptrics in Classical literature', *Arethusa* 22: 161–195.
Melchior-Bonnet, S. (2001), *The Mirror: A History*, trans. Katharine H. Jewett; with a Preface by Jean Delumeau, New York and London.
Nolan, E. P. (1990), *Now Through a Glass Darkly: Specular Images of Being and Knowing from Virgil to Chaucer*, Ann Arbor, MI.
Pendergrast, M. (2003), *Mirror Mirror: A History of the Human Love Affair with Reflection*, New York.
Pendergrast, M. (2008), 'Mirror mirror: A historical and psychological overview', in M. Anderson (ed.), *The Book of the Mirror: An Interdisciplinary Collection Exploring the Cultural Story of the Mirror*, Newcastle, 1–15.
Politis, N. G. (1975), 'Βυζαντιναί παραδόσεις', *Λαογραφικά σύμμεικτα* 2: 23–27.
Reinle, Ch. and Winkel, H. (eds) (2011), *Historische Exempla in Fürstenspiegeln und Fürstenlehren*, Frankfurt am Main.
Rorty, R. (1979), *Philosophy and the Mirror of Nature*, Princeton, NJ.
Schulte, J. M. (1999), *Speculum regis. Studien zur Fürstenspiegel-Literatur in der griechisch-römischen Antike*, Hamburg.
Simon, G. (1988), *Le regard, l'être et l'apparence dans l'optique de l'antiquité*, Paris.
Smith, A. M. (2014), *From Sight to Light: The Passage from Ancient to Modern Optics*, Chicago.
Stacey, P. (2007), *Roman Monarchy and the Renaissance Prince*, Cambridge.
Taylor, R. (2008), *The Moral Mirror of Roman Art*, Cambridge.
Tuczay, Ch. (2012), *Kulturgeschichte der Mittelalterlichen Wahrsagerei*, Berlin.
Ulrich, J. P. (2016), *Platonic Reflections in Apuleius*, University of Pennsylvania, PhD Thesis.

Vernant, J.-P. and Frontisi-Ducroux, F. (1997), *Dans l'Sil du miroir*, Paris.
Werness, H. B. (2009), *The Symbolism of Mirrors in Art from Ancient Times to the Present*, Lewiston, NY.

Chapter 1

Asmis, E. (1986), '"Psychagogia" in Plato's "Phaedrus"', *Illinois Classical Studies* 11(1/2): 153–72.
Bachvarova, M. R. (2012), 'The transmission of liver divination from East to West', *SMEA* 54: 143–64.
Burkert, W. (1992), *The Orientalizing Revolution: Near Eastern Influence on Greek Culture in the Early Archaic Age*, Cambridge.
Cain, R. B.. (2012), 'Plato on Mimesis and Mirrors', *Philosophy and Literature* 36(1): 187–95.
Charbonneaux, J. (1958), *Les bronzes grecs*, Paris.
Collins, D. (2008), 'Mapping the entrails: The practice of Greek hepatoscopy', *American Journal of Philology* 129(3): 319–45.
Congdon, L. O. K. (1985), 'Greek mirrors', *Notes in the History of Art*, 4(2/3) (Winter/Spring): 19–25.
Cornford, F. M. (1937), *Plato's Cosmology: The Timaeus of Plato*, London.
Durand, J-L. and Lissarrague, F. (1979), 'Les entrailles de la cite', *Héphaistos* I: 92–108.
Frontisi-Ducroux, F. and Vernant, J-P. (1997), *Dans l'oeil du miroir*, Paris.
Grummond, N. T. de (2002), 'Mirrors, marriage, and mysteries', *Journal of Roman Archaeology Supplementary Series* 47: 63–85.
Halliday, W. R. (1913), *Greek Divination: A Study of its Methods and Principles*, London.
Jastrow, M. (1907), 'The liver in antiquity and the beginnings of anatomy', *Transactions of the College of Physicians of Philadelphia* 29: 117–38.
Johansen, T. K. (2004), *Plato's Natural Philosophy: A Study of the Timaeus-Critias*, Cambridge.
Lamb, W. (1969), *Greek and Roman Bronzes*, New York.
Lloyd, G. E. R. (1987), *The Revolutions of Wisdom: Studies in the Claims and Practice of Ancient Greek Science*, Berkeley.
Loraux, N. (1987), *Tragic Ways of killing a Woman*. Cambridge, MA.
Lorenz, H. (2006), *The Brute Within: Appetitive Desire in Plato and Aristotle*, Oxford.
Netz, R. and Squire M. (2016) 'Sight and the perspectives of mathematics: The limits of ancient optics', in M. Squire (ed.), *Sight and the Ancient Senses*, London, 55–67.
Nutton, V. (2004), *Ancient Medicine*, London.
Onians, R. B. (1954), *The Origins of European Thought about the Body, the Mind, the Soul, the World, Time, and Fate*, Cambridge.
Rudolph, K. (2016), 'Sight and the Presocratics: Approaches to visual perception in early Greek philosophy', in M. Squire (ed.), *Sight and the Ancient Senses*, London, 36–53.
Sheppard, A. (2003), 'The mirror of the imagination: The influence of Timaeus 70eff.', *Bulletin of the Institute of Classical Studies* 46(S78): 203–12.
Shirazi, A. (2017), *The Mirror and the Senses: Reflection and Perception in Classical Greek Thought*, Dissertation, Stanford University.
Simon, G. (1988), *Le regard, l'être, et l'apparence dans l'optique de l'antiquité*, Paris.
Taylor, A. E. (1928), *A Commentary on Plato's Timaeus*, Oxford.
Tedlock, D. (1993), *Breath on the Mirror: Mythic Voices and Visions of the Living Maya*, San Francisco.
Thulin, Carl (1906), *Die Götter des Martianus Capella und der Bronzeleber von Piacenza*, Gieszen.
Van der Meer, L. B. (1987), *The Bronze Liver of Piacenza: Analysis of a Polytheistic Structure*, Amsterdam.

Bibliography

Chapter 2

Avotins, I. (1980), 'Alexander of Aphrodisias on vision in the atomists', *Classical Quarterly* 20: 429–54.
Berryman, S. (2012), '"It makes no difference": Optics and natural philosophy in Late Antiquity', *Apeiron* 45: 201–20.
Bruns, I. (ed.) (1887), 'Alexandri Aphrodisiensis de anima libri cum mantissa', in *Alexandri Aphrodisiensis praeter commentaria scripta minora* (CAG Suppl. Arist. 2.1), Berlin.
Burnyeat, M. (1992), 'Is an Aristotelian philosophy of mind still credible?' A Draft, in M. Nussbaum and A. Oksenberg Rorty (eds), *Essays on Aristotle's De anima*, Oxford, 15–26.
Burnyeat, M. (1995), 'How much happens when Aristotle sees red and hears middle C? Remarks on De anima 2.7–8', in M. Nussbaum and A. Oksenberg Rorty (eds), *Essays on Aristotle's De anima* (p'back edn), Oxford, 421–34.
Casati, R. (2012), 'Mirrors, illusions and epistemic innocence, in C. Calabi (ed.), *Perceptual Illusions. Philosophical and Psychological Essays*, London, 192–201.
Caston, V. (2005), 'The spirit and the letter: Aristotle on perception, in R. Salles (ed.), *Metaphysics, Soul, and Ethics in Ancient Thought*, Oxford, 245–320.
Caston, V. (2012), *Alexander of Aphrodisias: On the Soul I*, London.
Crampton, E. A. (2016), *Messengers, Mirrors and Light. Alexander of Aphrodisias on Visual Perception*, PhD dissertation, UCL.
Dooley, W. E. (1993), *Alexander of Aphrodisias: On Aristotle's Metaphysics 5*, London.
Duncombe, M. (2015), 'Aristotle's two accounts of relatives in Categories 7', *Phronesis* 60: 436–61.
Fotinis, A. P. (1979), *The De anima of Alexander of Aphrodisias*, Washington, DC.
Hahm, D. (1978), 'Early Hellenistic theories of vision and the perception of colour', in P. K. Machamer and R. G. Turnbull (eds), *Studies in Perception*, Columbus, OH, 60–95.
Harrari, O. (2011), 'The unity of Aristotle's category of relatives', *Classical Quarterly* 61: 521–37.
Hayduck, M. (ed.) (1891), *Alexandri Aphrodisiensis in Aristotelis metaphysica commentaria* (CAG 1), Berlin.
Ierodiakonou, K. (2018), 'Aristotle and Alexander of Aphrodisias on colour', in B. Bydén and F. Radovic (eds), *The Parva naturalia in Greek, Arabic and Latin Aristotelianism: Supplementing the Science of the Soul*, Darmstadt, 77–90.
Ierodiakonou, K. (forthcoming), 'Two puzzles in post-Aristotelian theories of vision', in B. G. Glenney and J. F. Pereira da Silva (eds), *History and Philosophy of Perception*, Oxford.
Ingenkamp, H. G. (1971), 'Zur stoischen Lehre vom Sehen', *Rheinisches Museum* 114: 240–46.
Lee, E. (1978), 'The sense of an object: Epicurus on seeing and hearing', in P. K. Machamer and R. G. Turnbull (eds), *Studies in Perception*, Columbus, OH, 27–59.
Long, A. A. and D. N. Sedley (1987), *The Hellenistic Philosophers* (2 vols), Cambridge.
Lorenz, H. (2007), 'The assimilation of sense to sense-object in Aristotle', *Oxford Studies in Ancient Philosophy* 33: 179–220.
Løkke, H. (2008), 'The Stoics on sense-perception', in S. Knuuttila and P. Kärkkäinen (eds), *Theories of Perception in Medieval and Early Modern Philosophy*, Dordrecht, 35–46.
Mugler, Ch. (1957), 'hexis, schesis et schēma chez Platon', *Revue des Etudes Grecques* 70: 72–92.
Sambursky, S. (1959), *Physics of the Stoics*, New York.
Sharples, R. W. (2002), 'Some problems in Lucretius' account of vision', *Leeds International Classical Studies* 1: 1–11.
Sharples, R. W. (2004a), *Alexander of Aphrodisias: Supplement to On the Soul*, London.
Sharples, R. W. (2004b), 'Alexander of Aphrodisias: What is a *Mantissa*?', in P. Adamson, H. Balthussen and M. Stone (eds), *Philosophy, Science and Exegesis in Greek Arabic and Latin Commentaries*, London, 51–69.
Sharples, R. W. (2005), 'Alexander of Aphrodisias on the nature and location of vision', in R. Salles (ed.), *Metaphysics, Soul, and Ethics in Ancient Thought*, Oxford, 345–62.

Sharples, R. W. (ed.) (2008), *Alexandri Aphrodisiensis de anima libri mantissa*, Berlin.
Sedely, D. (2002), 'Aristotelian relativities', in M. Canto-Sperber and P. Pellegrin (eds), *Le style de la pensé. Recueil de textes en hommage à Jacques Brunschwig*, Paris, 324–52.
Sorabji, R. (1991), 'From Aristotle to Brentano: the development of the concept of intentionality', *Oxford Studies in Ancient Philosophy*, suppl. vol.: 227–59.
Sorabji, R. (1992), 'Intentionality and physiological processes: Aristotle's theory of sense-perception', in M. Nussbaum and A. Oksenberg Rorty (eds), *Essays on Aristotle's De anima*, Oxford, 195–225.
Sorabji, R. (2005), 'Aristotle on sensory processes and intentionality', in D. Perler (ed.), *Ancient and Medieval Theories of Intentionality*, Leiden, 49–61.
Todd, R. B. (1974), 'ΣΥΝΕΝΤΑΣΙΣ and the Stoic theory of perception', *Grazer Beiträge* 2: 251–61.
Towey, A. (2000), *Alexander of Aphrodisias: On Aristotle on Sense Perception*, London.
Wendland, P. (ed.) (1901), *Alexandri Aphrodisiensis in librum de sensu commentarium* (CAG 3.1), Berlin.

Chapter 3

Addey, C. (2007), 'Mirrors and divination: Catoptromancy, oracles and Earth goddesses in antiquity', in M. Anderson (ed.), *The Book of the Mirror*, Cambridge, 33–46.
Algra, K. (1999), 'Walking images: Epicurean catoptrics in Lucretius *DRN* IV 318–323', *Elenchos* 20: 359–79.
Arrighetti, G. (1973), *Epicuro, opere*, 2nd edn, Turin.
Avotins, I. (1980), 'Alexander of Aphrodisias on vision in the atomists', *CQ* 30: 429–54.
Bailey, C. (1947), *Titi Lucreti Cari De rerum natura Libri Sex*, 3 vols, Oxford.
Bruns, I. (1887), *Alexandri Aphrodisiensis praeter commentaria scripta minora. De anima liber cum mantissa* (CIAG. Supplementum aristotelicum 2.1), Berlin.
Císar, K. (2001), 'Epicurean epistemology in Lucretius' *De rerum natura* IV 1–822', *LF* 124(1–2): 1–54.
Clay, D. (1983), *Lucretius and Epicurus*, Ithaca, NY.
de Grummond, N. T. (2002), 'Mirrors, marriage and mysteries', *Journal of Roman Archaeology* Suppl 81: 63–85.
Delatte, A. (1932), *La Catoptromancie grecque et ses derives*, Liège and Paris.
Dillon, M. (2017), *Omens and Oracles in Ancient Greece: Divination in Ancient Greece*, London and New York.
Fowler, D. P. (2002), *Lucretius on Atomic Motion: A Commentary on Lucretius De rerum natura 2.1–332*, Oxford.
Garani, M. (2007), *Empedocles redivivus: Poetry and Analogy in Lucretius*, New York and London.
Godwin, J. (1986), *Lucretius De rerum natura IV*, Warminster.
Hine, H. M. (2010), *Lucius Annaeus Seneca: Natural Questions. The Complete Works of Lucius Annaeus Seneca*, Chicago, IL and London.
Holwerda, D. (1977), *Scholia in Aristophanem. Pars I. Prolegomena de Comoedia scholia in Acharnenses, Equites, Nubes (Fasc. III 1). Scholia Vetera in Nubes*, Gröningen.
Hunink, V. J. C. (1997), *Apuleius of Madauros, Pro se de magia (Apologia)*, edited with a commentary (2 vols), Amsterdam.
Jones, A. (2001), 'Pseudo-Ptolemy *De Speculis*', *Sciamus* 2 (Sources and Commentaries in Exact Sciences 2), 145–86.
Jones, C. P. (2017), *Apuleius. Apologia. Florida. De Deo Socratis*, Loeb Classical Library 534, Cambridge, MA.

Bibliography

Kenney E. J. (2014), *Lucretius:* De Rerum Natura *Book III*, 2nd edn (1st edn 1971), Cambridge.
Koenen, M. H. (1996), 'Latusculana disputatio: Lucretius, *De rerum natura* IV 311–317 in its Philosophical context, especially its relation to Plato, *Timaeus* 46 b6–c2', in G. Giannantoni and M. Gigante (eds), *Epicureismo greco e romano*, Naples, 823–40.
Lloyd, G. E. R. (1982), 'Observational error in later Greek science', in J. Barnes, J. Brunschwig, M. Burnyeat and M. Schofield (eds), *Science and Speculation: Studies in Hellenistic Theory and Practice*, Cambridge and Paris, 128–64.
McCarty, W. (1989), 'The shape of the mirror: Metaphorical catoptrics in Classical literature', *Arethusa* 22: 161–96.
Marković, D. (2008), *The Rhetoric of Explanation in Lucretius'* De rerum natura, *Mnemosyne Suppl.* 294, Leiden.
Munro, H. A. J. (1893), *T. Lucreti Cari De Rerum Natura Libri Sex*, 4th edn rev., 2 vols, London and Cambridge.
Odgen, D. (2001), *Greek and Roman Necromancy*, Princeton, NJ.
Rouse, W. H. D. (1924), *Lucretius*, trans. W. H. D. Rouse (1924); rev. by M. F. Smith (1992), Loeb Classical Library 181, London and Cambridge, MA.
Schindler, C. (2000), *Untersuchungen zu den Gleichnissen im romischen Lehrgedicht: Lucrez, Vergil*, Manilius (*Hypomnemata* 129), Göttingen.
Schmidt, W. and Nix, L. (eds) (1900), *Heronis Alexandrini: Opera quae supersunt omnia, Vol. 2: Mechanica et catoptrica*, Leipzig.
Seaford, R. A. S. (1981), 'The mysteries of Dionysus at Pompeii', in H. W. Stubbs (ed.), *Pegasus: Classical Essays from the University of Exeter*, 52–67.
Sharples, R. (2002), 'Some problems in the theory of vision in *De Rerum Natura* 4', *Leeds International Classical Studies* 1(2).
Smith, M. F. (1993), *Diogenes of Oinoanda: the Epicurean Inscription*, edited with Introduction, Translation, and Notes (La Scuola di Epicuro Collezione di Testi Ercolanesi, Supplemento 1), Naples.
Taylor, R. (2008), *The Moral Mirror of Roman Art*, Cambridge.
Tybjerg, K. (2003), 'Wonder-making and philosophical wonder in Hero of Alexandria', *Studies in History and Philosophy of Science* Part A, 34(3): 443–66.
Tybjerg, K. (2005), 'Hero of Alexandria's mechanical treatises: Between theory and practice', in A. Schürmann (ed.), *Physik/Mechanik*, Stuttgart, 204–26.
Wendland, P. (1901), *Alexandri in Librum De Sensu Commentarium* (*Commentaria in Aristotelem Graeca* 3.1), Berlin.

Chapter 4

Bjørnbo, A. A. and Vogl, S. (1912), *Alkindi, Tideus und Pseudo-Euklid*, Leipzig and Berlin.
Brown, P. (1981), *Chaucer's Visual World: A Study of His Poetry and the Medieval Optical Tradition*, York University, Centre for Medieval Studies.
Burkert, W. (1977), 'Air-imprints or Eidola: Democritus' aetiology of vision', *Illinois Classical Studies* 2: 97–109.
Burnett, C. (2001), 'The coherence of the Arabic-Latin translation program in Toledo in the twelfth century', *Science in Context* 14(1–2): 249–88.
Carruthers, M. J. (2008), *The Book of Memory*, Cambridge.
de Lacy, P. (2005), *Galen: On the Doctrines of Hippocrates and Plato*, Berlin.
Hahm, D. (1978), 'Early Hellenistic theories of vision and the perception of color', in P. K. Machamer and R. G. Turnbull (eds), *Studies in Perception*, Columbus, OH, 60–95.
Haskins, C. H. (1928), *The Renaissance of the Twelfth Century*, Cambridge.

Heiberg, I. L. (1895), *Euclidis Opera omnia. 7, Optica. Opticorum recensio Theonis. Catoptrica. Cum scholiis antiquis*, Lipsiae.
Jones, A. (1994), 'Peripatetic and Euclidean theories of the visual ray', *PHYSIS. Rivista Internazionale di Storia della Scienza* 31(1): 47–76.
Leclerc, L. (1876), *Histoire de la médecine arabe*, Paris.
Lejeune, A. (1989), *L'optique de Claude Ptolemee dans la version latine d'apres l'arabe de l'emir Eugene de Sicile*, Leiden and New York.
Lindberg, D. C. (1975), *A Catalogue of Medieval and Renaissance Optical Manuscripts*, Toronto.
Lindberg, D. C. (1976), *Theories of Vision from al-Kindi to Kepler*, Chicago, IL.
Lindberg, D. C. (1996), *Roger Bacon and the Origins of Perspectiva in the Middle Ages*, Oxford.
Lindsay, W. M. (1913), *Sexti Pompei Festi De Verborum Significatu Quae Supersunt cum Pauli Epitome*, Lipsiae.
Long, A. A. and Sedley, D. N. (1987), *The Hellenistic Philosophers*, Cambridge.
Melchior-Bonnet, S. (2014), *The Mirror*, Oxford and New York.
Meyerhof, M. (1928), *The Book of the Ten Treatises on the Eye Ascribed to Hunain Ibn Is-Hâq (809–877 A.D.)*, Cairo.
Netz, R. and Squire, M. (2015), 'Sight and the perspectives of mathematics: The limits of ancient optics', in M. Squire (ed.), *Sight and the Ancient Senses*, London, 68–84.
Schöne, R. (1897), *Damianos: Schrift über Optik*, Berlin.
Simon, G. (1988), *Le regard l'être et l'apparence dans l'optique de l'antiquité*, Paris.
Smith, A. M. (2015), *From Sight to Light*, Chicago, IL.
Squire, M. (2015), *Sight and the Ancient Senses*, London.
Steinschneider, M. (1886), 'Euklid bei den Arabern. Eine bibliographische Studie', *Zeitschrift für Mathematik und Physik* 31. Hist.-Lit. Abt., 81–110.
Toomer, G. J. (1976), *Diocles on Burning Mirrors*, Berlin, Heidelberg and New York.
van Hoorn, W. (1972), *Ancient and Modern Theories of Visual Perception*, Amsterdam.

Chapter 5

Baratta, G. (2014), 'Gli specchietti votivi in piombo dedicati alla κυρίᾳ ἀγορᾶς', in Á. Martínez Fernández, B. Ortega Villaro, H. Velasco López and H. Zamora Salamanca (eds), *Àgalma. Ofrenda desde la Filología Clásica a Manuel García Teijeiro*, Valladolid, 709–13.
Bettini, M. and Pellizer, E. (2003), *Il mito di Narciso. Immagini e racconti dalla Grecia a oggi*, Turin.
Bonati, I. (2016), *Il lessico dei vasi e dei contenitori greci nei papiri. Specimina per un repertorio lessicale degli angionimi greci*, Berlin and Boston, MA.
Bonner, C. and Darby Nock, A. (1948), 'Neotera', *The Harvard Theological Review* 41(3): 213–15.
Bookidis, N. and Stroud, R. S. (1997), *The Sanctuary of Demeter and Kore: Topography and Architecture*, Princeton, NJ.
Budenz, J. (1858), *Das Suffix kos (ikos, akos, ykos) im griechischen: ein Beitrag zur Wortbildungslehre*, Göttingen.
Carpino, A. (2010), 'Mirrors', in M. Gagarin and E. Fantham (eds), *The Oxford Encyclopedia of Ancient Greece and Rome*, Vol. 4, Oxford, 444–46.
Chantraine, P. (1933), *La formation des noms en grec ancien*, Paris.
Chantraine, P. (1968), *Dictionnaire étymologique de la langue grecque. Histoire des mots*, Paris.
Concannon, C. W. (2017), *Assembling Early Christianity: Trade, Networks, and the Letters of Dionysios of Corinth*, Cambridge.
Congdon, L. O. K. (1981), *Caryatid Mirrors of Ancient Greece: Technical, Stylistic and Historical Considerations of an Archaic and Early Classical Bronze Series*, Mainz.

Bibliography

Congdon, L. O. K. (1985), 'Greek Mirrors', *Notes in the History of Art* 4(2/3): 19–25.
Cooney, J. D. (1973), 'Deluxe toilet objects', *The Bulletin of the Cleveland Museum of Art* 60(7): 215–21.
Darby Nock, A. (1953), 'Neotera, Queen or Goddess?', *Aegyptus* 33(2): 283–96.
Daris, S. (1968), *Spoglio lessicale papirologico*, I, Milan.
de Grummond, N. T. (1981), 'Reflections on the Etruscan mirror', *Archaeology* 34(5): 54–58.
de Grummond, N. T. (1985), 'The Etruscan mirror', *Notes in the History of Art* 4(2/3): 26–35.
de Grummond, N. T. and Hoff, M. (1982), 'Mirrors of the Mediterranean: Greek', in N. T. de Grummond (ed.), *A Guide to Etruscan Mirrors*, Tallahassee, FL, 32–33.
Debrunner, A. (1917), *Griechische Wortbildungslehre*, Heidelberg.
Depauw, M. and Stolk, J. (2015), 'Linguistic variation in Greek papyri. Towards a new tool for quantitative study', *Greek, Roman and Byzantine Studies* 55: 196–220.
Derriks, C. (2001), 'Mirrors', in D. B. Redford (ed.), *The Oxford Encyclopedia of Ancient Egypt*, Vol. 2, Oxford, 419–22.
Evans, T. V. (2010a), 'Identifying the language of the individual in the Zenon archive', in T. V. Evans and D. D. Obbink (eds), *The Language of the Papyri*, Oxford, 51–70.
Evans, T. V. (2010b), 'Standard Koine Greek in third century BC papyri', in T. Gagos (ed.), *Proceedings of the Twenty-Fifth International Congress of Papyrology (Ann Arbor 2007)*, Ann Arbor, MI, 197–206.
Frisk, H. (1970), *Griechisches Etymologisches Wörterbuch. Band II*, Heidelberg.
Frontisi-Ducroux, F. and Vernant, J. P. (1997), *Dans l'œil du miroir*, Paris.
Gignac, F. T. (1976), *A Grammar of the Greek Papyri of the Roman and Byzantine Periods, I (Phonology)*, Milan.
Grabes, H. (1982), *The Mutable Glass: Mirror-imagery in Titles and Texts of the Middle Ages and English Renaissance*, Cambridge.
Grassi, T. (1926), *Le liste templari nell'Egitto greco-romano secondo i papiri*, Milan.
Harrop, J. H. (1962), 'A Christian letter of commendation', *The Journal of Egyptian Archaeology* 48: 132–40.
Heath, S. (2006), 'A box mirror made from two antinous medallions of Smyrna', *American Journal of Numismatics* 18: 63–74.
Lee, A. D. (2000), *Pagans and Christians in Late Antiquity: A Sourcebook*, London and New York.
Lee, M. M. (2015), *Body, Dress, and Identity in Ancient Greece*, Cambridge.
Lee, M. M. (2017), 'The gendered economics of Greek bronze mirrors: Reflections on reciprocity and feminine agency', *Arethusa* 50(2): 143–68.
Leiwo, M. and Halla-Aho, H. (2002), 'A marriage contract: Aspects of Latin-Greek language contact (P. Mich. VII 434 and P. Ryl. IV 612 = ChLA IV 249)', *Mnemosyne* 55(5): 560–80.
Litinas, N. (2015), 'Inscription on a mirror', *Zeitschrift für Papyrologie und Epigraphik* 194, 158.
McCarty, W. (1989), 'The shape of the mirror: Metaphorical catoptrics in Classical literature', *Arethusa* 22(2): 161–95.
McGing, B. C. (1987), 'A papyrus listing stolen(?) objects, in the Library of Trinity College Dublin', *Hermathena* 143: 72–81.
Mastrocinque, A. (2012), 'Neotera and her iconography', in A. Mastrocinque and C. Giuffrè Scibona (eds), *Demeter, Isis, Vesta, and Cybele. Studies in Greek and Roman Religion in Honour of Giulia Sfameni Gasparro*, Stuttgart, 105–18.
Merker, G. S. (2003), 'An ivory mirror handle from Corinth', *Eretz-Israel: Archaeological, Historical and Geographical Studies. Hayim and Miriam Tadmor Volume*, Jerusalem, 129–35.
Milne, J. S. (1907), *Surgical Instruments in Greek and Roman Times*, Oxford.
Mitthof, F. (2005), 'Bemerkungen zu Papyri XVIII <Korr. Tyche>', *Tyche* 20: 259–61.
Økland, J. (2004), *Women in Their Place: Paul and the Corinthian Discourse of Gender and Sanctuary Space*, London and New York.

Bibliography

Pellizer, E. (1984), 'L'eco, lo specchio e la reciprocità amorosa. Una lettura del tema di Narciso', *Quaderni Urbinati di Cultura Classica* 17(2): 21-35.

Pellizer, E. (1991), 'Narciso e le figure della dualità', in M. Bettini (ed.), *La maschera, il doppio e il ritratto: strategie dell'identità*, Roma, 13-29.

Preisendanz, K. (1932), 'Review to S. Eitrem-L. Amundsen (1931), Papyri Osloenses II, Oslo: J. Dybwad', *Philologische Wochenschrift* 52: 227-34.

Reggiani, N. (2017), *Digital Papyrology I: Tools, Methods and Trends*, Berlin and Boston, MA.

Reggiani, N. (2018a), 'The *Corpus of the Greek Medical Papyri* and a New Concept of Digital Critical Edition', in N. Reggiani (ed.), *Digital Papyrology II: Case Studies on the Digital Edition of Ancient Greek Papyri*. Berlin and Boston, MA, 3-61.

Reggiani, N. (2018b), 'Linguistic and philological variants in the Papyri: A reconsideration in light of the digitization of the Greek Medical Papyri', in N. Reggiani (ed.), *Greek Medical Papyri: Text, Context, Hypertext. Proceedings of the DIGMEDTEXT Final Conference (Parma, 2-4 November 2016)*, Berlin and Boston, MA, forthcoming.

Reggiani, N. (2019), 'The digital edition of ancient sources as a further step in the textual transmission', in A. Novokhatko (ed.), *Proceedings of the Workshop 'Digital Classics III: Re-thinking Text Analysis' (Heidelberg, 11-13 May 2017)*, forthcoming.

Richter, G. (1938), 'An archaic Greek mirror', *American Journal of Archaeology* 42(3): 337-44.

Russo, S. (1999a), *I gioielli nei papiri di età greco-romana*, Florence.

Russo, S. (1999b), 'SPP XX 46r e gli ἐνέχυρα dei papiri di età greco-romana', *Comunicazioni dell'Istituto Papirologico 'G. Vitelli'* 3: 87-105.

Russo, S. (2005), 'Gli oggetti metallici nei παράφερνα', *Münstersche Beiträge zur Antiken Handelsgeschichte* 24: 213-41.

Russo, S. (2006), 'Note e correzioni a papiri documentari', *Zeitschrift für Papyrologie und Epigraphik* 155: 191-9.

Schefold, K. (1940), 'Griechische Spiegel', *Die Antike* 16: 11-37.

Scherer, J. (1976), 'Lettre d'Amadokos à Kléon', in A. E. Hanson (ed.), *Collectanea Papyrologica. Texts Published in Honor of H.C. Youtie*, I, Bonn, 79-89 (and Plate IV).

Schwarzmeier, A. (1993), 'A Greek box mirror in the Cleveland Museum of Art', *The Bulletin of the Cleveland Museum of Art* 80(9): 354-67.

Scholl, R. (1990), *Corpus der ptolemäischen Sklaventexte*, II, Stuttgart.

Stolk, J. V. (2018), 'Encoding linguistic variation in Greek documentary papyri. The past, present and future of editorial regularization', in N. Reggiani (ed.), *Digital Papyrology II: Case Studies on the Digital Edition of Ancient Greek Papyri*, Berlin and Boston, MA, 119-37.

Tsomis, G. (1999), *Zusammenschau der Frühgriechischen Monodischen Melik: Alkaios, Sappho, Anakreon*, Stuttgart.

Vandorpe, K. (1997), 'Seals in and on the Papyri of Greco-Roman and Byzantine Egypt', in M. F. Boussac and A. Invernizzi (eds), *Archives et Sceaux du monde hellénistique, Actes du colloque de Turin, Villa Gualino, 13-16 janvier 1993 (Bulletin de Correspondance Hellénique, Suppl. 29)*, Paris, 231-91.

Wunderlich, S. A. (1951), 'A Greek bronze mirror', *The Bulletin of the Cleveland Museum of Art* 38(1): 4-6.

Yiftach-Firanko, U. (2003), *Marriage and Marital Arrangements. A History of the Greek Marriage Document in Egypt. 4th century BCE-4th century CE*, Munich.

Chapter 6

Ambrosini, L. (ed.) (2012), *CSE Italia 7*, I, 1 Roma - Museo Nazionale Romano, Museo delle Antichità Etrusche e Italiche, Sapienza - Università di Roma, Collezione Gorga, Rome.

Bibliography

Aragosti, A., Cosci, P., Cotrozzi, A. M., Fantuzzi, M., and Lechi, F. (1985), *Gaio Plinio Secondo, Storia Naturale*, Vol. III, Libri XX–XXVII, Turin.

Beck, L. Y. (2005), *Pedanius Dioscorides of Anazarbus, De materia medica*, Altertumswissenschaftliche Texte und Studien, Vol. 38, Hildesheim, Zurich and New York.

Beschi, L. and Musti, D. (1982), *Pausania*, Guida della Grecia: libro I. L'Attica, Milan.

Carpino, A. (2009), 'Dueling Warriors on two Etruscan bronze mirrors from the fifth century BCE', in S. Bell and H. Nagy (eds), *New Perspectives on Etruria and Early Rome in Honor of Richard Daniel De Puma*, Madison, WI, 182–97.

Càssola, F. (1975), *Inni Omerici*, Verona.

Castagnoli, F. (1959), *Dedica arcaica lavinate a Castore e Polluce. Studi e materiali di storia delle religioni* 30: 109–117.

Castagnoli, F. (1983), 'L'introduzione del culto dei Dioscuri nel Lazio'. *Storia Romana* 31: 3–12.

Cateni, G. (2002), 'Nuovi contributi alla cronologia degli specchi con «Lasa» e «Dioscuri»', in A. Emiliozzi and A. Maggiani (eds), *Caelatores, incisori di specchi e ciste tra Lazio ed Etruria*, Atti della giornata di studio (Roma 2001), Rome, 41–57.

Colonna, G. (1996), 'Il Dokanon, il culto dei Dioscuri e gli aspetti ellenizzanti della religione dei morti nell'Etruria tardo arcaica', in L. Bacchielli and M. Bonanno Aravantinos (eds), *Scritti di antichità in memoria di Sandro Stucchi*, Studi Miscellanei 29: 165–84.

Colonna, G. (2005), 'Il Dokanon, il culto dei Dioscuri e gli aspetti ellenizzanti della religione dei morti nell'Etruria tardo arcaica', in *Italia ante romanum imperium. Scritti di antichità etrusche, italiche e romane (1958-1998)*, Pisa and Rome, 2085–2111.

Cristofani, M. (1985a), 'Il cosiddetto specchio di Tarchon: un recupero e una nuova lettura', *Prospettiva* 41: 4–20.

Cristofani, M. (1985b), 'Faone, la testa di Orfeo e l'immaginario femminile', *Prospettiva* 42: 2–12.

CSE, *Corpus Speculorum Etruscorum*.

de Grummond, N. T. (1991), 'Etruscan Twins and Mirror Images: The Dioskouroi at the Door', *Yale University Art Gallery Bulletin* 10: 10–31.

De Puma, R. D. (1973), 'The Dioskouroi on Four Etruscan Mirrors in Midwestern Collections', *Studi Etruschi* 41: 159–70.

De Puma, R. D. (1982), 'Greek Gods and Heroes on Etruscan Mirrors', in N. T. de Grummond (ed.), *A Guide to Etruscan Mirrors*, Tallahassee, FL, 89–100.

De Puma, R. D. (2013), 'Mirrors in art and society', in J. MacIntosh Turfa (ed.), *The Etruscan World*, London and New York, 1041–64.

Della Fina, G. M. (2002), 'La «Kranzspiegelgruppe». Criteri per la definizione delle officine»', in A. Emiliozzi and A. Maggiani (eds), *Caelatores. Incisori di specchi e ciste tra Lazio ed Etruria*, Atti della giornata di studio (Roma 2001), Rome, 51–58.

Edmonds, J. M. (1912), *The Greek Bucolic Poets*, London and New York.

Edmonds, J. M. (1922), *Lyra Graeca: Being the Remains of All the Greek Lyric Poets from Eumelus to Timotheus Excepting Pindar*, Vol. I, London and New York.

Evelyn-White, H. G. (1914), *Hesiod, the Homeric hymns, and Homerica*, London and New York.

Facchetti, G. (2015), *Tinas Cliniiaras, Annali del Dipartimento di Studi Letterari, Linguistici e Comparati. Sezione Linguistica, Università degli Studi di Napoli 'L'Orientale'*, 4: 141–182.

Fileni, M. G. (2015), 'Atena e la lampada: un passo "illuminante" dell'Odissea' (19: 31-43), in M. E. Micheli and A. Santinucci (eds), *Lumina, Convegno Internazionale di Studi*, Urbino 5–7 giugno 2013, Pisa, 109–25.

Gilotta, F. (1992), 'Una cista, il trionfo o la morte. Su alcuni aspetti di iconografie celebrative etrusco-italiche'. *Bollettino d'Arte del Ministero per i beni culturali e ambientali*, 74–75, 77–84.

Gilotta, F. (2007), in M. P. Baglione and F. Gilotta (eds), *CSE*, Italia, 6.1: Roma, Museo Nazionale Etrusco di Villa Giulia, Rome, 96–97.

Godley A. D. (1920), *Herodotus*, with an English translation by A. D. Godley. Books I and II, London and New York.

Guarducci, M. (1984), 'Le insegne dei Dioscuri', *Archeologia Classica XXXVI*, 133–54.
Izzet, I. (1998), 'Holding a mirror to Etruscan gender', in R. D. Whitehouse (ed.), *Gender and Italian Archaeology. Challenging the Stereotypes*, Accordia Research Institute and Institute of Archaeology, London, 95–126.
Jones, H. L. (1923), *The Geography of Strabo*, Vol. II, London and Cambridge, MA.
Lambrechts, R. (1987), *CSE* Belgique, 1, Rome, 47–49.
Maggiani, A. (2002), 'Nel mondo degli specchi etruschi', in A. Emiliozzi and A. Maggiani (eds), *Caelatores. Incisori di specchi e ciste tra Lazio ed Etruria*, Atti della giornata di studio (Roma 2001), Rome, 7–22.
Mangani, E. (1985), 'Le fabbriche di specchi nell'Etruria settentrionale', *Bollettino d'Arte del Ministero per i beni culturali e ambientali*, 21–40.
Mangani, E. (2002), 'Nuovi strumenti critici per la definizione delle officine degli incisori etruschi di specchi', in A. Emiliozzi and A. Maggiani (eds), *Caelatores, incisori di specchi e ciste tra Lazio ed Etruria*, Atti della giornata di studio (Roma 2001), Rome, 23–39.
Mansuelli, G. A. (1943), 'Materiali per un supplemento al «corpus» degli specchi etruschi figurati', *Studi Etruschi XVII*, 487–521.
Mansuelli, G. A. (1946–47), 'Gli specchi figurati etruschi', *Studi Etruschi XIX*, 9–137.
Massa-Pairault, H. F. (1985), *Recherches sur l'art et l'artisanat étrusco-italiques à l'époque hellénistique*, Rome.
Mavleev, J. (1990), 'Der Meister des Parisurteils I in der Ermitage', in H. Heres and M. Kunze (eds), *Die Welt der Etrusker: archaologische Denkmaler aus Museen der sozialistischen Lander: Staatliche Museen zu Berlin, Haupstadt der DDR Altes Museum, vom 4. Oktober bis 30. Dezember 1988*, Berlin, 175–77.
Moscati, P. (1986), *Analisi statistiche multivariate sugli specchi etruschi*, Rome.
Moullou, D. (2011), 'Lighting the fire and illumination in Antiquity', in I. Motsianos and E. Bintsi (eds), *Lighting the Fire and Illumination in Antiquity*, Catalogue of the exhibition, Thessaloniki, Folklife and Ethnological Museum of Macedonia-Thrace, 31 October 2011–11 June 2012, Thessaloniki, 45–57.
Naso, A. (2003), *I Bronzi Etruschi e Italici del Römisch-Germanisches Zentralmuseum*, Mainz.
Platt, V. J. (2018), 'Double vision: Epiphanies of the Dioscuri in Classical antiquity', *Archiv für Religionsgeschichte* 20(1): 229–56.
Rallo, A. (1974), *Lasa, Iconografia e esegesi*, Florence.
Rebuffat Emmanuel, D. (1984), 'Typologie général du miroir étrusque à manche massif', *Revue Archéologique* 2: 195–226.
Romeo, A. (1937), 'La pianta da lumini', *Annali della Facoltà di Agraria della Regia Università di Napoli, XV*, 155–59.
Salskov Roberts, H. (1983), 'Later Etruscan mirrors. Evidence for dating from recent excavations', *Analecta Romana Instituti Danici XII*, 31–54.
Sassatelli, G. (1993), 'Rappresentazioni di giochi atletici in monumenti funerari di area padana', in *Spectacles sportifs et scéniques dans le monde étrusco-italique* (Actes de la table ronde de Rome, 3–4 mai 1991). *Collection de l'École française de Rome* 172, 45–67.
Szilágyi, J. G. (1994), 'Discorso sul metodo. Contributo al problema della classificazione degli specchi tardo-etruschi', in M. Martelli (ed.), *Tyrrhenoi Philotechnoi* (Atti della giornata di studio, Viterbo 1990), Rome, 161–72.
Torelli, M. (1997), *Il rango, il rito e l'immagine: alle origini della rappresentazione storica romana*, Milan.
Valastro Canale, A. (2004), *Isidoro di Siviglia, Etimologie o Origini*, Turin.
Van der Meer F. (2001), 'Decorated Etruscan Stone Sarcophagi. A Chronological and Bibliographical Appendix to R. Herbig', *Babesch Bulletin Antieke Beschaving 76*, 79–100.
Wiman, I. M. B. (1990), *Malstria-Malena. Metals and motifs in Etruscan Mirror Craft*, Gothenburg.

Bibliography

Chapter 7

Adlin, J. (2013), 'Vanities: Art of the dressing table', *The Metropolitan Museum of Art Bulletin*: n.s., 71, no. 2.

Boucher, F. (2009), *Historia del trajeenoccidente. Desdelosorígenes hasta la actualidad*, Barcelona.

Bumke, J. (1991), *Courtly Culture: Literature and Society in the High Middle Ages*, Oakland, CA.

Burns, E. J. (2002), *Courtly Love Undressed. Reading through Clothes in Medieval French Culture*, Pittsburg, PA.

Camille, M. (1998), *The Medieval Art of Love: Objects and Subjects of Desire*, New York.

Capellanus, A., *De Amore, liber secundus*, in http://www.thelatinlibrary.com/capellanus/capellanus2.html

De Lorris, G. and De Meun, J. (1999), *The Romance of the Rose*, ed. and trans. F. Horgan, Oxford.

Frelick, N. (2016), *The Mirror in Medieval and Early Modern Culture: Specular Reflections*, Turnhout.

Frugoni, C. (2010), *Medioevosulnaso. Occhiali, bottoni e altreinvenzionimedieval*, Rome.

Goethe, J. W. V. (1990), *The Sorrows of the Young Werther*, New York.

Greenblatt, S. (2012), *Renaissance Self-Fashioning: From More to Shakespeare*, Chicago, IL.

Grethlein, J. (2016), 'Sight and reflexivity: Theorizing vision in Greek vase-painting', in M. Squire (ed.), *Sight and the Ancient Senses*, Oxford, 85–106.

Günther, J. (2019) 'Bening at his best: Miniatures of jewel-like execution', in https://guenther-rarebooks.com/artworks/categories/1/9444/

Lee, M. M. (2015), *Body, Dress, and Identity in Ancient Greece*, Cambridge.

Le Goff, J. (1988), 'Vestimentary and alimentary codes in Erec et Enide', *The Medieval Imagination*, Chicago, IL, 132–50.

L' Estrange, E. (2008), 'Gazing at Gawain: Reconsidering tournaments, courtly love, and the lady who looks', *Medieval Feminist Forum* 44(2): 74–96.

Melchior-Bonnet, S (2011), *The Mirror: A History*, London.

Mills, N. (1999), *Medieval Artefacts*, Essex.

Neufeld, C. (2013), 'Always accessorize: In defense of scholarly *Cointise*', in E. A. Joy and A. Klosowska (eds), *On style: An Atelier*, New York, 87–110.

Paris, G. (1883), 'Etudes sur les romans de la Table Ronde: Lancelot du Lac, II: Le conte de la charrette', *Romania* 12: 459–534.

Pendergrast, M. (2003), *Mirror, Mirror: A History of The Human Love Affair with Reflection*, New York.

Rebold, J (2009), *Materials, Methods, and Masterpieces of Medieval Art*, Santa Barbara, CA.

Rimell, V. (2006), '*Specular Logics*: Medicamina'. *Ovid's Lovers: Desire, Difference, and the Poetic Imagination*, Cambridge, 41–69.

Root, J. (2011), 'Marvelous crystals, perilous mirrors: *Le Roman De la Rose* and the discontinuity of the Romance subject', *The Romanic Review*, 102(1–2): 65–89.

Sand, A. (2011), 'The fairest of them all: Reflections on some fourteenth-century mirrors', in S. Blick and L. D. Gelfand (eds), *Push Me, Pull You. Imaginative and Emotional Interaction in Late medieval and Renaissance Art, Vol 1*, Leiden, 529–59.

Silver, C. (2017) '19th-Century "Lover's Eye" jewelry was the perfect accessory for secret affairs', *Atlas Obscura*, 15 September, in https://www.atlasobscura.com/articles/lovers-eye-jewelry

Smith, S. L. (2017), 'The Gothic mirror and the female gaze', in J. L. Carroll, A. G. Stewart (eds), *Saints, Sisters, and Sinners. Gender and Northern Art in Medieval and Early Modern Europe*, London, 73–93.

Stewart, S. (2017), *Painted Faces: A Colourful History of Cosmetics*, Stroud, Glos.

Chapter 8

Bettini, M. and Pellizer, E. (2003), *Il mito di Narciso: immagini e racconti dalla Grecia ad oggi*, Turin.
Bonnefoy, Y. (1991), *Mythologies*, Chicago, IL.
Bredbeck, G. (1994), 'Narcissus in the Wilde: Textual cathexis and the historical origins of queer camp', in M. Meyer (ed.), *The Politics and Poetics of Camp*, London, 51–74.
Bruhm, S. (2001), *Reflecting Narcissus: A Queer Aesthetic*, Mineapolis, MN.
Bruhm, S. (1995), 'Taking one to know one: Oscar Wilde and narcissism', *English Studies in Canada*, 21: 170-88.
Butler, S. (2013), 'Beyond Narcissus', in B. Shane and A. Purves (eds), *Synaesthesia and the Ancient Senses*, Oxford and New York, 185–200.
Carman, H. C. (2014), *Leon Battista Alberti and Nicholas Cusanus: Towards an Epistemology of Vision for Italian Renaissance Art and Culture*, London.
Cohen, Ed. (1987), 'Writing gone Wilde: Homoerotic desire in the closet of representation', *PMLA* 102(5): 801–13.
Constantine, P., Hadas, R. et al. (2010), *The Greek Poets: Homer to the Present*, New York.
Dickson, R. D. (1983), '"In a mirror that mirrors the soul": Masks and mirrors in *Dorian Gray*', *English Literature in Transition* 26(1): 5–15.
Dollimore, J. (1987), 'Different desires: Subjectivity and transgression in Wilde and Gide', in R. Gagnier (ed.), *Critical Essays on Oscar Wilde*, New York, 48–67.
Dundas, J. (1993), *Pencils Rhetorique: Renaissance Poets and the Art of Painting*, Newark, DE.
Ellis, H. (1927), 'The conception of narcissism', *Psychoanalytic Review* 14: 129–53.
Fong, B. and Beckson, K. (eds) (2000), *The Complete Works of Oscar Wilde. Volume 1: Poems and Poems in Prose*, Oxford.
Frankel, N. (ed.) (2011), *Oscar Wilde. The Uncensored Picture of Dorian Gray*, Harvard, MA.
Freud, S. (1957), 'On narcissism: An introduction', in J. Strachey (ed.), *The Standard Edition of the Complete Psychological Works. Vol 14*, London, 67–102.
Hart-Davis, R. (ed.) (1962), *The Letters of Oscar Wilde*, London.
Janes, D. (2014), 'Oscar Wilde, sodomy, and mental illness in late Victorian England', *Journal of the History of Sexuality* 23(1): 79–95.
Kenney, J. E. (ed.) (2009), *Ovid. Metamorphoses*, trans. A. D. Melville, Oxford.
Kosofsky-Sedgewick, E. (1985), *Between Men: English Literature and Male Homosocial Desire* (Gender and Culture), New York.
Kosofsky-Sedgewick, E. (1990), *Epistemology of the Closet*, Berkeley, CA.
Lacan, J. (1977), 'The mirror stage as formative of the function of the I', in A. Sheridan (ed. and trans.), *Écrits: A Selection*, New York, 1–7.
Lawrence, A. (1991), *Echo and Narcissus. Women's Voices in Classical Hollywood Cinema*, Berkeley, CA.
McCormack, J. (1997), 'Wilde's fiction(s)', in P. Raby (ed.), *The Cambridge Companion to Oscar Wilde*, Cambridge, 96–117.
McMahon, A. P. (trans.) (1956), *Leonardo Da Vinci's* Treatise on Painting, Princeton, NJ.
Manny, I. (2017), 'Oscar as (Ovid as) Orpheus: Misogyny and pederasty in *Dorian Gray* and the *Metamorphoses*', in K. Riley, A. J. L. Blanshard and I. Manny (eds), *Oscar Wilde and Classical Antiquity*, Oxford, 267–86.
Marcovitch, H. (2010), *The Art of the Pose: Oscar Wilde's Performance Theory*, Oxford.
Mighall, R. (ed.) (2000), *Oscar Wilde. The Picture of Dorian Gray*, Dunfermline.
Novak, A. D. (2008), *Realism, Photography and Nineteenth-Century Fiction*, Cambridge.

Bibliography

Nunokawa, J. (1995), 'The disappearance of the homosexual in *The Picture of Dorian Gray*', in G. E. Haggerty and B. Zimmerman (eds), *Professions of Desire: Lesbian and Gay Studies in Literature*, New York, 183-90.

Nunokawa, J. (1992), 'Homosexual desire and the effacement of the self in *The Picture of Dorian Gray*', *American Imago AIDS AND HOMOPHOBIA* 49(3): 311-21.

Pulver, E. S. (1970), 'Narcissism. The term and the concept', *Journal of the American Psychoanalytic Association* 18(2): 319-41.

Riquelme, J. P. (2000), 'Oscar Wilde's aesthetic Gothic: Walter Pater, dark enlightenment, and *The Picture of Dorian Gray*', *Modern Fiction Studies* 46(3): 609-31.

Rosner, V. (2005), *Modernism and the Architecture of Private Life*, New York.

Sinisgalli, R. (2006), *Il nuovo De Pictura di Leon Battista Alberti*, Italy.

Spencer, R. J. (ed.) (1966), *Leon Battista Alberti on Painting*, New Haven, CT.

Van Alphen, E. (2005), *Art in Mind. How Contemporary Images Shape Thought*, Chicago, IL and London.

Vinge, L. (1967), *The Narcissus Theme in Western European Literature up to the Early 19th Century*, Lund.

Walker, J. R. (2007), *Labyrinths of Deceit: Culture, Modernity and Identity in the Nineteenth Century*, Liverpool.

Wilde, O. (2010), *The Decay of Lying and Other Essays*, London.

Chapter 9

Addey, C. J. (2007), 'Mirrors and divination: Catoptromancy, Oracles and Earth goddesses in antiquity', in M. Anderson (ed.), *The Book of the Mirror: An Interdisciplinary Collection Exploring the Cultural Story of the Mirror*, Newcastle, 32-46.

Babb, L. A. (1981), 'Glancing: Visual interaction in Hinduism', *Journal of Anthropological Research* 37: 387-401.

Balensiefen, L. (1990), *Die Bedeutung des Spiegelbildes als ikonographisches Motiv in der antiken Kunst*, Tübingen.

Bartsch, S. (2006), *The Mirror of the Self: Sexuality, Self-Knowledge, and the Gaze in the Early Roman Empire*, Chicago, IL and London.

Bijker, W. E., Hughes, T. P. and Pinch, T. J. (eds) (1987), *The Social Construction of Technological Systems: New Directions in the Sociology and History of Technology*, Cambridge, MA and London.

Bowden, H. (2005), *Classical Athens and the Delphic Oracle, Divination and Democracy*, Cambridge.

Bowden, H. (2010), *Mystery Cults in the Ancient World*, London.

Bur, T. C. D. (2016), 'Mechanical miracles: Automata in Ancient Greek religion', MPhil diss., University of Sydney, Sydney.

Burghardt, W. J. (1961), 'The image of God in man: Alexandrian orientations', *The Catholic Theological Society of America* 16: 147-60.

Cain, R. B. (2012), 'Plato on mimesis and mirrors', *Philosophy and Literature* 36: 187-95.

Capra, A. (2017), 'Seeing through Plato's looking glass. Mythos and mimesis from republic to poetics', *Aisthesis* 10: 75-86.

Clark, S. (2016), *Plotinus: Myth, Metaphor, and Philosophical Practice*, Chicago, IL and London.

Cort, J. E. (2001), *Jains in the World: Religious Values and Ideology in India*, Oxford.

Delatte, A. (1932), *La Catoptromancie Grecque et ses Dérivés*, Liège and Paris.

Derrida, J. (1996), 'Foi et Savoir: Les deux Sources de la Religion aux Limites de la Simple Raison', in J. Derrida and G. Vattimo (eds), *La Religion*, Paris, 9-86.

Eck, C. A. van (2015), *Art, Agency and Living Presence: From the Animated Image to the Excessive Object*, Munich and Leiden.
Eck C. A. van, Gastel, J. J. van and Kessel, E. J. M. van (eds) (2014), *The Secret Lives of Art Works. Negotiating the Boundaries between Art and Life*, Leiden.
Eck, D. L. (1985), *Darśan Seeing the Divine Image in India*, 2nd edn, Chambersburg.
Eisenlohr, P. (2012), 'Media and religious diversity', *Annual Review of Anthropology* 41: 37–55.
Elsner, J. (2007), *Roman Eyes: Visuality and Subjectivity in Art and Text*, Princeton, NJ.
Engelke, M. (2007), *A Problem of Presence: Beyond Scripture in an African Church*, Berkeley, CA.
Engelke, M. (2010), 'Religion and the media turn: A review essay', *American Ethnologist* 37: 371–79.
Foster, H. (1988), 'Preface', in H. Foster (ed.), *Vision and Visuality*, Seattle.
Frontisi-Ducroux, F. and Vernant, J-P. (1997), *Dans L'œil du Miroir*, Paris.
Gazda, E. K. (2000), *The Villa of the Mysteries in Pompeii: Ancient Ritual, Modern Muse*, Ann Arbor, MI.
Gell, A. (1992), 'The technology of enchantment and the enchantment of technology', in J. Coote and A. Shelton (eds), *Anthropology, Art and Aesthetics*, Oxford, 40–66.
Gell, A. (1998), *Art and Agency: An Anthropological Theory*, Oxford.
Grethlein, J. (2016), 'Sight and reflexivity: Theorising vision in Greek vase-painting', in M. Squire (ed.), *Sight and the Ancient Senses*, London and New York, 85–106.
Grummond, N. T. de (2002), 'Mirrors, marriage, and mysteries', *Journal of Roman Archaeology Supplementary Series* 47: 62–85.
Hales, S. (2008), 'Aphrodite and Dionysus: Greek role models for Roman homes?', in S. Bell and I. L. Hansen (eds), *Role Models in the Roman World: Identity and Assimilation*. Ann Arbor, MI, 235–56.
Halliwell, S. (2002), *The Aesthetics of Mimesis: Ancient Texts and Modern Problems*, Princeton, NJ.
Heath, J. M. F. (2013), *Paul's Visual Piety: The Metamorphosis of the Beholder*, Oxford.
Heath, J. M. F. (2016), 'Sight and Christianity: Early Christian attitudes to seeing', in M. Squire (ed.), *Sight and the Ancient Senses*, London and New York, 220–36.
Houston, S. and Taube, K. (2000), 'An archaeology of the senses: Perception and cultural expression in ancient Mesoamerica', *Cambridge Archaeological Journal* 10: 261–94.
Johnston, S. I. (2001), 'Charming children: The use of the child in ancient divination', *Arethusa* 34: 97–117.
Jones, A. (1987), 'On some borrowed and misunderstood problems in Greek catoptrics', *Centaurus* 30: 1–17.
Jones, A. (2001), 'Pseudo-Ptolemy De Speculis', *SCIAMVS* 2: 145–86.
Keane, W. (1997), 'Religious language', *Annual Review of Anthropology* 26: 47–71.
Kindt, J. (2006), 'Delphic oracle stories and the beginning of historiography: Herodotus' Croesus Logos', *Classical Philology* 101: 34–51.
McCarty, W. (1989), 'The shape of the mirror: Metaphorical catoptrics in Classical literature', *Arethusa* 22: 161–95.
Magaloni Kerpel, D. (2015), 'Real and illusory feathers: Pigments, painting techniques, and the use of color in ancient Mesoamerica', in A. Russo, G. Wolf and D. Fane (eds), *Images Take Flight: Feather Art in Mexico and Europe*, Chicago, IL, 364–78.
Masià, R. (2015), 'On dating Hero of Alexandria', *Archive for History of Exact Sciences* 69: 231–55.
Meyer, B. (2006), 'Religious revelation, secrecy and the limits of visual representation', *Anthropological Theory* 6: 431–53.
Meyer, B. and Verrips, J. (2008), 'Aesthetics', in D. Morgan (ed.), *Key Words in Religion, Media and Culture*, New York and London, 20–30.
Morgan, D. (2008), *Key Words in Religion, Media and Culture*, New York and London.
Mudie Cooke, P. B. S. (1913), 'The paintings of the Villa Item at Pompeii', *JRS* 3: 157–74.

Bibliography

Nasrallah, L. S. (2010), *Christian Responses to Roman Art and Architecture: The Second-Century Church amid the Spaces of Empire*, Cambridge.

Netz, R. and Squire, M. (2016), 'Sight and the perspectives of mathematics: The limits of ancient optics', in M. Squire (ed.), *Sight and the Ancient Senses*, London and New York, 68–84.

Neugebauer, O. (1938), 'Über eine Methode zur Distanzbestimmung Alexandria-Rom bei Heron', *Det Kgl. Danske Videnskabernes Selskab. Historisk-filologiske Meddelelser* 26: 3–26.

Nilsson, M. (1957), *The Dionysiac Mysteries of the Hellenistic and Roman Age*, Lund.

Platt, V. (2011), *Facing the Gods: Epiphany and Representation in Graeco-Roman Art, Literature and Religion*, Cambridge.

Platt, V. (2015), 'Sight and the Gods: On the desire to see naked nymphs' in M. Squire (ed.), *Sight and the Ancient Senses*, London and New York, 169–87.

Platt, V. and Squire, M. (2018), 'Getting to grips with Classical art: Rethinking the haptics of Graceo-Roman visual culture', in A. Purves (ed.), *Touch and the Ancient Senses*, London and New York, 75–104.

Robbins, J. (2017), 'Keeping God's distance: Sacrifice, possession, and the problem of religious mediation', *American Ethnologist* 44: 464–75.

Russo, A., Wolf, G. and Fane, D. (eds) (2015), *Images Take Flight: Feather Art in Mexico and Europe*, Chicago, IL.

Saunders, N. (1998), 'Stealers of light, traders in brilliance: Amerindian metaphysics in the mirror of conquest', *RES Anthropology and Aesthetics* 33: 225–52.

Saunders, N. (2001), 'A dark light: Reflections on obsidian in Mesoamerica', *World Archaeology* 33: 220–36.

Saunders, N. (2003), 'Catching the light: Technologies of power and enchantment in pre-Columbian gold working', in J. Quilter and J. W. Hoopes (eds), *Gold and Power in Ancient Costa Rica, Panama, and Colombia*, Washington, DC, 15–47.

Schmidt, W. (1976), *Herons Von Alexandria: Vol II Mechanica et Catoptrica*, Leipzig.

Seaford, R. (1987), 'Pentheus' vision: Bacchae 918–22', *The Classical Quarterly* 37: 76–78.

Seaford, R. (1998), 'In the mirror of Dionysus', in S. Blundell and M. Williamson (eds), *The Sacred and the Feminine in Ancient Greece*, New York and London, 128–46.

Shaw, G. (1995), *Theurgy and the Soul: The Neoplatonism of Iamblichus*, Pittsburg, PA.

Sidoli, N. (2005), 'Heron's Dioptra 35 and analemma methods: an astronomical determination of the distance between two cities', *Centaurus* 47: 236–58.

Sidoli, N. (2011), 'Heron of Alexandria's date', *Centaurus* 53: 55–61.

Sinisgalli, R. (2012), *Perspective in the Visual Culture of Classical Antiquity*, Cambridge and New York.

Smith, A. M. (1996), 'Ptolemy's theory of visual perception: An English translation of the optics with introduction and commentary', *Transactions of the American Philosophical Society* 86: vii–300.

Smith, A. M. (2015), *From Sight to Light: The Passage from Ancient to Modern Optics*, Chicago, IL.

Souffrin, P. (2000), 'Remarques sur la Datation de la Dioptre d'Héron par l'Éclipse de Lune de 62', in G. Argoud, and J-Y. Guillaumin (eds), *Autour de La Dioptre d'Héron d'Alexandrie*, Saint-Étienne, 13–17.

Stang, C. (2016), *Our Divine Double*, Cambridge MA and London.

Stolow, J. (2005), 'Religion and/as media', *Theory, Culture & Society* 22: 119–45.

Taylor, R. (2008), *The Moral Mirror of Roman Art*, Cambridge.

Too, Y. (1996), 'Statues, mirrors, gods: Controlling images in Apuleius', in J. Elsner (ed.), *Art and Text in Roman Culture*, Cambridge, 133–52.

Tybjerg, K. (2003), 'Wonder-making and philosophical wonder in Hero of Alexandria', *Studies in History and Philosophy of Science* 34: 443–66.

Vries, H. de (2001), 'In Media Res: Global religion, public spheres, and the task of contemporary comparative religious studies', in H. De Vries and S. Weber (eds), *Religion and Media*, Stanford, CA, 3–42.

Chapter 10

Annas, J. (ed.) (2001), *Cicero, On Moral Ends*, trans. R. Woolf, Cambridge and New York.
Asmis, E. (1999), 'Epicurean EPISTEMOLOGY', in K. Algra et al. (eds), *The Cambridge History of Hellenistic Philosophy*, Cambridge, 260–94.
Bartsch, S. (2006), *The Mirror of the Self: Sexuality, Self-knowledge, and the Gaze in the Early Roman Empire*, Chicago, IL.
Bailey, C. (1950), *Titi Lucreti Cari De rerum natura libri sex*, Oxford.
Chantraine, P. (1999), *Dictionnaire étymologique de la langue grecque: Histoire des mots*, Paris.
Cherniss, H. and Helmbold, W. C. (1957), *Plutarch. Moralia*, Vol. 12, London and New York.
Eco, U. (1986), 'Mirrors', in *Semiotics and the Philosophy of Language*, Bloomington, IN, 202–26.
Ernout, A. and Meillet, A. (1980^4), *Dictionnaire étymologique de la langue latine. Histoire des mots*, Paris.
Frontisi-Ducroux, F. and Vernant, J.-P. (1997), *Dans l'œil du miroir*, Paris.
Gigon, O. and Straume-Zimmermann, L. (1988), *Marcus Tullius Cicero, Über die Ziele des menschlichen Handelns = De finibus bonorum et malorum*, Munich.
Heinze, R. (1897), *De rerum natura Buch III*, Leipzig.
Kenney, E. J. (1971), *Lucretius, De rerum natura, Book III*, Cambridge.
Kennedy, D. F. (2002), *Rethinking Reality: Lucretius and the Textualization of Nature*, Ann Arbor, MI.
Lloyd, G. E. R. (1966), *Polarity and Analogy. Two Types of Argumentation in Early Greek Thought*, Cambridge.
McCarty, W. (1989), 'The shape of the mirror: Metaphorical catoptrics in Classical literature' *Arethusa* 22(2): 161–95.
Marković, D. (2008), *The Rhetoric of Explanation in Lucretius' De Rerum Natura*, Leiden.
Moreschini, C. (2005), *M. Tullius Cicero, De finibus bonorum et malorum*, Munich.
Pellicer, A. (1966), *Natura, étude sémantique et historique du mot latin*, Publications de la Faculté des lettres et sciences humaines de l'Université de Montpellier 27, Paris.
Reinhardt, T. (2002), 'The speech of nature in Lucretius' *De Rerum Natura* 3.931–71', *CQ* 52(1): 291–304.
Schiesaro, A. (1990), *Simulacrum et imago: Gli argomenti analogici nel De rerum natura*, Pisa.
Sedley, D. N. and Long, A. A. (1987), *The Hellenistic Philosophers, I: Translations of the Principal Sources with Philosophical Commentary*, Cambridge.
Smith, M. F. and Rouse, W. H. D. (1992), *Lucretius, De rerum natura*, Cambridge, MA.
Stang, C. M. (2016), *Our Divine Double*, Cambridge, MA.
Taylor, R. (2008), *The Moral Mirror of Roman Art*, Cambridge and New York.
Wallach, B. P. (1976), *Lucretius and the Diatribe against the Fear of Death, De rerum natura III 830–1094*, Leiden.

Chapter 11

Afentoulidou, Ei. (2019), 'Philippos Monotropos in Byzantium and in the Slavonic world', in W. Hörandner, A. Rhoby and N. Zagklas (eds), *A Companion to Byzantine Poetry*, Leiden.

Bibliography

Afentoulidou-Leitgeb, Ei. (2012), *Philippos Monotropos' Dioptra and its Social Milieu: Niketas Stethatos, Nikolaos III Grammatikos and the Persecution of Bogomilism,* Parekbolai 2, 85-107.

Allies, M. H. (1898), *St. John Damascene: On Holy Images, Followed by Three Sermons on the Assumption,* London.

Anderson, M. (ed.) (2007), *The Book of the Mirror: An Interdisciplinary Collection Exploring the Cultural Story of the Mirror,* Cambridge.

Auvray, E. (ed.) (1875), *Les pleurs de Philippe,* Paris.

Avenarius, A. (1998), *Byzantský ikonoklazmus: storočie zápasu o ikonu.* Bratislava, English translation of A. Avenarius (2005), *The Byzantine Struggle over the Icon: On the Problem of Eastern European Symbolism,* Bratislava.

Benakis, L. (1982), 'The problem of general concepts in Neoplatonism and Byzantine thought', in D. J. O'Meara (ed.), *Neoplatonism and Christian thought,* Norfolk, VA, 75-86.

Bonnet, M. (ed.) (1898), 'Acta Ioannis', in M. Bonnet (ed.), *Acta apostolorum apocrypha,* Vol. 2.1, Leipzig (repr. Darmstadt, 1959), 151-216.

Bonnet, M. (ed.) (1903), 'Acta Thomae', in *Acta apostolorum apocrypha,* Vol. 2.2, Leipzig (repr. Hildesheim, 1972), 99-288.

Bradley, R. (1954), 'Backgrounds of the title speculum in mediaeval literature', *Speculum* 29(1): 100-15.

Cain, E. R. (2016), *Through a Mirror Darkly: Mystical Metaphors of Sight from Paul to Gregory of Nyssa and Augustine of Hippo.* Dissertation, New York.

Cameron, Av. (1970), *Agathias,* Oxford.

Caramico, A. (ed.) (2006), *Manuele File, Le proprietà degli animali II,* Naples.

Cattoi, Th. (2015), *Theodore the Studite: Writings on Iconoclasm,* New York.

Chronz, M. (ed.) (2009), Νεκταρίου, ἡγουμένου μονῆς Κασούλων (Νικολάου Ὑδρουντινοῦ), Διάλεξις κατὰ Ἰουδαίων, Athens.

Coulton, J. J. (2002), 'The dioptra of Hero of Alexandria', in C. J. Tuplin and T. E. Rihll (eds), *Science and Mathematics in Ancient Greek Culture,* Oxford, 150-64.

Courtonne, Y. (ed.) (1961), *Saint Basile. Lettres,* Vol. 2, Paris.

D'Aiuto, F. (ed.) (1994), *Tre canoni di Giovanni Mauropode in onore di santi militari,* Rome.

Dain, A. (1933), *La tradition du texte d'Héron de Byzance,* Paris.

De Stefani, A. (ed.) (1920), *Etymologicum gudianum,* Leipzig (repr. Amsterdam, 1965).

Fatouros, G. (ed.) (1992), *Theodori Studitae epistulae,* Vol. 1 Prolegomena et textum epp. 1-70 continens, Berlin.

Festa, N. (ed.) (1898), *Theodori Ducae Lascaris epistulae CCXVII,* Florence.

Gaselee, S. (ed.) (1917), *Achilles Tatius, with an English Translation,* London and New York.

Gautier, P. (ed.) (1972), 'Michel Italikos. Lettres et Discours', *Archives de l'Orient Chrétien* 14.

Giannouli, A. (2013), 'Catanyctic religious poetry', in A. Rigo (ed.), *Theologica Minora. The Minor Genres of Byzantine Theological Literature,* Turnhout, 86-109.

Giagkou, Th. and Papatriantafyllou-Theodoridi, N. (eds) (1999), Πανηγυρικὴ Α΄. Ἁγίου Νεοφύτου τοῦ Ἐγκλείστου Συγγράμματα, Vol. 3, Paphos.

Grabes, H. (1973), *Speculum, mirror und looking-glass: Kontinuität und Originalität der Spiegelmetapher in den Buchtiteln des Mittelalters und der englischen Literatur des 13. bis 17,* Tübingen.

Gutzwiller, K. L. (1998), *Poetic Garlands. Hellenistic Epigrams in Context.* Berkeley, CA.

Hugede, N. (1957), *La Metaphore du miroir dans les Épitres de saint Paul aux Corinthiens,* Neuchâtel.

James, M. R. (trans.) (1924), *The Apocryphal New Testament,* Oxford.

Jeffreys, E. (ed. and trans.) (1998), *Digenis Akritis: the Grottaferrata and Escorial versions,* Cambridge and New York.

Kambylis, A. (ed.) (1976), *Symeon Neos Theologos,* Berlin.

Bibliography

Karlsson, G. (1962), *Idéologie et cérémonial dans l'épistolographie byzantine*. Textes du Xe siècle analysés et commentés, Uppsala.
Koder, J. (ed.) (1969, 1971, 1973), *Syméon le Nouveau Théologien, Hymnes*. Introduction, texte critique et notes, Vols I–III, Paris.
Kolovou, F. (ed.) (1995), *Euthymios Tornikes als Briefschreiber*. Vier unedierte Briefe des Euthymios Tornikes an Michael Choniates im Codex Buc. gr. 508. *Jahrbuch der Österreichischen Byzantinistik* 45: 53–74.
Kotter, P. B. (ed.) (1975), *Die Schriften des Johannes von Damaskos*, Vol. 3, Berlin.
Kuehn, C. and Baggarly, J. (eds and trans.) (2007), *Anastasius of Sinai, Hexaemeron*, Rome.
Lampros, S. P. (ed.) (1880), *Μιχαὴλ Ἀκομινάτου τοῦ Χωνιάτου τὰ σωζόμενα*, Vol. 2, Athens.
Latte, K. (ed.) (1966), *Hesychii Alexandrini lexicon, epsilon – omikron*, Copenhagen.
Lewis, M. J. T. (2001), *Surveying Instruments of Greece and Rome*, Cambridge.
Miklas, H. and Fuchsbauer, J. (eds) (2013), *Die kirchenslavische Übersetzung der Dioptra des Philippos Monotropos*, Vol. 1, 'Überlieferung. Text der Programmata und des ersten Buches', Vienna.
Miller, E. (ed.) (1855–1857), *Manuelis Philae carmina*, Paris (repr. Amsterdam).
Müller, F. (ed.) (1958), *Gregorii Nysseni Opera*, Vol. III, 1, Leiden.
Nix, L. and Schmidt, W. (eds), (1900), *Heronis Alexandrini opera quae supersunt omnia*, Vol. 2.1, Leipzig.
Papadopoulos, I. V. (ed.) (1927), *Γρηγορίου Χιονιάδου τοῦ ἀστρονόμου ἐπιστολαί. Ἐπιστημονικὴ Ἐπετηρὶς Φιλοσοφικῆς Σχολῆς 1*, 151–206.
Papadopoulos-Kerameus, A. (ed.) (1904), *Θεόδωρος Στουδίτης, Μεγάλη κατήχησις*, St. Petersburg.
Papaioannou, S. (2010), 'Byzantine mirrors: Self-reflection in Medieval Greek writing', *Dumbarton Oaks Papers* 64: 81–101.
Patrologia Graeca: Migne, J.-P. (1857–1866) *Patrologiae cursus completus, Series graeca*, Vols 1–161, Paris.
Pignani, A. (ed.) (2007), *Teodoro Studita Catechesi-epitafio per la madre*, Naples.
Prochorov, G. M., Bil'djug, A. B., Miklas, H. and Fuchsbauer, J. (eds) (2008), *Dioptra Filippa Monotropa*. Antropologičeskaja enciklopedija pravoslavnogo srednevekov'ja, Moscow.
Reuss, J. (ed.) (1966), *Johannes-Kommentare aus der griechischen Kirche*, Berlin.
Sbordone, F. (ed.) (1936), *Physiologus*, Milan (repr. Hildesheim et al., 1991).
Schirò, G. (ed.) (1976), *Analecta hymnica Graeca e codicibus eruta Italiae Inferioris*. Vol. 4, Rome.
Schöne, H. (ed.) (1903), *Heronis Alexandrini opera quae supersunt omnia*, Vol. 3, Leipzig.
Seaford, R. (1984), '1 Corinthians XIII:12', *The Journal of Theological Studies N.S.* 35: 117–20.
Sinkewicz, R. E. (ed. and trans.) (1988), *Saint Gregory Palamas: The One Hundred and Fifty Chapters*, Toronto.
Spanos, A. (ed.) (2010), *Codex Lesbiacus Leimonos 11: Annotated Critical Edition of an Unpublished Byzantine Menaion for June*, Berlin and New York.
Spyridon Lavriotes (ed.) (1920), *Ἡ Διόπτρα*, Athens.
Stählin, O. and Früchtel, L. (eds) (1960), *Clemens Alexandrinus II. Stromata I–VI*, Berlin.
Stählin, O., Früchtel, L. and Treu, U. (eds) (1970), *Clemens Alexandrinus III. Stromata VII–VIII*, Berlin.
Sullivan, D., Talbot, A.-M. and McGrath, St. (eds) (2014), *The Life of Saint Basil the Younger. Critical Edition and Annotated Translation of the Moscow Version*, Washington, DC.
Talbot, A.-M. (1994), 'Epigrams of Manuel Philes on the Theotokos tes Peges and its art', *Dumbarton Oaks Papers* 48: 135–65.
Tittmann, I. A. H. (ed.) (1808), *Iohannis Zonarae Lexicon*, Leipzig (repr. Amsterdam, 1967).
Vilborg, E. (ed.) (1955), *Achilles Tatius. Leucippe and Clitophon*, Stockholm.
Vogt, A. (ed.) (1935), *Constantin VII Porphyrogénète. Le livre des cérémonies*. Vol. 1, Paris.
Way, Sr. A. C. (trans.) (1951), *Saint Basil, Letters*, Washington, DC.

Bibliography

Chapter 12

Agamben, G. (1981), *Stanze. Parole et fantasme dans la culture occidentale*, trans. Y. Hersant, Paris.

Akbari, S. C. (2004), *Seeing through the Veil: Optical Theory and Medieval Allegory*, Toronto.

Anderson, M. (ed.) (2007), *The Book of the Mirror: An Interdisciplinary Collection Exploring the Cultural Story of the Mirror*, Newcastle.

Arden, H. M. (1993), *The Romance of the Rose: An annotated Bibliography*, New York.

Ariani, M. and Gabriele, M. (eds) (1998), *Francesco Colonna, Hypnerotomachia Poliphili: introduzione, traduzione e comment*, 2 vols, Milan.

Baig, B. P. (1982), *Vision and Visualization: Optics and Light Metaphysics in the Imagery and Poetic Form of Twelfth and Thirteenth Century Secular Allegory, with Special Attention to the 'Roman de la Rose'*. PhD, University of California, Berkeley.

Bartsch, S. (2006), *The Mirror of the Self: Sexuality, Self-Knowledge, and the Gaze in the Early Roman Empire*, Chicago and London.

Benedetto, L. F. (1910), *Il 'Roman de la Rose' e la letteratura Italiana*, Halle a. S. M. Niemeyer.

Blamires, A. and Holian, G. C. (2002), *The Romance of the Rose Illuminated: Manuscripts at the National Library of Wales, Aberystwyth*, Cardiff.

Bowersock, G. W., Brown, P. and Grabar, O. (eds) (1999), *Late Antiquity: A Guide to the Postclassical World*, Cambridge, MA and London.

Brandt, O. (2006), 'The Lateran baptistery and the diffusion of octagonal baptisteries from Rome to Constantinople', *Atti del Congresso Internazionale di Archeologia Cristiana* 14: 221–27.

Carroll, L. (1871), *Through the Looking Glass and What Alice Found There*, London.

Clay, D. (1980), 'An Epicurean interpretation of dreams', *Americal Journal of Philology* 101(3): 342–65, Washington, DC.

Fleming, J. V. (1984), 'Further reflections on Oiseuse's mirror', *Zeitschrift für Romanische Philologie*, 100: 26–40.

Fleming, J. V. (1986), 'The garden of the Roman de la Rose: Vision of landscape or landscape of vision?', in E. B. MacDougall (ed.), *Medieval Gardens*, Washington, DC: Dumbarton Oaks Colloquium on the History of Landscape Architecture, 199–234.

Foucault, M. (1984) 'Des espaces autres: hétérotopies (conférence au Cercle d'études architecturales, 14 mars 1967)', *AMC – Architecture /Mouvement/Continuité* 5: 46–49. As reproduced in D. Defert and F. Ewald (eds), *Michel Foucault: Dits et écrits II. 1976–1988*, Paris.

Frappier, J. (1959), 'Variations sur le thème du miroir, de Bernard de Ventadour à Maurice Scève', *Cahiers de l'Association internationale des études francaises*, 11: 134–58.

George, A. R. (2010), *The Epic of Gilgamesh*, London.

Grace-Heller, S. (2000), *Robing Romance: Fashion and Literature in Thirteenth-Century France and Occitania*, PhD, Minneapolis, MN.

Grace-Heller, S. (2001), 'Light as glamour: The luminescent ideal of beauty in the Roman de la Rose', *Speculum*, 76: 934–59.

Harley, M. P. (1986), 'Narcissus, Hermaphroditus, and Attis: Ovidian lovers at the Fontaine d'Amors in Guillaume de Lorris's Roman de la Rose', *PMLA* 101: 324–37.

Horgan, F. (1994), *Guillaume de Lorris and Jean de Meun. The Romance of the Rose*, Oxford.

Hult, D. F. (1981), 'The allegorical fountain: Narcissus in the Roman de la Rose', *Romanic Review* 72: 125–48.

Hult, D. F. (1986), *Self-Fulfilling Prophecies: Readership and Authority in the First Roman de la Rose*, Cambridge.

Huot, S. (2010), *Dreams of Lovers and Lies of Poets: Poetry, Knowledge, and Desire in the Roman de la Rose*, London.

Jensen, R. M. (2011), *Living Water: Images, Symbols, and Settings of Early Christian Baptism*, Leiden.

Knoespel, K. (1985), *Narcissus and the Invention of Personal History*, New York.
Köhler, E. (1963), 'Narcisse, la Fontaine d'Amour et Guillaume de Lorris', *Journal des savants* 2: 86–103.
Kruger, S. (1992), *Dreaming in the Middle Ages*, New York.
Lees-Jeffries, H. (2006), 'Sacred and profane love: Four fountains in the *Hypnerotomachia* (1499) and the *Roman de la Rose*', *Word & Image* 22(1): 1–13.
Lefaivre, L. (1997), *Leon Battista Alberti's Hypnerotomachia Poliphili: Re-cognizing the Architectural Body in the Early Italian Renaissance*, Cambridge, MA.
Lewis, S. (1992), 'Images of opening, penetration and closure in the *Roman de la Rose*', *Word & Image* 8: 215–42.
Lewis, C. S. (1958), *The Allegory of Love: A Study in Medieval Tradition*, New York.
Lochrie, K. (2006), 'Sheer wonder: Dreaming Utopia in the Middle Ages', *Journal of Medieval and Early Modern Studies* 36(3): 493–516.
Lowry, M. (1979), *The World of Aldus Manutius: Business and Scholarship in Renaissance Venice*, Oxford.
Louis, R. (1974), *Le Roman de la Rose: Essai d'interpretation de l'allégorisme érotique*, Paris.
McCarty, W. (1989), 'The shape of the mirror: Metaphorical catoptrics in Classical literature', *Arethusa* 22: 161–95.
Nichols, S. G. (2003), 'Parler, penser, voir: le Roman de la Rose et l'étrange', *Littérature* 130: *Altérités du Moyen Âge*, 97–114.
Nolan, E. P. (1990), *Now through a Glass Darkly: Specular Images of Being and Knowing from Virgil to Chaucer*, Ann Arbor, MI.
Nordenfalk, C. (1985), 'The five senses in Late Medieval and Renaissance art', *Journal of the Warburg and Courtauld Institutes* 48: 1–22.
Notz, M.-F. (1978), 'Hortus Conclusus: Réflexions sur le rôle symbolique de la clôture dans la description romanesque du jardin', in F. Lecoy (ed.), *Mélanges de literature du Moyen Age au XXe siècle offerts à Jeanne Lods*, Paris, 459–72.
Nouvet, C. (2000), 'An allegorical mirror: the Pool of Narcissus in Guillaume de Lorris' *Romance of the Rose*', *Romanic Review* 91: 353–74.
Ovid (1993), *Metamorphoses*, ed. W. S. Anderson, Stuttgart.
Peklar, B. (2017), 'The imaginary self-portrait in the poem Roman de la Rose', *Ars & Humanitas* 11(1): 90–105.
Pérez-Gómez, A. (2006), *Built upon Love: Architectural Longing after Ethics and Aesthetics*, Cambridge, MA.
Polizzi, G. (1987), *Emblematique et géométrie: L' Espace et le Récit dans Le Songe de Poliphile*, PhD, Université de Provence.
Polizzi, G. (1990), 'Le devenir du jardin mèdieval? Du verger de la rose à Cythère', in *Senefiance* 28: *Vergers et Jardins dans l'Univers Medieval*, 267–88.
Pozzi, G. and Ciapponi, L. A. (eds) (1980), *Edizione critica e commento a cura di Hypnerotomachia Poliphili di Francesco Colonna*, 2 vols, Padua.
Preus, A. (1968), 'On "Dreams" 2, 459b24–460a33, and Aristotle's ὄψις', *Phronesis* 13(2): 175–82.
Priki, E. (2015), *Dream Narratives and Initiation Processes: A Comparative Study of the Tale of Livistros and Rodamne, the Roman de la Rose, and the Hypnerotomachia Poliphili*, PhD, University of Cyprus.
Richards, E. J. (1982), 'Reflections on Oiseuse's mirror: Iconographic tradition, luxuria and the Roman de la Rose', *Zeitschrift für Romanische Philologie* 98: 296–311.
Robertson, D. W. (1962), *A Preface to Chaucer: Studies in Medieval Perspectives*, Princeton, NJ.
Root, J. (2011), 'Marvelous crystals, perilous mirrors: Le Roman de la Rose and the discontinuity of the Romance subject', *The Romanic Review* 102(1–2): 65–89.
Stewering, R. (1996), *Architektur und Natur in der 'Hypnerotomachia Poliphili' (Manutius 1499) und die Zuschreibung des Werkes an Niccolò Lelio Cosmico*, PhD, University of Hamburg.

Bibliography

Strubel, A. (1992), *Guillaume de Lorris et Jean de Meun: Le Roman de la Rose*, Paris.
Taylor, R. M. (2008), *The Moral Mirror of Roman Art*, Cambridge and New York.
Trippe, R. (2004), *The Hypnerotomachia Poliphili and the Image of Italian Humanism*, PhD, The Johns Hopkins University.
White, I. (trans.) (unpublished), *Hypnerotomachia Poliphili (The Sleeping Amorous Struggle of Polia's Lover)*.
Winton, T. E. (2002), *A Skeleton Key to Poliphilo's Dream: The Architecture of the Imagination in the Hypnerotomachia Poliphili*, PhD, University of Cambridge.

Chapter 13

Balensiefen, L. (1990), *Die Bedeutung des Spiegelbildes als ikonographisches Motiv in der antiken Kunst*, Tübingen.
Barthes, R. (1981), *Camera Lucida*, New York.
Bartsch S. (2006), *The Mirror of the Self. Sexuality, Self-Knowledge, and the Gaze in the Early Roman Empire*, Chicago, IL.
Bazin, A. (ed. and trans. Hugh Gray) (2004), *What is Cinema? Vols 1 & 2*, Berkeley, CA.
Beretta, M. (2009), *The Alchemy of Glass: Counterfeit, Imitation, and Transmutation in Ancient Glassmaking*, Sagamore Beach, MA.
Bliquez, L. J. (2015), *The Tools of Asclepius: Surgical Instruments in Greek and Roman Times*, Leiden.
Cain, E. R. (2016), *Through a Mirror Darkly: Mystical Metaphors of Sight from Paul to Gregory of Nyssa and Augustine of Hippo*, PhD Thesis, New York.
Cain, R. B. (2012), 'Plato on Mimesis and mirrors', *Philosophy and Literature* 36(1): 187–95.
Camerota, F. (2002), 'Optics and the visual arts: The role of Σκηνογραφία', in J. Renn and G. Castagnetti (eds), *Homo Faber: Studies on Nature, Technology and Science at the Time of Pompeii*, Rome, 121–39.
Capra, A. (2017), 'Seeing through Plato's looking glass. Mythos and Mimesis from republic to poetics', *Aisthesis* 10: 75–86.
Clark, S. R. L. (2016), *Plotinus: Myth, Metaphor, and Philosophical Practice*, Chicago, IL and London.
Coulton, J. J. (2002), 'The dioptra of Hero of Alexandria', in C. J. Tuplin and T. E. Rihll (eds), *Science and Mathematics in Ancient Greek Culture*, Oxford, 150–64.
De Grummond, N. T. (2002), 'Mirrors, marriage and mysteries', *Journal of Roman Archaeology Supplement* 47: 63–85.
De Grummond, N. T. and M. Hoff (1982), 'Mirrors of the Mediterranean', in N. T. de Grummond, *A Guide to Etruscan Mirrors*, Tallahassee, FL, 52–58.
De Puma, R. D. (2013), 'Mirrors in art and society', in J. M. Turfa (ed.), *The Etruscan World*, London and New York, 1041–67.
Elsner J. (1995), *Art and the Roman Viewer: The Transformation of Art from the Pagan World to Christianity*, Cambridge.
Frede, D. (1992), 'The cognitive role of phantasia in Aristotle', in M. C. Nussbaum and A. O. Rorty (eds), *Essays on Aristotle's* De Anima, Oxford, 279–95.
Goldberg, B. (1985), *The Mirror and Man*, Charlottesville, VA.
Congdon, L. O. K. (1981), *Caryatid Mirrors of Ancient Greece: Technical, Stylistic and Historical Considerations of an Archaic and Early Classical Bronze Series*, Mainz.
Grabes, H. (1982), *The Mutable Glass*, Cambridge.
Greene, K. (2008), 'Inventors, invention, and attitudes towards technology and innovation', in J. P. Olesen (ed.), *Handbook of Engineering and Technology in the Classical World*, New York, 800–20.

Grethlein, J. (2017), *Aesthetic Experiences and Classical Antiquity. The Content of Form in Narratives and Pictures*, Cambridge.
Halliwell, S. (2002), *The Aesthetics of Mimesis: Ancient Texts and Modern Problems*, Princeton, NJ.
Hardie, Ph. (1988), 'Lucretius and the delusions of Narcissus', *MD* 20/21: 71–89.
Hirth, F. (1907), *Chinese Metallic Mirrors: With Notes on some Ancient Specimens of the Musée Guimet*, Paris.
Hub, B. (2008), *Die Perspektive der Antike. Archäologie einer symbolischen Form*, Frankfurt am Main.
Hulkes, R. (2007), 'The mirror as a metaphor for epistemology in Seneca's *De Clementia*', in M. Anderson, *The Book of the Mirror: An Interdisciplinary Collection Exploring the Cultural Story of the Mirror*, Newcastle upon Tyne, 47–59.
Hunink, V. (1997), *Apuleius of Madauros: Pro Se De Magia*, 2 vols, Amsterdam.
Huxley, G. (1959), *Anthemius of Tralles: A Study in Later Greek Geometry*, Cambridge.
Johansen, Th. K. (2012), *The Powers of Aristotle's Soul* (Oxford Aristotle Studies), Oxford.
Jones A. (2001), 'Pseudo-Ptolemy *De Speculis*', *Sciamus* 2: 145–86.
Jonsson, F. M. (1995), *Le Miroir, naissance d'un genre littéraire*, Paris.
Kauntze, M. (2007), 'Seeing through a glass darkly: The interpretation of a biblical verse in Augustine of Hippo', in M. Anderson (ed.), *The Book of the Mirror: An Interdisciplinary Collection Exploring the Cultural Story of the Mirror*, Newcastle.
Knorr, W. R. (1983), 'The geometry of burning-mirrors in antiquity', *Isis* 74: 53–73.
Knorr, W. R. (1985), 'Archimedes and the Pseudo-Euclidean "Catoptrics": Early stages in the ancient geometric theory of mirrors', *Archives internationales d'histoire des sciences* 35: 28–105.
Lada-Richards, I. (2005), '"In the Mirror of the Dance": A Lucianic metaphor in its performative and ethical contexts', *Mnemosyne* 58(3): 335–57.
Lapatin K. (2014), 'The materials and techniques of Greek and Roman art', in C. Marconi (ed.), *The Oxford Handbook of Greek and Roman Art and Architecture*, Oxford, 203–40.
Lejeune, A. (1948), *Euclide et Ploléméé: deux stades de l'optique geometrique grecque*, Louvain.
Lejeune A. (1957), 'Recherches sur la catoptrique grecque', *Memoires Acad. Bruxelles* 52(2).
Lejeune A. (1956), *L' Optique de Claude Ptolémée dans la version latine d' après l' arabe de l' émir Eugène de Sicile, Édition critique et exégétique*, Louvain.
Lewis, M. J. T. (2001), *Surveying Instruments of Greece and Rome*, Cambridge.
Libby, B. B. (2011), 'Moons, smoke, and mirrors in Apuleius' portrayal of Isis', *American Journal of Philology* 132: 301–22.
Lindberg D. C. (1976), *Theories of Vision from al-Kindi to Kepler*, London.
MacFarlane, A. and Martin, G. (2002), *Glass: A World History*, Chicago, IL.
McCarty, W. (1989), 'The shape of the mirror: Metaphorical catoptrics in Classical literature', *Arethusa* 22: 161–95.
Melchior-Bonnet, S. (2001), *The Mirror: A History*, trans. Katharine H. Jewett; with a Preface by Jean Delumeau, New York and London.
Mette, H.-J. (1983), 'Spiegelbildlichkeiten', *Würzburger Jahrbücher für die Altertumswissenschaft* NS 9: 81–87.
Moyer, A. (2012), *Deep Reflection: An Archaeological Analysis of Mirrors in Iron Age Eurasia*, PhD Thesis, University of Minnesota.
Myerowitz, M. (1992), 'The domestication of desire: Ovid's Parva Tabella and the Theater of Love', in A. Richlin (ed.), *Pornography and Representation in Greece and Rome*, Oxford, 131–57.
Nussbaum, M. C. (1978), *Aristotle's de Motu Animalium: Aristotle's de Motu Animalium. Text with Translation, Commentary, and Interpretive Essays*, Princeton, NJ.
Petridou, G. (2016), *Divine Epiphany in Greek Literature and Culture*, Oxford.
Perry, E. E. (2002), 'Rhetoric, literary criticism, and the Roman aesthetics of artistic imitation', *MAARSup* 1: 153–71.

Bibliography

Platt, V. (2001), *Facing the Gods: Epiphany and Representation in Graeco-Roman Art, Literature and Religion*, Oxford.
Platt, V. (2009), 'Virtual visions: Phantasia and the perception of the divine in Philostratus' *Life of Apollonius of Tyana*', in E. L. Bowie and J. Elsner (eds), *Philostratus*, Cambridge, 131–54.
Pollitt, J. J. (1974), *The Ancient View of Greek Art. Criticism, History, and Terminology*, New Haven, CT.
Porter, J. I. (2010), *The Origins of Aesthetic Thought in Ancient Greece: Matter, Sensation, and Experience*, Cambridge.
Rouveret, A. (1989), *Histoire et imaginaire de la peinture ancienne*, Rome.
Scheiter, K. M. (2012), 'Images, appearances, and phantasia in Aristotle', *Phronesis* 57: 251–78.
Schofield, M. (1992), 'Aristotle on the imagination', in M. C. Nussbaum and A. O. Rorty (eds), *Essays on Aristotle's De Anima*, Oxford, 249–77.
Seaford, R. A. S. (1998), 'In the mirror of Dionysus', in S. Blundell and M. Williamson (eds), *The Sacred and the Feminine*, London, 101–18.
Sheppard, A. (2003), 'The mirror of imagination: The influence of Timaeus 70eff.', in R. W. Sharples and A. Sheppard (eds), *Ancient Approaches to Plato's Timaeus*, London, 203–12 (BICS Supplements, vol. 78).
Sheppard, A. (2014), *The Poetics of Phantasia: Imagination in Ancient Aesthetic*, London.
Sheppard, A. (2015), 'Imagination', in P. Destree and P. Murray (eds), *A Companion to Ancient Aesthetics*, Chichester, 354–65.
Simon G. (1987), 'Behind the mirror', *Graduate Faculty Philosophy Journal* 12(1–2): 311–50 [special issue: *Topics in the History and Philosophy of Science*].
Simon, G. (1988), *Le regard, l'être et l'apparence dans l'optique de l'antiquité*, Paris.
Simon, G. (2003), *Archéologie de la vision*, Paris.
Sinisgalli, R. (2012), *Perspective in the Visual Culture of Classical Antiquity*, Cambridge.
Small, J. P. (2013), 'Skenographia in brief', in G. M. W. Harrison and V. Liapis (eds), *Performance in Greek and Roman Theatre*, Leiden and Boston, MA, 111–28.
Smith, A. M. (1996), 'Ptolemy's theory of visual perception: An English translation of the Optics with Introduction and Commentary', *Transactions of the American Philosophical Society* 86(2).
Smith, A. M. (2014), *From Sight to Light, The Passage from Ancient to Modern Optics*, Chicago, IL.
Steiner, D. T. (2001), *Images in Mind Statues in Archaic and Classical Greek Literature and Thought*, Princeton, NJ.
Stoichiță, V. I. (1997), *Short History of the Shadow*, trans. Anne-Marie Glasheen, London.
Takahashi, K. (1992), *Medieval Latin Traditions of Euclid's Catoptrica: A Critical Edition of 'De Speculis' with an Introduction, English Translation, and Commentary*, Fukuoka.
Tanner, J. (2006), *The Invention of Art History in Ancient Greece: Religion, Society and Artistic Rationalisation*, Cambridge.
Taylor, R. (2008), *The Moral Mirror of Roman Art*, Cambridge.
Too, Y. L. (1996), 'Statues, mirrors, gods: Controlling images in Apuleius', in J. Elsner (ed.), *Art and Text in Roman Culture*, Cambridge, 211–24.
Toomer, G. (trans.) (1976), *Diocles on Burning Mirrors*, New York.
Trimpi, W. (1978), 'The early metaphorical use of skiagraphia and skenographia', *Traditio* 34: 404–13.
Ulrich, J. P. (2016), *Platonic Reflections in Apuleius*, PhD Thesis, University of Pennsylvania.
Van der Eijk, P. J. (1994), *Aristoteles: De Insomniis. De Divinatione per Somnum (Aristoteles. Werke in deutscher Übersetzung 14/III)*, Berlin.
Vernant, J.-P. and Frontisi-Ducroux, F. (1997), *Dans l' Sil du miroir*, Paris.
Watson, G. (1988), *Phantasia in Classical Thought*, Galway.
Wedin, M. V. (1988), *Mind and Imagination in Aristotle*, New Haven, CT.

Chapter 14

Addey, C. (2007), 'Mirrors and divination: Catoptromancy, oracles and earth goddesses in antiquity" in M. Anderson (ed.), *The Book of the Mirror: An Interdisciplinary Collection Exploring the Cultural Story of the Mirror*, Newcastle upon Tyne, 32–46.

Baltrusaitis, J. (1978), *Le miroir: essai sur une légende scientifique: révélations, science-fiction et fallacies*, Paris.

Borges, J. L. (1970 [1945]), 'The Aleph', in *The Aleph and Other Stories, 1933–1969*, ed. and trans. by N. T. di Giovanni, New York, 15–30.

Cherniss, H. (1957), 'Concerning the face which appears in the Moon', in H. Cherniss and W. C. Helmbold (eds), *Plutarch* Moralia *Volume XII*, Cambridge, MA, 1–223.

Congdon, L. O. Keene (1985), 'Greek mirrors', *Notes in the History of Art* 4(2/3): 19–25.

Coulton, J. J. (2002), 'The *dioptra* of Hero of Alexandria', in C. J. Tuplin and T. E. Rihll (eds), *Science and Mathematics in Ancient Greek Culture*, Oxford, 150–64.

Couprie, D. L. (2011), *Heaven and Earth in Ancient Greek Cosmology: From Thales to Herclid es Ponticus*, New York, Dordrecht, Heidelberg and London.

Dällenbach, L. (1989), *The Mirror in the Text*, trans. by J. Whitely with E. Hughes, Chicago, IL.

Delatte, A. (1932), *La catoptromancie grecque et ses dérivés*, Liège and Paris.

Diels, H. (1920), 'Lukrezstudien II', *Sitzungsberichte der Preussischen Akademie der Wissenschaft*, 2–18.

Dillon, J. M. (2003), *The Heirs of Plato: A Study of the Old Academy (347–274 BC)*, Oxford.

Eisler, R. (1949), 'The polar sighting tube', *Archives Internationales d'Histoire des Sciences* 28: 312–23.

Frontisi-Ducroux, F. and Vernant, J.-P. (1997), *Dans l'oeil du miroir*, Paris.

Fusillo, M. (1999), 'The mirror of the Moon: Lucian's *A True Story* – from satire to Utopia', in S. Swain (ed.), *Oxford Readings in the Greek Novel*, Oxford, 351–81.

Gainsford, P. (2012), '*Odyssey* 20.356–357 and the eclipse of 1178 BCE: a response to Baikouzis and Magnasco', *TAPA* 142(1): 1–22.

García Santo-Thomás, E. (2017), *The Refracted Muse: Literature and Optics in Early Modern Spain*, trans. by V. Barletta, Chicago, IL.

Georgiadou, A. and Larmour, D. H. J. (1998), *Lucian's Science Fiction Novel* True Histories: *Interpretation and Commentary*, Leiden.

Georgiadou, A. and Larmour, D. H. J. (1994), 'Lucian and historiography: De historia conscribenda and *Verae Historiae*', *ANRW* II. 34.2. Berlin and New York, 1448–509.

Görgemanns, H. (1970), *Untersuchungen zu Plutarchs Dialog* De facie in orbe lunae, Heidelberg.

Grabes, H. (1982), *The Mutable Glass: Mirror-Imagery in Titles and Texts of the Middle Ages and English Renaissance*, trans. by G. Collier, Cambridge.

Graham, D. W. (2013), *Science before Socrates: Parmenides, Anaxagoras, and the New Astronomy*, Oxford and New York.

Hadot, P. (1995), *Philosophy as a Way of Life. Spiritual Exercises from Socrates to Foucault*, ed. A. I. Davidson and trans. M. Chase, Malden, MA, Oxford and Victoria.

Hamilton, Sir W. and Tischbein, J. H. W. (1795), *Collection of engravings from ancient vases mostly of pure Greek workmanship: discovered in sepulchres in the Kingdom of the Two Sicilies but chiefly in the neighbourhood of Naples during the course of the years MDCCLXXXIX and MDCCLXXXX. Now in the possession of Sir Wm. Hamilton . . . with remarks on each vase by the collector . . . Mr. Wm. Tischbein Director of the Royal Academy of Painting at Naples*, Vol. 3.

Hill, D. E. (1973), 'The Thessalian trick', *RhM* 116(3/4): 221–38.

Huxley, G. (1963), 'Eudoxian topics', *GRBS* 4(2): 83–105.

Keyser, P. T. (1992), 'Xenophanes' sun (frr. A32, 33.3, 40 DK6) on Trojan Ida (Lucr. 5.660–5, D.S. 17.7.5–7, Mela 1.94–5),' *Mnemosyne* 45: 299–311.

Bibliography

König, J. and Whitmarsh, T. (eds) (2007), *Ordering Knowledge in the Roman Empire*, Cambridge.
Koppenfels, W. von (1981), 'Mundus alter et idem. Utopiefiktion und menippeische Satire', *Poetica* 13: 16–66.
Lada-Richards, I. (2005), '"In the mirror of the dance": A Lucianic metaphor in its performative and ethical contexts', *Mnemosyne* 58(3): 335–57.
Lewis, M. J. T. (2001), *Surveying Instruments of Greece and Rome*, Cambridge, 51–108.
McCarty, W. (1989), 'The shape of the mirror: Metaphorical catoptrics in Classical literature', *Arethusa* 22: 161–95.
Mansfeld, J. and Runia, D. T. (2009), *Aëtiana. The Method and Intellectual Context of a Doxographer*, Vol. III, Leiden and Boston, MA.
ní Mheallaigh, K. (2014), *Fakes, Freaks and Hyperreality: Reading Fiction with Lucian*, Cambridge.
ní Mheallaigh, K. (2019), 'Looking back in wonder: Contemplating home from the *Iliad* to *Pale Blue Dot*', in T. Biggs and J. Blum (eds), *The Epic Journey in Greek and Roman Literature*, Cambridge, 263–91.
ní Mheallaigh, K. (forthcoming), *The Moon in the Greek and Roman Imagination: Selenography in Myth, Literature, Science and Philosophy*, Cambridge.
von Möllendorff, P. (2000), *Auf der Suche nach der verlogenen Wahrheit. Lukians* Wahre Geschichten, Tübingen.
Neve, M. (2004), 'Glazy reflections. Notes on the role of glass as a *sensorium communis* [sic] in the formation of some geographical paradigms', in M. Beretta (ed.), *When Glass Matters: Studies in the History of Science and Art from Graeco-Roman Antiquity to Early Modern Era*, Florence, 283–320.
Plantzos, D. (1997), 'Crystals and lenses in the Graeco-Roman world', *American Journal of Archaeology* 101(3): 451–64.
Préaux, C. (1973), *La lune dans la pensée grecque*, Brussels.
Sayili, A. (2007), 'The "observation well"', *Foundation for Science, Technology and Civilisation* 636: 1–7.
Schibli, H. S. (1993), 'Xenocrates' daemons and the irrational soul', *CQ* 43: 143–67.
Taub, L. (2008), *Aetna and the Moon: Explaining Nature in Ancient Greece and Rome*, Corvallis.
Taylor, R. (2008), *The Moral Mirror of Roman Art*, Cambridge and New York.
Temple, R. (2000), *The Crystal Sun. Rediscovering a Lost Technology of the Ancient World*, London.
Wälchli, P. (2003), *Studien zu den literarischen Beziehungen zwischen Plutarch und Lukian*, Leipzig.
Wasserstein, A. (1967), 'An unpublished treatise by Demetrius Triclinius on lunar theory', *Jahrbuch der österreichischen byzantinischen Gesellschaft* 16: 153–74.
Webster, C. (2014), *Technology and/as Theory: Material Thinking in Ancient Science and Medicine*. PhD Diss., Columbia University.
Whitaker, E. A. (1999), *Mapping and Naming the Moon: A History of Lunar Cartography and Nomenclature*, Cambridge.
Williams, G. D. (2012), *The Cosmic Viewpoint. A Study on Seneca's Naturales Quaestiones*, Oxford and New York.

Chapter 15

Alpatov, M. V. (1978), *Early Russian Icon Painting*, Moscow.
Baltzly, D. and M. Share (trans.) (2018), *Hermeias: On Plato Phaedrus 227A–245E*, London.
Bekker, I. (ed.) (1838), Pseudo-*Symeon Magistros Chronicon, Theophanes Continuatus*, CSHB, Bonn.
Belting, H. (1994), *Likeness and Presence. A History of the Image before the Era of Art*, trans. E. Jephcott, London.

Bibliography

Bernard, H. (trans.) (1997), *Hermeias von Alexandrien, Kommentrar zur Platons Phaidros*, Tübingen.

Betancourt, R. (2018), *Sight, Touch, and Imagination in Byzantium*, Cambridge.

Cain, E. R. (2016), *Through a Mirror Darkly: Mystical Metaphors of Sight from Paul to Gregory of Nyssa and Augustine of Hippo*. Diss. New York.

Cameron, A. (1983), 'The history of the image of Edessa: The telling of a story', in Okeanos. Essays Presented to Ihor Ševčenko, *Harvard Ukranian Studies* 7: 80–94.

Constas, N. (1997), 'Icons and the imagination', *Logos. A Journal of Catholic Thought and Culture* 1(1): 114–25.

Cormack, R. (1997), *Painting the Soul. Icons, Death Masks and Shrouds*, London.

Couvreur, P. (ed.) (1901), *Hermiae Alexandrini in Platonis Phaedrum scholia*, Paris.

Cuscin, M. (2009), *The Image of Edessa*, Leiden.

Cutler, A. (1985), *The Craft of Ivory. Sources, Techniques, and Uses in the Mediterranean World: A.D. 200–1400*, Washington, DC.

Cutler, A. (1994), *The Hand of the Master. Craftsmanship, Ivory and Society in Byzantium (9th–11th Centuries)*, Princeton, NJ.

Dagron, G. (1991), 'Holy images and likeness', *Dumbarton Oaks Papers* 45: 23–33.

De Imagine Edessena CP. Translata, PG 133: cols 424–54, esp. 444–48.

Dobschutz, E. (1899), *Christusbilder. Untersuchungen zur christlichen Legende*, Leipzig.

Dubable, A.-M. (1997), 'L'homélie de Grégoire le Référendaire pour la reception de l'image d'Édesse', *Revue des etudes byzantines* 55: 5–51.

Elkins, J. (1999), *Why are Our Pictures Puzzles? On The Modern Origins of Pictorial Complexity*, New York.

Elsner, J. (2003), 'Visualising women in Late Antique Rome: The Projecta casket', in C. Entwistle (ed.), *Through a Glass Brightly. Studies in Byzantine and Medieval Art and Archaeology Presented to David Buckton*, Oxbow.

Engberg, S. G. (2004), 'Romanos Lekapenos and the Mandilion of Edessa', in J. Durand and B. Flusin (eds), *Byzance et les reliques du Christ*, Paris, 123–42.

Evans, H. C. and Wixon, W. D. (eds) (1997), *The Glory of Byzantium. Art and Culture of the Middle Byzantine Era A. D. 843–1261*, New York.

Evans, H. C., Holcomb, M. and Hallman, R. (2001), 'The Arts of Byzantium', *The Metropolitan Museum of Art Bulletin* 58(4) (Spring).

Fee, G. D. (1987), *The First Epistle to the Corinthians*, Grand Rapids, MI.

Frazer, M. E. (1974), 'Hades stabbed by the cross of Christ', *Metropolitan Museum Journal* 9: 153–61.

Frelick, N. M. (ed.) (2016), *The Mirror in Medieval and Early Modern Culture. Specular Reflections*, Turnhout.

Goldin, F. (1967), *The Mirror of Narcissus in the Courtly Love Lyric*, New York.

Goldschmidt, A. and Weitzmann, K. (1934), *Die byzantinischen Elfenbeinsculpturen des X.–XIII. Jahrhunderts*, Vol. II, Berlin.

Gombrich, E. H. (1996), *Art & Illusion. A Study in the Psychology of Pictorial Representation*, Phaidon Press, 89.

Grabar, A. (1931), *La Sainte Face de Laon: Le Mandylion dans l'art orthodoxe. Seminarium Kondakovianum*, Prague.

Howard, K. (1994), *The Metropolitan Museum of Art Guide*, New York.

James, L. and Webb, R. (1991), '"To understand ultimate things and enter secret places": Ekphrasis and art in Byzantium', *Art History* 14: 1–17.

Kalavrezou, I. et al. (eds) (2003), *Byzantine Women and Their World*, London.

Kee, J. (2012), 'Detail', *The Art Bulletin* 94(4): 499–501.

Kessler, H. L. and Wolf, G. (eds) (1998), *The Holy Face and the Paradox of Representation*, Bologna.

Bibliography

Kitzinger, E. (1995), 'The Mandylion at Monreale', *Arte Profana e Arte Sacra a Bisanzio*, A Iacobini and E. Zanini (eds), Rome, 575–590 [reprinted in E. Kitzinger, *Studies in Late Antique Byzantine and Medieval Western Art*, Vol. II, London, 2003, no. XXXVIII, 1158-18].

Lazarev, V. N. (1976), *Novgorodian Icon Painting*, Moscow.

Lucarini, C. M. and Moreschini, C. (eds) (2012), *Hermias Alexandrinus: In Platonis Phaedrum scholia*, Berlin.

Magdalino, P. (2004), 'L'église du Phare et les reliques de la Passion à Constantinople (VIIe/VIIIe–XIIIe siècles)', in J. Durand and B. Flusin (eds), *Byzance et les reliques du Christ*, Paris, 15–30.

Madgalino, P. (2013), 'Knowledge in authority and authorized history: The Imperial Intellectual Programme of Leo VI and Constantine VII', in P. Armstrong (ed.), *Authority in Byzantium*, London, 187–210.

Melchior-Bonnet, S. (2001), *The Mirror. A History*, New York.

Mondzain, M.-J. (2005), *Image, Icon, Economy. The Byzantine Origins of the Contemporary Imaginary*, trans. R. Franses, Stanford, CA.

O'Neill, J. P. (ed.) (1987), *The Metropolitan Museum of Art. Europe in the Middle Ages*, New York.

Onians, J. (1980), 'Abstraction and Imagination in Late Antiquity', *Art History* 3(1): 1–24.

Papaioannou, S. (2010), 'Byzantine mirrors. Self-Reflection in Medieval Greek writing', *Dumbarton Oaks Papers* 64: 81–101.

Ragusa, I. (1991), 'Mandylion-Sudarium: The translation of a Byzantine relic to Rome', *Arte Medievale* II(2): 97–106.

Runciman, S. (1929), *The Emperor Romanus Lecapenus and his Reign. A Study in Tenth-Century Byzantium*, Cambridge.

Seaford, R. (1984), 1 'Corinthians XIII:12', *The Journal of Theological Studies (Notes and Studies)* 35: 117–120.

Stein, W. A. (2016), *How to Read Medieval Art*, New York.

Tilghman, B. C. (2011), 'The shape of the word: Extralinguistic meaning in insular display lettering', *Word & Image* 27(3): 292–308, esp. 300.

Trilling, J. (1998), 'The image not made by hands and the Byzantine way of seeing', in H. L. Kessler and G. Wolf (eds), *The Holy Face and the Paradox of Representation*, Bologna, 109–27.

Tronzo, W. (2018), 'Justinian's Hagia Sophia, Angels and Restlessness', in J. N. Napoli and W. Tronzo (eds), *Radical Marble. Architectural Innovation from Antiquity to the Present*, London and New York, 23–42.

Webb, R. (2007), 'Accomplishing the picture. Ekphrasis, mimesis and martyrdom in Asterios of Amaseia', in L. James (ed.), *Art and Text in Byzantine Culture*, Cambridge, 13–32.

Webster, C. (2014), 'Technology and/as Theory: Material Thinking in Ancient Science and Medicine' (unpublished diss.), Columbia.

Weitzmann, K. (1960), 'The Mandylion and Constantine Porphyrogennetos', *Cahiers Archéogiques* XI: 163–84.

Wolf, G. (1998), 'From Mandylion to Veronica', in H. L. Kessler and G. Wolf (eds) (1998), *The Holy Face and the Paradox of Representation*, Milan, 153–79.

Wolf, G. et al. (eds) (2004), *Mandylion: Intorno al Sacro Volto, da Bisanzio a Genova*, Skira.

Chapter 16

Acerbi, F. (2011), 'The geometry of burning mirrors in Greek antiquity: Analysis, heuristic, projections, lemmatic fragmentation', *Archive for History of Exact Sciences* 65(5): 471–97.

Beebe, W. (1938), *923 Meter unter dem Meerespiegel*, Leipzig.

Brockhaus, H. (1891), *Die Kunst in den Athos-Klöstern*, Leipzig.

Bibliography

Busch, G. (1804), *Handbuch der Erfindungen*, Vol. 2, Eisenach.
Calas, N. (1942), *Confound the Wise*, New York.
Calas, N. (1975), *Mirrors of the Mind*, New York.
Daguerre, L. (1839), *Histoire et description des procédés de Daguerréotype et du Diorama*, Paris.
Della Porta, G. (1558), *Magiae Naturalis*, Naples.
Didron, N. (1845), *Manuel d'iconographie chrétienne grecque et latine*, Paris.
Dimaras, K. Th. (1937-1938), 'Θεοφάνους του εξ Αγράφων βίος Διονυσίου του εκ Φουρνά', *Ελληνικά* 10: 273-79.
Donndorf, J. (1818), *Geschichte der Erfindungen*, Vol. 5, Leipzig.
Dräseke, J. (1893), *Vom Dionysioskloster auf dem Athos*, in: *Byzantinische Zeitschrift*, Vol. 2.1, Jan. 1893, 79-95.
Dupuy, L. (1777), *Fragment d' un ouvrage grec d'Anthémius, sur des paradoxes de mécanique*, s. l.
Dutens, L. (1775), *Du miroir ardent d'Archimede*, Paris.
Edgerton, S. (2009), *The Mirror, the Window, and the Telescope*, Ithaca, NY.
Gedeon, M. (1876), 'Ποικίλη Στοά. Αθωνική αγιογραφία. Τοιχογραφίαι Πανσελήνου', *Πρωία* vol. Α΄, 2, Nr. 7, 18. Oct. 1876, 53-54.
Gedeon, M. (1885), *Ο Άθως*, Constantinople.
Grafton, A. (1991), *Fälscher und Kritiker: Der Betrug in der Wissenschaft*, Berlin.
Hetherington, P. (1974), *The Painter's Manual of Dionysius of Fourna*, London.
Hockney, D. (2001), *The Secret Knowledge*, London.
Huxley, G. (1959), *Anthemius of Tralles: A Study in Later Greek Geometry*, Cambridge.
Kakavas, G. (2008), *Dionysios of Phourna (c. 1670-c. 1745). Artistic Creation and Literary Description*, Leiden.
Kirchner, A. (1646), *Ars magna lucis et umbrae*, Rome.
Kladaki-Vratsanou, E. (2009), 'Καλοδούκας Κυραμαριός του Νικολάου', *Symaikon Vima* Sept.-Oct., 342: 5.
Kladaki-Vratsanou, E. (2010), 'Ο ηγετικός ρόλος της Σύμης', *Symaikon Vima* May-June: 5.
Knorr, W. R. (1983), 'The geometry of burning-mirrors in antiquity', *Isis* 74: 53-73.
Lefèvre, W. (ed.) (2007), *Inside the Camera Obscura: Optics and Art under the Spell of the Projected Image*, preprint 333, Berlin.
Lykurgos, A. (1856), *Enthüllungen über den Simonides-Dindorfschen Uranios. Unter Beifügung eines Berichtes von Herrn Prof. Tischendorf*, Leipzig.
Millet, G. (1927), *Monuments de l' Athos, Les peintures*, Paris.
Milliner, M. (2016), 'Man or metaphor? Manuel Panselinos and the Protaton frescoes', in Johnson, Papalexandrou and Ousterhout (eds), *Approaches to Byzantine Architecture and its Decoration*, Burlington, Ontario, 221-35.
Müller, Diamantopoulou, Gastgeber and Katsiakiori-Rankl (eds) (2017), *Die getäuschte Wissenschaft. Ein Genie betrügt Europa*, Vienna.
Niebuhr, B. G. (1828), *Corpus Scriptorum Historiae Byzantinae*, Pars III: Agathias, Bonn.
Oikonomos, K. (1849), *Περί των ερμηνευτών*, Athens.
Omont, H. (1888), *Inventaire sommaire des manuscrits grecs de la Bibliotheque nationale et des autres bibliotèques de Paris et des Départements, III*, Paris.
Papadopoulos-Kerameus, A. (1909), *Διονύσιου του εκ Φουρνά ερμηνεία της ζωγραφικής τέχνης*, St Petersburg.
Pyatnitsky, Y. (2011), 'An imperial eye to the past: Byzantine exhibitions in the State Hermitage museum, 1861-2006', *Tyragetia, serie nouă* V[XX](2): 71-98.
Rangavis, A. R. (1851), 'Σιμωνίδου χειρόγραφα', *Pandora* 23 (Feb. 1851): 551-55; 24 (March 1851): 565-73; 25 (April 1851): 595-602; 26 (May 1851): 621-27.

Bibliography

Restle, M. (1995), 'Malerbücher', in Marcell Restle and Klaus Wessel (eds), *Reallexikon zur byzantinischen Kunst* V: 1222–73.
Risner, F. (ed.) (1572), *Opticae Thesaurus Alhazeni*, Basel.
Russo, L. (2005), *Die vergessene Revolution oder die Wiedergeburt antiken Wissens*, Berkeley, CA.
Sathas, K. (1868), *Νεοελληνική φιλολογία. Βιογραφίαι εν τοις γράμμασι διαλαμψάντων Ελλήνων από της καταλύσεως της βυζαντινής αυτοκρατορίας μέχρι της ελληνικής εθνεγερσίας (1453-1821)*, Athens.
Simms, D. L. (1977), 'Archimedes and the burning mirrors of Syracuse', *Technology and Culture* 18: 1–24.
Simonides, K. (1848), *Περί Ηλιοτυπίας και ανεκδότων τινών αρχαίων χειρογράφων νεωστί ανακαλυφθέντων*, Athens.
Simonides, K. (ed. and trans.) (1864), *The Periplus of Hannon*, London.
Simonides, K. (ed.) (1849), *Συμαΐς ή Ιστορία της εν Σύμη Απολλωνιάδος Σχολής [...] υπό Μελετίου ιερομονάχου του εκ Χίου*, Athens.
Simonides, K. (ed.) (1850), *Γεωγραφικά τε και Νομικά την Κεφαληνίαν αφορώντα [...] Ευλύρου Κεφαλλήνος του Πυλαρέως*, Athens.
Simonides, K. (ed.) (1853), *Ερμηνεία των ζωγράφων ως προς την εκκλησιαστικήν ζωγραφιάν*, Athens.
Simonides, K. (ed.) (1861 and 1862), *Facsimiles of Certain Portions of the Gospel of St. Matthew*, London.
Siniosoglou, N. (2016), *Αλλόκοτος ελληνισμός*, Athens.
Toomer, G. (trans.) (1976), *Diocles on Burning Mirrors*, New York.
Tsigaridas, E. (2008), *Οι τοιχογραφίες του παρεκκλησίου του Αγίου Ευθυμίου (1302/03) στον Ναό του Αγίου Δημητρίου: Έργο του Μανουήλ Πανσέληνου στην Θεσσαλονίκη*, Thessaloniki.
Unger, Fr. W. (1870), 'Christlich-griechische oder byzantinische Kunst', in H. Brockhaus (ed.), *Griechenland. Geographisch, geschichtlich und culturhistorisch, Bd. 5*, Leipzig, 291–474.
Van Helden, A., Dupré, S. and Van Gent, R. (2010), *The Origins of the Telescope*, Amsterdam.
Vasilaki, M. (1999), *Ο Μανουήλ Πανσέληνος και η εποχή του*, Athens.
Vlachos, K. (1903), *Η χερσόνησος του Αγίου Όρους και εν αυτή μοναί και οι μοναχοί πάλαι τε και νυν*, Volos.
Westermann, A. (1839), *Παραδοξογράφοι [Paradoxographoi], Scriptores rerum mirabilium Graeci*, Braunschweig and London (= Amsterdam 1963).
Willach, R. (2008), *The Long Route to the Invention of the Telescope*, Philadelphia.
Xanthakis, A. (1991), *Ιστορία της ελληνικής φωτογραφίας*, Athens.

INDEX

Note: Headings in italics are book titles or non-English terms. Page numbers in italics refer to illustrations; those followed by n. refer to a note with its number.

Abgar, King of Edessa 185–6
acheiropoietic icons 178–81, 182, 184–7
Achilles Tatius 133, 167–8
acoustics 173–4
Acts of John 134–5
Acts of Thomas 134
Aëtius 171
air (as medium)
    and distance 36–8
    and vision 2, 22, 24–7, 34, 44–5, 46, 50–2
Alberti, Leon Battista 96
Alcaeus of Mytilene 60, 109
Alexander of Aphrodisias
    De Sensu 24–5, 26, 37
    Mantissa 19–20, 22, 23, 25
    On the Soul 19, 20–1, 21–4
Alhacen, *De aspectibus* 1
Alhazen, *Book of Optics* 192
Amant (*Le Roman de la Rose*) 140, 142–3, 145–8
amour courtois (fin' amor) 81, 82–6, 87, 90
Amour (*Le Roman de la Rose*) 145–7
analogical reasoning 41–2, 120, 123, 125, 228 n.6
Anaxagoras 125
animals 121–2, 123–4
Anthemius of Tralles 115, 191–2
Antiochus of Ascalon 123
ants 123–4
appetites 9–10, 15–16, 203 n.38, 203 n.41
Apuleius 175
    Apologia 159–60, 162
Arabic texts 47–8, 191
Archimedes 192
Aristophanes 117, 206 n.3
    Acharnians 112–13
    Clouds 166–8
Aristotle
    Categories 25–6
    De insomniis (*On Dreams*) 14, 163, 202 n.29
    On the generation of animals 173–4
    Metaphysics 21
    Meteorology 19
    On Sense Perception 19, 24, 27–8
    theory of vision 23–7

Ars Amandi 87, 89–90
artworks. *See* paintings
Athos, Mount 189–90, 193, 195, 196, 244 n.35
atomic world 32–3, 42, 119

Bacon, Roger 49, 210 n.34, 211 n.47
Barlaam the Calabrian 130
Basil of Caesarea 131
beauty 134, 146–7
    female 4, 68, 81, 86–8, 141
    male 99–101, 102
    of the soul 96, 131
    See also cosmetic mirrors
Benedetto, Luigo Foscolo 141
Bernardino de Sahagún 108, 224 n.9
Bjørnbo, Axel Anthon 47, 49
Book of Wisdom 127–8, 130
books, as mirrors 136
box mirrors 69
bronze mirrors
    Corinthian 179
    Etruscan 73–80
    in Graeco-Roman Egypt 67–70
    Greek 11, 14, 201 n.12
    surfaces 13, 202 n.29, 202 n.30
Brown, Peter 49
burning mirrors 191–3
Burns, E. J. 89
Busch, Wilhelm Benjamin 191
Byzantium
    culture 183–4
    literature 2, 127–8
    mirrors 179
    theology 128–31, 184–7

Calas, Nikolas 1, 189, 197, 242 n.1
Calchas 13, 202 n.27
Cambridge change 26, 206 n.24, 206 n.25
camera obscura 194–5
Camille, Michael 81, 86
Capellanus, Andreas, *De Amore* 81, 87, 89–90
Carroll, Lewis 139
caryatid mirrors 69
case mirrors 69

Index

Castor and Pollux 73, 74–8
catoptrics 1–2, 110–12
   animism 162–4
   catoptric moon 165–75
   devices 207 n.16
   Epicurean philosophy 29–35, 36–42
   mimesis 99, 157–62
   in religious context 114–17, 180
   See also reflection
catoptromancy 32, 112–14, 132, 173, 206 n.3
   See also reflection
children 121–3
Chionates, Michael 136
Chioniades, Gregory 131
Christianity
   Metropolitan Crucifixion Ivory 177–87
   and mirrors 4, 117, 127–31, 134–5, 178–9
Cicero, *De Finibus* 121–3
clamshell mirrors 69
Clement of Alexandria 117
Colonna, G. 75
colours
   mirror images 21–7, 52
   vision 44, 46, 211 n.45
concave mirrors 47, 172–3
cones (visual) 43–4, 45–7, 211 n.55
Constantine VII Porphyrogennetos 136, 184–7, 242 n.54
convex mirrors 47, 68, 124, 172–3
cosmetic mirrors
   in antiquity 68, 79
   Middle Ages 81, 82–3, 86, 89–90
   See also beauty
courtly love (*fin' amor*) 81, 82–6, 87, 90
Cristofani, M. 76
cryptomorphs 180–1, 182, 184, 187
crystals 143–4, 145–7, 233 n.26
curved mirrors 2, 47, 68, 124, 172–3
   catoptric animism 162–4
Cutler, Anthony 182

Da Vinci, Leonardo 96
death 75, 139
   Epicurean philosophy on 119–20
   underworld 77, 170, 181
deception 1, 109, 127, 158, 175, 189
   See also illusions
decoration
   Etruscan mirrors 73–4
   scenes of courtly love 84–6
deformation. *See* distortion
de Lorris, Guillaume 81, 87, 141, 148
Demeter 113, 173
de Meun, Jean 81, 87–9, 90, 141
Demosthenes 110
Didron, Adolph 193–4, 196

Digenis Akrites 127
Diocles 209 n.24
Diogenes of Oinoanda 31–2
Dionysius 75
   Dionysiac Mysteries 32, 108, 116, 117
dioptra 60–1, 127–8, 131, 133–4, 135–7
   seeing tube 173–4
Dioscuri 73, 74–8
direct vision 43–5, 50–3
distance 34, 36–8, 54
distortion 2, 34, 46–7, 54, 113, 157, 162
   See also refraction
divination 134–7
   books as mirrors 136
   catoptromancy 32, 112–14, 132, 173, 206 n.3
   hepatoscopy 10–14
   lecanomancy 116, 132, 135
divine epiphany 76, 112, 116–17, 163
divine presence 107, 112, 115, 116–17
diving bells 190–1
double folded mirrors 68–9
dreams 21, 139–40, 203 n.40
   Hypnerotomachia Poliphili 149–54
   Le Roman de la Rose 140, 141–8, 153–4
Durand, Paul 193–4

earth, and the moon 169–75
Echo 93, 95, 96–7
Edessa, image of. *See* Mandylion
Egypt 59
   Greek language in 61, 64–5
   women's daily life 67–71
elements 53
embodied soul 9–10, 12, 15–16
Empedocles 36
Encheiridion (Painter's Manual) 193–4
encomia 131–2
enoptromancy. *See* catoptromancy
Epicurean philosophy 32, 33–4, 36, 40
   and death 119–20, 121, 124–5
   mirrors of nature 120–5
   reflection 36–42
   theory of vision 19–20, 31–2
epiphany 112, 116–17, 163
   of Dioscuri 76
epistolography 131–2
Etruscans
   mirrors 13, 73–80
   religion 77
etymology 60–7, 124–5, 133–4, 139
   See also Greek language; Latin language
Euclid
   Catoptrica 115
   De Speculis 161, 162, 164
   theory of vision 43–4

Index

Eudoxus of Cnidos 240 n.52
Exodus 135
extramission theory 43
eyes (human) 43–6, 51–2, 53, 209 n.20, 211 n.45

female. *See* women
fin' amor 81, 82–6, 87, 90
flames 77–9
flat mirrors 2, 157–8
    catoptric mimesis 158–62
    multiple 38–41, 114
floral imagery 73, 77
Florentine Codex 108, 111, 224 n.9
folding mirrors 68–70
forgeries 189–97
Foucault, Michel 3, 139–40
fountains
    Narcissus' fountain 141–2, 143–7
    Salmacis 142–3, 146
Freud, Lucian 96
Freud, Sigmund 94–5

Galen, Claudius
    De Placitis Hippocratis et Platonis 44–5, 48–9
    mirrors 208 n.12
    theory of vision 43, 44–6, 209 n.20, 211 n.54
gardens 140–1, 143, 146–8
gaze
    direction of 60, 61
    fin' amor 83, 84–5, 87
    lecanomancy 116, 132, 135
    in mythology 60, 110
    religious 108–9, 130, 157
    women and mirrors 13, 15, 83, 179, 240 n.8
gender objects, mirrors as 59, 67–8, 70–1
    See also women
geometrical optics 43–4, 110–12, 115, 117
Gerard of Cremona 47–8
glass mirrors 81, 139, 199 n.4
Graeco-Roman world 59, 67–71, 107–17
Greek culture
    ancient Greek religion 112–17
    hepatoscopy 11–12
    technological achievements 191–7
Greek language 139
    mirrors in 60–71, 124–5, 133–4
    use in Egypt 61, 64–5
    See also etymology
Greenblatt, Stephen 82
Gregory of Nyssa 133
Gregory the Referendarius 186
Guillaume de Lorris 81, 87, 141, 148

Hades 77, 170, 181. *See also* death
Hegesianax of Alexandria Troas 171
heliotypia 193–4

hepatoscopy 10–14
Hermaphroditus 142, 146
Hermias 178
Herodotus 78–9
Hero of Alexandria (Pseudo-Hero)
    Catoptrica 111–12, 113–15, 207 n.16, 226 n.29
    De Speculis 158, 161–4, 244 n.33
Hero of Byzantium (Hero the Younger) 137
hesychasm 129
heterosexuality 96–7
heterotopias 3, 139–40
    oneiric heterotopias 140–1, 148–9
Hinduism 108–9
homosexuality 94–5, 98–9, 100–1, 102–3
Hypnerotomachia Poliphili 140–1, 148–53
    mirrors 152, 153–4

Iamblichus 109
Ibn-Ishaq, Hunayn 48, 209 n.20
icons 128, 184
    acheiropoietic icons 178–81, 182, 184–7
    iconoclasm 2, 129
    painting 189–90, 193–4
Idleness (Oiseuse, *Le Roman de La Rose*) 87–8, 141–3
illusions 3, 34, 157–8, 163, 167
    See also deception; magic; reality
images
    controlling appetite 16
    idols (*simulacra*) 30–2, 33–5, 36–9, 139
insects 123–4
intentionalist interpretation 23–4
iron mirrors 50
Italikos, Michael 132
ivory
    Metropolitan Crucifixion Ivory 181–2
    mirror cases 81, 83–7
    mirror handles 69, 215 n.65
    qualities of 85, 91

Jain mirror ritual 108
John Chrysostom 136
John of Damascus 129

katoptron 60–2, 119, 127, 134, 136
Kircher, Athanasius 191
Kosofsky Sedgwick, Eve 94–5, 101
Koumanoudis, Stefanos 193

Lacan, Jacques 3, 98, 99
lamp wicks 77–9
Latin language 47–8, 139
    mirrors in 64, 66–7, 124–5
    in Roman Egypt 65
    style of Lucretius 35–6, 40–2
    See also etymology; Roman culture

Index

lecanomancy 32, 116, 132, 135
left-right inversion 2, 24–7, 38–9, 115
letters 131–2
light 21–7
    and dark 98–9
    and the Dioscuri 76
    divine 130, 133, 135
    MesoAmerican society 108–9
    Tideus' theory of reflection 43, 45–7, 50, 52–5
    See also lamp wicks
liminal spaces
    human and divine 75, 107, 108–9
    in *Hypnerotomachia Poliphili* 150–3
    living and dead 77
    in *Le Roman de la Rose* 139–40, 141, 145–7
literature, as mirror 136
liver
    bronze 11, 201 n.13
    in embodied soul 9–10
    hepatoscopy 10–14
    liver-mirror analogy 9–17, 163, 170
Lorenz, H. 15
Lorris, Guillaume de 81, 87, 141, 148
love tokens 69, 81, 83–7, 90–1, 221 n.15
Lucian
    Icaromenippus 166, 171, 172–5
    True Histories 113–14, 165–6
Lucretius
    De Rerum Natura 29–42, 119–21
    scientific method 35–6, 41–2
    use of language 35–6, 40–1
lunar. *See* moon

magic 2, 36, 102, 142–3, 167–8
    See also illusions
Mandylion 181, 184–7
marriage contracts 62–4, 65, 67
Maximoú 127, 132
medieval period. *See* Middle Ages
Medusa 110
Meletios of Chios 189–90
MesoAmerican society 108–9
metal mirrors 53, 81, 157–8, 235 n.21
    bronze mirrors 11, 13–14, 67–70, 73–80, 179, 201 n.12, 202 n.29, 202 n.30
    iron mirrors 50
    silver mirrors 68, 69, 70
metaphors (mirrors as) 2–4, 110, 127, 132, 135, 179
    title metaphors 136–7
Metropolitan Crucifixion Ivory 177–87
Middle Ages
    fin' amor 81, 82–7, 90
    mirrors 2, 4, 81, 82–7, 89, 90–1, 136

mimesis
    artistic 158–62, 178, 184, 244 n.36
    and religious aura 107
mirror images 3, 157–8
    colour 21–7
    reality of 19–21
    temporary nature 161, 163–4
mirroring process 19
    paintings 95–6, 99–102, 131–2, 158–61, 203 n.39
mirror of nature 119–25
mirrors 1, 6
    Etruscan mirrors 79–80
    folding mirrors 68–70
    in Graeco-Roman Egypt 68–71
    as medium 4, 132–3, 161–2
    mirrors of nature 119–25
    multiple mirrors 38–41, 113–14, 161
    portable 69, 81, 82–7, 90–1
    size of mirrors 46–7, 53–5, 159
    See also curved mirrors; flat mirrors; reflection; reflective surfaces
moon
    and the earth 169–75
    great lunar mirror 165–7
    reflection of the sun 167–8
morality 87–9, 119
motion 159–60
Mount Athos 189–90, 193, 195, 196, 244 n.35
multiple mirrors 38–41, 113–14, 161

Narcissus 60, 84, 110
    fountain of 141–2, 143–7
    and *The Picture of Dorian Gray* 93–8, 100, 102–3
Neophytos the Recluse 135, 136
Nicean Creed 128
Nicholas of Otranto 135

observatories 174, 240 n.52
obsidian 108–9
Oiseuse (*Le Roman de La Rose*) 87–8, 141–3
ontology of reflection 19–21, 109–12, 117
    See also reality
open door analogy 34–5, 36, 37
optical illusions. *See* illusions
osyptrum 60, 62–7, 127–8, 133–4, 136
Ovid, *Metamorphoses* 93–4, 96–8, 102, 142, 146, 233 n.26

paintings 15–16, 21
    mirroring process 95–6, 99–102, 131–2, 158–61, 203 n.39
    Painter's Manual 193–4
    school of Symi 189–90
Palamas, Gregory 130

Index

Panselinos, Manouel 193–4, 196, 244 n.27
Papadopoulos-Kerameus, A. 193
Papaioannou, Stratis 136
papyri (Graeco-Roman) 59, 67–8
    words for mirror 60–7, 68–71
Parmenides 169
Parthenius 93
Paul (Apostle)
    Letters to the Corinthians 129, 130–1, 133, 178–9
    Letter to the Hebrews 128
Pausanius 93, 113, 115–16, 163–4
perception
    illusions 157–8
    of mirror images 19–21
    perceptibility of God 128–9, 130, 137–8
    visual 23–7, 30–1, 44, 51–2, 130
    See also vision
phantasia 6, 20, 158, 163
Philes, Manuel 129, 134, 135–6
Philippos 137
Philo of Alexandria 163
phlomis 77–8, 219 n.53
Physiologus 128
plane mirrors. *See* flat mirrors
Plato
    Respublica 9, 109, 110, 117, 158–9
    Theaetetus 26
    Timaeus 9–11, 12–17, 202 n.34
pleasure 42, 121–2
Pliny the Elder 77–8, 121, 210 n.38
Plutarch
    The Cleverness of Animals 123–4
    De facie 168–71, 173
    De Pythiae oraculis 160
    Moralia 123–4
pneuma 20, 44, 49, 208 n.8, 211 n.54
    psychic *pneuma* 44–6
Poliphilo. *See Hypnerotomachia Poliphili*
Polizzi, Gilles 141
Pollux and Castor 73, 74–8
polyptoton 40–1
polytheoron 114
portable mirrors 69, 81, 82–7, 90–1, 221 n.15
portals 150–1, 152–3
portraits
    of Dorian Gray 95–100
    sculpture 160–1
    See also paintings
Posidonius 240 n.52
Prometheus 13, 191, 197
prophecy. *See* divination
psychosomatic experiences 16
Ptolemy, Claudius 43–4, 161

rainbows 19
Rangavis, Alexandros 193, 196

reality 1, 3
    mirror images 19–21, 27–8, 34–5, 101, 107, 110–11, 159
    paintings 102
    See also illusions; ontology of reflection
reason 9–10, 15–16, 202 n.38
reflection
    Lucretius' theories 37, 38–40, 42
    ontology 109–12, 117
    in paintings 95–100
    religious aura 74, 107–9, 112–17, 137–8
    repeated 38–41
    self-knowledge 2–3, 83, 98, 119, 136, 144–5, 150–1
    Tideus' theories 43, 45–7, 53–5
    See also catoptrics; catoptromancy; mirrors
reflective surfaces 108–9, 113, 157–8
    in dream spaces 140, 141, 144–6, 153–4
    lecanomancy 32, 116, 132, 135
    liver 14, 15
    three-dimensional surfaces 35
    unspotted mirror 127–8, 130–1
    water 135, 168
    See also mirrors
refraction 2, 44, 147, 173
    See also distortion
Reggio di Calabria 48, 209 n.22
relation (*schesis*) 22, 24–7, 205 n.21
relationships, in *The Picture of Dorian Gray* (Wilde) 95–100
religion
    Christianity 117, 127–31, 137–8
    Etruscan 74, 77
    Hinduism 108–9
    Jainism 108
    and reflection 107–9, 112–17, 137–8
religious artefacts
    Metropolitan Crucifixion Ivory 177–87
    relics 184–7
    votive offerings 67–8, 70–1
    See also icons
Renaissance 95–6, 141
    mirrors 2, 82
revelation, using mirrors 127, 133, 135–6, 137, 178–9
rhetorical devices 40–1
riddles 129, 132–3
right-left inversion 2, 24–7, 38–9, 115
ritual use of mirrors 112–13
    Dionysiac Mysteries 32, 116, 117
    Jain mirror ritual 108
Roman culture 117, 119, 121, 124–5, 167, 191
    Villa of the Mysteries, Pompeii 32, 116
    See also Graeco-Roman world; Latin language
Le Roman de la Rose 81, 83, 140–8
    mirrors 87–9, 141–3, 153–4
Romanos I Lecapenos 184–5, 186–7

Index

St Elmo's fire 76
St Hilarion 135
St Paul (the Apostle)
    Letters to the Corinthians 129, 130–1, 133, 178–9
    Letter to the Hebrews 128
Salmacis 142, 143, 146, 233 n.26
schesis (relation) 22, 24–7, 205 n.21
sculpture 160–1
see-through veil 127, 133–4
self-fashioning 82
self-knowledge 2–3, 98, 119, 136
    fin' amor 140, 150–2
Seneca 29, 42, 161
senses 9–10, 29–30, 33–4, 151–2
    See also vision
sexuality 93
    heterosexuality 96–7
    homosexuality 94–5, 98–9, 100–1, 102–3
sight. *See* vision
silver mirrors 68, 69, 70
Simonides, Konstantinos 189–97
simulacra. *See under* images
Socrates 26, 109, 158–9
soul. *See* embodied soul
specula literature 2
spherical mirrors. *See* curved mirrors
spirit 9–10
spiritualist interpretation 23–4
stand mirrors 69
Stoic theory of vision 19–20, 44
sun, relationship with the moon 169–71
surfaces. *See* reflective surfaces
Symais 189–97
Symeon the New Theologian 135

Tarquinian tombs 75
telescopes 174, 190
temples 114–16
terminology for mirrors
    Greek language 60–7, 124–5, 133
    Latin language 124–5
Theodore II Laskaris 134
Theodore the Studite 129, 131
theophany 135
Thessalian trick 167

threefold mirrors 69–70
Tideus
    De Speculis 43–8, 50–5, 209 n.20
    identity of 48–9, 209 n.24
tombs, Tarquinian 75
Tornikes, Euthymios 131
Triclinius, Demetrius 171–2
tripartite soul. *See* embodied soul

underworld 77, 170, 181
    See also death
unspotted mirror 127–31

Varro 124
verbascum 77–8, 219 n.53
Vergil 124
Veronica 187, 242 n.55
Villa of the Mysteries, Pompeii 32, 116
virtual images 109, 111, 117, 157–8
vision 24–7, 130, 183
    aids to 137–8
    direct vision 43–5, 50–3
    theories of 19–21, 23–4, 43–5, 50
    See also perception
visualization 14–15, 16–17
Vogl, Sebastian 47, 49
votive offerings 67–8, 70–1

Wälchli, P. 172–3
water 53
    fountains 141–7
    reflection in 135, 168
wells 113, 165–6, 173–4
Wilde, Oscar 103
    The Picture of Dorian Gray 93, 94–103
wine, as mirror 60, 109
women
    mirror gazing 13, 15, 83, 84–5, 179, 240 n.8
    mirrors and *fin' amor* 82–6, 90
    possession of mirrors in antiquity 13, 59, 67–8, 70–1, 74, 75–6, 79
    See also gender objects
wonder 37–8, 111–12, 157

Xanthopoulos, Nicephoros Callistos 136